Australia

WORLD BIBLIOGRAPHICAL SERIES

General Editors:
Robert L. Collison (Editor-in-chief)
Sheila R. Herstein
Louis J. Reith
Hans H. Wellisch

VOLUMES IN THE SERIES

VOLUME 46

Australia

I. Kepars
Compiler

CLIO PRESS

OXFORD, ENGLAND · SANTA BARBARA, CALIFORNIA.
DENVER, COLORADO

217491

British Library Cataloguing in Publication Data

Kepars, I.
Australia. – (World bibliographical series; 46)
1. Australia – Bibliography
I. Title II. Series
016.94406'3 Z4011

ISBN 0-903450-83-6

Clio Press Ltd.,
55 St. Thomas' Street,
Oxford OX1 1JG, England.

ABC-Clio Information Services,
Riviera Campus, 2040 Alameda Padre Serra,
Santa Barbara, Ca. 93103, U.S.A.

Designed by Bernard Crossland
Typeset by Berkshire Publishing Services
Printed in Great Britain by
Billing and Sons Ltd., Worcester

THE WORLD BIBLIOGRAPHICAL SERIES

This series will eventually cover every country in the world, each in a separate volume comprising annotated entries on works dealing with its history, geography, economy and politics; and with its people, their culture, customs, religion and social organization. Attention will also be paid to current living conditions – housing, education, newspapers, clothing, etc. – that are all too often ignored in standard bibliographies; and to those particular aspects relevant to individual countries. Each volume seeks to achieve, by use of careful selectivity and critical assessment of the literature, an expression of the country and an appreciation of its nature and national aspirations, to guide the reader towards an understanding of its importance. The keynote of the series is to provide, in a uniform format, an interpretation of each country that will express its culture, its place in the world, and the qualities and background that make it unique.

SERIES EDITORS

Robert L. Collison (Editor-in-chief) is Professor Emeritus, Library and Information Studies, University of California, Los Angeles, and is currently the President of the Society of Indexers. Following the war, he served as Reference Librarian for the City of Westminster and later became Librarian to the BBC. During his fifty years as a professional librarian in England and the USA, he has written more than twenty works on bibliography, librarianship, indexing and related subjects.

Sheila R. Herstein is Reference Librarian and Library Instruction Coordinator at the City College of the City University of New York. She has extensive bibliographic experience and recently described her innovations in the field of bibliographic instruction in 'Team teaching and bibliographic instruction', *The Bookmark*, Autumn 1979. In addition, Doctor Herstein co-authored a basic annotated bibliography in history for Funk & Wagnalls *New encyclopedia*, and for several years reviewed books for *Library Journal*.

Louis J. Reith is librarian with the Franciscan Institute, St. Bonaventure University, New York. He received his PhD from Stanford University, California, and later studied at Eberhard-Karls-Universität, Tübingen. In addition to his activities as a librarian, Dr. Reith is a specialist on 16th century German history and the Reformation and has published many articles and papers in both German and English. He was also editor of the *American Society for Reformation Research Newsletter*.

Hans H. Wellisch is Associate Professor at the College of Library and Information Services, University of Maryland, and a member of the American Society of Indexers and the International Federation for Documentation. He is the author of numerous articles and several books on indexing and abstracting, and has most recently published *Indexing and abstracting: an international bibliography*. He also contributes frequently to *Journal of the American Society for Information Science, Library Quarterly*, and *The Indexer*.

Contents

Contents

Contents

Foreword

This bibliography directs the reader to books on all aspects of Australia, its people and its place in the world. The selection concentrates on sources that emphasize those aspects of Australia which in the compiler's view express its unique qualities and background. It is hoped that the works included will stimulate the reader's curiosity regarding the fifth continent and so encourage further reading.

The book is intended for the informed general reader as well as the scholar who wishes to obtain background information in a field other than his own. It should benefit both short- and long-term visitors and also people intending to migrate to Australia. It will serve as a reference for librarians, booksellers and others who are frequently asked to recommend books in a particular subject area, and can be used as a selection tool by overseas libraries wishing to assemble or develop a basic collection of Australiana.

The selection of suitable titles for inclusion in the bibliography was lightened enormously by the compiler's involvement for more than a decade in the editorship of *Australian books: a select list of recent publications and standard works in print*, published annually by the National Library of Australia. Although on a different scale and more richly annotated, the present bibliography is similar in its objectives to *Australian books*, from which the preliminary selection of titles was made. This experience and easy access to the national book collection enabled the compiler to make a final choice from a detailed examination of each book, supported wherever possible by reviews.

The bibliography includes classic accounts, general surveys, thorough summaries, and books which, for want of a better phrase, add 'local colour' and hopefully will kindle a spark of curiosity in the reader to delve deeper and further. Such a keen reader will find that many of the listed titles contain extensive bibliographies or suggestions for further reading. He or she may wish to go on and consult Sir John Ferguson's monumental seven-volume *Bibliography of Australia* which lists Australian printed works comprehensively for the period 1784-1900.

Foreword

From 1936 to the present the National Library has published *The Australian National Bibliography* which from 1936 to 1960 was known as *Books Published in Australia* and *Annual Catalogue of Australian Publications*.

Following the truism that 'a picture is worth a thousand words', quality pictorial works and those generously illustrated have an honoured place in the bibliography.

In an introductory survey some material necessarily has to be excluded, and this bibliography omits works of the imagination by individual authors. Interested readers have access to Australian novels, poetry and short stories through many of the books included in the literature section. As a rule biographies, because of their large numbers and the consequent difficulty in choosing the best, are not included. Some individual biographies which throw light on the wider field of endeavour of the biographee, or which fill a gap in the literature on a certain field, have been listed within certain subject sections. Collected biography is included. Highly specialized, abstruse works are not listed.

As far as is possible the arrangement of books within each section is hierarchical. The general introductions or surveys of the subject are followed by works of specialized interest and increasing complexity. Often the intended audience of a book is indicated in the annotation. Although the bibliography concentrates mainly on books, there are sections listing the more important newspapers, periodicals and magazines in a variety of fields. Periodical articles may be accessed through *APAIS, Australian Public Affairs Information Service: a subject index to current literature*, published monthly and cumulated annually by the National Library of Australia, which should be available in large libraries overseas.

Throughout this bibliography the emphasis is on recent publications which should be available for sale in the larger bookshops in English-speaking countries or by writing directly to the publishers. Many of the large international publishing houses are represented in Australia and some have large local lists. Many of the books may also be available at Australian embassies which have representative collections on the country. Those in London and Washington house comprehensive collections of Australiana. Older works and recent ones which are out of print should be available on interlibrary loan from national, large public and university libraries, especially those that have some involvement with Australian studies.

Finally, I am grateful for the assistance given to me by Maija Kepars who unselfishly acted the part of the 'informed general reader' by critically commenting on the language, content and general comprehensibility of the annotations which describe each selection.

Australia: a backward glimpse

by Geoffrey Blainey

Each year a holiday marks the landing, on January 26, 1788, of the first British colonists at Sydney harbour. We call the day Australia Day. We are still slow to recognize that the real Australia Day occurred at least fifty thousand years ago when the first Aboriginals landed. We are slow to realize that the land has had at least two separate histories and that the history which began with the raising of the British flag represents, at most a fragment of our history.

The ancestors of the Aboriginals lived at one time in the south east of Asia and must have moved slowly across the Indonesian archipelago, passing from island to island until, countless generations later, they found this continent. It was then a larger continent, embracing New Guinea to the north and Tasmania to the south. Less than 8,000 years ago the slow rising of the seas separated Australia from New Guinea, and thus isolated Australia at the very time when most regions of the globe were beginning that transition from nomadic groups to those settled societies which kept herds and cultivated gardens, lived in permanent villages and towns, and formed larger political units. Thus when the British reached Australia in 1788 with their fast sailing ships, their firearms, their livestock and seeds, their books and charts, their clocks and surveying instruments, and the first products of the industrial revolution, they found nomads who possessed no pottery and metals and no permanent villages, and were divided into hundreds of tribal groups each with its own language or dialect.

The tragedy of this confrontation between the first industrial nation of the world and the last continent of nomads, was that neither civilization could understand the other. Only in the last twenty years has a widening circle of white Australians come to appreciate the achievements of the black Aboriginals; and even that appreciation stems in part from the current phase of disillusionment with western civilization and its cult of high technology. In most years the migratory Aboriginal tribes probably had a high standard of living though they planted no crops, built no granaries or warehouses, and used the simplest home-made equipment of wood, bone, fibre and stone. In many districts Aboriginals ate more than a hundred different plant foods as well as fish, meat, eggs and insects. Perhaps 300,000 Aboriginals lived in the continent, and that small population – a mere fiftieth of Australia's present population – helps to explain why they lived in abundance and why they had the leisure in which to pursue a complex social life.

When the British began to place a few settlements on the eastern coast and later to move inland with their sheep and cattle, the small Aboriginal societies succumbed at almost every point of contact. They had no immunity to smallpox, influenza, measles and other diseases which came with the invaders. Disease and demoralization were the main killers but in hundreds of isolated clashes many Aboriginals were killed or maimed by gunshot and bullets. Tribe after tribe vanished, and even in 1910 many scientists believed that the Aboriginal race would ultimately be extinguished. The Aboriginals are now multiplying, and will ultimately exceed the prehistoric peak. Eventually they will gain in their own homeland that respect and status which was too long denied them.

Colonists coming from the British Isles were not easily acclimatised. They found the vegetation dull and monotonous, the native animals bizarre, and they felt their isolation. The seasons were upside down; and Christmas came in summer and Easter in autumn. People thought the summers were too hot; and in search of shade they built wide verandahs around the larger houses and planted shade trees, preferably the trees which reminded them of home. The summer heat made many outdoor workers prefer a shorter working day to higher wages; and in the mid 1850s the stonemasons and building workers of the larger cities won the eight-hour day. For long the anniversary of the first winning of the 8-hour day was celebrated as a public holiday in the main cities, though not on the farms where the working day remained long. Fear of the hot sun deterred most settlers from the large tropical zone. There in the last quarter of the nineteenth century the sugar fields were worked by black islanders recruited from the South West Pacific, and the Chinese miners outnumbered the Europeans on most of the tropical goldfields and in the hot interior much of the cartage fell into the hands of the camel teamsters who, though known as 'Afghans', came from the present Pakistan. Fear of the hot sun has faded, and the prejudice against living in the tropics has faded too. But the two-fifths of the continent which lies in the tropics is peopled sparsely, and that region – as large as India – holds less than one million of Australia's fourteen million people.

The emotional acclimatisation has been even slower than the physical. In learning to feel at home the Europeans in Australia were

Australia: a backward glimpse

often taught by artists. The young poet Adam Lindsay Gordon, who committed suicide near the seashore in Melbourne in 1870, was to become for about thirty years more influential in Australia than was perhaps any contemporary poet in England. His influence came partly from the fact that his ballads formed a half-way house for the emotions, accommodating those who were homesick for Britain and yet were attracted to their adopted land. Gordon celebrated the native tree, the wattle, and the blue distant ranges*, but he also wrote of Australia as a land 'where bright blossoms are scentless'; and a later generation, feeling much more at home, has not forgiven him for his mild floral insult. In the 1880s a small group of painters — now known as the Heidelberg School — caught the colours and strong light of the rural landscape of the summertime in the coolest corner of Australia; and they slowly persuaded several generations of Australians to see their summer, and their dry landscape, with friendlier eyes. In the 1920s and 1930s artists painted for perhaps the first time the strong red colours of desert. Slowly the vast dry inland has become less forbidding to typical Australians, partly through technological change and partly through new emotional attitudes. One suspects that even Australians of the fifth generation do not yet feel at home as securely as their descendants will feel in the year 2100 A.D.

The land itself is enormous and, in its diversity, difficult to visualise. It is the fifth largest country in the world, coming behind the Soviet Union, China, Canada, and Brazil. It has massive mineral deposits but many of the deposits lie in unpopulated country, far from the sea and require a huge investment before they can export their first minerals to overseas markets. Most of Australia's soil is poor; and even that narrow crescent of wheat land which runs for a thousand miles in the south-east corner is deficient in phosphate, and so most of these crops which provide bread for tens of millions of people in Australia and China would be meagre but for the addition of artificial fertilisers. Most of Australia is dry, and most rivers which appear on inland maps are empty for much of the year.

Occasionally even the more fertile districts suffer from drought. The worst drought in the last two centuries ran from about 1895 to 1903. It halved the number of sheep and almost halved the cattle. In a vast area the grass ceased to grow and winds whipped up the topsoil and drove it away. On some windy days, cities on the coast were darkened by dust-filled air in the middle of the day. Clouds of dust were carried across

---

* Gordon's father had served in the Bengal Lancers and was a scholar of Hindustani. Home again in England, he perhaps gave his young son a more sympathetic attitude to hot climates and exotic places.

the sea to New Zealand where the brown fall-out coated the snow. Drought tinges the literature of the turn of the century. Henry Lawson and *The Bulletin* school of writers saw Nature as harsh partly because it was especially harsh during their prime. We now know enough about the climate in the south-east quarter of Australia, where nearly all *The Bulletin* writers lived, to conclude that in their childhood the climate was relatively favourable but in their adult years was less reliable. From the late 1880s to the mid 1940s there were frequent droughts in most rural areas of Victoria, South Australia, New South Wales, and southern Queensland.

For long the country, 'the bush', was the dominant theme in literature and the common theme in painting. Most writers and artists, however, worked in coastal cities. The tendency to live in a coastal city rather than the town or countryside was observed even in 1850. Australia was first occupied by the British as a convict settlement — 160,000 convicts arrived in the eighty years after 1788 — and a gaol is often an urban activity. The catching of deep-sea whales in the early years built up the coastal cities, for there the whaling ships were repaired and equipped, and there the owners and crews spent their money. Later the government railways fanned out from the coastal cities and the civil servants clustered there. Most migrants fresh from the British Isles were nervous of the lonely bush, and the migrant with wife and children found the cost-of-living was cheaper in the coastal city.

Sydney and Melbourne today hold four of every ten Australians and even by world standards they are large cities. They are about 600 miles apart, and outwardly alike. They have long been rivals; and in the gold rushes of the 1850s Melbourne quickly passed the older Sydney and became for half a century the larger city. About 1900 Sydney regained the lead but in the last thirty years Sydney's lead over Melbourne has been narrowing. The simplest sign of their rivalry is Canberra, the federal capital city: it was established in 1927, a new town with a parliament house and long grass and little else. It exists because neither Melbourne nor Sydney would allow the other to be the capital.

British Australia was a child of the industrial revolution. It enjoyed its first wave of prosperity because it supplied wool for the textile mills of Yorkshire, whale oil for the engines and oil lamps of the industrial towns, gold for great finance houses of London, and copper for the smelters of Wales. It was colonised by people who were not averse to technical change, who often craved it, and who themselves discovered new ways of making and doing. Significantly most of our bank notes depict the portraits of Australian innovators: a pioneer breeder of a

Australia: a backward glimpse

new species of wheat, a grandfather of aeronautics, the father of the fine-wool industry, an early aviator, and a scientist who co-discovered the first antibiotic, the drug penicillin. The high standard of living of the average Australian has owned much to inventiveness, to a willingness to find new ways of growing or making or transporting commodities. Many educated Australians today condemn their country as conservative, comprehensively conservative, forgetting that the political arena is only one of many arenas of national life.

The main physical and economic changes came before the Second World War. The fastest changes in loyalties, attitudes and alliances came after that war. Britain is no longer the main source of popular culture and new technology and capital. Britain has been replaced by the United States as our main military ally and by Japan as the main trading partner. Since the late 1940s Australia has attracted far more migrants from southern and western Europe than from the British Isles, the traditional source of migrants. Whereas the great majority of Australians once felt intense pride in their British ancestry, and on many public occasions attributed their nation's successes to the qualities of the British race and to divine guidance, both Britain and God appear less and less in public orations and on foundation stones. A dogmatic belief in the supremacy of European civilization and peoples has also waned, and Australian tourists flock to south and east Asia, and Asian immigrants have become citizens in unprecedented numbers, and Aboriginals have belatedly become citizens of their own country.

In the very recent history of any nation we can't be certain of what is illusion and what is reality. The new opera house in Sydney mirrors that uncertainty. It is widely seen as the new symbol of the nation, a symbol of how Australians would like their land to be seen by the larger world. But for most Australians the sail-like roof of the opera house is more appealing than the music sung within.

The above article, originally published in 'The Literary Criterion', is reproduced with the permission of Dr. Geoffrey N. Blainey, A.O., Ernest Scott Professor of History, University of Melbourne, Melbourne, Victoria, Australia.

The Country and Its People

1 **Australia.**
   Sir Keith Hancock.   Brisbane: Jacaranda, 1961. 3rd ed. 282p.
   bibliog.

Although published fifty years ago, this classic is acclaimed by many critics as one of the best modern interpretations of Australia and Australians. The themes developed by Professor Hancock have been borrowed and perpetuated as the great myths of Australian society by most of the later commentators on national identity. Briefly Hancock's themes are: the idea of a democratic and egalitarian ethos, 'Australia is a classless community'; the idea that the Australian political process is 'a see-saw between a party of initiative and parties of resistance', and that Australian politics is a non-ideological struggle to gain economic advantage for one's group – 'a struggle of group interest almost totally devoid of ideas'; the idea that the history of Australia has been 'the history of Australia's growing up' and 'coming of age as a nation' in the international community; the idea that Australian egalitarianism leads to mediocrity and a 'she'll be right' attitude; and the idea that Australia's leaders are incompetent and that the country lacks an élite of leaders with ideas and vision.

2 **Inventing Australia: images and identity 1688-1980.**
   Richard White.   Sydney: Allen & Unwin, 1981. 205p. bibliog.

Traces some of the efforts to explain what it means to be Australian. It is the author's view that all attempts to find a national identity are necessarily futile, and are nothing more than myth-making by dominant groups in society, such as historians, intellectuals, and those who wield economic power. Nevertheless White's story of the endeavours to define the Australian experience makes this an illuminating book. An excellent bibliography of sources and further reading completes the text.

3 **Intruders in the bush: the Australian quest for identity.**
   Edited by John Carroll.   Melbourne: Oxford University Press, 1982.
   242p.

This collection of essays by leading Australian historians, sociologists and critics is the most recent examination of the national character. The essays range from the classical legends of Australian identity through more recent visions of Australia as reflected in drama, film, painting and the work of Nobel Prize winner, novelist Patrick White, to the editor's own concept of an Australian identity. This is a convenient and stimulating summary of the variety of views about the Australians' preoccupation with themselves which at times borders on an obsession.

1

4 **This is Australia.**
Olaf Ruhen (and others). Sydney: Lansdowne Press, 1982. 4th ed.
363p.

In its fourth edition since it first appeared in 1975, this large volume contains
twelve chapters on contemporary Australia, its aspirations and its heritage, accompanied by splendid photographs. The chapters cover: the land, the economy,
cities, politics, religion, the environment, the arts, science, education, leisure,
sport and foreign relations.

5 **The Australian people.**
Craig McGregor. Sydney: Hodder & Stoughton, 1980. 334p.

The Australian people revises the author's 1966 book *Profile of Australia*. This
state-of-the-nation study deals with every facet of Australia and its people – life
in the cities and the country, the significant changes in the class structure in the
last decade, politics, popular culture, the arts, minority groups such as Aborigines
and immigrants, the future of the country as well as the events of recent years
which have dramatically changed Australian life. In short, this is an excellent
introduction to the country for the serious reader. Twelve penetrating profiles of
prominent Australians illustrate each chapter and the book is worth reading for
these alone.

6 **The Australia book: the portrait of a nation by our greatest writers.**
Edited by T. Inglis Moore. Melbourne: Currey O'Neil, 1982. 267p.

An attempt to provide a representative picture of Australia – of the country
itself, its people and its history, and the national ways of life and thought –
through the writing of Australia's leading authors. The editor, who has been
involved with literature all his life, has chosen the pieces for inclusion well, and
browsing in this book is a delightful experience.

7 **The stockyard and the croquet lawn: literary evidence for Australian
cultural development.**
G. A. Wilkes. Melbourne: Arnold, 1981. 153p. bibliog.

The purpose of this study is to examine Australian literature as evidence of Australian cultural development. It is usually seen in terms of an emergent nationalism
or the clash between the authentic Australian and the imported English – the
stockyard and the croquet lawn. Wilkes' approach is to see how the 'literary
evidence' – the poetry and the fiction – fits these stereotypes. The argument
provides for very entertaining reading. A well-selected, short bibliography points
the way to further reading.

8 **The lucky country.**
Donald Horne. Sydney: Angus & Robertson, 1968. 2nd rev. ed.

An influential interpretation of Australian national character, frequently
reprinted. While it restages many of the familiar myths such as egalitarianism and
mediocre leadership, it is written in a wise, vigorous style with many original
insights, thus making the book both provocative and readable. For this reason it
is recommended as one of the best general introductions to Australia.

9 **Money made us.**
Donald Horne. Melbourne: Penguin Books, 1976. 256p. bibliog.

An enormously readable and entertaining account of how economic values have shaped Australian society. Horne argues that throughout Australia's history human values have been sacrificed to the need for development, for exports, for profits, for economic growth. His writing derives from observations and insights gained during extensive travels through Australia, and for this reason chapters on country towns, farmers and farming, water development and mineral exploitation are unsurpassed by other commentators on this Australian scene.

10 **The Australian legend.**
Russel Ward. Melbourne: Oxford University Press, 1970.
2nd ed. 283p. bibliog.

When this book first appeared in 1958 it was an important breakthrough in terms of what Australian historians then regarded as respectable evidence. Among Ward's souces were folksongs, popular ballads and imaginative literature as well as contemporary eye witness accounts. The work was also strikingly original in its theme, which was to 'try to trace and explain the development of the Australian self-image' or 'national mystique'. The basic argument is that a specifically Australian outlook originated among the rural or 'bush' workers and that this small group has influenced the attitudes of the whole Australian community. A controversial work in 1958, it still excites debate among the professionals, and should certainly be read by anyone interested in knowing what being an Australian means. This pioneering book has gone through many reprints and editions, with a new illustrated edition in 1978, which comprises 8 pages in full colour and over 160 black-and-white prints. The scholarly journal *Historical Studies* devoted a whole issue to re-examining the continuing power and validity of Ward's ideas (vol. 18, 1978, entitled *The Australian legend revisited*).

11 **Sports.**
Keith Dunstan. Melbourne: Cassell, 1973. 367p.

This, the author's third in a trilogy of exposés of some of what he considers to be the more objectionable national characteristics, looks at the Australians' obsession with sport. For sheer entertainment and readability it is a worthy successor to his popular *Wowsers* published in 1968, a study of the persistence of puritanical killjoys in Australian society and *Knockers*, 1972, a collection of adverse comment on just about every aspect of Australian life by both local critics and foreign visitors. A paperback edition of *Sports* was published in 1981 by Sun Books, Melbourne.

12 **Land of the long weekend.**
   Ronald Conway. Melbourne: Sun Books, 1978. 372p. bibliog.

An analysis of contemporary Australian national character. The author, a psychologist, burst into print in 1971 with his *The great Australian stupor* (Melbourne:
Sun Books) that attacked what he saw as the essential spiritual emptiness of
Australian life. The themes raised in that book are elaborated here. For Conway
the family is paramount in maintaining a secure, creative society, but the Australian nuclear family is under serious threat and stress mainly because of the heavy
drinking rituals of Australian males, their verbal and emotional reserve, the
'apartheid of sex roles' and the conditions which are synonymous with Australian
life: 'alienation, loneliness, aggressive legalitarianism and materialism, resentment
of authority and . . . lack of openness to others . . . '. His conclusion is that
Australia has produced a conformist society of selfishness and greed, a place
where the national and individual effort is aimed at attaining monetary and
material supremacy and scrambling up some illusory status ladder.

13 **The U-jack society: an experience of being Australian.**
   Ian Moffitt. Sydney: Ure Smith, 1972. 232p.

A lively book about Australia by a practising journalist. The author is highly
critical of Australians' lack of concern for a sane ecology and their preoccupation
with materialistic self-indulgence, while increasingly leaving the running of the
country to foreign interests. The book is worth reading if only for his chapter on
the national automobile madness. To quote: 'The Australian's loving preoccupation
with his car has become a commonplace: he fondles each nut and bolt in intermi-
nable conversations in the pub, strips it, lays it on the lawn, and greases its nipples
while his wife wonders whether he will ever better his indoor average of one-a-
month. But put him behind the wheel and he becomes the world's most heedless
driver – not as terrifying, perhaps, as a Taipei taxi driver, not quite as insane as a
Turk, but more openly agressive than any of them. So many Australians equate
driving with masculinity: pass them and they suffer instant emasculation. Scores
of them are undetected murderers . . .'.

14 **The Australianization of John Bull.**
   Joe Rich. Melbourne: Longman, 1974. 237p. bibliog.

A popular attempt to explain the historical origins of the Australian character. It
is an entertaining fluent narrative enhanced throughout with contemporary
quotations.

15 **Rites, black and white.**
   Robert Brain. Melbourne: Penguin Books, 1979. 228p.

A comparison of the cultural traditions of black Australians – the Aborigines –
and white Australians from an anthropological viewpoint. The author argues that
the rites typically ascribed to blacks are in fact representative of 'passage rites'
shared universally by all humankind. In the process the reader learns a great deal
about the lifestyles of both the Aborigines and the white population of Australia.

Geography

General

16 **Australia: a geography.**
Edited by D. N. Jeans. Sydney: Sydney University Press, 1977.
571p. maps. bibliog.
This is the first ever definitive systematic geography of Australia. The authors, all academics, are recognized leaders in their respective fields and they present the accumulated research of recent decades in twenty-four authoritative and balanced chapters. Topics covered are: climate; physiographic regions; hydrology; early landform evolution; fluvial landforms; desert lands; coast; soils; vegetation; rural land use; climate and primary production; pastoral Australia; tropical Australia; fisheries; population; social geography of Aboriginal Australia; space, politics and territorial organization; capital cities; the urban system; minerals and mining; manufacturing; transport; recreation; and Australia in the Pacific Islands. The text is well supported with illustrative material including 149 figures, 104 tables and 62 plates.

17 **Regional landscapes of Australia: form, function and change.**
N. Learmouth, A. Learmouth, maps by P. Daniel. Sydney:
Angus & Robertson, 1971. 493p. bibliog.
This massive volume of descriptive geography is aimed at the intelligent layman as well as at the student. It contains a wealth of detailed information on the five main regions of the continent which the authors see as the south-east, north-east, central, north-west and south-west. The text has been made very readable by separating statistical information from the long descriptive passages. There are over 150 black-and-white photographs, 16 pages of colour photographs and a superb series of monochrome and colour maps dealing with relief, geology, temperature and evaporation, rainfall, water resources, land cover, exploration and settlement, conservation and soil erosion and population. Although bulky and clearly not intended for the purpose, the book would be an excellent guide for the traveller to and around Australia.

5

18 **Australia.**

R. L. Heathcote.   London: Longman, 1975. 246p. maps. bibliog.
(The World's Landscapes).

A new methodology is used to interpret Australia's geography – the device applied being the concept of the 'landscapes of Australia'. Dr. Heathcote's first task is to reconstruct the 'quiet' continent before the advent of the white man; then he goes on 'to describe the continent as it was in the early 1970s, emphasizing the contrasts with the original condition and analysing in some detail aspects of European settlement from 1788 to the 1970s, which have produced the significant modifications of the original scenes'. The final chapters bring together the wealth of material presented into five major types of vision of Australia: the scientific, the romantic, the colonial, the national and the ecological, which serve to stress the complexity of attitudes to landscape in what is often taken to be the 'simplest' of continents.

19 **Australia's resources and their development.**

R. K. Wilson.   Sydney: Department of Adult Education,
University of Sydney, 1980. 406p. maps. bibliog.

A comprehensive economic geography of Australia. The information is up to date and the text is profusely illustrated with maps and figures.

20 **The Australian environment.**

Edited by G. W. Leeper.   Melbourne: CSIRO, in association with
Melbourne University Press, 1970. 4th ed. 163p. maps. bibliog.

Although somewhat dated as regards statistical data and, especially, the bibliographies, this book can still be used as an introductory text to Australia's rural industries and their physical setting. The chapters are pithy and well written and provide essential information on landforms, climates, soils, water and irrigation, vegetation, pastures, field and forest crops, animal production and native fauna. The book's success over a long period suggests the need for a new edition.

21 **Australian climate patterns.**

J. Gentilli.   Melbourne: Nelson, 1972. 285p. maps. bibliog.

As a generalization it is accepted that most of the Australian continent is hot and dry and the further one goes inland the hotter and drier it becomes, yet the range of climatic variation is fairly wide and the climatic pattern itself is complicated. Dr. Gentilli surveys the pattern in this handy single-volume treatise. Introductory chapters on climatic regions and their delineation are followed by thirteen regional chapters. There is a short concluding chapter on climatic change. The text is generally clear and is enlivened with many original quotations from earlier works. Informative diagrams, maps and tables aid understanding, and an extensive bibliography is an additional feature of the book.

22 **Ancient Australia: the story of its past geography and life.**
C. F. Laseron, revised by R. O. Brunnschweiler. Sydney: Angus
& Robertson, 1969. 2nd ed. 253p.

Like the author's other book, *The face of Australia*, this one 'on the geological
history of the Australian continent has been and remains popular, not only
because of the wealth of scientific information it contains, but because he
succeeded in making this store of knowledge available in a form that can be
understood by everybody, scholar and layman alike'. Dr. Brunnschweiler, a Swiss
geologist, has rearranged and rewritten large parts of the book and has also added
entirely new chapters to take into account the greatly increased knowledge about
the geology of Australia since the first edition appeared in 1954. Many photographs and drawings aid the reader's understanding of the text.

23 **The face of Australia: the shaping of a continent.**
C. F. Laseron, revised by J. N. Jennings. Sydney: Angus &
Robertson, 1972. 200p. maps.

This book not only describes the scenic beauty of Australia, but also explains
how the distinctive features of the land were fashioned by natural processes. As
a popular, easily understood introduction to the geology of Australia it has not
been surpassed since it first appeared in 1953. The present edition has been completely revised by a professional geographer to include recent discoveries and
research into the nature and development of Australian landforms. The essential
character of the book – its popular appeal – has been retained. New photographs
and maps enhance the updated text.

24 **Island continent: aspects of the historical geography of Australia
and its territories.**
A. Grenfell Price. Sydney: Angus & Robertson, 1972. 283p.
bibliog.

A collection of essays on aspects of the historical geography of Australia which
have been of particular concern to the author throughout a long working life.
Lively and provocative, the book can be read for sheer entertainment as well as
for its information content.

25 **Australia's first frontier: the spread of settlement in New South
Wales, 1788-1829.**
T. M. Perry. Melbourne: Melbourne University Press in association
with the Australian National University, 1963. 163p. bibliog.

A historical geography of the first forty years of settlement in Australia.

Maps and atlases

26 **Reader's Digest atlas of Australia.**
Sydney: Reader's Digest Services, with the Division of National
Mapping, Department of National Resources, 1978. 288p. maps.
bibliog.

This is the most comprehensive atlas of Australia currently available, with 160
colour maps each at a scale of 1:1,000,000. Given the scale, the maps are surprisingly detailed. They are arranged in sequence, and a key appears at the beginning
of the sequence so that each double page gives the effect of one large map with
some overlap rather than two separate maps. The rest of the volume contains
material common to atlases such as maps, and data on weather and climate,
geology, flora and fauna. In addition there is a comprehensive description of the
social and economic geography of Australia and of particular cities and regions
within the country.

27 **Philip's illustrated atlas of Australia.**
Melbourne: Philip & O'Neil, 1981. rev. ed. 178p.

Although designed primarily for school use, this atlas provides an excellent
picture of Australia for the general reader. It combines more than 100 maps with
many beautiful colour illustrations, detailed text and comprehensive statistics.

28 **A continent takes shape.**
Egon Kunz, Elsie Kunz. Sydney: Collins, 1971. 175p. maps.

This is a cartographic history of Australia. Dr. Kunz and his wife have put together
more than 100 maps, chart' and aerial photographs of Australia ranging from the
12th century to the present. The quality of reproduction of the maps, many of
which are in colour, is excellent. There is a brief accompanying text consisting
mainly of quotations from contemporary sources.

29 **The discovery of Australia: the charts and maps of the navigators
and explorers.**
T. M. Perry. Melbourne: Nelson, 1982. 159p.

A large-format volume of reproductions of historic maps and charts, with a text
combining the history of Australian cartography and a history of exploration of
the continent.

Discovery and exploration

30 The discovery of Australia.
G. A. Wood, revised by J. C. Beaglehole, foreword by O. H. K.
Spate. Melbourne: Macmillan, 1969. 391p. maps. bibliog.

Still unexcelled as a clear, comprehensive and very readable narrative of the exploration of the south-west Pacific, from the earliest theories about the possible existence of a continent there to the detailed charting of the coast of Australia by Matthew Flinders in the years 1796-1803. Portuguese, Spanish, Dutch, French and English explorations, as well as the voyages of the great navigators Quiros, Torres, Tasman, Dampier and Cook are described in detail. The book was published in 1922 and was based on a series of lectures given five years before, but the story is as exciting today as it was then. Professor Beaglehole, the great authority on James Cook, revised the text for this new edition, incorporating corrections which Wood himself made for a new edition and modifying references where recent research has brought to light new maps and diaries. Professor O. H. K. Spate has written the foreword showing how in spite of research done in recent years, Wood's original interpretations still hold strong.

31 The discovery and exploration of Australia.
Erwin H. J. Feeken, Gerda E. E. Feeken, O. H. K. Spate.
Melbourne: Nelson, 1970. 318p. map. bibliog.

Here the exploits of all the significant Australian explorers have been gathered into one volume. The biographical sketches are not only informative but also can be read solely for pleasure and entertainment. As Erwin Feeken is a cartographer it is not surprising to find a most useful series of coloured maps on which the routes of the explorers are traced. A key details every geographical feature named by the explorers. Completing the cross-references, a gazetteer lists about 4,000 place and feature names revealing their origins. Professor Oskar Spate, a historical geographer, has written an excellent introductory essay on the sea and land exploration of Australia. The bibliography lists the sources of quotations used in the historical text and gazetteer. The book is lavishly illustrated, including portraits of the explorers mentioned.

32 Australian explorers: a selection of their writings with an introduction.
Compiled by Kathleen Fitzpatrick. London: Oxford University
Press, 1958. 503p. maps. bibliog. (World's Classics, 559).

The literature of Australian land exploration is extensive as most of the explorers' journals, or narratives based upon them, have been published. Kathleen Fitzpatrick has made an excellent selection of extracts from the journals of the principal land explorers from 1813 to 1876. The book provides the reader with insight into the personalities of the men who had to cope with the extremes of climate and terrain of the huge continent which they were attempting to map. The author's scholarly introduction touching on the human as well as the geographical aspects of Australian exploration adds greatly to the value of the book.

33 **Crossing the dead heart.**
C. T. Madigan. Adelaide: Rigby, 1974. 171p.

It is remarkable that the Simpson Desert, a 145,000 square kilometre wasteland of arid, red sand ridges, was crossed for the first time just forty odd years ago. In 1939 Cecil Madigan, geologist and one-time Antarctic explorer, led a party of nine men and nineteen camels through what he called 'the last untrodden area in Australia' in thirty-one days. The author gives a straightforward account of a potentially dangerous but in fact largely uneventful journey. The real value of the book lies in its description of the eerie, desolate landscape so typical of much of the interior of the continent, unfamiliar even to most Australians, four-fifths of whom live in the cities or near the coastline.

34 **Australia unveiled: the share of the Dutch navigators in the discovery of Australia.**
Günter Schilder, translated from the German by Olaf Richter.
Amsterdam: Theatrum Orbis Terrarum, 1976. 424p. bibliog.

The story of the Dutch discovery of Australia in the 17th century, and the mapping of the north, west and south coasts of the continent. This single volume contains most of the pictorial representations of Australia from ancient times to the voyages of Tasman. The author has analysed and annotated them and added findings of his own. A standard work on the myths about the Great South Land – Terra Australis – and its eventual discovery.

35 **France Australe: a study of French explorations and attempts to found a penal colony and strategic base in south western Australia 1503-1826.**
Leslie L. Marchant. Perth: Artlook Books, 1982. 384p. bibliog.

The first major investigation of early French involvement in the discovery and exploration of Western Australia. According to the author, France has an arguable claim to Western Australia on precisely the same basis as the 'prescriptive right' Argentina uses in claiming the Falkland Islands. The book is lavishly illustrated with the work of artists and mapmakers who accompanied the various expeditions.

Natural disasters

36 **Natural hazards in Australia.**
Edited by R. L. Heathcote, B. G. Thom. Canberra: Australian Academy of Science, 1979. 531p. bibliog.

These are the edited papers of a symposium sponsored by the Academy of Science, the Institute of Australian Geographers and the Academy of Social Sciences. The volume covers an enormous range of Australian natural disasters and their social and economic consequences.

37 **Winds of fury: the full true story of the great Darwin disaster.**
Keith Cole. Adelaide: Rigby, 1977. 211p.

Cyclone Tracy struck Darwin on 25 December 1974 and within a few hours destroyed over 10,000 houses; damaged all public utilities; rendered 45,000 people homeless; killed 66 people and injured 140. The author and his wife saw their own house being gradually torn apart around them and this is a vivid description of their experience. Also included are a number of other eyewitness accounts of that night of terror. Other aspects of the cyclone and its aftermath to come under the author's scrutiny include the attitudes and behaviour of the armed forces and police, political ineptitude and allegations of bureaucratic bungling. Although very subjective the book is nonetheless a fascinating study of a major disaster from the viewpoint of an ordinary citizen. There are 16 pages of black-and-white photographs which illustrate the almost unbelievable destruction wrought by Tracy.

38 **Cyclone.**
Hector Holthouse. Adelaide: Rigby, 1977. 179p. (Seal Books).

In the wet season, December to April, the northern third of the continent experiences severe cyclones, with wind velocities exceeding 160 kilometres an hour. They are usually accompanied by torrential rain which results in severe flooding. Although these great storms devastate agricultural lands and cause great property damage as well as loss of life, they can sometimes penetrate deep enough inland to bring relief to huge areas of arid land. The author has collected details of some of the more spectacular cyclones to hit the east coast of Australia during the last century. The stories of shipwrecks, drownings, massive seas and floods, record rainfalls, miraculous escapes and bravery are enlivened by interviews with survivors. An important part of the book deals with the history of early weather forecasting in Australia, a period dominated by the Queensland meteorologist Clement Wragge, a colourful character who delighted in naming cyclones after girls and political leaders for whom he held little respect.

39 **Drought: causes, effects, solutions.**
D. Campbell. Melbourne: Cheshire, 1968.

Australia's climate is characterized by prolonged periods of dry weather which occur regularly and often cover vast areas of the continent. In short, there is always drought somewhere in Australia. Frequently these dry spells cause huge agricultural losses with a serious effect on the national economy. Don Campbell believes that Australians have become passive and fatalistic about drought. His book is a polemical attempt to stir the populace from its apathy. The author offers many worthwhile suggestions for cushioning the effects of drought, including research at national level; surveying and building dams and irrigation schemes; building adequate transport links between drought-prone areas and regions of more reliable rainfall; creating fodder reserves; and arranging finance for these schemes.

40 **Bushfire: history, prevention, control.**
Red Foster. Sydney: Reed, 1976. 247p.

Bushfires in Australia have a grim record of death and destruction. Seventy-one people perished in a horror blaze in Victoria in January 1939. Millions of hectares of forest and grazing land were wiped out as were whole towns and many farms. In 1967 fires destroyed 1,100 buildings on the outskirts of Hobart, the capital of Tasmania, and 62 people lost their lives. The author witnessed the deaths of three fellow volunteer firefighters in a bushfire in 1968 in the Blue Mountains, not far from Sydney, Australia's largest city. The experience prompted him to fill the big gap in information available about this recurring natural hazard. The result is a detailed and richly illustrated book which examines the history, prevention and control of bushfires. Throughout the book the author emphasizes a much neglected Australian institution, the voluntary fire brigades, which have over 250,000 members.

41 **Bushfire disaster: an Australian community in crisis.**
R. L. Wettenhall. Sydney: Angus & Robertson, 1975. 320p.
maps. bibliog.

Tornadoes, cyclones, floods, fires, droughts and to a lesser extent earthquakes are natural disasters which can strike suddenly anywhere in the populated areas of the Australian continent. On 7 February 1967 Hobart and its environs were swept by bushfires which within a few hours caused the deaths of 62 people and the destruction of 1,300 houses and other property adding up to a total damage bill of $40 million. Dr. Wettenhall analyses the Hobart experience in which he was personally involved, setting it against the background of disaster in Australia in general, and drawing from it conclusions about the necessity for preparedness and community organization in the event of emergency, conclusions which the Brisbane-Ipswich floods of 1974 and the Darwin cyclone of Christmas Day of the same year have borne out only too well. A dramatic series of photographs illustrate the havoc wrought by the fires in and around Tasmania's capital city.

42 **They all ran wild: the story of pests on the land in Australia.**
Eric C. Rolls. Sydney: Angus & Robertson, 1977. 415p. bibliog.
(A & R Non-Fiction Classics).

Rabbit infestation in Australia reached plague levels in the years after the Second World War. The epidemic was eventually controlled by the establishment of the South American virus disease myxomatosis. The author devotes a good half of his book to the story of the rabbit, from its painstaking introduction and acclimatization, its northward invasion that left the pastures bare and decimated trees and native plants, to its final control. The rest of the book deals with some of the other introduced plagues – foxes, rats, donkeys, pigs, sparrows – and takes a look at the problems posed by the indigenous kangaroos, dingoes and the well-meaning yet often incredibly naive Acclimatization Societies, which devoted themselves to the introduction of exotic, mainly European fauna to Australia. There is a more extensive bibliography in the first edition published in 1969. An entirely rewritten edition for young readers appeared in 1973, entitled *Running wild* (Sydney: Angus & Robertson).

Travel guides

43 Australia.
Robin Mead. London: Batsford, 1983. 173p.

A popular guide to Australia published in the Batsford travel books series.

44 Explore Australia: touring for leisure and pleasure.
Sydney: Currey O'Neil, 1980. 400p.

A motorist's delight! A comprehensive guide for touring the continent, it combines in one volume 176 pages of road maps, detailed guides to every capital city, descriptions of over 700 towns and a gazetteer of more than 9,000 places. There are special features on Australia's most exciting holiday areas such as the Great Barrier Reef, the Red Centre, the Murray River, the Flinders Ranges and the wine-growing areas to name just a few. The book is lavishly illustrated with black-and-white and colour photographs. Indispensable for anyone exploring Australia by car and a valuable up-to-date reference to all cities and towns in Australia.

45 Reader's Digest motoring guide to Australia.
Edited and designed by Reader's Digest Services, 1982. 383p.

An excellent road touring guide with many detailed maps, road signs in several languages, a section on safe driving, one on routine maintenance and roadside repairs. A useful list of annual events such as festivals, sporting fixtures, carnivals, shows and street fairs is included. An indispensable companion for the motor tourist.

46 Right way, don't go back: travels in Australia.
Donald Horne. Melbourne: Sun Books, 1978. 163p.

This well-known social commentator takes his family to examine the traveller's Australia. Horne's other books on the state of the nation draw heavily on descriptions and insights gained on his extensive travels and here we see how he goes about this task.

47 Sydney: the harbour city handbook.
Robyn Stone. Sydney: Allen & Unwin, 1981. 252p.

An up-to-date convenient pocket-book providing a complete guide to Australia's largest and most exciting city. There is valuable information for the visitor on a low budget as well as for the more affluent tourist.

48 The Bulletin book of Australian wineries.
Richard Beckett, Donald Hogg. Sydney: Gregory's, 1979. 276p.

A comprehensive guide to over 220 Australian wineries. The book is particularly useful for the touring wine lover who wants to taste and perhaps to buy. Maps of each wine-making district show the locations of all wineries.

Description and travel

49 The book of Australia.
Robert Wilson, photography by Ray Joyce, Reg Morrison.
Sydney: Lansdowne, 1982. 487p. bibliog.

A thorough geographical guide to Australia with more than 1,000 colour photographs depicting the landscape, the people and the flora and fauna. Over 50 maps pinpoint the location of places mentioned in the text. There is a detailed index and a short bibliography for further reading. A book for the tourist as well as for the armchair traveller.

50 Australia the greatest island: an aerial exploration of the Australian coastline.
Robert Raymond, photography by Reg Morrison. Sydney: Ure Smith, 1979. 352p.

A collection of superb photographs of the Australian coastline taken at low altitudes from a seaplane. The pictures effectively convey the diversity and expanse of the Australian continent. The expedition of the two airborne authors started from Cape Leeuwin in the south-west corner and took them in an anti-clockwise direction around the entire coastline following the route Matthew Flinders took in 1801 in his attempt to circumnavigate the continent.

51 A day in the life of Australia: March 6, 1981.
Sydney: DITLA, 1981. 288p.

On March 6, 1981, one hundred of the world's leading photojournalists were commissioned to try to capture on film, across the continent, one day in the life of Australia. There were sixty-seven photographers from nineteen countries as well as thirty-three Australians. This huge book is the product of their labours.

52 Australia: a timeless grandeur.
Photography by Reg Morrison, text by Helen Grasswill. Sydney: Lansdowne, 1981. 304p. bibliog.

A large-format book with many fine, coloured photographs of remote, wild places in Australia. The text outlines the geological structure, climate, vegetation and wildlife of each area.

53 Seven cities of Australia.
Sydney: John Ferguson, 1978. 182p.

In 1977 the *Bulletin* magazine asked seven noted Australian writers to take an extended look at the capital city with which each was connected in some way. Ian Moffitt made an affectionate assessment of Sydney; Hal Porter gave a brilliant portrait of the smallest capital, Hobart; Robert Macklin wrote about Brisbane; Keith Dunstan, Melbourne newspaper columnist, took a close look at his native city; Geoffrey Dutton, noted literary figure, examined Adelaide; Robert Drewe made an expatriate's return to remote Perth in Western Australia; and Alan Fitzgerald, Canberra's resident satirist, wrote about the nation's capital. The articles have been collected as a permanent record of Australia's capital cities in the late 1970s. Black-and-white illustrations accompany the text.

54 The heritage of Australia: the illustrated register of the national estate.
Melbourne: Macmillan, with the Australian Heritage Commission, 1981. 1,248p.

This unique publication has 6,500 entries, 200 maps and 8,500 photographs backed by authoritative essays as well as complete indexes. All the presently listed elements that make up the National Estate and are destined for preservation are included. They range from historic sites and buildings to national parks and sacred Aboriginal sites.

55 Southern walkabout.
Vincent Serventy. Sydney: Reed, 1969. 160p.

The author's *Nature walkabout*, published in 1967, described the Serventy family's travels from Perth northwards, traversing the top of Australia and south to Sydney, a journey of some 25,000 kilometres which took six months. In this book Serventy, with his wife and their three children, complete the circuit of the continent, from Sydney back to Perth. The main object of the journeys was to record and photograph wildlife, thus gathering material for the author's articles and books on natural history. The books abound with fascinating Australiana: history, folklore, geology, accounts of early navigators and explorers and insights into the natural inhabitants – animals, plants and men. The text is further enhanced by many informative colour photographs. A strong conservation theme runs through the book.

56 The book of the Murray.
Edited by G. V. Lawrence, G. Kinross Smith. Adelaide: Rigby, 1975. 264p. bibliog.

The Murray is the largest river of the driest continent on earth. Although its length of over 2,000 kilometres and the area of its basin rank the Murray among the main rivers of the world, the volume of its flow is quite small compared to such giants as the Amazon, Nile and Mississippi. However, since its flow has been gradually brought under control by the building of storages in its upper reaches, weirs at the mouth and a system of locks along its length, it has brought that scarce Australian resource – water – to the inhabitants of three states: New South Wales, Victoria and South Australia. Besides emphasizing the economic significance of the Murray, the book has authoritative chapters by sixteen expert contributors on the history, geography, anthropology, zoology and botany of the river. The volume is amply illustrated, many photographs being reproduced in colour. There is a bibliography but, sadly, no index.

Geography. Description and travel

57 **Australia's greatest river.**
John Larkins, photographs by Steve Parish. Adelaide: Rigby, 1982. 231p. bibliog.

A glossy magnificently illustrated volume following the 2,530-kilometre-long Murray downstream from its source in the Australian Alps to its entrance into the sea in South Australia. The text, a blend of history, reminiscences and description, is informative as well as entertaining.

58 **Some came early, some came late.**
Nancy Phelan. Melbourne: Macmillan, 1970. 219p.

The author is a prolific writer of travel books, who this time has turned her attention to her own country. The book is as much concerned with people as places and she focuses mainly on immigrant communities and how they have fitted into the Australian way of life. A perceptive, easy-to-read account which also instructs.

59 **Australian pub crawl.**
Douglass Baglin, Yvonne Austin. Sydney: Child & Henry, 1980. rev. ed. 160p.

Even if you don't like beer, you'll like the book! It can certainly serve as the drinking man's touring guide to watering holes in a dry land, but it is also a travel book and a valuable record of social and architectural history. It is the result of a twenty-year pub crawl by the authors and is a nostalgic tribute to what is perhaps Australia's best-loved institution – the pub, or hotel. The colour photographs by one of Australia's best practitioners are a delight.

60 **The Great Dividing Range.**
Jeff Toghill. Sydney: Reed, 1982. 288p.

The Great Dividing Range is Australia's greatest mountain chain stretching for 4,000 kilometres along the entire east coast from the tip of Cape York Peninsula almost to the border of South Australia with Victoria. The name, a heritage from the original settlers and early map makers, is inappropriate, as the Divide is nowhere 'great' in comparison with the world's big ranges, and it is not a range in the accepted meaning of the word. For the most part it consists of soft, undulating hills, vast wheat-covered plains and a small area of snow-covered alpine country in its highest part. Being near the coast it is part of the narrow coastal area that receives more or less reliable rainfall and therefore supports many settlements and farming communities in stark contrast to the huge, arid inland. The book portrays the range in many colour photographs with a supportive text.

61 **Reader's Digest book of historic Australian towers.**
Photographs by Robin Morrison. Sydney: Reader's Digest
Services, 1982. 334p.

Fifty towers are described, each chosen because of its historical significance, either as convict settlement, port, goldfield tower, commercial or agricultural centre, and because of the wealth of images that it conveys. There are more than 1,000 magnificent photographs and descriptions of the people and lifestyles that created these communities. Altogether a delightful evocation of Australia's past.

62 **All things wild.**
Jeff Carter. Adelaide: Rigby, 1977. 151p.

Carter is an indefatigable traveller and prolific writer of travel books about Australia's wild places and the colourful people who live there. His yarns are breezy, easy to read and provide a good introduction to the atmosphere of the vast country that lies beyond the populated coastal fringe. He has published more than a dozen books. Two others are *Wild country* (Rigby, 1971), and *People of the inland* (Rigby, 1966). All books are illustrated by the author's own photographs.

Natural History, Flora and Fauna

Natural history

63 **Land of wonder: an illustrated anthology of the best Australian nature writing.**
Selected and edited by Alec H. Chisholm. Sydney: Angus & Robertson, 1979. 284p.

This is the illustrated edition of a work first published in 1964. The author has collected a diversity of material, which ranges from official reports prepared by officers of the First Fleet to the work of modern novelists and scientists. It should appeal to a wide readership with an interest in the unique flora and fauna of Australia.

64 **Wild places of Australia.**
Photographs by Lee Pearce, text and directory by Lawrence Durrant, Valerie Parv. Sydney: Bay Books, 1983. 224p.

An excellent, up-to-date guide to Australia's national parks. The text describes the major parks according to types of environment (coasts and islands, highlands and forests, outback and the Centre), paying particular attention to wildlife and special features such as Aboriginal rock art. A directory gives detailed information on nearly 300 national parks, where each one is, how to get to it, and what there is to do and see there. The text is supplemented with magnificent photographs taken specially for the book.

65 **The singing land: 22 natural environments of Australia from surging ocean to arid desert.**
Vincent Serventy. Sydney: Angus & Robertson, 1972. 95p. bibliog.

A broad overview for the layman of the environmental variations on the continent. The book examines how the animals and plants have adapted themselves to their environment. The text is accompanied by colour illustrations.

66 **Dryandra: the story of an Australian forest.**
    Vincent Serventy. Sydney: Reed, 1970. 205p.

Dryandra is a state forest reserve of some 50,000 acres situated 200 kilometres south-east of Perth in Western Australia. It was reserved originally for mallet trees, used for tannin production, but has served also as a sanctuary for many native animals and plants nearly extinct in other areas where they once thrived. The author traces, month by month, the sequence of the four seasons and their effect on the forest and its inhabitants. A fascinating book for the nature lover, enhanced by many colour illustrations.

67 **The great gardens of Australia.**
    Howard Tanner, assisted by Jane Begg. Melbourne: Macmillan,
    1976. 198p. bibliog.

The first published survey of Australian public and private gardens by someone professionally trained and involved in the shaping of the physical environment. Tanner, an architect, is good on plans, spaces, volumes and tones but is weak on botanical science and historical perspective. The book is profusely illustrated.

68 **Wildlife of eastern Australia.**
    Stanley Breeden, Kay Breeden. Sydney: Collins, 1973. 224p.
    bibliog.

This husband-and-wife team of dedicated naturalists stress the interdependence of plant and animal communities, their adaptation to a particular environment and climatic features, while at all times considering the degree of specialization that Australia's long isolation fostered. The text is free of jargon and written for popular appeal while being scientifically accurate. The present volume contains most of the text of the first two volumes of the Breedens' major work *A natural history of Australia*, a much more profusely illustrated work than the present handy volume. Volume 1 is *Tropical Queensland*, published in 1970; volume 2 is *Australia's south east*, 1972; volume 3 is *Australia's north*, 1975. All were published by Collins in Sydney and London.

69 **Australian seashores: a guide for the beach-lover, the naturalist,
    the shore fisherman, and the student.**
    William J. Dakin, assisted by Isobel Bennett, Elizabeth Pope.
    Sydney: Angus & Robertson, 1976. 372p.

This classic work on the botany and zoology of the Australian seashore, first published in 1952, has been reissued once again in the Australian Natural Science Library series. Professor Dakin devoted a lifetime to the study of his subject. His great communicative skills are evident in this easy-to-read yet scholarly work. Less accessible to the general reader is *The fringe of the sea*, by Isobel Bennett (photography by F. G. Myers, Keith Gillett. Adelaide: Rigby, 1974. rev. ed.).

70 **The Great Barrier Reef.**
Isobel Bennett, photography by the author. Sydney: Lansdowne
Press, 1981. 184p. bibliog.

The Barrier Reef is the largest structure on earth created by living organisms. This
scholarly work comprehensively covers the story of the reef, its history, structure,
plants and animals and its ecological relationships. It is a popular scientific book
presented in language intelligible to the interested reader. Included are a great
number of magnificent coloured illustrations.

71 **Australia's Great Barrier Reef.**
Robert Endean. Brisbane: University of Queensland Press, 1982.
348p.

The most recent comprehensive and authoritative study of this remarkable natural
formation in all its aspects. There are over 300 coloured illustrations.

Flora

72 **People and plants in Australia. Plants and man in Australia.**
Edited by D. J. Carr, S. G. M. Carr. Sydney: Academic Press,
1981. 2 vols.

These two companion volumes present thirty-one essays on the history of Australian botany. The discipline started with the many amateur collectors who sent
their gatherings of exotic specimens to professional botanists in Europe. The
profession blossomed in later years when Australian botanists became world
leaders in certain aspects of the science.

73 **Flora of Australia: volume 1: introduction.**
Bureau of Flora and Fauna, Canberra. Canberra: Australian
Government Publishing Service, 1981- .

This is the introductory volume to a series planned to comprise approximately
fifty volumes to be published over a twenty-year period and intended to cover the
names, characteristics, distribution and habitat of Australian plants.

74 **The vegetation of Australia.**
   Noel C. W. Beadle. Cambridge, England: Cambridge University
   Press, 1981. 690p. bibliog.

The Australian flora is usually regarded as unique, chiefly because it contains a high proportion of endemic genera and partly because two genera, eucalyptus and acacia, with a total of over 1,000 species, dominate most of the continent. This is the first scholarly account of the vegetation of the whole of the continent. The author presents an analysis of the flora, its origin, development and composition. The book contains 378 black-and-white photographs of plant communities, 90 tables of data and 38 distribution maps, including a unique vegetation map of the continent, showing the distribution of some 90 plant communities. The volume should be of particular value to all botanists, ecologists and plant geographers.

75 **Australian vegetation.**
   Edited by R. H. Groves. Cambridge, England: Cambridge
   University Press, 1981. 449p. bibliog.

In this major review of the vegetation of the continent all main species of the Australian flora are described. Each chapter is written by an expert on a particular vegetation type. Chapters on plant geography, history, alien plants and conservation are included. The book is intended mainly as a text for students and professional botanists.

76 **Wild flowers of Australia.**
   Thistle Y. Harris, illustrated by Adam Forster. Sydney: Angus &
   Robertson, 1979. 8th ed. rev. 207p. bibliog.

A popular book which has been in print since 1938. It portrays over 250 Australian wild flowers which are commonly found in all states. As far as possible non-technical descriptions are used and each plant is illustrated by magnificent paintings for easy identification.

77 **Native trees and shrubs of south-eastern Australia.**
   Leon Costermans. Adelaide: Rigby, 1981. 422p.

Written for the non-specialist, while retaining scientific accuracy, this large, comprehensively illustrated volume makes an indispensable aid for any field observer or armchair traveller to the larger species of vegetation of the fertile south-eastern corner of the continent.

78 **Native trees of Australia.**
   Mervyn Millet, colour photography by Jutta Hösel. Sydney:
   Lansdowne Press, 1971. 112p. bibliog.

An introductory book to thirty-four of the most common Australian native trees, with some general material on botany and botanists.

79 **Forests of Australia.**
Alexander Rule. Sydney: Angus & Robertson, 1967. 213p.
A comprehensive examination of Australian forest regions and forest-based industries.

80 **The gift of the forest.**
Pictorial editor and project co-ordinator Jutta Hösel, library editors Rosemary Brissenden, Robert Brissenden. Melbourne: Currey O'Neil, with Australian Conservation Foundation, 1982. 148p. bibliog.
Today about two-thirds of the forest lands in existence at the time of first settlement in Australia have disappeared. This handsome volume is a celebration of the remaining forest, and presents a selection of the best artistic photographs, poems and prose, both past and present.

81 **Acacias of Australia.**
Marion H. Simmons, photographs by John G. Simmons. Melbourne: Nelson, 1981. 325p. bibliog.
Acacias (also known as wattles) are the most widespread and numerous of all Australian plants. Quick-growing, showy, and tolerating a wide range of conditions, it is a popular plant for cultivation. This is the first book for the general reader, which illustrates the species from each state showing flowers, foliage and the rarely-drawn pods.

82 **Emigrant eucalypts: gum trees as exotics.**
Robert Fyfe Zacharin. Melbourne: Melbourne University Press, 1978. 137p. bibliog.
Native eucalyptus trees dominate the Australian landscape and provide by far the larger proportion of its forest products. The author tells the story how eucalypts, planted as exotics, were dispersed throughout the world after the first seeds arrived in England in 1770. The text is backed up by many interesting illustrations.

83 **Useful wild plants in Australia.**
A. B. Cribb, J. W. Cribb. Sydney: Fontana/Collins, 1982. 269p. bibliog.
One of a series of three books by the same authors on similar themes. The other two volumes are *Wild medicine in Australia* (Sydney: Collins, 1981); and *Wild food in Australia* (Sydney: Fontana/Collins, 1982. rev. ed.). The three books provide a different and popular approach to the diverse and unique plant life of Australia.

Fauna

84 **Australian shells: illustrating and describing 600 species of marine gastropods found in Australian waters.**
B. R. Wilson, Keith Gillett. Sydney: Reed, 1980. new ed. 152p.

The shores of the Australian island continent are famous for the diversity of marine molluscs. This book lists and illustrates the better-known of the tens of thousands species living there. It is a good reference tool for the collector and shoreline fossicker to identify what to buy or find. *Shell collecting in Australia* (Neville Coleman. Sydney: Reed, 1976) is a practical book, which describes methods of getting the shells by trawling, scuba diving and rainforest collecting. It also warns about potential dangers of the hobby and gives advice about cleaning shells and keeping aquariums.

85 **Insects of Australia.**
John Goode, illustrated by R. J. Tillyard. Sydney: Angus & Robertson, 1980. 260p. bibliog.

Included in the book are all the common insects and some rarer species considered to be of particular interest owing to their unusual characteristics. Enough basic information is given in the text to enable the collector or nature observer to identify any Australian insect. Illustrations are from the classic *The insects of Australia and New Zealand.*

86 **Butterflies of Australia.**
T. F. B. Common, D. F. Waterhouse. Sydney: Angus & Robertson, 1981. rev. ed. 682p. bibliog.

First published in 1972, this book has been substantially revised and expanded. It is an authoritative and up-to-date reference on the Australian species with many coloured plates, numerous line drawings and distribution maps. The informative text is well complemented by a glossary, bibliography and index.

87 **Australian sea fishes north of 30°S.**
Neville Coleman. Sydney: Doubleday, 1981. 297p.

A companion volume to *Australian sea fishes south of 30°S*, published in 1980. Together the books provide an identification guide to the marine fishes in Australian waters. The colour photographs feature live fish in their natural environment. Each illustration is accompanied by a detailed description of the fish and its habits.

88 **Shark attack.**
V. M. Coppleson. Sydney: Angus & Robertson, 1962. 2nd ed. 269p.

A comprehensive account about sharks and shark attacks on humans. The author ranges world-wide, but the focus is on Australia, where preventive measures are also discussed. There are maps, tables, lists of recorded attacks and photographs, some of them quite gruesome.

89   **Reptiles and amphibians of Australia.**
       Harold G. Cogger.   Sydney: Reed, 1979. 608p. bibliog.

The standard reference for identification of Australia's 664 species of frogs, crocodiles, turtles and tortoises, lizards and snakes. The descriptive text for each species is accompanied by a distribution map, 192 colour photographs taken in the field and 594 black-and-white photographs. Line drawings are provided where necessary.

90   **Reader's Digest complete book of Australian birds.**
       Consultant editor H. J. Frith.   Sydney: Reader's Digest Services,
       1977. 615p.

The most complete book of Australian avifauna ever published contains detailed references to over 700 species. Most of the beautiful colour photographs have been selected from the National Photographic Index of Australian birds, a project begun in 1969 to collect colour prints of every Australian species of birds. The book gives authoritative easy-to-read detail on each bird's location, nesting and eating habits, male and female characteristics and ornithological name. As a magnificent production it was chosen Best Designed Book of the Year by The Australian Book Publishers' Association. A similar large format book is *Every Australian bird illustrated* (Adelaide: Rigby, 1975).

91   **Wildlife of Australia.**
       Vincent Serventy.   London: Hamish Hamilton, 1977. 216p.
       bibliog.

Serventy is a prolific author of nature books and an activist in the conservation movement. In this large, well-illustrated volume he covers Australia's unique fauna in detail.

92   **A guide to the native mammals of Australia.**
       W. D. L. Ride, drawings by Ella Fry.   Melbourne: Oxford
       University Press, 1970. 249p. bibliog.

Recognized as the standard work on the subject, this book is also a contribution to the problems of conservation. All the native Australian mammal fauna is included, from kangaroos to pygmy-possums and from seals to desert mice, with full descriptions and excellent line drawings of each species. The text is written in everyday language and with anecdotal sidelights for a wide readership. An appendix containing detailed bibliographical references to definitive anatomical descriptions renders it useful for the professional. An earlier book published in 1941 and issued in a revised and abridged edition in 1973, outdated in some of its classifications but including much interesting historical information, is *Furred animals of Australia* (Ellis Troughton. Sydney: Angus & Robertson, 1973).

93 A treasury of Australian wildlife: selected studies from *Australian Natural History*.
   Edited by D. F. McMichael. Sydney: Ure Smith, 1967. 354p.

A selection of articles which have appeared over twenty years in *Australian Natural History*, a magazine published by the Australian Museum. Although written by subject specialists, the material was compiled for the general reader and succeeds in being accessible, informative and often fascinating. With 235 illustrations it is a multi-purpose book: it can be read right through, it can be 'dipped into', and it can serve as a reference book.

94 **Adventures with Australian animals.**
   Harry Franca, photographs by Harry Franca, Claudy Franca.
   Adelaide: Rigby, 1976. 164p.

The author has worked since 1960 as a full-time naturalist, writer and photographer. In this book he records the highlights of fifteen years spent roaming the Australian bush in search of material for his publications. There are many black-and-white and colour photographs taken by his wife and himself. A non-technical, easy-to-read book.

95 **The lyrebird.**
   L. H. Smith. Melbourne: Lansdowne Press, 1968. 115p.

Probably the most spectacular native bird is the lyrebird. Its colourful, spreading gossamer fan is as astonishing as a peacock's, it is an artful copyist and sound mimic, a ceremonial dancer and a master-builder of mounds for performances. Dr. Smith spent thirty-five years studying and photographing these birds, mainly in Sherbrooke Forest near Melbourne, Victoria. This fascinating work presents the results of a lifetime's study in lively text and excellent photography.

96 **Paradoxical platypus: hobnobbing with duckbills.**
   David Fleay. Brisbane: Jacaranda, 1980. 150p.

A most entertaining account of the habits of one of Australia's shyest creatures, the duckbilled platypus. The author has spent forty-seven years observing, feeding and breeding the animal. Over a 100 magnificent photographs, many in colour, add to the text. Another informal account of the animal is *The platypus*, by Harry Burrell (Adelaide: Rigby, 1974).

97 **Dingoes don't bark.**
   Lionel Hudson. Adelaide: Rigby, 1974. 80p.

The dingo or native dog is Australia's most maligned animal. There is a bounty on its head, and 10,000 kilometres of fencing has been erected to keep the dingoes out of sheep country. Hudson's book is a sympathetic account of the dingo which dispels a number of myths about the animal. The author is not a naturalist, but the work is based on his travels in dingo country while making a documentary film about the animals, and on his experience in raising a dingo pup in his suburban home.

98 **Possum moods.**
Paule Ridpath. Sydney: Ure Smith, 1967. 72p.

The author lived for four years in the forest-covered foothills of Mount Welling-ton near Hobart. Some of the many possums inhabiting the surrounding bush visited her house, especially after she encouraged them with bread and honey, and the author here sets down her observations of these nocturnal visitors. She has a sensitive appreciation of animals and a fine ability to convey her observations and feelings in words. The book should have great appeal to anyone interested in the habits of wild animals as well as being a valuable reference to professional students of animal behaviour, and there are many excellent photographs. Another light-hearted account of possums in the rain forests of northern Queensland is *Spotlight on possums* (Rupert Russell. Brisbane, Australia: University of Queens-land Press, 1980).

99 **The year of the kangaroo.**
H. D. Williamson, illustrated by Roy B. Doyle. Sydney: Reed, 1977. 187p. bibliog.

An interesting account of the life cycle of the kangaroo during the four seasons. The story is based on fact and personal observation although it is presented in fictional form, and is suitable for a wide readership from children to adults. Williamson has published a similar book on the other favourite denizen of the Australian bush, *The year of the koala* (illustrated by William T. Cooper. New York: Scribner's, 1975). A third popular work by Williamson is *Fierce encounter: life and death in the Australian bush* (illustrated by William Cooper. Sydney: Reed, 1970).

100 **Kangaroos.**
H. J. Frith, J. H. Calaby. Melbourne: Cheshire, 1969. 209p. bibliog.

A scientific study of the biology and basic conservation needs of the kangaroo, the best-known native animal of Australia. The book is suitable for the informed layman. A short, popular account with many photographs is available in *The life of the kangaroo*, by Stanley and Kay Breeden (Sydney: Angus & Robertson, 1966).

101 **Our dying fauna: a personal perspective on a changing environment.**
Athol M. Douglas. Perth: Creative Research, with the Biological Services, 1980. 170p.

A book about wildlife conservation in Australia, written by a naturalist who has had a lifelong association with the Western Australian Museum. The style is free of jargon and scientific mystique, which makes the book very accessible to anyone interested in the fate of Australia's unique wildlife. Unlike most books on the subject, this one also considers the invertebrates, which are usually excluded from popular accounts of conservation.

102 **Australian endangered species: mammals, birds and reptiles.**
Derrick Ovington. Sydney: Cassell, 1978. 183p. bibliog.

A description in text and paintings of twenty-three mammals, eighteen birds and two reptiles which the author considers to be threatened by extinction. He also suggests methods of preserving these animals, and gives examples of previous successful conservation programmes.

History

Reference works

103 **Dictionary of Australian history.**
Brian Murphy. Sydney: McGraw-Hill, 1982. 304p.

Designed as a reference work for schools and universities, the book is useful to everyone needing information about key figures and events in Australian history. The text is factual rather than interpretative.

104 **Australia: a chronology and fact book 1606-1976.**
Compiled and edited by Alex C. Castles. Dobbs Ferry, New York: Oceana, 1978. 151p. bibliog.

A chronology of Australia in the World Chronology series. Besides some other documents, the book includes the full text of the Australian constitution.

105 **The manufacture of Australian history.**
Rob Pascoe. Melbourne: Melbourne University Press, 1979. 207p. bibliog.

The author manages to include most of the major writers as well as some of the minor ones in this unique survey of Australian historiography in the twentieth century. All books cited in the text are listed in a bibliography. An excellent guide to further reading.

106 **Historical disciplines and culture in Australasia: an assessment.**
Edited by John A. Moses. Brisbane: University of Queensland Press, 1979. 291p.

A collection of essays by leading practitioners on the state of historiography in Australia, who have usually been remarkably reluctant to engage themselves in introspection. This book is therefore very welcome for illuminating their views on the art and science of history.

107 **New history: studying Australia today.**
Edited by G. Osborne, W. F. Mandle. Sydney: Allen & Unwin, 1982. 216p. bibliog.

While traditional areas of historiography such as narrative, general and political history still flourish, recently considerable effort has been devoted to certain specialist areas. These essays investigate some of this new work and suggest where future research might lead. Fields covered include: Aboriginal history, women's history, oral history, medical history, sports history, history of post-war immigration, labour history, the Australian mandate in New Guinea, transport and urban history.

108 **Such was life: select documents in Australian social history.**
Russel Ward, John Robertson. Sydney: Alternative Publishing Cooperative, 1978-80. 2 vols. Vol. 1, 1788-1850, 337p. Vol. 2, 1851-1913, 352p.

A stimulating selection from contemporary sources about life in Australia. Besides official documents there are descriptions by ordinary people of town and country life, Aboriginals, seafaring, bush-ranging, sheep, cattle and the unique wildlife. The excerpts bring to life the ways in which the early settlers lived, their hardships and the shortcomings of the society. Short explanatory prefaces to each document show how they fit into the overall story. Recommended as a companion to the reading of general histories. Other worthwhile collections of source materials are: F. K. Crowley's *A documentary history of Australia, 1788-1970* (Melbourne Nelson, 6 vols.), C. M. H. Clark's *Select documents in Australian history, 1788-1900* (Sydney, Angus & Robertson, 1977. 2 vols.), and Clark's *Sources of Australian history* (London, 1957). Other more specialist document collections are listed in Crowley's preface to his *Documentary history*.

109 **The Australian dream: a collection of anticipations about Australia from Captain Cook to the present day.**
Selected and introduced by Ian Turner. Melbourne: Sun Books, 1968. 358p.

The introduction states that 'this is a book about Australia's future – or more precisely about how people in both the distant and recent past have seen Australia's future'. It is an anthology of what the author considers to be significant speculations about Australia's future from Erasmus Darwin to present day commentators. Professor Turner introduces the documents with a brilliant essay on the Australian dream.

General works

110 **A short history of Australia.**
Manning Clark. Melbourne: Macmillan, 1981. 2nd illustrated ed.
256p.

A very personal, often provocative interpretation of the story of Australia. Always interesting, most readable and very enjoyable, this short, popular history is based on the material collected for the writing of Professor Clark's five-volume *A history of Australia*. The second edition is enhanced by well-chosen illustrations. Five volumes of this monumental work have now been published bringing the story up to the evacuation of the Australian forces from Gallipoli. The author interprets the history of Australia through the personalities of tragic individuals to ordinary people. He handles his theme with the skill of a great novelist – indeed, the work is capable of being read as a great novel and has won many literary awards. Anyone with any interest in Australian history at all must read this unique work. The five volumes of *A history of Australia*, all published by Melbourne University Press, are: Volume I – *From the earliest times to the age of Macquarie,* 1962; Volume II – *New South Wales and Van Diemen's Land 1822-38,* 1968; Volume III – *The beginnings of an Australian civilization 1824-51,* 1973; Volume IV – *The earth abideth for ever 1851-88,* 1978; Volume V – *The people make laws 1888-1915,* 1981.

111 **The story of Australia.**
A. G. L. Shaw. London: Faber, 1972. 4th ed. 336p. bibliog.

An introductory history of Australia paying equal attention to economic and political development. There is a very good annotated bibliography.

112 **A concise history of Australia.**
Robert Lacour-Gayet, translated by James Grieve. Melbourne: Penguin Books, 1976. 484p. bibliog.

A general history of Australia, interesting because it is one of the few such works written from the perspective of the outsider, an eminent French historian.

113 **Australia since the coming of man.**
Russel Ward. Sydney: Lansdowne, 1982. 254p. bibliog.

This is a revised, updated and expanded version of the author's *Australia: a short history*, first published in 1965. Like the earlier edition, it is an eminently readable and invaluable introduction to the history of Australia. The theme of the book is the development of a distinctive Australian nationality. Many well-chosen illustrations support the text.

114 **Australia.**
R. M. Crawford. Melbourne: Hutchinson, 1979. 4th rev. ed.
199p. bibliog.

The latest edition of this popular book, first published in 1952, updates the text to the middle 1970s.

115 **Australia: the quiet continent.**
Douglas Pike. Cambridge, England: Cambridge University Press, 1970. 2nd ed. 244p.

A general history of Australia, particularly useful because it highlights the importance of regional history. Pike gives relatively more weight to the history of the outer states than most historians who usually emphasize developments in the populous states of New South Wales and Victoria.

116 **A new history of Australia.**
Edited by F. K. Crowley. Melbourne: Heinemann, 1974. 639p. bibliog.

An academic, large-scale general history of white men's activities in Australia from their penal origins in 1788 to 1972. Professor Crowley has divided Australian history into logical periods and engaged academic specialists in each period to give their version of events based on latest thinking and research. The result is twelve views of twelve consecutive periods of Australia's history. Inevitably, with a dozen authors involved, the book suffers from the absence of a unifying theme, but each period is covered to a much greater depth than in most other single volume works currently available. There is also an extensive bibliography and an excellent detailed index.

117 **The tyranny of distance: how distance shaped Australia's history.**
Geoffrey Blainey. Melbourne: Macmillan, 1982. rev. ed. 365p. bibliog.

A fascinating and original work, which shows the influence of isolation on Australia's development. Blainey argues that the vast distances within Australia, and between it and Europe, shaped the pattern of European settlement in Australia to a much greater degree than historians had previously acknowledged. The book is written in the author's usual lively style and is an excellent starting point to more elaborate histories of the country. There is also an illustrated coffee-table edition published in 1974.

118 **The Australian people: biography of a nation.**
Donald Horne. Sydney: Angus & Robertson, 1973. 285p. bibliog.

A witty, readable but opinionated history, by this well-known social commentator, of how Australians became what they are.

119 **Class structure in Australian history: documents, narrative and argument.**
R. W. Connell, T. H. Irving. Melbourne: Longman Cheshire, 1980. 378p.

The authors explore the development of class relations and the transformation of the ruling class in Australia. The book is in fact an interpretation of Australian history seen in the light of the class struggle. The argument is supported throughout with lengthy extracts from documents selected from such diverse sources as magistrate records, personal letters of citizens, government reports and appropriate novels of the times. This is an important book which throws new light on the development of Australian society since the foundation of the nation.

Foundation

120 **The foundation of Australia (1786-1800); a study in English criminal practice and penal colonization in the eighteenth century.**
Eris O'Brien. Sydney: Angus & Robertson, 1950. 2nd ed. 327p. bibliog.

A classic work which was first published in 1937. It is in two parts, the first covers the discussions in England about establishing a penal colony in Australia, and the second deals systematically and in great detail with the main subject, the actual foundation.

121 **The founding of Australia: the argument about Australia's origins.**
Edited by Ged Martin. Sydney: Hale & Iremonger, 1981. rev. ed. 313p.

Why did Britain establish a penal colony in Australia? The obvious answer is – for penal reasons. After the loss of the American colonies the British had nowhere to dump their convicts, and Australia, recently claimed for the Crown by James Cook, provided the obvious solution. However, there has been a long line of historians who have questioned this traditional explanation about the origins of British settlement in Australia. The present book is a collection of articles from a number of historical periodicals and extracts from books, with an introduction and some linking comments provided by the editor bringing together conflicting theories on the founding of Australia. It is a delightful book which allows the reader to make up his or her mind as to what the reasons for settlement may have been.

122　**Convicts and empire: a naval question, 1776-1811.**
　　Alan Frost.　Melbourne: Oxford University Press, 1980. 240p.
　　bibliog.

The commonly accepted reason for Australia's settlement is as a convenient dumping ground for England's excessive number of convicts, and the official documents of the time tend to support this view. Frost, on the other hand, argues that New South Wales was founded as a strategic support for English power in the eastern hemisphere. According to reports of earlier voyages it seemed likely that Botany Bay would make a good base for a squadron and that timber for masts could be found in the vicinity and flax could be grown for sails and cordage.

123　**Trade, tactics and territory: Britain in the Pacific, 1783-1823.**
　　Margaret Steven.　Melbourne: Melbourne University Press, 1983.
　　155p.

The settlement of Australia seen in the context of British commercial interests in the South Pacific region. Steven argues that in the pursuit for resources, especially the fur, sealing and whaling trades, Britain courted war with Spain and entered into rivalry with France and America. These new strategic considerations suggest new motives for the sending of the First Fleet to Botany Bay to create a British base in the South Seas.

124　**The First Fleet: the convict voyage that founded Australia, 1787-88.**
　　Jonathan King.　Melbourne: Macmillan, 1982. 186p.

An account of the eight-month voyage to Australia of the original fleet of eleven little ships bearing 1,350 people: officers, seamen, soldiers, men and women convicts as well as livestock. The author has compiled the story from the original diaries of those who actually took part in the voyage. He has done the job skilfully and the result is a lively narrative further enhanced by contemporary illustrative material.

125　**Australia: the first twelve years.**
　　Peter Taylor.　Sydney: Allen & Unwin, 1982. 220p.

A popular account of the first twelve years of settlement, 1788-1800, based on the recorded experiences of the early colonists. It is a fascinating story of how an isolated community, six sailing months away from the mother country and consisting of soldiers, civil officers and British criminals, survived to lay the foundations of today's Australia. At the end of the twelve-year period Sydney had grown into a town with a harbour, the surrounding interior had been explored and farming was established. On a sadder note the seeds of conflict with the Aborigines were established as well.

Colonial period

126 A land half won.
Geoffrey Blainey. Melbourne: Macmillan, 1980. 388p. bibliog.

This is a companion volume to the author's *Triumph of the nomads: a history of ancient Australia* (Sun Books, 1977), a history of the 40,000 years before European settlement in 1788. Professor Blainey shows that contrary to the white man's belief that the pre-settlement era had no history, the Aboriginal society was remarkably successful in its adaptation to and survival in the harsh and inhospitable environment. In the present book he continues with what he regards as the second phase of Australia's history – the story of just over a century of colonial settlement from 1788 to 1900. His conclusion is that at that time most Australians were still strangers to the continent, they had mastered the land physically but had as yet failed to relate to it emotionally. It is a pragmatic view of Australia's development, but is interesting because it shows how often neglected factors such as geology, botany and climate have influenced Australia's history. Like his other thirteen books, *A land half won* is gripping reading because of Blainey's facility for bright ideas and unusual perspectives.

127 Transported in place of death: convicts in Australia.
Christopher Sweeney. Melbourne: Macmillan, 1981. 185p. bibliog.

The story of the convict phase of Australia's history, written with popular appeal. The book is pleasantly produced and contains many contemporary illustrations.

128 Protest and punishment: the story of the social and political protesters transported to Australia, 1788-1868.
George Rudé. Oxford, England: Clarendon Press, 1978. 270p. bibliog.

Until serious research exploded the myth, there was widespread belief among Australians that all the convicts transported to Australia were either innocent men and women crushed by an unjust society and a harsh penal code, or radicals and martyrs being punished for their dissidence. Professor Rudé writes about the 2-3 per cent of the people who fall into the latter category. He estimates there were 3,600 of them, or about one in forty-five of all tranportees. He discusses their background, the reasons for their protest against the establishment at home, their trials and their punishment.

129   **The convict settlers of Australia: an enquiry into the origin and character of the convicts transported to New South Wales and Van Diemen's Land, 1787-1852.**
L. L. Robson.   Melbourne: Melbourne University Press, 1965. 257p. bibliog.

For many years after Australia was established as a penal colony prisoners made up most of its population. Between 1787 and 1868 nearly 162,000 men and women were transported as convicts to the British colonies of New South Wales, Victoria, Western Australia and Van Diemen's Land (present Tasmania). This pioneering work, using statistical sampling, examines the convicts' social and economic background, age, religion, occupation and the sort of life they led in Australia. There are exhaustive appendixes which tabulate Robson's findings and discuss his methods of processing the copious but erratic convict records.

130   **Convicts and the colonies: a study of penal transportation from Great Britain and Ireland to Australia and other parts of the British Empire.**
A. G. L. Shaw.   Melbourne: Melbourne University Press, 1977. Original edition in London: Faber, 1966. 399p. bibliog.

A dispassionate investigation into the history of convict transportation to Australia. Shaw's study, based on detailed research on the character of the convicts, resolves the long argument about the criminality of Australia's first settlers. He demonstrates conclusively that the great majority of the convicts were in fact urban petty criminals who had been in and out of gaol in England before transportation.

131   **The convict ships, 1787-1868.**
Charles Bateson.   Glasgow: Brown & Ferguson, 1969. 2nd ed., Sydney: Reed, 1974. 421p.

Convict ships sailed to Australia for more than 80 years and carried some 160,000 prisoners sentenced to transportation. Bateson describes the appalling conditions prevailing on the ships, which were normally of only 400 to 600 tons and undertook a voyage of about 20,000 kilometres with 200 convicts, 30 or so soldiers as guards and a further 30-40 sailors. This definitive work carries extensive appendixes of statistical data of all the ships involved as well as detailed notes and references to source material.

132   **The colonial Australians.**
David Denholm.   Melbourne: Penguin Books, 1979. 202p.

Starting from seemingly trivial details, the author reinterprets some of the conventional explanations of 19th-century Australian behaviour. The underlying purpose is to give Australians a better understanding of their national identity by looking at the lives of their forebears. A fascinating book — its readability is doubtless explained by the fact that the author is also a novelist.

133 **The Australian colonists: an exploration of social history, 1788-1870.**
K. S. Inglis. Melbourne: Melbourne University Press, 1974. 316p. bibliog.

In the first of a proposed four-volume work, Professor Inglis lists some of the more important events of Australia's early years that have, in his opinion, contributed to the formation of a national identity and to the development of uniquely Australian characteristics. The 91 illustrations are carefully chosen to support the well-written text.

134 **Australia in the Victorian age.**
Michael Cannon. Melbourne: Nelson, 1971-1975. 3 vols. bibliogs.

A popular, profusely illustrated social history of Australia in the 19th century. Recommended to the general reader for its readability and information content. Volume 1: *Who's master? Who's man?*; volume 2: *Life in the country*; volume 3: *Life in the cities.*

Federation

135 **Federation.**
Edited by Scott Bennett. Melbourne: Cassell, 1975. 251p. bibliog.

A selection of documentary extracts, linked with commentary by the editor, relating to the history of the federation and the drafting of the constitution.

136 **The making of the Australian constitution.**
J. A. La Nauze. Melbourne: Melbourne University Press, 1972. 369p. bibliog.

A thorough, scholarly study of the framing of the constitution, this book draws on source materials not available to Quick and Garran when they wrote their classic study *Annotated constitution of the Australian Commonwealth* (q.v.) in 1901. It is intended for historians, political scientists and constitutional lawyers, but is also accessible to the interested general reader, because of the author's easy style.

137 **Essays in Australian federation.**
Edited by A. W. Martin. Melbourne: Melbourne University Press, 1969. 206p. bibliog.

A collection of six essays offering novel insights into the history of the federation movement and the constitution-drafting process.

138 **Prosper the Commonwealth.**
Sir Robert Garran. Sydney: Angus & Robertson, 1958. 444p.

The author was a participant in the drafting of the constitution and became the first Commonwealth Attorney-General. In this autobiography he presents a lively first-hand description of the foundation of the Commonwealth and its first parliament and government, as well as many comments on developments since 1901. The text is accompanied by many black-and-white photographs of prominent Australians, including Prime Ministers.

139 **The federal story: the inner history of the federal cause, 1880-1900.**
Alfred Deakin, edited and introduced by J. A. La Nauze.
Melbourne: Melbourne University Press, 1963. 2nd ed. 182p.

An intimate account of the activities of the federal movement during the years 1880-1901 by one of the founding fathers of the Australian Federation who was three times Prime Minister of the new Commonwealth of Australia between 1901 and 1910.

140 **The emergent Commonwealth. Australian federation: expectations and fulfilment, 1889-1910.**
R. Norris. Melbourne: Melbourne University Press, 1975. 273p.

This study re-examines the constitutional convention and the deals and compromises that were made from which the constitution grew. It defines some of the expectations of the makers of the document, and plots some of the deviations from it in the first decade of federation, when radical legislation was enacted on the exclusion of coloured immigrants, popularly known as the White Australia Policy, defence and social welfare.

Post-Federation (20th century)

141 **A nation for a continent: the history of Australia, 1901-1975.**
Russel Ward. Melbourne: Heinemann Educational, 1977. 515p.
bibliog.

A survey of the history of Australia in the 20th century from 1901, when the colonies federated, to 1975. As in his other books Ward's underlying theme is the development of a national consciousness.

142 **Australia since federation: a narrative and critical analysis.**
Fred Alexander. Melbourne: Nelson, 1980. 4th ed. 445p.
bibliog.

Intended for senior high school and undergraduate students, the book is also a
useful introductory text for general readers. It is a narrative of political and social
change by a historian who has witnessed many of the events he describes. The
latest edition straddles the traumatic developments that came with the Labor
Party's return to office after an absence of twenty-three years in 1972 and its
subsequent dismissal by the governor-general in 1975. The book is illustrated with
photographs, cartoons and maps, and there is a very useful annotated list of major
historical and contemporary works for further reading.

143 **Lion and kangaroo: Australia, 1901-1919, the rise of a nation.**
Gavin Souter. Sydney: Collins, 1978. 344p. bibliog.

A journalist's account of the first nineteen years of federated Australia, a period
when almost all of the country's national institutions came into being. Souter
cleverly juxtaposes the growth of a national consciousness with the still prevailing
pro-British sentiment. It is a witty, well-written book enhanced by well-chosen
illustrations – photographs, cartoons and paintings.

144 **Time of hope: Australia, 1966-72.**
Donald Horne. Sydney: Angus & Robertson, 1980. 186p.

Horne, the prolific social commentator, recognizes that the seven years from 1966
to 1972 were the time of critical change. The changes in social and political
attitudes of those years prepared the way for Australia's first reform government
in twenty-three years – The Whitlam Labor administration from 1972 to 1975.
The text is characterized by Horne's well-known iconoclastic wit and is illustrated
by well-chosen black-and-white photographs.

145 **Days of wine and rage.**
Frank Moorhouse. Melbourne: Penguin Books, 1980. 446p.

An anthology of pieces written by the author and others, published in various
journals and newspapers, which illustrate the life and thought of the bohemian
counter-culture in Sydney and a few other Australian cities in the 1970s.

146 **Australia's yesterdays: a look at our recent past.**
Cyril Pearl. Sydney: Reader's Digest Services, 1979. 2nd ed.
360p.

A large-format, popular social history of Australia in the 20th century. The book
is splendidly illustrated and the linking text is by Cyril Pearl, noted social historian
and prolific author. Altogether this is a delightful volume for reading or for
browsing.

147 **Social sketches of Australia, 1888-1975.**
Humphrey McQueen. Melbourne: Penguin Books, 1978. 255p.
bibliog.

Intended basically as a text book for secondary schools, this book can be thoroughly recommended to the general reader. It is a complete departure from the conventional, dry representations of parliamentary and constitutional history. McQueen concentrates on source materials that illuminate the lives and attitudes of ordinary people. So the reader learns what the people wore and ate, what type of houses they lived in, what they learned at school and how they were affected by natural disasters, diseases and working conditions in the developing industrial society. Extensively illustrated with many previously unpublished pictures, *Social sketches* is a fascinating account of the social history of the Australia of the last hundred years.

148 **Australia, New Zealand and the Pacific Islands since the First World War.**
Edited by William S. Livingston, William Roger Louis. Canberra: Australian National University Press, 1979. 249p.

A collection of essays assessing the significant historical developments in the south-west Pacific since the First World War. It is set against a background dominated by the simultaneous dwindling of British power and rising American influence, and burgeoning nationalism in the region. Geoffrey Sawer's analysis of federal-state relations is written with admirable clarity and demonstrates the complexity of the Australian political structure.

149 **The fabulous century.**
Peter Luck. Sydney: Lansdowne Press, 1980. 399p.

Based on an award-winning TV series, this coffee-table book is interesting for the more than 200 contemporary photographs, which illustrate Australian social history in the 20th century. Highlights of politics, sport, fashion, people and disasters are featured.

Special topics

150 **The prehistory of Australia.**
D. J. Mulvaney. London: Thames & Hudson, 1969. 276p.
bibliog. (Ancient Peoples and Places).

The author, who is a practising archaeologist himself, surveys the continent's 30,000 years of prehistory and ethno-history. The book is illustrated with many excellent black-and-white photographs. There is a chronological table based upon radio-carbon dating and a bibliography of sources surveying knowledge in the field up to the late 1960s.

151 **A prehistory of Australia, New Guinea and Sahul.**
J. Peter White, with James F. O'Connell, illustrations by Margrit
Koettig. Sydney: Academic Press, 1982. 286p. bibliog.

A prehistory of the continent of Sahul, during the period dating from first
human occupation about 50,000 years ago until the severance of the land masses
now called New Guinea, Australia and Tasmania by the rising of the sea, from
about 12,000 years ago. The book also treats the prehistory of these land masses
separately and in some detail. This work is much more up to date with the latest
research than John Mulvaney's excellent *Prehistory of Australia* (see above).

152 **From deserts the prophets come: the creative spirit in
Australia, 1788-1972.**
Geoffrey Serle. Melbourne: Heinemann, 1973. 274p. bibliog.

Professor Serle concentrates on the development of literature, art, music, theatre
and architecture with some reference to science and scholarship in their Australian
context. In fact this book is the first general cultural history of Australia and is
therefore a standard reference for anyone interested in this aspect of Australian
life.

153 **A maritime history of Australia.**
John Bach. Sydney: Pan Books, 1982. 481p. bibliog.

To Australia, an island continent, sea transport has been and still is of primary
importance; indeed maritime history is essential for a complete understanding
of Australia's development as a nation. The title is somewhat misleading, because
the author limits himself to 'the commercial transportation of cargo and passengers' omitting all aspects of naval history, fishing and the exploitation of other
marine resources, tugs and ferry services and water-based recreational activities.
Within these self-imposed Lmits the book is a comprehensive history covering the
period 1788-1975. It is based on painstaking research, and the many paintings,
ancient photographs and modern pictures are a fascinating collection in their
own right and support the text well.

154 **A new Britannia: an argument concerning the social origins of
Australian radicalism and nationalism.**
Humphrey McQueen. Melbourne: Penguin Books, 1975.
rev. ed. 261p. bibliog.

A provocative demolition of such Australian myths as anti-British nationalism,
mateship and the socialist nature of radicalism in the late 19th and early 20th
centuries in Australia. McQueen sustains interest at all times because of his
vigorous, often amusing argument and new interpretations of well-known facts.

155 **The real Matilda: woman and identity in Australia, 1788 to 1975.**
Miriam Dixson. Melbourne: Penguin Books, 1976. 280p. bibliog.

A feminist history of the role of woman in Australia, which like Anne Summers'
book *Damned whores and god's police* (see below) assails the masculinist assumptions upon which almost all previous Australian histories have been based.

156 **Damned whores and god's police: the colonization of women in Australia.**

Anne Summers. Melbourne: Penguin Books, 1975. 494p.

Until the publication of this work nearly all previous books on Australian history and society were written by men who tended to exclude women from their accounts. Summers has produced the first detailed history of ordinary woman in Australia from a feminist point of view. The author believes that women have been 'colonized' and have as yet not found ways to overcome their oppression. The book outlines the situation of the 'colonized' in contemporary Australia; it identifies the 'colonization' process; and finally it offers an explanation for its lasting success.

157 **Worth her salt: women at work in Australia.**

Edited by Margaret Bevege, Margaret James, Carmel Shute.

Sydney: Hale & Iremonger, 1982. 453p.

Until the 1970s most Australian history was written by men about men. *Worth her salt* contains the edited papers presented to the second Women and Labour Conference held in Melbourne in 1980. The papers bring together research and recollection which illuminate the female experience in Australia and demonstrate that women played a significant role in the country's development.

158 **Colonial Eve: sources on women in Australia, 1788-1914.**

Edited by Ruth Teale. Melbourne: Oxford University Press, 1978. 288p. bibliog.

Women's history began with the publication of Anne Summers' *Damned whores and god's police* (q.v.) in 1975, and Miriam Dixson's *The real Matilda* (q.v.) in 1976. Since then several collections of source materials for women's studies have appeared. *Colonial Eve* concentrates on the period from European settlement to the outbreak of the First World War and contains a selection of short extracts from parliamentary papers, private diaries, court reports, cartoons, advertisements and a wide range of other sources. The book makes entertaining reading and proves that there is no paucity of materials about Australian women. A similar book is *The world moves slowly: a documentary history of Australian women,* edited by Beverly Kingston (Sydney: Cassell, 1977).

159 **Women, class and history: feminist perspectives on Australia, 1788-1978.**

Edited by Elizabeth Windschuttle. Melbourne: Fontana/Collins, 1980. 605p.

A broad collection of the most recent feminist research and writing about Australian society since its beginnings. There are twenty-five articles by some of the nation's most prominent feminist historians as well as some non-academics. The latter are mainly accounts of personal experience.

160 **The gold seekers.**
Norman Bartlett. London: Jarrolds, 1965. 240p. bibliog.

An easy-to-read, popular account of the early Australian gold rushes from 1851 to 1854. The book re-creates admirably the atmosphere of frenetic excitement and the varied experiences of the gold diggers.

161 **Gold fever: the Australian goldfields 1851 to the 1890s.**
Edited by Nancy Keesing. Sydney: Angus & Robertson, 1967. 412p.

A collection of descriptions of life on the Australian gold fields written by men and women who worked and lived there or visited them between 1851 and the 1890s. Nancy Keesing, a poet and author, has selected the pieces well, and overall the reader is able to absorb the atmosphere of those exciting days. The book is lavishly illustrated with drawings, prints and paintings of the period.

162 **Australian imperialism in the Pacific: the expansionist era, 1820-1920.**
Roger C. Thompson. Melbourne: Melbourne University Press, 1980. 289p. bibliog.

An account of Australian colonial tendencies towards the islands of the southwest Pacific. This sub-imperialism was expressed on behalf of the British Empire and consisted mainly of frequent urgings by Australia to get the British government to add the Pacific islands to the jurisdiction of the Crown. These colonial sentiments led to the one concrete example of Australian imperialism − taking over Papua from Britain, and later, at Versailles, getting German New Guinea and Nauru converted to 'C' class League of Nations mandates administered by Australia.

163 **The Australian trusteeship Papua New Guinea, 1945-75.**
Ian Downs. Canberra: Australian Government Publishing Service, 1980. 587p. bibliog.

A semi-official history of thirty years of Australian endeavours for effective administration in Papua New Guinea which eventually through international pressure and rising indigenous expectations led to self-government. Downs was for more than three decades administrator, farmer and politician in the territory. Although much scholarly research has gone into the book its virtues are mainly due to his first-hand knowledge of what he describes. The book is illustrated.

164 **A time for building: Australian administration in Papua and New Guinea, 1951-1963.**
Paul Hasluck. Melbourne: Melbourne University Press, 1976. 452p.

Sir Paul Hasluck was Minister for Territories for the period he discusses in the book. It is a work of detail and reflection, controlled by the author's craftsmanship as a writer and historian, and a valuable record of how he went about deciding and implementing Australian government policy in Papua New Guinea.

165 **Hubert Murray: the Australian pro-consul.**
Francis West. Melbourne: Oxford University Press, 1968. 296p.
bibliog.

Murray was appointed the first Lieutenant-Governor of Papua, when the British
handed over the territory to Australia in 1908, and he remained in office until
his death in 1940. In his lifetime he achieved a great reputation as a humane
administrator, although a later generation has regarded him as a benevolent despot.
From the study of Murray the reader learns much about Australian colonial
practice. West has also edited a selection of Murray's letters *Selected letters of
Hubert Murray* (Melbourne: Oxford University Press, 1970).

166 **Taim bilong masta: the Australian involvement with Papua
New Guinea.**
Hank Nelson. Sydney: Australian Broadcasting Commission,
1982. 224p.

This book is based on an edited version of a 24-part radio series of the same name
broadcast by the Australian Broadcasting Commission. It consists of interviews
recorded mostly in 1980 with people who had been part of the Australian involvement in Papua New Guinea, and is fascinating in the detail of people's experiences,
offering a better perception of what life in Papua New Guinea was really like than
many so-called 'learned' accounts might do. The pidgin-English title means 'Time
belongs to my master' – or 'I am my master's slave'. An exciting exercise in the
use of oral history.

167 **Australian liberalism and national character.**
Tim Rowse. Melbourne: Kibble Books, 1978. 293p. bibliog.

An intellectual history of Australia in the 20th century, in particular the decades
from the 1920s to the 1960s. Rowse's methodology is to examine a succession of
Australian intellectuals who have endeavoured to explain Australian society or
redirect it. After introducing the reader to liberal social theory, the book divides
its material into four 'episodes': the Workers' Education Association experiment
– to provide a civic education for the working class; the revision of New Liberal
optimism implied in Hancock's *Australia* (q.v.); the thinking behind the Australian
Labor Party's plans for post-war social reconstruction in the 1940s and the
definition of 'Australianism' that went with it, and, lastly, the reversals suffered
by this 'radical' definition during the 1950s and 1960s. Recommended for the
serious reader who wants to understand how and why the liberal tradition has
been dominant in Australian historiography.

168 **Room for manoeuvre: writings on history, politics, ideas and play.**
Ian Turner, selected and edited by Leonie Sandercock, Stephen
Murray-Smith. Melbourne: Drummond, 1982. 335p.

A collection of writings by Professor Ian Turner – historian, socialist and political
activist – the book is a good sample of the thinking and attitudes of the intellectual Left in Australia of the post-war era.

169 **Occasional writings and speeches.**
Manning Clark. Melbourne: Fontana/Collins, 1980. 269p.

This collection is important because it shows how Australia's most eminent historian views the writing of history and the role of the historian in the wider social context.

170 **Nellie Melba, Ginger Meggs and friends: essays in Australian cultural history.**
Edited by Susan Dermody, John Docker, Drusilla Modjeska.
Melbourne: Kibble Books, 1982. 288p.

Historians and critics not only discuss novels, poems and literary culture but also dwell on films, television, popular literature and comic strips. Many of the essays are written from standpoints informed by feminism, contemporary cultural theories and Marxism.

171 **Australian popular culture.**
Edited by Peter Spearritt, David Walker. Sydney: Allen & Unwin, 1979. 255p. bibliog.

A collection of essays on the tools of mass entertainment, such as music, film, theatre and popular literature, and mass urban events such as the opening of the Sydney Harbour Bridge in 1932 and the passing of the celebration of Empire Day. The text is complemented with well-chosen illustrations and a bibliography of popular culture in Australia, 1900-1960. An entertaining and informative book.

172 **Australian album – the way we were: Australia in photographs, 1860-1920.**
Daniel O'Keefe. Sydney: O'Keefe. 1982. 224p.

A collection of photographs arranged in themes covering sixty years of Australian life as seen through the lens of the camera. Overall this large-format volume presents a fine evocation of Australia's past.

173 **Country life in old Australia.**
Introduced by Geoffrey Dutton. Melbourne: Currey O'Neil, 1982.

A large-format illustrated book of some 150 interesting photographs from a variety of archival sources. Dutton's introduction provides historical background and all the pictures have explanatory notes. The photographs depict life in south-eastern Australia in the early days of settlement and feature settlers, timber cutters, prospectors, miners, quarriers, shearers, swaggies, bullockies, bush children and pioneer families. Overall the illustrations capture the flavour of the period very well.

174 **The drovers.**
Keith Willey. Melbourne: Macmillan, 1982. 154p. bibliog.

Drovers are men who drive livestock to market over long distances. A romantic aura has always surrounded these 'outback heroes' who have featured prominently in folklore and balladry. They became the focus of legend and their individuality expressed the restlessness, the sardonic humour and stoicism considered to be typical Australian characteristics. There are not many drovers left, as their place has been taken over by motor transports and stock trains. The author, who knew many drovers, tells their story vividly thus ensuring that they will not be forgotten. Vivid first-hand reminiscences of droving can be found in *Droving days*, by H. M. Barker (Melbourne: Pitman, 1966).

175 **The shearers.**
Patsy Adam-Smith. Melbourne: Nelson, 1982. 416p.

In the 19th and early 20th centuries the Australian economy was based on the export of fine wool and it was said that the country rode on the sheep's back. This book records the experience and the folklore of the men who shore the sheep — the shearers. They travelled the great shearing routes of the vast outback country of inland Australia and through the years became the stuff of legends. The author toured every state of the country visiting shearing sheds, tracking down old shearers, their 'mates' (or friends) and their families to record their reminiscences. The result is a passionate account of the way of life of the shearers and their place in Australian history. Many historic drawings and photographs complement the text.

Regional and local history

176 **Australian capital cities: historical essays.**
Edited by J. W. McCarty, C. B. Schedvin. Sydney: Sydney University Press, 1978. 201p.

Since their inhabitants account for more than 75 per cent of the total population of Australia, the history of the six state capitals reflects largely the history of the nation. The ten historical essays collected here discuss various aspects of the urban development of these large metropolitan areas.

177 **Canberra: history of Australia's national capital.**
Lionel Wigmore. Canberra: Dalton Publishing, 1972. rev. ed. 236p. bibliog.

An updated edition of the history published in 1963 as *The long view* to commemorate the city's 50th anniversary. For a description of the development of Canberra from the town planning perspective the reader should consult *Tomorrow's Canberra: planning for growth and change* (Canberra: National Capital Development Commission, 1970).

178 **The bush capital: how Australia chose Canberra as its federal city.**
Roger Pegrum. Sydney: Hale & Iremonger, 1983. 192p.

This book covers two aspects of the emergence of Canberra as the national capital: firstly, it gives an historical account of the events which led to the choice of a site for the capital in 1909; and secondly it describes the selection of the Walter Burley Griffin place for the design of Canberra.

179 **Sydney since the twenties.**
Peter Spearritt. Sydney: Hale & Iremonger, 1978. 294p. bibliog.

The story of Australia's largest and most cosmopolitan city during the period of its greatest growth when Sydney was transformed from a walking-distance city to a sprawling metropolis. The book is brought to life by the superb photographs, cartoons, sketches and maps which the author has painstakingly collected.

180 **Twentieth-century Sydney: studies in urban & social history.**
Edited by Jill Roe. Sydney: Hale & Iremonger, with the Sydney History Group, 1980. 272p. bibliog.

The second collection of studies in the history of Sydney by the Sydney History Group. It follows *Nineteenth-century Sydney: essays in urban history*, edited by Max Kelly, (Sydney: Sydney University Press, in association with the Sydney History Group, 1978). Collectively the studies try to locate the diverse forces shaping the modern city and city life.

181 **The history and description of Sydney harbour.**
P. R. Stephensen, Brian Kennedy. Sydney: Reed, 1981. 352p.

This is an update by Brian Kennedy of the original work by Stephensen published in 1966. Often referred to as the world's greatest and most beautiful waterways, this great expanse of water which meanders through the city and its outlying suburbs not only serves as a haven for ships, but also as a water playground for Sydney's 3½ million citizens.

182 **Newcastle: the making of an Australian city.**
J. C. Docherty. Sydney: Hale & Iremonger, 1983. 191p. bibliog.

For almost a century Newcastle has been Australia's sixth largest city. A centre for the coal trade during the 19th century it has since become a base for heavy industry. The book traces the city's industrial and economic development as well as the social and urban trends to the present day. Many tables, diagrams and photographs support the text.

183 **Silver, sin and sixpenny ale: a social history of Broken Hill, 1883-1921.**
Brian Kennedy. Melbourne: Melbourne University Press, 1978. 202p. bibliog.

Broken Hill is a remote and unique mining town in the far west of New South Wales. It owes its origin to the discovery in 1883 of one of the world's richest deposits of silver, lead and zinc. Conflict between the miners and owners of the mine often erupted into industrial unrest, which came to a head in 1919 with a bitter nineteen-month strike. This book is a lively social history of Broken Hill from its beginnings to the end of the big strike in 1921. Another book focusing on mining history at the mine is Geoffrey Blainey's *The rise of Broken Hill* (Melbourne: Macmillan, 1968).

184 **Discovering Monaro: a study of man's impact on his environment.**
W. K. Hancock. Cambridge, England: Cambridge University Press, 1972. 209p.

Monaro, a region of nearly 10,000 square kilometres, is in the high country of Australia's south-east corner. The book is a fascinating local history of this region and at the same time shows how 600 generations of black Australians and 6 generations of white settlers have supported themselves on the grassy uplands and alpine watersheds, and what changes they have inflicted on the physical environment. An interesting book by one of Australia's foremost historians.

185 **The rush to be rich: a history of the colony of Victoria, 1883-1889.**
Geoffrey Serle. Melbourne: Melbourne University Press, 1971. 392p. bibliog.

Together with his earlier work *The golden age: a history of the colony of Victoria, 1851-1861* (1963), the two books provide an excellent, readable account of two important periods in the history of Victoria – the gold rush which transformed Victoria in the 1850s from a minor pastoral settlement to the most celebrated British colony, and the heady 1880s which led to an unprecedented boom from 1887 to 1889, a period also important because of the seeds of interaction between the Australian colonies which eventually led to federation.

186 **The rise and fall of marvellous Melbourne.**
Graeme Davidson. Melbourne: Melbourne University Press, 1978. 304p. bibliog.

A social history of Melbourne during the 'boom and bust' of the 1880s and 1890s. The book is lavishly illustrated with contemporary line drawings, etchings and photographs. A must for anyone interested in Australian urban development. Another classic book of the period which has gone through many editions is Michael Cannon's *The land boomers* (Melbourne: Nelson, 1976. new illustrated ed.).

47

187 **Port Phillip gentlemen and good society in Melbourne before
the gold rushes.**
Paul de Serville. Melbourne: Oxford University Press, 1980.
256p. bibliog.

Not all the early settlers were convicts or of the lower classes. From 1836 to 1842
the colonial gentlemen of breeding and rank attempted to re-create a society
based on blood, privilege and the principle of exclusion. In this they were defeated
by their liberal opponents. An interesting and well-written book which illuminates
a forgotten episode in Australian history.

188 **Men of yesterday: a social history of the western district of
Victoria, 1834-1890.**
Margaret Kiddle. Melbourne: Melbourne University Press, 1962.
573p. bibliog.

Widely recognized as being among the outstanding works of Australian history. It
tells, superbly, the story of the passing of the first generation of settlers – the
transplanted English, Irish and Scots. Highly recommended for the serious reader
looking for a deeper understanding of Australia's settlement.

189 **Lucky city: the first generation at Ballarat, 1851-1901.**
Weston Bate. Melbourne: Melbourne University Press, 1978.
302p. bibliog.

The city of Ballarat, in the state of Victoria, grew to urban prominence during the
1850s gold rush. The miners' rebellion at the Ballarat diggings known as the
Eureka Stockade has acquired a mythological importance in Australian history as
a stand against established authority. While Bate gives a superb and definitive
account of this event, his richly illustrated and eminently readable book is also a
major achievement in city biography and regional study. Similar though less
spectacular urban development took place during the second half of the
19th-century gold discoveries in another Victorian town, Bendigo – see *Bendigo:
a history*, by Frank Cusack (Melbourne: Heinemann, 1973).

190 **Paradise of dissent: South Australia, 1829-1857.**
Douglas Pike. Melbourne: Melbourne University Press, 1967.
2nd ed. 580p.

A scholarly study of the colony of South Australia from its foundation to the
establishment of responsible government. Unlike the other colonies South
Australia had no convict transportation. Many of the free settlers were dissenters
and nonconformists with a passion for the religious and civil liberty which they
believed England had denied them. They made South Australia the first colony in
the British Empire to separate church from state. The book broadens the view of
Australian history which more often than not is seen from the aspect of the two
populous states on the east coast – New South Wales and Victoria.

191   **Adelaide and the country, 1870-1917: their social and political relationship.**
J. B. Hirst.   Melbourne: Melbourne University Press, 1973.
266p. bibliog.

The relationship between city and hinterland remains one of the least studied aspects of colonial life. In this study of Adelaide, the capital of South Australia, the author stresses the complementary character of urban and rural life. Adelaide, like the other Australian colonial capitals, experienced rapid growth in the second half of the 19th century. By the end of the period covered by Hirst, Adelaide had half of South Australia's total population of a half million.

192   **Adelaide, 1836-1976: a history of difference.**
Derek Whitelock.   Brisbane: University of Queensland Press,
1977. 342p. bibliog.

Unlike the other state capitals, Adelaide, in South Australia, was founded as a result of an ambitious social plan. It was envisaged as 'an Athens of the South' – a model society free of both English flaws and colonial convictism. It became pious, industrious and grave, the shrine of middle-class respectability. The Adelaide sense of difference, the author feels, still lives and thrives. The text is generously supplied with photographs, sketches and maps.

193   **The call of the land: a history of Queensland to the present day.**
W. Ross Johnston.   Brisbane: Jacaranda, 1982. 229p.

Queensland today is generally considered to be Australia's most conservative state. In this general survey of the development of Queensland, the author attempts to explain how the present system of priorities in community and government attitudes has arisen.

194   **From the dreaming to 1915: a history of Queensland.**
Ross Fitzgerald.   Brisbane: University of Queensland Press, 1982.
354p.

Fitzgerald sees the history of Queensland, Australia's second largest state, in terms of the white settlers' commitment to material progress: an overwhelming sense of duty to develop the vast territory, to tame the wilderness. The central themes which emerge in this history – racism, authoritarianism, despoliation of the environment – are still the themes of contemporary state politics. There are many well-selected illustrations in this interesting work, which the author intends to complete with a second volume on 20th-century developments.

195 **Brisbane in the 1890s: a study of an Australian urban society.**
Ronald Lawson. Brisbane: University of Queensland Press,
1973. 373p. bibliog.

By 1900, just over 100 years from its foundation, Australia was one of the world's most urbanized countries, with a large proportion of the population living in the six state capitals of Melbourne, Sydney, Adelaide, Brisbane, Perth and Hobart. This social history of Brisbane, the capital of Queensland, discusses and illustrates many aspects of city life: working conditions, family life, educational opportunities, the care of the needy, sporting, cultural and other leisure activities and so on.

196 **The cry for the dead.**
Judith Wright. Melbourne: Oxford University Press, 1981. 303p.
bibliog.

This celebrated Australian poet describes the occupation of the vast pastoral lands of Queensland by the white settlers in the second half of the 19th century. The story has been told before, but for the first time the stories of the Aborigines and the white invaders are run side by side, showing how the Aborigines bravely battled against the white man's guns, disease and poison. It is not only a story of the extermination of the original inhabitants of the continent, but also a chronicle of the rape of the land itself. The once-fertile land had by the turn of the century become a virtual wasteland through excessive pastoral practices. The book is based on the original records of the author's ancestors.

197 **A history of Tasmania: Volume I. Van Diemen's Land from the earliest times to 1855.**
Lloyd Robson. Melbourne: Oxford University Press, 1983.
632p. bibliog.

This is the first scholarly history of Van Diemen's Land, Tasmania, Australia's small island state. The period covered in the book was a particularly brutal one, marked by bloody clashes between the settlers and the Aborigines and the exploitation of the convict system to the full in the service of the colony's developing economy. The second volume will cover Tasmania as a colony and state from the 1850s to the present day.

198 **Urbanization: the evolution of an Australian capital.**
R. J. Solomon. Sydney: Angus & Robertson, 1976. 434p.
bibliog.

A scholarly study in historical geography: the development of Hobart, capital of the island state of Tasmania. It is a book of enormous value to the student of urban growth and the town planner, and not without interest to the general reader in social history. A much less specialized general history is Peter Bolger's *Hobart Town* (Canberra: Australian National University Press, 1973).

199 **A new history of Western Australia.**
Edited by C. T. Stannage. Perth: University of Western Australia
Press, 1981. 836p. bibliog.

This thematically organized book contains four chapters on Aboriginal prehistory
and black-and-white relations; four on demographic and economic history; six on
political history; and seven on aspects of social history. In a final chapter Professor
G. C. Bolton reflects on historical writing about Australia's largest state. Another
book, published in 1960 but still relevant reading, is F. K. Crowley's *Australia's
Western third*, a history of Western Australia from the first settlements to modern
times.

200 **The people of Perth: a social history of Western Australia's
capital city.**
C. T. Stannage. Perth: Perth City Council, 1979. 364p. bibliog.

Published on the occasion of Perth's 150 years of white settlement, this is an
excellent urban history.

201 **Far country: a short history of the Northern Territory.**
Alan Powell. Melbourne: Melbourne University Press, 1982.
301p.

A history of the vast, remote administrative unit of the Northern Territory, a
region more than 1¼ million square kilometres in area with a population of some
125,000 people. Often referred to as Australia's last frontier it is a capricious land
of extremes of climate and of sometimes bitter conflict between the white
residents and the Territory's relatively large population of Aborigines. Often
neglected in general histories of Australia the Northern Territory gets its full due
in this volume.

Law and Constitution

202 **Legal research: materials and methods.**
Enid Campbell, E. J. Glasson, Ann Lahore. Sydney: Law Book Company, 1979. 2nd ed. 276p.

The standard Australian source book for legal literature. To find the law as applied in Australia this guide is indispensable. It discusses in great detail federal and state law reports, digests, statute law and non-legal literature relevant to the law. Where still applicable English sources are also included.

203 **Australia's constitution: time for change?**
John McMillan, Gareth Evans, Haddon Storey. Sydney: Law Foundation of New South Wales, with Allen & Unwin, 1983. 422p.

The authors state in the preface: 'This book is intended to stimulate a serious national debate on the desirability and possibility of changing the Australian constitution. Its aim is not to argue for any particular change but simply to expose the problems that appear to exist in the present operation of the constitution, to identify possible solutions to those problems, and to suggest some ways in which constructive debate might actually be encouraged.' The aim that the authors have set themselves is admirably achieved and the book is useful for all those interested in constitutional review or just wanting to know more about how the Australian constitution works.

204 **Australian constitutionalism.**
R. D. Lumb. Sydney: Butterworth, 1983. 170p. bibliog.

Constitutional change is much discussed in Australia but, according to the author, it is conducted 'without a true understanding of the influence of political theory: much of it appeals to slogans, catchcries and glib phrases'. The book examines the sources and growth of Australian constitutionalism, especially the British and American systems on which the Australian constitution is modelled. Then the present system is discussed to determine what values it incorporates and what inadequacies may be found in it. A clear, up-to-date treatise recommended to all who want to understand the Australian constitutional framework.

205 **Australia's constitution.**
Colin Howard. Melbourne: Penguin Books, 1978. 216p. bibliog.
In this brief but comprehensive survey the author explains in an easy, readable style the contents of the Australian constitution, how it affects the political life of the country and the affairs of its citizens and how it may be changed. A useful, short chapter on books for further reading is included.

206 **The annotated constitution of the Australian Commonwealth.**
J. Quick, R. R. Garran. Sydney: Angus & Robertson, 1901.
Reprinted, Sydney: Legal Books, 1976. 1,008p.
Originally published immediately after federation, this book was written well before judicial interpretation of the constitution commenced. It is still an indispensable tool for understanding the intentions of the framers of the constitution. There are two parts: a general historical account of the making of the document, and a commentary on the meaning of each section, with further historical references. The credentials of the two authors are impeccable: Sir John Quick was himself a delegate to the Constitutional Convention of 1897-98 which drafted and debated the document through to its almost final form, and Sir Robert Garran was secretary to the drafting committee of the convention.

207 **An introduction to the Australian constitution.**
P. H. Lane. Sydney: Law Book Company, 1977. 2nd ed. 350p.
This introduction is intended to be an easily read paperback for those who want some general knowledge of government in Australia. It is also meant to be an inducement towards further study of the subject. The Convention Debates of the 1890s are discussed as well as later attempts at reform, including the Constitutional Convention of the 1970s. A list of leading cases has been included for further reading. It is altogether a conservative and cautious view of the constitution.

208 **The future of Australian federalism: a commentary on the working of the constitution.**
Gordon Greenwood. Brisbane: University of Queensland Press, 1976. 2nd ed. 361p. bibliog.
The text of this edition remains unchanged from the original issue in 1946, when it was a landmark on constitutional history and analysis. Its special value lies in the fact that it was the earliest study by a non-lawyer and that the issues Greenwood raised a generation ago are as relevant today as they were then.

209 **Conventions, the Australian constitution and the future.**
L. J. M. Cooray. Sydney: Legal Books, 1979. 235p.

The events leading up to November 1975, when the Governor-General, Sir John Kerr, dismissed the Prime Minister Mr. Whitlam from office and created a bitter constitutional debate. Professor Cooray subjects the Commonwealth constitution and most of the conventions that have developed with it to a penetrating examination. The focus is on the events of 1975 and the author's main theme is the prospects of constitutionalism in the future. Recommended to readers who want to acquire a deeper insight into the problems of government machinery in Australia.

210 **Labor and the constitution, 1972-1975: essays and commentaries on the constitutional controversies of the Whitlam years in Australian government.**
Edited by Gareth Evans. Melbourne: Heinemann, 1977. 383p.

The best book on the constitutional aspects of the turbulent political events during the Labor government's term in office from 1972 to 1975, which led to its dismissal from office by the Governor-General. The essays are of a uniformly high standard and range widely over federalism, parliament and the executive, the electorate and the judiciary. Although it is not a work for beginners, it is both readable and informative.

211 **Federation under strain: Australia, 1972-1975.**
Geoffrey Sawer. Melbourne: Melbourne University Press, 1977. 237p.

After twenty-three years of conservative rule the reformist Australian Labor Party was elected to govern again in 1972. After three turbulent years in office the Governor-General dismissed the government in November 1975. This event, unprecedented in Australian political history, created wide public controversy and led to a questioning of the Australian constitution. The author, an eminent authority on constitutional law, gives a legal interpretation of the political issues during the Labor administration. It is a scholarly study, yet written in terms accessible to the lay reader. Understandably, the pros and cons of the issues involved in the dismissal of the popularly elected government have generated a large body of literature, information on which can be gained through a detailed bibliography which appears in Ruth Atkins's *Governing Australia* (q.v.).

212 **Australian federalism in the courts.**
Geoffrey Sawer. Melbourne: Melbourne University Press, 1967. 262p.

A layman's survey of the High Court's interpretation of the constitution up to early 1967. The High Court of Australia is at the apex of the country's judicial system and occupies a preferred position in relation to suits that involve the interpretation of the constitution.

213 **The constitutions of the Australian states.**
R. D. Lumb. Brisbane: University of Queensland Press, 1976.
4th ed. 136p.

The constitutions of the states, like the Australian constitution originate from British statutes. This book traces constitutional developments in each of the former colonies, which after federation became self-governing states. The division of powers between the Australian and state parliaments follows the American model. The powers of the Australian parliament and government are specified: all other powers are left to the states. A federal law, if valid, overrides any state law not consistent with it.

214 **The Australian legal dictionary.**
S. E. Marantelli. Melbourne: Hargreen, 1980. 242p.

A dictionary for the layman. All entries commence with a brief definition, followed by a succinct summary of the law as it stands. References to statutes and case law are given with an emphasis on Victorian statutes.

215 **An Australian legal history.**
Alex C. Castles. Sydney: Law Book Company, 1982. 550p.

The first comprehensive Australian legal history, this book surveys the history of the profession, the development of the courts in the various states and the Commonwealth, and the Australian development and the application in Australia of the English common law.

216 **Australian courts of law.**
James Crawford. Melbourne: Oxford University Press, 1982. 297p.

Traces the development of the Australian court systems from their English and colonial origins and provides an up-to-date account of the modern system. All major courts are dealt with: magistrates', district and supreme courts, the Federal Court, High Court and Privy Council, and the main specialist courts such as the industrial courts and commissions, the Family Court, children's courts and small claims courts. The courts of all six states, the Australian Capital Territory and the Northern Territory are included.

217 **Freedom in Australia.**
Enid Campbell, Harry Whitmore. Sydney: Sydney University Press, 1973, new ed. 488p.

Directed primarily at the layman, *Freedom in Australia* is an excellent general survey of law relating to civil liberties and individual freedom. It covers such areas as police, arrest, bail, prosecution, freedom of movement, treatment of the sick, obscenity, the media, theatre, demonstrations, government information and a bill of rights. The underlying philosophy is that Australians need more freedom and ought to make a more determined effort to pursue the ideals of democracy.

218 **The divided legal profession in Australia: history, rationalisation and rationale.**
J. R. S. Forbes. Sydney: Law Book Company, 1979. 300p.
A history of the legal profession in Australia.

219 **The legal mystique: the role of lawyers in Australian society.**
Michael Sexton, Laurence W. Maher. Sydney: Angus & Robertson, 1982. 196p.

The theme of the book is the inordinate influence that lawyers have on Australian society. They not only practise law, but also are entrusted with a wide range of social and economic questions that affect the distribution of power and resources. They are involved in politics, the bureaucracy and the business world. They are appointed to run enquiries into drugs, the police, nuclear energy, human relationships and the secret service; to head bodies such as the Prices Justification Tribunal, Academic Salaries Tribunal and the Australian Security Intelligence Organization. Presumably they are entrusted with all this responsibility because of the 'myth of neutrality'. The authors examine the backgrounds of 56 judges and find that they come from a narrow privileged part of society; they are inherently conservative men – no women – and judge issues, consciously or unconsciously, from a certain point of view. This is one of the most important books about the legal system to be published in Australia.

220 **Your rights, 1980.**
John Bennett. Melbourne: John Bennett, 1980. 7th ed. 73p.

This popular pamphlet is a very useful reference on civil rights, written by the long-time secretary of the Victorian Council for Civil Liberties. A similar publication is *All about citizen's rights* (Melbourne: Nelson, 1976) by Ken Buckley, the president of the Council for Civil Liberties of New South Wales.

221 **An introduction to law.**
D. P. Derham, F K. H. Maher, P. L. Waller. Sydney: Law Book Company, 1983. 4th ed. 210p.

Intended mainly as a beginner's guide towards a more serious study of law the book can nevertheless appeal to laymen who are interested in the Australian legal system. It is particularly good at explaining the variations between Australian state laws. An appendix instructs on how to go about finding the law.

222 **A layman's guide: you and the law in Australia.**
Barry Williams. Adelaide: Rigby, 1979. 185p.

This book is presented as a guide to Australian law in so far as it affects the ordinary citizen. The aim is to identify likely problems that arise in common legal situations and then to make clear one's basic legal position. These include among others, buying property, accidents at work or during leisure, crashing a car, children's rights, damaging property, divorce or separation, making a will, starting or winding up a business.

223 **Law for the people: a citizen's guide to the law in Australia and New Zealand.**
Edited by Stan Ross, Mark Weinberg, with contributions by members of the Faculty of Law at the University of New South Wales. Melbourne: Penguin Books, 1976. 408p.

A good and lively survey of the basic principles of Australian and New Zealand law, it concentrates on instructing the layman on the deficiencies in the legal system of both countries.

224 **The Australian and the law.**
Geoffrey Sawer. Melbourne: Penguin Books, 1972. rev. ed. 293p.

For many years Professor Sawer's book was the only layman's introduction to the basic features of the Australian legal system and the basic principles of Australian law, both civil and criminal, in all six states. It remains to this day one of the more lucid and civilized guides, and no doubt a new edition bringing the work up to date with changing laws will eventually be published.

225 **Too much order with too little law.**
Frank Brennan. Brisbane: University of Queensland Press, 1983. 303p. bibliog.

A scholarly study of the history of public protest in Queensland. The book concentrates on the post-1966 period, when the first major clashes over demonstrations against Australian involvement in the Vietnam War took place. During the 1971 South African Rugby tour of Queensland, the state government declared a state of emergency to control protests against apartheid. Following a comparative study of the public order machinery in the various Australian states, the authors find that the measures taken in Queensland are the most drastic.

Politics

General

226 Dictionary of Australian politics.
Edited by P. J. Boyce. Melbourne: Longman Cheshire, 1980.
292p.

A very useful tool for quick reference to 'the most significant or distinctive institutions, personalities, procedures and idiom of government in Australia. The scope is national, state and municipal, with the emphasis extending beyond such obviously central entities as parliaments and parties, to include bureaucracies, corporations, trade unions, pressure groups and the media'. Another very similar work, that should be used in conjunction with the above, is *The Macmillan dictionary of Australian politics*, by Dean Jaensch and Max Teichmann published in Melbourne in 1979. It has a very useful appendix which lists governors-general, prime ministers, federal leaders of the opposition and state premiers since federation.

227 Australia's government and parliament.
David Solomon. Melbourne: Nelson, 1981. 5th ed. 168p.

The author has an intimate knowledge of how the process of government in Australia operates. For many years he was a member of the parliamentary press gallery in Canberra and in 1975 he was public relations officer to the then Prime Minister Gough Whitlam. This first-hand experience has enabled him to write an excellent introductory text to Australian government and politics. The popularity of the book is evidenced by the fact that it is now in its fifth edition since it was first published in 1973. Recommended for the general reader with little previous knowledge of Australian politics and political institutions. The text of the Australian constitution is given in an appendix.

228 **Australian politics: a fifth reader.**
Edited by Henry Mayer, Helen Nelson. Melbourne: Longman Cheshire, 1980. 593p.

A successor to four earlier Australian politics readers, the fifth edition is shorter and is tightly structured around the basic institutions and processes of the political system. Part 1 examines the context of Australian politics; part 2 covers the constitution, federalism and the bureaucracy; part 3 deals with political parties and elections; part 4 is about pressure groups, Aborigines, women and trade unions; part 5 is an entirely new section on the media and information. There are also valuable notes listing all earlier editions and including a select list of chapters that do not appear in this edition but are still useful.

229 **The pieces of politics.**
Edited by Richard Lucy. Melbourne: Macmillan, 1983. 3rd ed. 532p.

This book of readings contains essays carefully chosen to reflect the major contemporary issues in Australian politics. The volume has eight parts: political parties, pressure groups and trade unions, parliament, bureaucracy, federalism, elections, issues and political analysis.

230 **Platforms for government: the national platforms and policies of Australia's political parties analysed and compared.**
Edited by David Combe, Greg Hartung, Geoffrey Hawker. Canberra, ACT: Yarralumla Soft, with David Combe and Associates, 1982. 347p.

An essential guide to understanding government policies and their implications and the alternatives. All four major Australian political parties — The Liberal Party of Australia, The National Country Party of Australia, the Australian Labor Party, and the Australian Democrats — are represented.

231 **How we are governed.**
C. R. Forell. Melbourne: Longman Cheshire, 1982. 9th ed. 142p. bibliog.

A primer on the working of parliamentary democracy in Australia for young readers, but can serve as a basic introductory text for any beginner in the subject.

232 **Governing Australia: an introduction.**
Ruth Atkins. Brisbane: Wiley, 1980. 218p. bibliogs.

'Designed to help beginners in the study of Australian government by providing some background information, explanations of some terms and a generous supply of references many of them annotated'. The bibliographies are very useful, especially one on the constitutional crisis of 1975 when the Governor-General dismissed the elected Labor government. The book also includes the text of the Australian constitution.

Politics. General

233   **Australian political institutions.**
Don Aitkin, Brian Jinks.   Melbourne: Pitman, 1982. 2nd ed.
283p. bibliog.

An excellent introduction to Australian politics. Although intended as a textbook
at university entrance level, the book stands apart from other texts because of its
plain language and sufficient comment which make it readable and at times
provocative. It achieves admirably the aims set out in the preface: to provide the
essential facts about the main institutions of Australian politics and government,
to convey enough history to put these in perspective, to discuss some of the
talking-points about the institutions and to indicate problems and possible
changes in the processes of government. The chapter on the electoral system is
probably the best thing ever published on this subject.

234   **Government and politics in Australia: democracy in transition.**
William J. Byrt, Frank Crean.   Sydney: McGraw-Hill, 1982.
2nd ed. 302p. bibliog.

A useful introduction written in simple language suitable for the general reader
with no previous knowledge of the subject. Frank Crean was a minister in the
Labor government of 1972-75. Each chapter is concluded by a short list of books
for further reading.

235   **Australian government today.**
Geoffrey Sawer.   Melbourne: Melbourne University Press, 1977.
12th ed. 142p.

Professor Sawer's book was first published in 1948 and has not been out of print
since. As a work of elementary reference it is without equal and is a masterpiece
of good prose and lucid explanation. Obviously it is the text for anyone interested
in acquainting himself quickly with the Australian political system.

236   **Australian national government.**
L. F. Crisp.   Melbourne: Longman Cheshire, 1978. 4th ed. 523p.
bibliog.

One of the standard general works of Australian parliamentary government, this
has been through many revisions and editions since its original publication in
1965. The text of the constitution is reproduced in an appendix and a very useful
select bibliography of up-to-date books and articles and official publications
appears in each edition. Other similar works published recently are: *The politics
of Australian democracy* by Hugh Emy (Melbourne: Macmillan, 1978); *The pieces
of politics* edited by R. Lucy (Melbourne: Macmillan, 1978. 2nd ed.); *Cabinet
government in Australia* by S. Encel (Melbourne: Melbourne University Press,
1974).

237 **A constitutional history of Australia.**
W. G. McMinn. Melbourne: Oxford University Press, 1979.
213p. bibliog.

This book traces the stages by which the autocratic régimes in the Australian colonies acquired democratic constitutions based on the Westminster model. It is concerned more with the working and evolution of the Australian system of government than with the strict law of the constitution or with the fine detail of colonial, state or federal politics. It is a work for the serious student of Australian affairs. A useful bibliographical note concludes the book.

238 **Australian federalism: future tense.**
Edited by Allan Patience, Jeffrey Scott. Melbourne: Oxford University Press, 1983. 217p.

A collection of readings specially written for the book, which examine the issue of Australian federalism and its future. The contributors include prominent politicians, two previous Prime Ministers and two state Premiers who have dealt with federal relations in practice and some leading academics − one economist, one constitutional lawyer and five political scientists who look at federalism from a theoretical perspective. The views expressed are diverse, but all agree that federalism must evolve in new ways to cope with the uncertain economic future.

239 **What rough beast? The state and social order in Australian history.**
Sydney Labour History Group. Sydney: Allen & Unwin, 1982. 282p.

A collection of well-argued essays which investigate the reality of state power expressed historically in Australia. They explore the methods by which that power has been used to create and maintain a preferred social order, and to suppress real and imagined threats to that particular order.

240 **Illusions of power: the fate of a reform government.**
Michael Sexton. Sydney: Allen & Unwin, 1979. 305p. bibliog.

An examination of how a government elected to office with a moderate programme of reform encountered some of the realities of power in Australia. After being out of power for twenty-three years the Labor Party was elected to govern again in 1972 but in 1975 it was dismissed from office by the Governor-General, Sir John Kerr. The book shows how the Labor government was subject to the limits imposed by other power-holders − bureaucrats, manufacturers, trade unions, banks, mining companies and media groups. It is a very readable account with many illustrations of the leading personalities mentioned in the text. The bibliography concluding the book lists the large body of literature generated by the three eventful years of Labor government.

241 **The politics of patriotism: the pressure group activities of the Returned Servicemen's League.**
G. L. Kristiansen. Canberra: Australian National University Press, 1966. 286p. bibliog.

An in-depth examination of the ways in which the largest veterans' organization in Australia attempts to influence the federal government on matters that concern its members – pensions, medical benefits, war-service homes, soldier settlement, employment preference as well as controversial subjects such as defence and anti-communism.

242 **Interest groups and public policy.**
Roger Scott. Melbourne: Macmillan, 1980. 248p. bibliog.

Presents case-studies on Australian pressure groups as they operate at the state level. There is an essay on each state (two on New South Wales) on topics in the fields of education, social services, Aborigines and land rights, rural producer groups, urban planning and environmental protection. General theoretical questions are taken up in the opening and closing essays. A useful select bibliography on pressure groups in Australia concludes the book.

243 **Rooted in secrecy: the clandestine element in Australian politics.**
Joan Coxsedge, Ken Coldicutt, Gerry Harant. Melbourne: Committee for the Abolition of Political Police (CAPP), 1982. 250p.

Although some of the material in the book can only be informed speculation, overall it is an admirable effort to list all clandestine police forces and intelligence-gathering agencies operating in Australia and to record some of the ramifications of their work. As the authors see it, the worst aspect of these agencies is their uncontrolled routine espionage and surveillance of the lives of what must add up to millions of Australians.

244 **Responsible government in Australia.**
Edited by Patrick Weller, Dean Jaensch. Melbourne: Drummond, for the Australasian Political Studies Association, 1980. 276p.

An authoritative collection of essays on the theory and practice of responsible government in Australia. Chapters examine parliament, statutory authorities, the public service, local government and the community. Overseas comparisons are also made and each chapter is accompanied by lists of references.

245 **Australian democracy in crisis: a radical approach to Australian politics.**
Andrew Theophanous. Melbourne: Oxford University Press, 1980. 450p. bibliog.

Dr. Theophanous, a Member of Parliament and former lecturer in politics, has written a pioneering study of the Australian political system. He combines empirical material on institutions and recent political events with a well-defined theoretical framework from which to evaluate them. The framework is derived partly from the democratic principles upheld by all sides of Australian political life and partly from European neo-Marxism. An essential text for the serious reader who wants to preserve some balance with the more traditional interpretations of the structure and processes of Australian government and politics.

246 **The Whitlam venture.**
Alan Reid. Melbourne: Hill of Content, 1976. 465p.

Alan Reid has been a political journalist for more than forty years and his experience shows in this narrative of the events which led to the dismissal of the Whitlam-led Labor government by the Governor-General in 1975. He is the author of two other books of recent political history – *The power struggle* (Sydney: Shakespeare Head Press, 1969) is the story of the election of comparatively little-known Senator John Gorton as Prime Minister after the dramatic disappearance, while swimming in the ocean, of the then Prime Minister Harold Holt in December 1967; *The Gorton experiment* (Sydney: Shakespeare Head Press, 1971) is an account of Gorton's years in power until he was voted out from the leadership of the Liberal Party and the Prime Ministership in March 1971 on his own casting vote. While the books are by no means the fairest or the most objective reports of events, they are certainly well informed and provide gripping reading even for people who are usually not very interested in politics. All three books are illustrated with black-and-white photographs of people mentioned in the text.

247 **From Whitlam to Fraser: reform and reaction in Australian politics.**
Edited by Allan Patience, Brian Head. Melbourne: Oxford University Press, 1979. 320p.

This work analyses the politics of the Federal governments in Australia from 1972 to 1978. The election of the first Labor government in twenty-three years and the subsequent return to power of the Liberal-National Country Party coalition in 1975 provide a rare opportunity to compare the parties in action and not simply election promises. Each chapter is written by a specialist who examines the record of both parties in a particular policy area, such as the economy, social welfare, health, education, Aborigines, immigration, minerals and energy, foreign policy and others.

Politics. General

248 **Rehearsals for change: politics and culture in Australia.**
Dennis Altman. Melbourne: Fontana/Collins, 1980. 215p.

A survey of socio-cultural developments in Australia in the 1960s and 1970s. Altman does not believe that governments in Australia can achieve effective change and argues for social changes based on grass-roots participation and the new social movements which evolved in the last twenty years.

249 **Poor little rich country: the path to the eighties.**
Maximilian Walsh. Melbourne: Penguin Books, 1979. 232p.

This is essentially a political and economic history of Australia during the 1970s. The author is editor of Australia's foremost financial newspaper *The Financial Review* and has a talent for demystifying economic issues. His message is that the events of the '70s such as the world economic crisis and internal social and political upheavals shattered Australia's basic assumptions of assured prosperity and social tranquility based on its natural wealth. Although the latter remains, Australians have not learned from experience but have moved toward short-sighted selfishness, cynicism and declining standards of public and private conduct. A pessimistic book, but written with such vigour and astuteness that it sustains interest to the last page.

250 **The split: Australian Labor in the fifties.**
Robert Murray. Melbourne: Cheshire, 1970. 388p.

A detailed examination of the split in the Australian Labor Party in the 1950s, which led to the creation of the Democratic Labor Party. The split kept the Labor Party out of federal government until 1972. This is a book for readers needing a deeper understanding of Australian post-war politics, but it is also a thrilling story in its own right.

251 **A fractured federation? Australia in the 1980s.**
Edited by Jennifer Aldred and John Wilkes. Sydney: Allen & Unwin, 1983. 106p.

A selection of papers read at the 48th Summer School of the Australian Institute of Political Science held at Canberra in early 1982. States' rights in the Australian federation have been the subject of a continuous debate and political action ever since the Commonwealth of Australia came into existence in 1901. These papers examine the question of federalism from different perspectives and political viewpoints. The book must be read by anyone who wants to understand the complexity of Australian affairs.

252 **The new conservatism in Australia.**
Edited by R. Manne. Melbourne: Oxford University Press, 1982. 290p.

A collection of thirteen essays written by some of the more prominent Australian conservative intellectuals in the areas of Australian politics, society and international relations. As a result it is not a book about the Right, but expounds the Right's viewpoint on important issues of public affairs.

253 **Australia and the new Right.**
Edited by Marian Sawer. Sydney: Allen & Unwin, 1982.
181p. bibliogs.

An examination of the impact on Australian politics of the general shift to the Right in the English-speaking democracies. On the whole the contributors are critical of the arguments put forward by these vocal opponents of the welfare state and economic planning.

254 **From Barton to Fraser: every Australian prime minister.**
Brian Carroll. Melbourne: Cassell, 1978. 176p.

A large-format volume with many illustrations on all Australian prime ministers since federation. The text concentrates on the political facts, not on their personalities, and as a result the author has produced sketches of the office-holders rather than full portraits. The book serves well its purpose of easy reference.

255 **Mr. Prime Minister: Australian prime ministers, 1901-1972.**
Colin A. Hughes. Melbourne: Oxford University Press, 1976.
208p.

An account of the twenty-one men who held the office before Gough Whitlam who was Prime Minister from 1972 to 1975 and Malcolm Fraser who has held office since 1975. This book is an excellent introduction for anyone who needs a quick introduction to the strengths and weaknesses of the men and outlines of their terms of office.

Parliament and elections

256 **Inside the Australian parliament.**
David Solomon. Sydney: Allen & Unwin, 1978. 211p. tables.
bibliog.

David Solomon has intimate knowledge of how the Australian parliament operates. He is a journalist who spent more than ten years in Parliament House in Canberra, first as a reporter and commentator, then as a political correspondent, and finally as a member of staff of a prime minister. This is therefore not a theoretical study, but an account of happenings inside the House. Solomon says that he has 'attempted to look beyond the formal standing orders and formal purposes to what actually happens – how ministers, members, governments and oppositions approach and are affected by the various procedures and proceedings in both parliament and Parliament House'.

257 **Servant of the House.**
Frank C. Green. Melbourne: Heinemann, 1969. 173p.

A personal account of how the Australian parliament and government operates by the Clerk of the House of Representatives from 1937 until 1955.

258 **Parliamentary privilege in Australia.**
Enid Campbell. Melbourne: Melbourne University Press, 1966.
218p.

A legal study about the privileges of the Houses of Parliament, federal and state, and of their members, officers and committees. Throughout, the emphasis is upon the delimitations of these privileges by legislative enactment and judicial decisions, and upon the procedures for enforcement of parliamentary privileges both in parliament and in the courts.

259 **Parliament and bureaucracy: parliamentary scrutiny of administration: prospects and problems in the 1980s.**
Edited by J. R. Nethercote. Sydney: Hale & Iremonger, with the
Australian Institute of Public Administration, 1982. 363p.

A collection of papers most of which were delivered at the 1981 national conference of the Australian Institute of Public Administration. The strength of the book is that it brings together the perspectives, views and opinions of a wide range of people including several parliamentarians and officials for whom the subjects being analysed are of daily concern.

260 **The Parliament of New South Wales, 1856-1965.**
G. N. Hawker. Sydney: Government Printer, 1971. 377p.
bibliog.

A record of the working of Australia's oldest parliament, the Lower House or Legislative Assembly and the Upper House or Legislative Council of New South Wales. This very detailed history is based on all available official sources, published material and unpublished documents and theses.

261 **Australia votes: the 1958 federal election.**
D. W. Rawson. Melbourne: Melbourne University Press on
behalf of the Australian National University, 1961. 259p.

This was the first full analysis of a federal election. Attention is focused on two electorates, one in the country in New South Wales and the other in Brisbane, Queensland's capital. The book provides an intimate glimpse into the electoral process in Australia.

262 **Elections 1980.**
Malcolm Mackerras. Sydney: Angus & Robertson, 1980. 355p.

This is a further edition of the book originally known as *Australian general elections* which appeared in 1972 prior to the election that year. In 1975 a fresh edition under the title *Elections 1975* was issued, which became a guide to that election. The book is essentially a compilation of electoral statistics for all federal elections held since 1958, with a seat-by-seat analysis of the 1977 election. There are electoral maps, records of past voting and swing patterns in each seat and state. The author's well-known comprehensive swing chart and electoral pendulum are included. In addition there are useful descriptive chapters on recent elections, opinion polls and other informative material.

263 **Australia at the polls: the national elections of 1975.**
Edited by Howard R. Penniman. Washington, DC: American
Enterprise Institute for Public Policy Research, 1977. 373p.
(AEI Studies, 142).

A dispassionate study of the election following the constitutional crisis that
culminated in the Governor-General's unprecedented dissolution of Parliament
and dismissal of the sitting Labor government of Prime Minister Gough Whitlam.
The thirteen contributors are all experts on Australian government and politics.
The Institute in 1979 published an account of the subsequent election – *The
Australian national elections of 1977.*

264 **Time of testing: the Bob Hawke victory.**
Craig McGregor. Melbourne: Penguin Books, 1983. 257p.

One of several books on the March 1983 federal election campaign, which resulted
in the defeat of the Liberal-National Party coalition and the election of the Labor
government with Bob Hawke as the new Prime Minister. Three other books are:
Gamble for power, by Anne Summers (Melbourne: Nelson, 1983); *31 days to
power*, by Robert Haupt, Michelle Grattan (Sydney: Allen & Unwin, 1983);
and, *The things we did last summer: an election journal* (Melbourne: Fontana/
Collins, 1983).

265 **Anatomy of an election.**
Edited by P. R. Hay, Ian Ward, John Warhurst. Melbourne:
Hill of Content, 1979. 268p.

An account of the 1979 Victorian state election campaign. State elections in
Australia are contested by the same parties which operate at the national level,
but they concentrate on local issues. There have been few major studies of state
elections but some further books of interest are: *In firm hands: the Western
Australian state elections, 1977*, edited by B. Hamilton, (Perth: Politics Department, University of Western Australia, 1979); *Images and issues: the Queensland
state elections of 1963 and 1966*, by Colin Hughes (Canberra: Australian National
University Press, 1969); *Politics in a suburban community: the N.S.W. state
election in Manby, 1965*, edited by John Power (Sydney: Sydney University
Press, 1968), a study of election politics in one particular electorate; *The South
Australian elections, 1959*, by R. Hetherington, R. L. Reid (Adelaide: Rigby,
1962).

266 **Communism and democracy in Australia: a survey of the 1951
referendum.**
Leicester Webb. Melbourne: Cheshire, 1954. 214p.

In 1951 the Australian government sought by referendum the power to suppress
the Australian Communist Party and to remove Communists from office in trade
unions. By a small majority of 52,000 votes Australians rejected the proposition.
Webb's book is a first-rate analysis of the referendum campaign and its background.

Politics. Political parties

267 **Stability and change in Australian politics.**
Don Aitkin. Canberra: Australian National University Press,
1982. 2nd ed. 400p.

The 1977 edition of this book was based on two massive surveys of some 2,500 people in 1967 and 1969 in order to find out the political attitudes and behaviour of Australians. The 2nd edition is based on the findings of a new survey carried out in 1979, which, in the author's opinion, confirms the general thesis of the first volume – that the stability of the Australian political system can be attributed to the voters' 'relatively unchanging feelings of loyalty' to a chosen political party and its 'generalised ideology'.

268 **Society and electoral behaviour in Australia: a study of three decades.**
D. A. Kemp. Brisbane: University of Queensland Press, 1978.
401p. bibliog.

An analysis of three decades of Australian voting patterns and attitudes since 1945. Kemp's basic findings are that established factors indicating how people would vote, such as class, wealth, occupation, religion are declining because of increased education affluence and mobility of the Australian electorate.

Political parties

269 **Political parties in Australia.**
Graeme Starr, Keith Richmond, Graham Maddox. Melbourne:
Heinemann Education, 1978. 399p. bibliogs.

An exposition of the Australian party system suitable for both the student and the general reader. There are chapters on the 'Liberal Party of Australia', the 'National Country Party', the 'Australian Labor Party' and a chapter on the minor parties such as the 'Democratic Labor Party', the 'Australia Party', 'Council for the Defence of Government Schools', the 'Liberal Movement', the 'Workers' Party', 'Australian Democrats', 'Australian Communist Party', the 'Nazi parties' and 'Conservative groups'.

270 **The Australian party system.**
Dean Jaensch. Sydney: Allen & Unwin, 1983. 235p. bibliog.

The focus of this study, unlike other books on the subject, is the analysis of the Australian party system and not individual political parties. It is concerned with the interrelationships among the parties with regard to representation, responsibility, socialization, participation, persuasion, deliberation, policy formation and communication.

271 **The emergence of the Australian party system.**
Edited by P. Loveday, A. E. Martin, R. S. Parker. Sydney: Hale
& Iremonger, 1977. 536p. bibliog.

The 20-year period from about 1890 to 1910 saw a dynamic change in the
political scene of the Australian colonies and the newly founded commonwealth.
This scholarly book examines the changes and the processes which produced
functioning political parties at both the state and federal levels. The work is indispensable for the political historian but it can be read with interest by the serious
student of Australian affairs.

272 **Party politics: Australia, 1966-1981.**
James Jupp. Sydney: Allen & Unwin, 1982. 232p. bibliog.

A study of the various parties since 1966 when Prime Minister Sir Robert Menzies
retired after a record term in office of eighteen years. Like its predecessor, *Australian political parties*, published in 1964, this book is also an excellent introduction
to Australian politics for the general reader and student, both in Australia and
overseas.

273 **The ALP: a short history of the Australian Labor Party.**
Brian McKinlay. Melbourne: Drummond/Heinemann, 1981.
168p. bibliog.

The Australian Labor Party has the longest continuous existence of any political
party in this country. It dates from 1891 and is one of the oldest democratic
socialist parties in the world. The author is also editor of *A documentary history
of the Australian labor movement, 1850-1975* (Melbourne: Drummond, 1979).

274 **Machine politics in the Australian Labor Party.**
Edited by Andrew Parkin, John Warhurst. Sydney: Allen &
Unwin, 1983. 281p.

The Australian Labor Party has existed for nearly a hundred years and features
complex politics within its organization. This collection of essays looks at the
internal politics of the party at the federal, state and local levels.

275 **A liberal nation: the Liberal Party & Australian politics.**
Marian Simms. Sydney: Hale & Iremonger, 1982. 224p.
bibliog.

An analysis of the theory and practice of the Liberal Party of Australia since its
foundation in 1944. The party has been in government ever since it first came to
power in 1949, except for the period 1972-75, when the Australian Labor Party
formed the government and again in 1983 when the Labor Party regained power.

69

276 **Politics, power and persuasion: the Liberals in Victoria.**
Peter Aimer. Sydney: Bennett, 1974. 248p. bibliog.

Until recently the state of Victoria has been the power base of the Liberal Party in Australia, and the Victorian division of the party has been one of Australia's more electorally successful bodies by any standards. Aimer's concern is not so much with political issues or personalities, as with the structure and functioning of the party organization. He investigates the growth of the Liberal Party out of the defeated United Australia Party and then traces its activities in Victoria between the years 1945 and 1971.

277 **The foundation of the Australian Country Parties.**
B. D. Graham. Canberra: Australian National University Press, 1966. 320p. bibliog.

From the early years of the 20th century agrarian parties have been the third force in the Australian political system. As long-standing partners in governing coalitions both at state and federal levels, they have succeeded in gaining benefits for their rural electorates that far outweigh their numerical representation. Graham's study traces in considerable detail the history of these parties in the formative years during which they developed their characteristics and worked out their strategies. An unashamedly partisan account of the party is Ulrich Ellis' *A history of the Australian Country Party* (Melbourne: Melbourne University Press, 1963).

278 **Revolutionaries and reformists: Communism and the Australian labour movement, 1920-55.**
Robin Gollan. Canberra: Australian National University Press, 1975. 330p. bibliog.

A history of the Communist Party of Australia through its heyday in the 1930s and 1940s to the middle-1950s when it disintegrated into several minor Left parties, none of which can claim to be its true successor.

279 **The Communist Party of Australia: a short history.**
Alastair Davidson. Stanford, California: Stanford University, 1969. 214p. bibliog. (Hoover Institution Studies, 26).

A history spanning the fifty years since the party's formation in 1920 to the late 1960s when much of its influence, except in certain trade unions, had dissipated.

Public Administration

280 **Government administration in Australia.**
R. N. Spann. Sydney: Allen & Unwin, 1979. 524p.

A major re-write of Spann's classic study *Public administration in Australia* originally published more than twenty years ago. This new book is a complete survey of the federal state and local governments. It is suitable for students, practitioners and the general reader.

281 **An introduction to Australian public administration.**
Kenneth W. Wiltshire. Melbourne: Cassell, 1974. 279p. bibliog.

Describes and analyses the structure, size and operation of both national and state government bureaucracies. The author explores the role of the public servant in policy formulation and discounts the traditional idea of the public servant as a passive, neutral instrument of government. Although somewhat overtaken by events, such as the restraints put on the growth of their public services by governments in the late 1970s and early 1980s, the book is worthwhile as an introductory text, because of its clear and simple explanation of public administration in Australia.

282 **Understanding public administration.**
Edited by G. R. Curnow, R. L. Wettenhall. Sydney: Allen & Unwin, 1981. 292p. bibliog.

A wide-ranging review of the state of public administration in Australia up to 1980. It is a collection of articles by a number of specialists in the field of administration written to commemorate the work of two distinguished colleagues.

283 **Public service inquiries in Australia.**
Edited by R. F. I. Smith, Patrick Weller. Brisbane: University of Queensland Press, 1978. 381p.

A collection of papers devoted to four recent enquiries into public bureaucracies: three state investigations (South Australia, Victoria and New South Wales) and the Royal Commission on Australian Government Administration. Together they provide a stimulating and wide-ranging debate on essential aspects of the public service and the need for reform.

Public Administration

284 **Politics between departments: the fragmentation of executive control in Australian government.**
Martin Painter, Bernard Carey. Brisbane: University of Queensland Press, 1979. 132p.

A study of bureaucratic politics at the federal level and their effect on government policy during the Labor administration from 1972 to 1975. It is the only work to investigate in detail the operation and role of interdepartmental committees in Australian government. Of particular interest to the serious student of public policy formation in the Australian context.

285 **Innovation and reaction: the life and death of the Federal Department of Urban and Regional Development.**
C. J. Lloyd, P. N. Troy. Sydney: Allen & Unwin, 1981. 282p. bibliog.

The Department of Urban and Regional Development (DURD) was created in 1972 by the incoming Whitlam Labor government to bring into effect the Labor Party's policy on the cities and regions. Both authors played an active role in the creation of DURD and the basic source material was the correspondence, memoranda and working papers of Tom Uren, the responsible minister. The book is an intimate record of public administration and bureaucracy at work, a subject not well represented in Australian literature on administration.

286 **The establishment of the Department of Trade: a case-study in administrative reorganization.**
R. P. Deane. Canberra: Australian National University, 1963. 103p. bibliog.

A case-study which attempts to describe, analyse and explain the reasons for certain changes made in 1956 with the trade and industry functions of the federal government. Comparisons are made with administrative theory about the purposes and methods of departmental organization. The work gives an insight into how public administration functions at the federal level in Australia.

287 **Governments of the Australian States and Territories.**
Brisbane: University of Queensland Press, 1976- .

Published under the general editorship of Colin Hughes, this series consists of the most recent surveys of the various systems of Australian state government administrations. They are: *The government of Tasmania,* by W. A. Townsley; *The government of Victoria,* by Jean Holmes; *The government of South Australia,* by Dean Jaensch; *The government of the Australian Capital Territory*, by Ruth Atkins; *The government of the Northern Territory*, by Alistair Heatley; *The government of New South Wales*, by R. S. Parker; *The government of Queensland*, by Colin A. Hughes. Each volume explores the ways in which each state's system differs from the others and why it differs. The two territory volumes anticipate how each territory is expected to achieve self-government.

288 **Public servants and patronage: the foundation and rise of the New South Wales Public Service, 1786-1859.**
Arthur McMartin. Sydney: Sydney University Press, 1983. 345p. bibliog.

A comprehensive history of the oldest of the Australian bureaucracies, from its foundation in 1786 to its emergence as an integral part of the machinery of responsible government in 1856. It is an important addition to the small list of works on Australian administrative history.

289 **Local government and the people: challenges for the eighties.**
M. A. Jones. Melbourne: Hargreen, 1981. 275p. bibliog.

A companion volume to the author's *Australian local government* (1977). It investigates local government and anticipates the pressures it will face during the next decade from a troubled economy and public spending cutbacks at the national level. The author suggests that there will be new opportunities from a revitalized local government as disillusionment spreads with big government on the national and state levels.

290 **Albany to Zeehan: a new look at local governments.**
Ruth Atkins. Sydney: Law Book Company, 1979. 147p. bibliog.

The author attacks some popular myths and misunderstandings about local government in Australia and provides international comparisons. She discusses problems, such as party politics, rates, amalgamations, malpractice and maladministration. There is an interesting appendix giving brief information about a number of very different and widely scattered local authorities throughout Australia.

291 **Local government in Australia: reformation or regression?**
Donald M. Purdie. Sydney: Law Book Company, 1976. 200p. bibliog.

The Australian Federation has a three-tier system of government; the national government and parliament, the state governments and their legislatures, and about 900 local government bodies at the city, town, municipal and shire level. Local governments have important functions such as providing essential services, amenities, community facilities and controls, negotiating with state or federal authorities and adjudicating local conflicts. Purdie, an experienced municipal official, explores the problems facing local government in Australia and suggests reforms and reorganization while expressing disappointment about resistance to change. There is a useful bibliographical section.

292 **Governing the cities: the Australian experience in perspective.**
Andrew Parkin. Melbourne: Macmillan, 1982. 147p.

Describes and evaluates the government of metropolitan areas, where more than 85 per cent of Australia's population of 15 million live. It is not often realized that Australia is one of the most urbanized countries in the world.

293 **The civic frontier: the origin of local communities and local government in Victoria.**
Bernard Barrett. Melbourne: Melbourne University Press, 1979. 329p. bibliog.

A scholarly study of the structural development of Victorian communities. The author uses case-studies of the processes of growth in the city of Melbourne, its suburbs and country areas during the first generation of white settlers in Victoria between 1834 and 1870. It can be said to provide 'an archaeology of existing institutions' and thus lead to a better understanding of them not only in Victoria but other states as well.

294 **Police in Australia: development, functions and procedures.**
Kerry Milte, assisted by Thomas A. Webber. Sydney: Butterworth, 1977. 511p.

In the Australian federal system the six state police forces enforce state laws, and the Australian Federal Police are responsible for the enforcement of federal laws throughout Australia and the provision of general police services in the Australian Capital Territory. *Police in Australia* surveys them all. A strong legal bias is evident in the book, no doubt reflecting the authors' legal training.

Foreign Relations

295 **Independence and alliance: Australia in world affairs, 1976-80.**
Edited by P. J. Boyce, J. R. Angel. Sydney: Allen & Unwin,
with the Australian Institute of International Affairs, 1983. 368p.

This is the sixth in the indispensable series of volumes published by the Australian
Institute of International Affairs, which for twenty-five years has provided an
authoritative, analytical record of Australia's overseas interests and the government's handling of foreign policy. Each volume covers a 5-year period, starting
with 1950-55. Previous volumes were edited by Gordon Greenwood, Norman
Harper and W. J. Hudson. The series is designed not only for the specialist scholar
or academic reader but rather for all people interested in politics generally and in
Australia's role in international affairs in particular.

296 **Australia in peace and war: external relations, 1788-1977.**
T. B. Millar. London: Hurst, 1978. 578p. bibliog.

This is the only general history of Australia's foreign policy development. The
emphasis is on the last forty years, the period in which Australia evolved its own
independent attitude towards the world. The book is intended for a wide
audience: undergraduates, secondary students and general readers.

297 **Australia's Asian policies: the history of a debate, 1839-1972.**
A. W. Stargardt. Wiesbaden, GFR: Institute of Asian Affairs in
Hamburg, with Otto Harrassowitz, 1977. 404p.

An interesting account of the development of Australian foreign policy. The book
demonstrates how Australia's relations with other countries were defined by her
loyalties to Britain and later the United States. Stargardt criticizes the policy of
dependence and argues that unquestionable loyalty has not always served
Australia's best interests.

298 **Prime ministers and diplomats: the making of Australian foreign policy, 1901-49.**
P. G. Edwards. Melbourne: Oxford University Press, with the Australian Institute of International Affairs, 1983. 240p. bibliog.

A history of the evolution of Australian foreign policy from federation to the immediate post-Second World War years by which time independence from the British in international politics had been achieved. The approach of the author is less concerned with the nature of the policy than with the nature of the men who shaped it and tried to carry it out. Anyone interested in Australia's foreign relations will want to read this book.

299 **The frightened country.**
Alan Renouf. Melbourne: Macmillan, 1979. 555p.

In his thirty-six years of diplomatic service the author served in twelve Australian missions abroad, held six ambassadorial appointments and served as head of the Foreign Affairs Department from 1973-76, when he was appointed Australian ambassador to the United States until his retirement in 1979. He characterizes Australia as 'the frightened country' whose obsession with security has led to a confused foreign policy, which in turn has jeopardized relations with her Asian and Pacific neighbours and compromised her status in world affairs. Overall the book is a scathing criticism of official policy-making and must be read by everyone with an interest in Australia's role in world affairs. Renouf has also published an entertaining, anecdotal account of his diplomatic career in *The champagne trail* (Melbourne: Macmillan, 1980).

300 **The evolution of Australian foreign policy, 1938-65.**
Alan Watt. Cambridge, England: Cambridge University Press, 1967. 387p. bibliog.

Sir Alan Watt, a former diplomat and administrative head of the Australian Foreign Affairs Department, has traced the development of Australian foreign policy for the period 1938-65. In 1938 Australia had only one diplomatic representative in a non-Commonwealth country; she relied primarily on British sources of official information and tended to follow the British line in foreign affairs. Thus the book describes the coming of age of an independent Australian foreign policy. Although intimately involved in the events he describes, the author has tried to rely on published material only. He has much more to say about the personalities of the men with whom he was involved during his long career in *Australian diplomat: memoirs of Sir Alan Watt* (Sydney: Angus & Robertson, 1972).

301 **An introduction to Australian foreign policy.**
J. A. Camilleri. Brisbane: Jacaranda, 1979. 4th ed. 177p.
bibliog.

A clear and acute commentary on the history of Australian foreign policy. The author emphatically criticizes Australia's dependence on the American alliance which has been the cornerstone of all Australian policy initiative for the past forty years. The American alliance is the sole subject of a more recent book by Camilleri: *Australian-American relations: the web of dependence* (Melbourne: Macmillan, 1980).

302 **Diplomatic witness: Australian foreign affairs, 1941-1947.**
Paul Hasluck. Melbourne: Melbourne University Press, 1980.
306p.

The Rt. Hon. Sir Paul Hasluck, now retired, became Governor-General of Australia after a long record of service as a cabinet minister in the portfolios of territories, defence and external affairs. From 1941 until his resignation in 1947 he was an officer of the infant Department of External Affairs. The book's interest lies in its insights into wartime administration, post-war policy planning, the birth and infancy of the United Nations and wartime personalities — both Australian and foreign, not least the brilliant but erratic Dr. H. V. Evatt, then Minister for External Affairs, President of the United Nations General Assembly 1948-49 and later Leader of the Labor Opposition, 1951-60.

303 **Documents on Australian Foreign Policy.**
Canberra: Australian Government Publishing Service for the
Department of Foreign Affairs, 1976- . 5 vols to date.

These are the first five volumes, covering the years 1937 to June 1942, in a series planned to span the period 1937 to 1949. This was a vital period in the nation's development, when its very survival was at stake. The documents are meticulously edited and are indispensable to all serious students of Australia's external relations. Here the interested general reader can profit by recapturing the ideas and thoughts of a past period. Another collection of contemporary source material is *Documents on Australian international affairs, 1901-1918*, edited by Gordon Greenwood, Charles Grimshaw (Melbourne: Nelson, 1977).

304 **Agenda for the eighties: contexts of Australian choices in foreign and defence policy.**
Edited by Coral Bell. Canberra: Australian National University
Press, 1980. 256p.

A useful guide to the areas of defence and foreign policy in which Australian governments, of whatever party, will have to make decisions over the next decade. Some of the problems analysed are those of the central balance of power (Australia's relations with the United States and the Soviet Union), nuclear policy, Antarctica, China and Japan, the Persian Gulf and the Indian Ocean littoral. An appendix provides a selection of documents which may remain relevant during the 1980s: The ANZUS (Australia, New Zealand, United States Security Treaty) Treaty, the North West Cape Agreement, the Antarctic Treaty, and the Model Agreement on Nuclear Materials.

Foreign Relations

305 **Australian foreign minister: the diaries of R. G. Casey, 1951-60.**
Edited by T. B. Millar. London: Collins, 1972. 352p.

The edited diaries of Lord Casey who was Australia's Minister for External Affairs from 26 April 1951 to 22 January 1960. This covers an important period of realignment for Australia: the American alliance was forged by the signing of the Australia, New Zealand, United States Security (ANZUS) Treaty; and the importance of Asia in Australian foreign relations was recognized and institutionalized in the South East Asia Treaty Organization (SEATO).

306 **The last domino: aspects of Australia's foreign relations.**
Malcolm Booker. Sydney: Collins, 1976. 254p. bibliog.

The author, a long-serving career diplomat, argues the case for independence from the American alliance and the necessity for Australia to regard itself as a geographical part of Asia, and to follow an essentially neutral foreign policy. The author has also published another equally pessimistic book: *Last quarter: the next twenty-five years in Asia and the Pacific* (Melbourne University Press, 1978).

307 **Isolationism and appeasement in Australia: reactions to the European crises, 1935-1939.**
E. M. Andrews. Canberra: Australian National University Press, 1970. 236p. bibliog.

An examination of public opinion and to a lesser extent government policy towards the aggressions which led to the Second World War in Abyssinia, Spain, Austria, Czechoslovakia and Poland. The study ranges from early support for the League of Nations to the change to a policy of appeasement, culminating in the Munich crisis of 1938, and the Australian reaction to it.

308 **Australia and the League of Nations.**
W. J. Hudson. Sydney: Sydney University Press, with the Australian Institute of International Affairs, 1980. 224p. bibliog.

It was in the League of Nations that Australia served its diplomatic apprenticeship and became accepted eventually as an independent if still 'British' voice in world affairs. The book describes and evaluates Australia's contributions to the creation, development and ultimate failure of the League.

309 **Australian external policy under Labor: content, process and the national debate.**
Henry S. Albinski. Brisbane: University of Queensland Press, 1977. 373p. bibliog.

An analysis of Australian external policy under the first Labor Party government elected to federal office after nearly a quarter of a century. It governed from 1972 to 1975 and initiated some radically new policies, such as recognition of China and the establishment of diplomatic relations with North Vietnam. On coming to power Labor also emphasized the contrast with the previous Liberal government's policies in the areas of anti-racism and anti-colonialism, and stressed the government's support for social changes that would reduce poverty, inequalities and injustices in developing countries. Professor Albinski, an American academic, has written other works on Australian affairs that merit attention: *Politics and foreign policy in Australia: the impact of Vietnam and conscription* (Durham, North Carolina: Duke University Press, 1970); and *The Australian America security relationship* (Brisbane, Australia: University of Queensland Press, 1981).

310 **Australia and the colonial question at the United Nations.**
W. J. Hudson. Sydney: Sydney University Press, 1970. 214p. bibliog.

An examination of Australia's attitude in the United Nations to the colonial question, notably its own administration of Papua and New Guinea, Indonesian independence and the West Irian question. Overall Australia's diplomatic response to a changing anti-colonial world is seen to have been conservative and defensive.

311 **Australia and the United Nations.**
Norman Harper, David Sissons. New York: Manhattan Publishing, 1959. 423p.

A scholarly examination of Australia's involvement with the United Nations from its inception at the San Francisco Conference to 1957.

312 **Billy Hughes in Paris: the birth of Australian diplomacy.**
W. J. Hudson. Melbourne: Nelson, 1978. 147p. bibliog.

William Morris Hughes, the Prime Minister, fought hard to achieve representation for Australia at the Paris Peace Conference in 1919. Once there Hughes had considerable success, and came home with New Guinea under Australian control (with some compensation), white Australia safe, and Japanese expansionism partly neutralised — altogether quite a triumph for a young nation of dominion status in its début at international diplomacy.

313 **Australia and Britain: studies in a changing relationship.**
Edited by A. F. Madden, W. H. Morris-Jones. Sydney: Sydney
University Press, with the Institute of Commonwealth Studies,
University of London, 1980. 195p.

A series of essays by various academics on the traditional strength of British
influence in Australia, despite the widening gap between the interests of the two
countries over the last thirty years.

314 **Australia & America, 1788-1972: an alternative history.**
L. G. Churchward. Sydney: Alternative Publishing Cooperative,
1979. 261p. bibliog.

A survey of American-Australian relations from the foundation of New South
Wales, when American merchantmen started trading with the new colony and
American whalers plied their trade in Australian waters, until 1972, when in the
author's opinion American economic and cultural penetration of Australia had
become firmly established.

315 **Unequal allies: Australian-American relations and the Pacific War.**
Roger J. Bell. Melbourne: Melbourne University Press, 1977.
278p. bibliog.

A very good book on Australian-American relations in the 1940s, based on
recently released American, Australian and British official documents. Contrary
to popular belief, Bell's conclusions are that the wartime alliance between the
USA and Australia was transitory and did not lead to an 'unconditional and
enduring' relationship with the new protector. He drives home the lesson, not
properly understood even by many Australian policy makers, that the United
States government will consider its first duty to be to its own people, and that
therefore its readiness to give military or economic help to Australia, or any other
country, will depend upon its assessment of how far that will promote and
protect American, not Australian, interests.

316 **Approaches to Asia: Australian post-war policies and attitudes.**
Gordon Greenwood, with the assistance of Pamela Bray.
Sydney: McGraw-Hill, 1974. 612p. bibliog.

An examination of Australia's participation in, and response to, the more important Asian issues since the Second World War. The historical narrative is supported
by copious extracts from original documents. The book shows Australia's increasing concern with Asian countries, as the government assumed a more independent
foreign policy stance during and after the war. It is essential reading for anyone
wanting to understand present Australian policy towards Asia.

317   The Australia and New Zealand nexus.
      Alan Burnett, Robin Burnett.   Canberra: Australian Institute
      of International Affairs and New Zealand Institute of Inter-
      national Affairs, 1978. 289p.

A study of the intergovernmental arrangements between the two countries with
respect to: movement of peoples, defence, trade relations and trans-Tasman
transport. Special emphasis is laid upon the network of bilateral arrangements
between two closely associated but independent countries.

318   Australia's northern neighbours: independent or dependent?
      Edited by P. Wolfers. Melbourne: Nelson, 1976. 276p.

The papers in this book are the edited proceedings of the fifth national conference of the Australian Institute of International Affairs in May 1975. The underlying theme of the conference was to examine the impact of foreign aid and
investment on development in South-East Asia, a region of vital importance to
Australia's security. The overall consensus reached by the participants was that
the less developed countries have not benefited from the aid, trade and investment of the richer nations, on the contrary, their activities have added to racial
and regional differences and have led to the entrenchment of local élites.

319   Australia and the Indonesian revolution.
      Margaret George. Melbourne: Melbourne University Press, with
      the Australian Institute of International Affairs, 1980. 221p.
      bibliog.

An historical analysis of the development of Australia's diplomatic interest in the
Netherlands East Indies, subsequently Indonesia, under the Labor governments in
the period 1942-49.

320   Australia: the Asia connection.
      Jim Hyde. Melbourne: Kibble Books, 1978. 140p. bibliog.

A Marxist interpretation of Australian foreign policy which highlights the Labor
government's policies between 1972 and 1975. The concept of the 'Pacific Rim
Strategy' is introduced and explained — events since the end of the Second World
War in Asia and the Pacific are seen in terms of United States economic imperialism.

321   Confronting the nuclear age: Australian responses.
      Compiled by John Hinchcliff. Sydney: Pacific Peacemaker,
      1982. 119p.

A collection of a wide range of Australian opinion deploring the nuclear arms race
between the superpowers and stressing the importance of nuclear disarmament
and the need for collective efforts to achieve it.

322 **The secret state: Australia's spy industry.**
Richard Hall. Sydney: Cassell, 1978. 252p.

A pioneering exposé of the Australian security and intelligence system.

323 **Truth will out: ASIO and the Petrovs.**
Michael Thwaites. Sydney: Collins, 1980. 214p. bibliog.

Australia's most notorious espionage scandal was the defection in 1954 of Vladimir Petrov, third secretary at the Soviety Embassy in Canberra. The story of the defection has been told several times. *Nest of traitors: the Petrov affair* by Nicholas Whitlam and John Stubbs (Brisbane: Jacaranda, 1974) took the view held throughout widespread sections of the Australian community that the official enquiry involved a party political conspiracy in which ASIO, the Australian Security Intelligence Organization, played a most dubious role. Thwaites tells the story from the ASIO side – he is well qualified to do so, because at the time he was head of counter-espionage and supervised Petrov's defection.

324 **Sub-rosa: memoirs of an Australian intelligence analyst.**
R. H. Mathams. Sydney: Allen & Unwin, 1982. 127p.

A personal account of the evolution and role of national intelligence-gathering activity in Australia by a senior official now retired from the service.

Defence and Military History

Military history

325 **The Australians in nine wars: Waikato to Long Tan.**
Peter Firkins. Adelaide: Rigby, 1971. 448p. bibliog.

A popular history of military campaigns in which Australians have been involved: the Maori wars in New Zealand during the 1860s; the Sudan campaign in 1885-6; the Boer War at the turn of the century; the suppression of the Boxer Rebellion in China in 1900-1; the First and Second World Wars; the Korean War; the emergency in Malaysia and the confrontation of Indonesia and, finally, the Vietnam War. The tone throughout is nationalistic and emphasizes the fighting prowess of the Australian soldier. A good selection of illustrations accompanies the text.

326 **The broken years: Australian soldiers in the Great War.**
Bill Gammage. Canberra: Australian National University Press, 1974. 301p. bibliog.

A compilation of extracts from the letters and diaries of one thousand front-line soldiers of the Australian Imperial Force, mainly from the collection in the Australian War Memorial Library. The author provides a running commentary which reconstructs in turn the motives and expectations which led the men to volunteer, the agonizing realities of active service abroad, and the radically changed outlook brought home by the survivors. A popular and immensely readable book which has gone through several printings, it should be read in conjunction with the official war histories.

327 **Our war: Australia during World War I.**
Brian Lewis. Melbourne: Melbourne University Press, 1980; Penguin Books, 1981. 328p.

A book of unusual interest, written from a young boy's perspective who lived in a middle-class family in well-to-do Melbourne during the First World War. Lewis combines newspaper accounts of the war with his own and others' reminiscences to produce a vivid account of the 'home front'. He shows the initial patriotism and optimism, the split over conscription, the reaction against the local Germans, the sectarian and moral struggles involving both class and religion, and the contributions to the war effort of women, the press and the schools.

328 **The Australian people and the Great War.**
Michael McKernan. Melbourne: Nelson, 1980. 242p.

An entertaining and well-illustrated book which examines the First World War as
it impinged on the 'ordinary' Australian. On a higher plane it can be regarded as
an Australian case-study in the anatomy of mass paranoia afflicting all the participant nations in that great conflict.

329 **Of Nautilus and eagles: history of the Royal Australian Navy.**
Peter Firkins. Melbourne: Cassell, 1975. 269p.

A comprehensive history dating from February 1909 when *Parramatta*, first
warship of the Australian Navy, was launched on the Clyde. Two-and-a-half years
later the king approved the title Royal Australian Navy.

330 **The first A.I.F.: a study of its recruitment, 1914-1918.**
L. L. Robson. Melbourne: Melbourne University Press, 1982.
227p. bibliog.

The Australian Imperial Force of 417,000 men was raised to fight beside Britain
in the First World War. The Australian government of the day held two unsuccess-
ful referenda for the right to introduce conscription to recruit the force. This is a
scholarly study showing how the plebiscites, amid the sectarian bitterness which
followed the Irish Easter Rising, shattered the Australian Labor Party and deeply
divided the whole community. The events of those years left a bitter legacy that
influenced politics and social life in Australia for many years afterwards.

331 **The Royal Australian Navy: an illustrated history.**
George Odgers. Sydney: Child & Henry, 1982. 224p.

A well-written narrative history, liberally illustrated with photographs and
paintings, of the RAN since the times of Cook's discovery of the east coast of
Australia in 1770.

332 **Warships of Australia.**
Ross Gillett, Colin Graham, with Anthony Macdougall. Adelaide:
Rigby, 1977. 293p.

The most comprehensive review of the history of the Royal Australian Navy ever
undertaken. Every ship is given a technical description, picture and line drawing
and a full history. There is also a section which outlines the history of the
Australian navies. The Fleet Air Arm is described, listing every squadron since its
formation and the types and numbers of the aircraft flown.

333 **Military aircraft of Australia, 1909-1918.**
Keith Isaacs. Canberra: Australian War Memorial, 1971. 190p.

A detailed history of Australian military aviation, including a full account of its participation in aerial warfare during the First World War. Each aeroplane is described from its wheels up, engine, horsepower, performance, characteristics and deficiencies. A faithful line drawing of each machine is included. All First World War 'aces' are chronicled. It is intended to publish further volumes of this definitive work to bring the story to the present. In the meantime another work, much less detailed, can be used for the subsequent period. It is *Aircraft of the R.A.A.F., 1921-78,* by Geoffrey Pentland and Peter Malone (Melbourne: Kookaburra Technical Publications, 1978).

334 **Australian air force since 1911.**
N. M. Parnell, C. A. Lynch. Sydney: Reed, 1976. 216p. bibliog.

A profusely illustrated history of the Royal Australian Air Force.

335 **A pictorial history of the Royal Australian Air Force.**
George Odgers. Sydney: Ure Smith, 1977. 2nd ed. 160p.

The RAAF was born in the army as the Australian Flying Corps in 1914. Commencing with its baptism of fire during the First World War, the author continues the story of the air force's exploits during the Second World War, the Korean War, the Malayan emergency and in Vietnam. The text is illustrated with both colour and black-and-white photographs.

336 **Australian military uniforms, 1800-1982.**
Monty Wedd. Sydney: Kangaroo Press, 1982. 144p. bibliog.

A work of military history showing the evolution of the Australian military forces and their uniforms from the early colonial days to the present. There are forty magnificent full colour plates and numerous black-and-white drawings depicting in great detail uniforms, badges, arms and accoutrements.

337 **The ANZACS.**
Patsy Adam-Smith. Melbourne: Nelson, 1978. 372p. bibliog.

A view of the Great War from the men in the trenches, as expressed in their letters and personal diaries. The author allows the men to tell the story and is always sympathetic when interposing her own conclusions. It is a 'gripping yarn' which does away with the myths that have grown around the ANZAC's (Australian and New Zealand Army Corps). The book is also notable for the inspired use of photographs and captions to support the text.

338 **Australia in the war of 1939-1945**.
  Edited by G. Long. Canberra: Australian War Memorial,
  1952-1977. 22 vols.

The Australian War Memorial in Canberra commemorates Australia's involvement
in wars. It maintains a large collection of relics and documents, many of which are
on permanent display, and also commissions the writing of official histories of
the conflicts in which Australia participated. Besides the present work on the
Second World War the War Memorial has published *The official history of Australia
in the War of 1914-1918*, edited by C. E. W. Bean in 12 volumes, and other
shorter works on the Boer War, Korean War and on special aspects of the armed
services.

339 **Australia at war, 1939-1945**.
  John Robertson. Melbourne: Heinemann, 1981. 269p. bibliog.

An admirably concise book, which, without breaking any new ground, retells
clearly the story of Australia's participation in the Second World War. The author
discusses the major issues in war policy and strategy, inept leadership, disastrous
campaigns and the country's contribution to the Allied cause. Eminently suited
for the student and the general reader.

340 **High command: Australia and Allied strategy, 1939-1945**.
  D. M. Horner. Sydney: Allen & Unwin, with the Australian
  War Memorial, 1982. 556p. bibliog.

A detailed study of Australian strategy and its relationship to Allied grand strategy
in the Second World War. It is the story of the political skirmishing among the
Allies behind the military battles.

341 **Australia's Vietnam: Australia in the second Indo-China war**.
  Edited by Peter King. Sydney: Allen & Unwin, 1983. 226p.

A collection of essays which examine several aspects of Australia's involvement
in the Vietnam War over the period 1961-71. As in the US, the war unleashed a
strong organized opposition to Australia's involvement.

342 **War for the asking: Australia's Vietnam secrets**.
  Michael Sexton. Melbourne: Penguin Books, 1981. 212p.

The author argues and presents evidence against the conventional wisdom that
Australian troops were asked by the South Vietnamese to enter the war in
Vietnam. Quite on the contrary he shows how Australian politicans and diplomats
put pressure on the United States administration to ensure that Australia was
invited to a war in which the Vietnamese hosts and possibly even Australia's
American sponsors never really wanted Australia to participate.

343 **The thirty niners.**
Peter Charlton. Melbourne: Macmillan, 1981. 279p. bibliog.

An examination of the character, motivations and ordeals of the voluntary founding members of the Australian Imperial Force – those who enlisted in the Sixth Division and its ancillary units in 1939. To add authenticity to his narrative Charlton makes extensive use of memories, diaries and letters of the participating soldiers. A fascinating and different story of Australians at war.

344 **The puzzled patriots: the story of the Australia First Movement.**
Bruce Muirden. Melbourne: Melbourne University Press, 1968.
200p. bibliog.

During the Second World War two organizations – the Communist Party of Australia and Jehovah's Witnesses – were declared illegal on the grounds of alleged subversive activity. Although a third organization, the Australia First Movement, was never banned, twenty-one of its members were prosecuted. This is an account of the movement and the trial of its members. It presents an interesting study of civil rights in Australia during a period of national insecurity.

345 **Over-sexed, over-paid & over here: Americans in Australia, 1941-1945.**
John Hammond Moore. Brisbane: University of Queensland Press, 1981. 303p. bibliog.

During the Second World War about a million American servicemen were stationed for some time in Australia. During the swift Japanese advance in the Pacific the American troops were welcomed with open arms. This honeymoon, however, did not last long and Australian servicemen as well as civilians became actively resentful of the free-spending assertive 'Yanks'. There was widespread social bitterness and tension which eventually led to physical violence. All this upheaval is chronicled by the author, a visiting American academic, with dispassionate and accurate detail. Elsewhere the book provides a comprehensive review of military co-operation between the two countries. There are black-and-white photographs.

Defence policy

346 **Cold war two and Australia.**
Dennis H. Phillips. Sydney: Allen & Unwin, 1983. 122p.

An examination of Australia's participation in the Cold War as an uncritical ally of the United States. The book argues for the adoption of an independent foreign policy stance by Australia.

347 **Australia and imperial defence: a study in air and sea power.**
John McCarthy. Brisbane: University of Queensland Press, 1976.
227p. bibliog.

Since settlement in 1788 it has been assumed that in case of war England would
send its fleet to defend Australia. Yet in 1942 with the British surrender in Singa-
pore Australia found itself almost defenceless against the predictable Japanese
attack. If Australia was let down by Britain then, how much can she rely on any
other country for support in wartime? Is there over-reliance on the American
alliance today? Besides considering this vital question, the book provides a unique
account of Australia's armed services, the formation of a local aircraft industry
and the formulation and implementation of defence policy in the period between
the two world wars.

348 **The search for security in the Pacific, 1901-14: a history of
Australian defence and foreign policy, 1901-23, Vol. 1.**
Neville Meaney. Sydney: Sydney University Press, 1976. 306p.
bibliog.

It has been a widely held view that Australia in its early years depended entirely
on Britain for its foreign policy. In a detailed and thoroughly researched analysis,
Meaney argues strongly that this attitude is at best a hazy folk myth. He states
convincingly that in the period between federation and the First World War,
successive Australian statesmen like Deakin, Fisher and Hughes endeavoured to
formulate a uniquely Australian foreign and defence policy. In the second volume
the author plans to deal with Australian policy during and after the First World
War.

349 **Rethinking Australia's defence.**
Ross Babbage. Brisbane: University of Queensland Press, 1980.
312p. bibliog.

The author argues that the era of forward defence is over and the days when
Australia could rely on a universal security guaranteed by the United States are
also past. Babbage is critical of the failure of Australian governments to respond
to the new security challenges.

350 **Australian defence policy for the 1980s.**
Edited by Robert O'Neill, D. M. Horner. Brisbane: University
of Queensland Press, 1982. 308p.

Seventeen leading defence analysts and commentators examine the major aspects
of current Australian defence policy and offer views on its future development.

351 **Strategy & defence: Australian essays.**
Edited by Desmond Ball. Sydney: Allen & Unwin, 1982. 402p.
bibliog.

A collection of essays by Australian academics in the fields of international
relations, military strategy and defence policy, written from an Australian
perspective and addressing issues of Australian concern.

352 **A suitable piece of real estate: American installations in Australia.**
Desmond Ball. Sydney: Hale & Iremonger, 1980. 180p.

A detailed discussion of American defence, scientific and technical intelligence installations in Australia. Successive Australian governments have accepted these facilities without adequate knowledge of their functions or aims and without effective participation or control over them. Ball's book, backed by extensive research, is a landmark in the examination of an area of Australian public policy that has for far too long been the province of secret groups whose ignorance is masked by appeals to national security that forbid them to publicly explain and justify policies which could involve Australia in nuclear war.

353 **The military and Australia's defence.**
Edited by F. A. Mediansky. Melbourne: Longman Cheshire, 1979. 165p. bibliogs.

A collection of papers on the role of the military in the development and maintenance of Australia's defence capability. The book is divided into two parts. The first examines the formulation of defence policy, in particular the roles played by military officers in making policy decisions. The second part deals with the education and training of military officers.

354 **The ANZUS Treaty alliance.**
J. G. Starke. Melbourne: Melbourne University Press, 1965. 315p. bibliog.

The Australia, New Zealand, United States Security Treaty is a tripartite military alliance signed in September 1951 and regarded by all Australian governments since then as the cornerstone of this country's security policy. Although written some years ago, the book can be regarded as the definitive work on the treaty's text, historical background and purpose. The book's only shortcoming is that in parts it has an approach which may be overly legalistic and academic for a popular audience.

355 **Conscription: necessity and justice. The case for an all voluntary army.**
Glenn Withers. Sydney: Angus & Robertson, 1972. 168p.

No other public issue in Australia has caused more enduring division and bitterness than conscription for overseas military service. In 1972 the incoming Labor government suspended conscription following the bitter controversy during the Vietnam conflict. Withers' book presents a powerful indictment of all compulsory military service. A detailed history of how conscription was first introduced in Australia in peacetime in the early 20th century is *Compulsory citizen soldiers* by Thomas W. Tanner (Sydney: Alternative Publishing Co-operative, 1980).

356 **Australia's military alliances: a study in foreign and defence policies.**
B. Chakravorty. New Delhi: Sterling, 1977. 292p. bibliog.

The central concern of the book is the facilitating role which Australia plays to American interests in the region. The author offers an Indian perspective to Australia's foreign policy and argues for non-alignment and an independent defence capacity. He also examines the formidable obstacles, domestic and external, to such changes.

Religion and Philosophy

357 **Philosophy in Australia since 1958.**
S. A. Grave. Sydney: Sydney University Press for the Australian Academy of the Humanities, 1976. 24p.

A concise yet detailed survey of the study of philosophy in Australian institutions of higher learning. All important monographs and journals are identified by author and title and commented on briefly.

358 **Contemporary philosophy in Australia.**
Edited by Robert Brown, C. D. Rollins. London: Allen & Unwin, 1969. 216p.

A collection of essays selected to display some of the variety of subject matter, viewpoint and method of argument in modern Australian philosophy. It is not a book for the layman, but the introduction briefly ranges over the practice of philosophy in Australia and mentions some of the schools, names, tendencies and publications which may be of interest to the serious student of the field.

359 **Religions in Australia: the *Pix* series extended to 41 beliefs.**
Tess van Sommers. Adelaide: Rigby, 1966. 248p.

Originally these articles appeared in the popular periodical *Pix* and were aimed at the general public. They are interesting, clear and simple and concentrate more on the lesser-known sects and groups than the better-known established faiths.

360 **The shape of belief: Christianity in Australia today.**
Dorothy Harris, Douglas Hynd, David Millikan. Sydney: Lancer, 1982. 293p. bibliog.

Twenty opinion leaders in the Australian church describe, explain and evaluate contemporary Australian expressions of religious belief. Included is a comprehensive bibliography on the subject covering the literature of the last twenty years.

361 **Religion in Australia: a sociological investigation.**
Hans Mol. Melbourne: Nelson, 1971. 380p. bibliog.

This book presents the findings in 1966 of a religious survey of more than 4,000 adults. Much information, previously unavailable, is presented about the religious attitudes of Australians. Overall Mol finds that the essential characteristic of this attitude is ambivalence.

362 **Religious studies in Australia since 1958.**
Eric Osborn. Sydney: Sydney University Press for the Australian
Academy of the Humanities, 1978. 13p.
A concise survey of recent academic religious studies in Australia.

363 **Unto God and Caesar: religious issues in the emerging Commonwealth, 1891-1906.**
Richard Ely. Melbourne: Melbourne University Press, 1976.
162p. bibliog.
The author shows how churchmen hoped to reinforce their influence by attaching
themselves to the federation movement, a new force in late 19th-century Australian life. He also demonstrates how they failed in their hope to enhance their
status in the new Federation.

364 **The Catholic Church and community in Australia: a history.**
Patrick O'Farrell. Melbourne: Nelson, 1977. 463p. bibliog.
Catholics constitute a quarter of the population of Australia, making them by far
the largest active religious group in Australia. Originally they were mostly of
Irish origin although immigration, especially since the Second World War, has
brought many Catholics of other nationalities into the country. Since Australia's
foundation, Catholics have exercised a powerful and sometimes controversial
influence on Australian society. This work surveys the Catholic religion in the
Australian community from early colonial society to the 1970s.

365 **The Roman mould of the Australian Catholic Church.**
John N. Moloney. Melbourne: Melbourne University Press,
1969. 209p. bibliog.
There has always been a debate on the characteristics of the Catholic Church in
Australia as to whether it was moulded by the Irish priests or whether Rome
exercised the dominant influence. The author in a lively study claims that the
latter established and now maintains the spirit of the Church in Australia.

366 **Builders and crusaders.**
T. R. Luscombe. Melbourne: Lansdowne, 1967. 253p.
A survey for the general reader of the careers of outstanding Roman Catholic
priests, prelates and laymen in Australian history and how they have affected
their Church and their country's social and political development.

367 **Rockchoppers: growing up Catholic in Australia.**
Edmund Campion. Melbourne: Penguin Books, 1982. 241p.
bibliog.
An insider's view of movements within Roman Catholicism in Australia over the
past thirty years. It is an excellent autobiographical social history and must be
read by anyone who wants to understand Australian society and politics.

368　**The myth of the universal church: Catholic migrants in Australia.**
Frank W. Lewins.　Canberra: Faculty of Arts, Australian
National University, 1978. 164p. bibliog.

This book examines the role of the common faith among Australian Catholics
and the one million post-war Catholic immigrants and their children. The author
concludes that the common faith is of little or no consequence in the settlement
of Catholic migrants in Australia. The Australian Catholic Church is more
Australian than Catholic: an institution whose ideology avows internationalism
and whose morality predicates that the brotherhood of man is ethnocentric in
action.

369　**Mr. Santamaria and the bishops.**
Gerard Henderson.　Sydney: St. Patrick's College, 1982. 2390p.
bibliog. (Studies in Christian Movement, no. 7).

An examination of the involvement of the Australian Catholic Church in social
and political issues from the 1940s to the 1960s. The activities and attitudes of
the chief protagonists such as B. A. Santamaria, Cardinal Gilroy, Dr. Mannix and
Bishop James Carroll are analysed in detail against the background of the perennial
problem on the proper relationship between religion and politics.

370　**The Movement.**
Paul Ormonde.　Melbourne: Nelson, 1972. 198p.

The Movement was a body of Catholics, acting with the moral and financial
support of their bishops, which secretly operated within the Australian Labor
Party and most of the country's major industrial unions in opposition to the
perceived threat of Communism. This activity led to the split of the Australian
Labor Party, which allowed the conservative coalition to govern for the next
twenty years. This history of the Movement is of primary importance in the study
of Australia's political and religious history.

371　**Church and state: changing government policies towards religion
in Australia: with particular reference to Victoria since
separation.**
J. S. Gregory.　Melbourne: Cassell, 1973. 283p. bibliog.

This book is about the shifts in community attitudes towards organized religion.
It focuses on the 1860s and 1870s in Victoria when state aid was withdrawn from
the churches and the government took up full responsibility for elementary
education, the state aid debate is a perennial one in Australia and crops up
frequently. After a 90-year interval in 1964, state aid to church schools was re-
established by the federal and state governments, and the issue was raised again
in the 1983 federal election.

372 **Convicts, clergymen and churches: attitudes of convicts and ex-convicts to the churches and clergy in New South Wales from 1788 to 1851.**
Allan M. Grocott. Sydney: Sydney University Press, 1980. 322p. bibliog.

The theme of the book is the attitude of the convicts towards organized religion which ranged from apathy to cynicism and distrust to violent hostility. This is not to be wondered at, as the men of God were always associated with the governing class and with punishment handed down by clerical magistrates. A worthy contribution to the social history of colonial Australia.

373 **With pen and tongue: the Jesuits in Australia, 1865-1939.**
Ursula M. L. Bygott. Melbourne: Melbourne University Press, 1980. 423p. bibliog.

A history of the Jesuit contribution to the growth of the Catholic Church in Australia. An integral part of that contribution was the recognition by the Jesuits of the need for an active lay movement and the importance of an intellectual élite from which the Church might draw its future leaders.

374 **Booth's drum: the Salvation Army in Australia, 1880-1980.**
Barbara Bolton. Sydney: Hodder & Stoughton, 1980. 287p. bibliog.

A well-written general account of the Army's development in Australia.

375 **Other temples, other gods: the occult in Australia.**
Nevill Drury, Gregory Tillett. Sydney: Methuen 1980. 176p. bibliog.

The authors list and describe an astonishing number of cults apparently flourishing in Australia, although they do not attempt to estimate the number of their adherents. Judging from the many bookshops and organizations listed in the back there must be considerable interest in the occult in Australia. The text is lavishly illustrated.

Economy

376 **State of play 2: the INDECS Economics special report.**
Sydney: Allen & Unwin, 1982. 176p. bibliog.

A group of economists — Indecs Economics — have combined to produce this simply written, up-to-date account on the Australian economy. It is not a textbook, but describes recent developments on key aspects of the economy — inflation, unemployment, wages, the balance of payments — and discusses the policies which have been used by the government and the alternative policies advocated by its critics. Recommended by the experts as the best available introduction to the state of the Australian economy.

377 **Exit full employment.**
Barry Hughes. Sydney: Angus & Robertson, 1980. 235p.

The author attempts to explain the events and ideas that have led to stagflation in Australia — rising unemployment and inflation. The resulting book is a readable, polemical account of recent economic and political history in Australia.

378 **Crisis in abundance.**
Peter Sheehan. Melbourne: Penguin Books, 1980. 264p.

Analyses the economic factors behind the recession besetting Australia in the early 1980s.

379 **Economic crisis, cities & regions: an analysis of current urban and regional problems in Australia.**
Frank J. B. Stilwell, with contributions by Graham Larcombe.
Sydney: Pergamon, 1980. 182p.

An analysis, using a political economic approach, of the effect of economic crisis at the urban and regional levels in Australia in the 1980s. The author published an earlier book on this subject which can still be read as an introduction to the subject — *Australian urban and regional development* (Sydney: Australia & New Zealand Book Co., 1974).

380 **Earning a crust: an illustrated economic history of Australia.**
Brian Carroll. Sydney: Reed, 1977. 176p. bibliog.

A popular, plain language account of Australia's economic history. There are many interesting black-and-white illustrations in this large-format book.

381 **The economic development of Australia.**
A. G. L. Shaw. Melbourne: Longman Cheshire, 1980. 7th ed.
223p. bibliog.

An updated version of this popular text, first published in 1944. Intended primarily for students it is equally suitable for the general reader as an introduction to Australia's economic history.

382 **Descriptive economics: Australian economic institutions and problems.**
F. T. Nankervis, 11th ed. edited by Alan Gregory. Melbourne: Longman Cheshire, 1978. 11th ed. 344p. bibliog.

A popular book, first published in 1950, which discusses in plain non-technical language the workings of the Australian economic system. It meets the needs of students, and the general reader who has little knowledge of the theory of economics but is interested in economic problems. The text is clearly presented and the frequent editions keep it up to date.

383 **The process of economic development in Australia.**
W. A. Sinclair. Melbourne: Cheshire, 1976. 266p. bibliogs.

The most up-to-date economic history covering the whole period of white settlement in Australia and taking into account everything that has been published on the subject since the Second World War. The book is especially valuable for bringing together in one volume all these published arguments and empirical studies on Australia's economic development.

384 **An economic history of Australia.**
Edward Shann. Cambridge, England: Cambridge University Press, 1948. 456p.

This classic text was first published during the Great Depression, and its author saw Australia's history as an example of what could be achieved by individual initiative, if uninhibited by government regulation. According to Professor Shann the entrepreneurs are the heroes, the bureaucrats and other preachers of restriction are the villains, and the freely operating price mechanism is in the best interest of the economy. In short, Shann belongs to the classical school of economics and the latter part of the book descends into polemic. It is well-written, however, and since the market economists' views are in vogue again the argument can be read with interest.

385 **British imperialism and Australia, 1783-1833: an economic history of Australasia.**
Brian Fitzpatrick. London: Allen & Unwin, 1939. Reissued by Sydney University Press, 1971. 396p. bibliog.

This classic interpretation views Australia's history as an episode in the imperialistic exploitation by Britain of her colonies. A second volume, entitled *The British Empire in Australia: an economic history, 1834-1939*, published by Melbourne University Press in 1941, updated the story to 1939. A second revised and abridged edition was published in 1949 and reissued by Macmillan in 1969.

386 **Australian capitalism in boom and depression.**
R. Catley, B. McFarlane. Sydney: Alternative Publishing
Cooperative, 1981. 249p.

Essentially this book is an economic history of Australia interpreted from a
radical socialist perspective. It provides a contrast to the views of Australian
economic development and the political system expressed in most other books on
the subject.

387 **Government and capitalism: public and private choice in
twentieth century Australia.**
N. G. Butlin, A. Barnard, J. J. Pincus. Sydney: Allen & Unwin,
1982. 369p. bibliog.

A wide-ranging study of the ways in which government, since federation, has
come to play an ever-increasing role in the affairs of Australians and how
individuals have become increasingly dependent on government. The authors trace
the interrelationships between public and private decision-making in areas such as
investment and borrowing, public enterprise services and infrastructure, regulation
of rural, manufacturing, service and labour markets and the evolution of the social
welfare system.

388 **Gone tomorrow: Australia in the 80s.**
Humphrey McQueen. Sydney: Angus & Robertson, 1982. 256p.
bibliog.

A lively polemic about Australian capitalism in the 1970s. The two major themes
of the book are de-labourisation and foreign control. According to McQueen
de-labourisation is the process by which hundreds of thousands of Australians are
thrown out of work by the technological and market demands of national and
transnational corporations. The author especially castigates Australia's failure to
control and derive long-term benefit from the exploitation of the non-renewable
resources.

389 **Twentieth century economic development in Australia.**
E. A. Boehm. Melbourne: Longman Cheshire, 1979. 2nd ed.
368p. bibliog.

A comprehensive treatment, concentrating on the post-war period, of the
major changes which have taken place in the structure and institutions of the
Australian economy. It is not a highly interpretative book, but presents a useful
arrangement of the available statistical and other evidence quite accessible to the
'intelligent layman'.

Economy

390 **Australian economic development in the twentieth century: essays.**
Angus Sinclair (and others), edited by Colin Forster. New York: Praeger, 1971. 334p.

A book of readings, each of the six chapters being devoted to one aspect of the development of the Australian economy during the period from 1890 to the 1960s. These include capital formation, trade and economic structure, economies of scale and Australian manufacturing, the market structure of Australian manufacturing, the services ensemble and some perspectives of Australian economic development.

391 **Foundations of the Australian monetary system, 1788-1851.**
S. J. Butlin. Sydney: Sydney University Press, 1968. 727p. bibliog.

This is the standard economic history of Australia up to 1851. The book was first published in 1953.

392 **Surveys of Australian economics.**
Edited by F. H. Gruen for the Academy of the Social Sciences in Australia. Sydney: Allen & Unwin, 1978-1983. 3 vols.

A series of three volumes containing state-of-the-art-literature surveys of the Australian economic scene, commissioned by the Academy of Social Sciences in 1975. Issues examined in volume 1 are: monetary policy, wages policy inflation, agricultural policy and protection policy. Volume 2 includes income distribution and poverty, urban economics, economics of education, radical economics and Australian economics, 1968-78. Volume 3 concludes with economics of regulation, resources and Australian economic development, health economics and Australian taxation policy. Non-specialists will find many of the essays difficult, but for readers versed in economics, the work is one of the best introductions to the issues covered.

393 **Australia: a client state.**
Greg Gough, Ted Wheelwright. Melbourne: Penguin Books, 1982. 255p.

A study of the influence exercised by transnational corporations on the economic, social, political and cultural life of Australia.

394 **Will she be right? The future of Australia.**
Herman Kahn, Thomas Pepper. Brisbane: University of Queensland Press, 1980. 199p. bibliog.

In the late 1970s fourteen of Australia's biggest companies commissioned the prestigious Hudson Institute to conduct a study of Australia's long-term economic prospects in a world-wide context. This book is the result of that endeavour.

395 **Multinationals take over Australia.**
Len Fox. Sydney: Alternative Publishing Corporation, 1981.
226p.

All aspects of foreign take-overs mostly Japanese and US sourced, are dealt with, ranging from mining to cars, oil, computers, food, chemicals, communications and so on. While there is no reason to dispute these well-known facts, the author claims that the process has gone beyond the industrial scene and concludes that Australia already has lost much of its independence to powerful multinational corporations and their allies in such forms as government and intelligence services.

396 **Incomes policy in Australia.**
Edited by Keith Hancock. Sydney: Harcourt, 1981. 405p.

An excellent assembly of arguments for and against an incomes policy in Australia, originating in a conference held in 1979. The question of whether wages and prices should be controlled or allowed to find their own levels is subject to a continuous debate in Australia, and the book is recommended to anyone who wants to understand the economic and political environment in Australia.

397 **Wage indexation: a study of Australian wage issues, 1975-1980.**
David H. Plowman. Sydney: Allen & Unwin, 1981. 193p.
bibliog.

Wage indexation, the adjustment of wages in line with inflationary movements to preserve their real value, has generated much heated debate in Australia. The book examines the implementation, operation and tribulations of wage indexation from its tentative introduction in April 1975 to the abandonment of the wage indexation principles in January 1981.

398 **Life insurance in Australia: an historical and descriptive account.**
A. C. Gray. Melbourne: McCarron Bird, 1977. 316p. bibliog.

An historical view of the industry in Australia together with a comprehensive account of the changing nature of the insurance business in the last twenty-five years and of the investment policies of the various life insurance offices.

399 **Australia and the Great Depression: a study of economic development and policy in the 1920s and 1930s.**
C. B. Schedvin. Sydney: Sydney University Press, 1970. 419p.
bibliog.

The depression of the 1930s was a traumatic experience for many Australians and shaped social and political attitudes which have persisted to the present. Schedvin's book is a comprehensive study of the Great Depression in Australia in the context of the international economy.

Economy

400 **Weevils in the flour: an oral record of the 1930s depression in Australia.**
Wendy Lowenstein. Melbourne: Hyland House, 1978. 464p. bibliog.

Two hundred well-selected interviews with survivors of the 1930s depression make up this excellent record of the social conditions of the period. The compiler introduces each group of recordings with an explanatory historical background sketch and follows them all with an appendix outlining chronologically the main events of the depression from 1927 to 1939.

401 **The wasted years? Australia's Great Depression.**
Edited by Judy Mackinolty. Sydney: Allen & Unwin, 1981. 273p. bibliog.

Twelve essays on the impact of the Great Depression, which also re-examine the causes and the panaceas advanced to solve the economic difficulties. The remedies sound very much like the theories in vogue which have been proposed to overcome the present recession. There is a comprehensive bibliography.

402 **Unemployed workers: a social history of the Great Depression in Adelaide.**
Ray Broomhill. Brisbane: University of Queensland Press, 1978. 220p. bibliog.

A fine study of the impact of the depression in Adelaide, capital of South Australia, where nearly 50 per cent of workers lost their jobs, 25 per cent were forced to accept part-time employment and the remainder had their wages cut by 20 per cent. The book sets the South Australian experience of the depression into a general sociological framework showing the appalling effect of hard times on people in any industrialised society. A work of special interest during a period of world-wide recession.

Business and Industry

403 The Australian company: studies in strategy and structure.
W. J. Byrt. London: Croom Helm, 1981. 171p.

There are almost 2,000 public companies listed on the Australian stock exchanges and there are nearly as many proprietary and non-listed companies. In addition there are many public or statutory corporations. As in other modern capitalist countries they exert a strong influence on the economic, political and social life of the nation. This book presents an analysis about the strategies and structures of some of the largest and most important corporations.

404 The corporation and Australian society.
Edited by K. E. Lindgren, H. H. Mason, B. L. J. Gordon.
Sydney: Law Book Co., 1974. 334p.

A collection of writings which explore the operations of corporations in Australia and their impact on the lives of Australians. It is an important study of entities which exert great influence in all democratic capitalist societies.

405 Small business in Australia: problems and prospects.
B. L. Johns, W. C. Dunlop, W. J. Sheehan. Sydney: Allen & Unwin, 1983. 2nd ed. 197p.

Small firms are found in almost every sphere of business activity in Australia. They account for more than 40 per cent of private-sector employment. The purpose of this work is to provide information about the economic and social aspects of small businesses in Australia. The second edition is totally revised and updated. The original structure of the argument is retained but substantial portions of the text are rewritten. The new information in this edition was obtained from an in-depth survey of more than 5,000 small firms. Case-studies are presented of several individual traders and industries in which small firms predominate.

406 **Australian industry policy.**
Edited by T. G. Parry. Melbourne: Longman Cheshire, 1982.
320p.

A collection of fourteen papers published between 1974 and 1980 arranged into four categories: industrial organization and competition policy, foreign investment, technology, and structural adjustment and industry policy. Each section has a self-contained introduction, complete with references, to supplement the readings.

407 **Economics and Australian industry.**
F. G. Davidson, B. R. Stewardson. Melbourne: Longman
Cheshire, 1979. 2nd ed. 309p.

A study of manufacturing industry in Australia by means of five case-studies illustrating the various forms of market competition. There is a monopoly in iron, steel and possibly paper, an oligopoly in motor vehicles, and monopolistic competition in retailing, but the production of wool is governed by competition only. The book includes a general introducton to the Australian economy and a theoretical discussion of market forms.

408 **Industrialization and dependence: Australia's road to economic development, 1870-1939.**
Peter Cochrane. Brisbane: University of Queensland Press, 1980.
171p. bibliog.

A history of economic development in Australia. The author concentrates on the British influence on Australian manufacturing before 1939 and endeavours to demonstrate that Australian industrialization was a continuation of dependence on Britain rather than a break from it.

409 **Industrial awakening: a geography of Australian manufacturing 1788 to 1890.**
G. J. R. Linge. Canberra: Australian National University Press, 1979. 845p. bibliog.

A comprehensive, scholarly history of the development of manufacturing in Australia up to 1890. Subsequent volumes are intended to bring the work up to the present. Well documented with illustrations, charts and statistical tables.

410 **Promoting industry: recent Australian political experience.**
P. Loveday. Brisbane: University of Queensland Press, 1982.
223p. bibliog.

A study of the relationships between secondary industry and government, especially government departments. Industries and bureaucrats in Australia have evolved into a system of mutual dependence and the author lists the many ways in which the two sectors are connected. He argues that the politicians have very little input or control over policy towards industry.

411   **Jobs or dogma: the Industries Assistance Commission and Australian politics.**
John Warhurst.   Brisbane: University of Queensland Press, 1982.
255p. bibliog.

The Industries Assistance Commission plays a major role in providing advice to the government on tariffs. By means of institutional analysis and case-studies, the book explains tariff policy, the workings of the Australian bureaucracy, and the nature of Australian federalism. The IAC is a statutory body nominally independent of government, and this relationship is also explored by examining the methods, often indirect, by which a government can exert pressure on such bodies. Overall the book deals extensively with public policy, economics and public administration in Australia.

412   **Northern Australia: patterns and problems of tropical development in an advanced country.**
P. P. Courtenay.   Melbourne: Longman Cheshire, 1982. 335p.
bibliog.

Although northern Australia occupies half of the continent its population is only 5 per cent of the Australian total. Like northern Canada it is a huge region rich in minerals but beset by environmental problems that have made settlement and development difficult. The book is a scholarly in-depth study of the problems as well as development prospects of this vast tropical region.

413   **'What's good for Australia . . . !' The story of B.H.P.**
Alan Trengove.   Sydney: Cassell, 1975. 263p. bibliog.

Broken Hill Proprietary Co. Ltd. is the country's biggest company and has a monopoly on Australia's iron and steel production. It is no wonder that this giant private concern with such a significant influence on the national economy has throughout its lifetime created much controversy and passionate feelings – both for and against. The author, a journalist, tries to steer a middle course in a most readable and lively account of the history of the company. Many interesting photographs accompany the text.

414   **Fisheries of Australia.**
Peter Pournall.   Farnham, England: Fishing News Books with Fisheries Division, Department of Primary Industry, Canberra, 1979. 149p. bibliog.

A history of fishing in Australia from Captain Cook's 1770 voyage of discovery to the 20th century. The book describes in a general way the present-day industry including the major fisheries vessels, gear and methods used.

415   **Whaling around Australia.**
Max Colwell.   Adelaide: Rigby, 1969. 168p. bibliog.

A history of Australia's first maritime industry built around whaling in the 1790s. Since the publication of the book the killing of whales has been abandoned. They are now a protected species in Australian territorial waters.

Commerce

416 **Australia in the world economy.**
J. O. N. Perkins. Melbourne: Sun Books, 1979. 3rd ed. 182p.
bibliog.

This book discusses the principal problems in the field of international economic policy which are of importance to Australia. It has been designed to meet the requirements of both students and informed laymen.

417 **Wealth, poverty and survival: Australia in the world.**
Edited by John Langmore, David Peetz. Sydney: Allen &
Unwin, with the Australian Labor Party, 1983. 225p. bibliog.

This book focuses on poverty and militarism as the two gravest threats to world survival and contributes an Australian perspective to a strategy for reducing these threats and injustices in the world order. It is in two parts. The first part deals with relations between the industrial countries (the North) and the developing countries (the South). Reference is made to the differences and conflict between the industrial capitalist countries (the West) and the industrial communist countries (the East). The second part of the book deals with the interplay between Australian domestic and international economic policies.

418 **The E.E.C. and Australia.**
J. D. B. Miller. Melbourne: Nelson, 1976. 137p.

A book written for the general reader to acquaint him or her with the workings of the European Economic Community, why it is important to Australia, and how it might affect Australian interests in the future.

419 **Import control and industrialisation: a study of the Australian experience.**
G. G. Moffatt. Melbourne: Melbourne University Press, 1970.
188p.

Moffatt carefully appraises the impact of import control on the domestic economy. The question of tariffs and other import controls needed to facilitate the operation of Australian industry has been hotly debated for many years. Currently the fashionable argument is that tariffs lead to inefficiency and prevent necessary structural changes in local industries. A historical survey of tariff policy, for readers interested in the origins of import controls, is *The tariff in the Australian colonies, 1856-1900*, by G. D. Patterson (Melbourne: Cheshire, 1968).

420 **Australia-New Zealand economic relations – issues for the 1980s.**
Edited by Robin Burnett, Alan Burnett. Canberra: Australian
National University, 1981. 183p. (Public Affairs Conferences,
no. 1).

The papers in this volume were given at a Public Affairs Conference organized by
the Australian National University in 1980. The purpose of the conference was to
bring people from industry, government and trade unions together to discuss the
essential issues of closer economic relations in the 1980s.

421 **The Sydney traders: Simeon Lord and his contemporaries,
1788-1821.**
D. R. Hainsworth. Melbourne: Melbourne University Press,
1981. 2nd ed. 264p. bibliog.

The author proves that, contrary to conventional belief, commercial enterprise
flourished in the first forty years of settlement. This period was the social and
economic seed-time of Australia, during which the foundations of Australian
economic development were laid.

Banking and Finance

422 The Australian financial system after the Campbell Report.
J. O. N. Perkins. Melbourne: Melbourne University Press, 1982.
141p. bibliog.

The Campbell Report of the Committee of Inquiry into the Australian Financial
System tabled in Federal Parliament in November 1981 has sparked considerable
community debate. The report is lengthy and unlikely to be read in full except
by specialists. Professor Perkins has prepared this 'guidebook' not only for
students but also for general readers. It concentrates on the major issues of public
interest only and does not summarize all of the recommendations and proposals
contained in the report. Another guide to the report including the full conclusions
and recommendations is *The new money jigsaw*, edited by Fred Breuchley and
P. P. McGuiness (Sydney: Magazine Publications, 1981).

**423 Money, work and social responsibility: the Australian financial
system.**
Edited by G. J. Crough. Sydney: Transnational Corporations
Research Project, University of Sydney, 1980. 215p.

The Transnational Corporations Research Project was established in 1975 to
conduct research into various aspects of foreign investment and the activities of
transnational corporations in Australia. This collection of papers on the Australian
financial system advocates more social responsibility on the part of the financial
institutions. An appendix lists the publications so far issued by the project.

424 The Australian trading banks.
H. W. Arndt, W. J. Blackert. Melbourne: Melbourne University
Press, 1977. 5th ed. 206p.

The fifth edition of the standard text on the Australian banking system maintains
the high standards of its predecessors. Although this edition is somewhat dated
itself, no doubt a new edition will not be long in appearing.

425 **The battle for the banks.**
A. L. May. Sydney: Sydney University Press, 1968. 229p.
bibliog.

The attempt by the Chifley Labor government to nationalize the private trading banks in the period 1947-49 was 'probably the most controversial move by any Australian government in the history of the Commonwealth'. This book tells the story of the campaigns for and against the nationalization legislation, which was eventually rejected in the courts. It also contributed to the Labor government's defeat in the 1949 federal elections.

426 **Bank of New South Wales: a history. Volume 1: 1817-1893. Volume 2: 1894-1970.**
R. F. Holder. Sydney: Angus & Robertson, 1970. 2 vols.
bibliog.

A chronicle of Australia's first bank, founded in 1817. Recently it merged with the Commercial Bank of Australia and became the Westpac Banking Corporation and now handles around 24 per cent of Australia's banking business.

427 **Australia and New Zealand Bank: the Bank of Australasia, and the Union Bank of Australia Limited, 1828-1951.**
S. J. Butlin. Melbourne: Longman, 1961. 459p.

This work, while ostensibly treating the development of certain individual banks, is virtually a history of banking in Australia and, by extension, the history of Australia's economic development.

428 **Australian monetary policy, 1950-1975.**
D. C. Rowan. Sydney: Allen & Unwin, 1980. 313p. bibliog.

Monetary policy has been an extremely important element in Australia's overall macro-economic policy and, more specifically, in attempts at economic stabilization. This technically orientated book provides an analysis based on data gathered from twenty years of the use of monetary policy in Australia for stabilization purposes.

429 **Australian monetary economics.**
Edited by K. T. Davis, M. K. Lewis. Melbourne: Longman Cheshire, 1981. 396p.

A book of selected readings on monetary policy discussion in Australia since 1968. The authors' earlier study *Monetary policy in Australia* (Melbourne: Longman Cheshire, 1980) complements this book.

430 **Intergovernmental relations in Australia.**
Edited by R. L. Mathews. Sydney: Angus & Robertson, 1974.
310p.

A collection of seminar papers by various experts on the problems of the Australian federal system. The contributors consider the financial, constitutional, judicial, political and organizational problems of federalism and attempt to show how the system may be adapted to make it serve the needs of Australians more effectively.

431 **The development of Australian fiscal federalism: selected readings.**
Edited by W. Prest, R. L. Mathews. Canberra: Australian
National University Press, 1980. 518p.

A collection of articles and documents produced during the first sixty years of federation which most clearly illustrate the origins and development of Australian fiscal federalism. Certain economic and fiscal initiatives originating in Australia have resulted in the creation of institutions or the development of processes many of which remain unique in federal countries. These include the Australian Loan Council, the Commonwealth Grants Commission, the co-ordination of taxation policy in general and uniform tax in particular, and the establishment of independent statutory commissions to advise on intergovernmental specific purpose grants.

432 **Federal finance: intergovernmental financial relations in Australia since federation.**
R. L. Mathews, W. R. C. Jay. Melbourne: Nelson, 1972. 370p.

An examination of the development of intergovernmental financial relations in Australia with special reference to the uniquely Australian institutions which have evolved for the purpose of dealing with taxation and grants arrangements between commonwealth and state governments (the Premier's Conference), equalization grants to financially weaker states (the Commonwealth Grants Commission), payments to the states for specific purposes such as roads and education (agencies such as the Commonwealth Bureau of Roads and the Australian Universities Commission), and borrowing by commonwealth, state and local governments (the Australian Loan Council).

433 **Public finance in Australia: theory and practice.**
Peter Groenewegen. Melbourne: Prentice-Hall, 1979. 282p.
bibliog.

Although it is written as a textbook, this is a clear description of how taxation and public expenditure in Australia fit together and also how it fits into the context of theoretical and applied economic analysis of public finance. The emphasis of the book is on taxation, the financing of the public debt and intergovernmental financial relations.

434   **The Australian Loan Council in federal fiscal adjustments,
      1890-1965.**
      R. S. Gilbert.   Canberra: Australian National University Press,
      1973. 337p. bibliog.

An analysis of the purpose and the functions of the Loan Council in the financial
relations between the federal government and the six states. Covering constitutional law, economics and politics the author endeavours 'to shed new light'
on the intentions the founders had for the Australian federal system.

435   **Financing the small states in Australian federalism.**
      R. J. May.   Melbourne: Oxford University Press, 1971. 235p.
      bibliog.

The Commonwealth Grants Commission is a uniquely Australian institution. The
commission was set up in the early 1930s to allocate funds from the federal
government to the smaller states in order to bring the standard of their services up
to those of the populous states of New South Wales and Victoria after the same
net sacrifice, in terms of state taxes and charges, had been made. Dr. May's book
traces the history of special grants from the federal government to the smaller
states since federation.

436   **The New International Economic Order and implications for
      Australia.**
      Russell G. Rollason.   Sydney: Alternative Publishing
      Co-operative, 1981. 218p.

In 1974 the United Nations General Assembly adopted the Declaration and
Action Programme on the establishment of a New International Economic Order.
This book examines these proposals and their likely implications for Australia.
It pleads the case for greater international co-operation and a more equitable
distribution of the earth's resources amongst the world's people.

437   **The money miners: Australia's mining boom, 1969-70.**
      Trevor Sykes.   Sydney: Wildcat Press, 1978. 388p.

An experienced financial journalist gives an account of the speculative excesses
of the 1969-70 mining boom involving thousands of ordinary Australians. Millions
of dollars were won and lost in a matter of hours, although in the end almost
everyone lost. The author demonstrates how the stock exchanges run by members
of the securities industry, were highly selective in both their supervision of the
market and the dissemination of information. Official enquiries into the mal-
practices of the period led to the establishment of a National Companies and
Securities Commission more than ten years after the event.

438 **The politics of taxation.**
Edited by John Wilkes. Sydney: Hodder & Stoughton, 1980.
320p.

This book consists of papers read at the 46th Summer School of the Australian Institute of Political Science, held at Canberra ACT, 26-28 January 1980. There is a diversity of approach and treatment in the seven contributions on the political economy of taxation in Australia.

439 **Other peoples' money: economic essays.**
H. C. Coombs. Canberra: Australian National University Press, 1971. 190p.

A book of essays which reveals the author's views on banking and monetary policy when he was governor of Australia's central banks – the Commonwealth Bank and the Reserve Bank between 1949 and 1968. The essays are perceptive and reflect Dr. Coombs's sense of humour and humanity.

Employment and Manpower

440 I want to work.
Mick Young. Sydney: Cassell, 1979. 159p. bibliog.

A book about Australia's unemployment crisis by the then opposition party's spokesman on employment and industrial relations. He projects a political perspective on the problem and his work is especially interesting, because the Australian Labor Party has since been elected to government in March 1983. Mr. Young became Special Minister of State and a Cabinet member.

441 Stuck! Unemployed people talk to Michele Turner.
Michele Turner. Melbourne: Penguin Books, 1983. 263p.

This is an important record of a serious social predicament in Australia in the 1980s when more than 10 per cent of the labour force are unemployed. The individual reasons for unemployment are discussed in the introduction and the difficulties affecting 38 men and women aged between 17 and 50 are simply presented in their own words.

442 Out of work, out of sight: a study of the impact of unemployment on a group of Australian people.
Graeme Brewer. Melbourne: Brotherhood of St. Lawrence, 1980. 104p. bibliog.

The author is Senior Research Officer at the Brotherhood of St. Lawrence, an independent organization concerned with the social effects of unemployment. He has interviewed a broad sample of jobless workers and uses their first-person stories as the basis for his presentation of the plight of jobless people in Australia. A short, readable account, free from sociological jargon, of a major problem of the 1980s.

443 Hidden unemployment: the Australian experience.
Peter Stricker, Peter Sheehan. Melbourne: Institute of Applied Economic and Social Research, University of Melbourne, 1981. 234p. bibliog.

A specialist study of a phenomenon that is not shown up in the official statistics on unemployment. If the authors are correct then unemployment in Australia in early 1983 is nearer to 1½ million than the official figure of 750,000. They also show that older men, non-English speaking migrants and women suffer most from hidden unemployment.

Employment and Manpower

444   Working for the Company: work and control in the Whyalla
       shipyard.
       Roy J. Kriegler.   Melbourne: Oxford University Press, 1980.
       308p.

An account of life at the Broken Hill Proprietary Company's shipyards at Whyalla,
South Australia. The text is built around extensive quotations taken from interviews with workers, after the author had spent three months working at the yards
to gain first-hand experience. The book focuses on working conditions, worker-
employer relations, company policy and practice on compensation, the role of the
unions, but it is also a fascinating document about ordinary people's lives in a
company town.

445   **Automation and unemployment: papers presented at an
       ANZAAS Symposium, Sydney 28 July 1979.**
       Sydney: Law Book Company, 1979. 164p.

The Symposium was convened by the Australian and New Zealand Association
for the Advancement of Science, NSW Division, to bring together the views of the
leading protagonists in the public debate on the future of employment prospects
in the era of micro-electronics and the silicon chip. Representatives from government, management and employee organizations presented papers.

446   **Women at work.**
       Kay Hargreaves.   Melbourne: Penguin Books, 1982. 402p.

A comprehensive treatment of the major issues confronting working women, such
as the problem of 'the double working life', the relationship between the women's
movement and the labour movement, equal opportunities and rewards, a healthy
work environment and the right to work.

447   **Gentle invaders: Australian women at work, 1788-1974.**
       Edna Ryan, Anne Conlon.   Melbourne: Nelson, 1975. 196p.

A fascinating record of progress in the struggle for industrial justice by women in
Australia.

448   **My wife, my daughter and poor Mary Ann: women and work
       in Australia.**
       Beverley Kingston.   Melbourne: Nelson, 1975. 158p. bibliog.

Concentrates on the ordinary women in the work-force forgotten until now by
the historians, the factory workers, domestic servants, nurses, teachers and shop-
girls as well as women in the home between 1860 and 1930. A well-written,
original study.

Trade Unions, Labour Movements and Industrial Relations

449 **Australian unions: an industrial relations perspective.**
Bill Ford, David Plowman. Melbourne: Macmillan, 1983. 576p.
bibliog.

A collection of readings on Australian trade unions written with the purpose of broadening the readers' understanding of these important organizations in Australian industrial life.

450 **Trade unions in Australia: who runs them, who belongs – their politics, their power.**
Ross M. Martin. Melbourne: Penguin Books, 1980. 2nd ed. 165p.

Since some 55 per cent of all wage and salary earners belong to Australia's more than 300 unions, the movement plays an important role in the country's affairs. Martin's book is a straightforward introductory survey of contemporary Australian trade unions.

451 **Unions and unionists in Australia.**
D. W. Rawson. Sydney: Allen & Unwin, 1978. 166p. bibliog.

A broad investigation of trade unionism in Australia based on an intensive survey of rank and file union members, this book demolishes many of the popular misconceptions held about trade unions and their members. It analyses the political impact of Australian unionism, the relations between unions and elected governments, and the special connection between the Australian Labor Party and many unions. It also looks at the broader issues of past and present trade unionism and the probable role of the movement in the kind of society which is likely to develop in Australia for the remainder of this century.

452 **In union is strength: a history of trade unions in Australia,
1788-1978.**
Ian Turner. Melbourne: Nelson, 1978. 2nd ed. 152p. bibliog.

This is a brief history of the Australian working class and trade union movement
from convict times to the present. Written from a socialist position, it is
recommended for laymen as it is written in simple language, is uncluttered with
detail and provides a general account which is also an interpretation.

453 **Unions in crisis.**
Clyde Cameron. Melbourne: Hill of Content, 1982. 375p.

This book is a product of the author's fifty years experience in Australian unions
and federal politics. Mr. Cameron was Minister for Labour and Immigration and
then Science and Consumer Affairs Minister in the 1972-75 Labor government,
thus he brings to this discussion extraordinary practical experience. It is a partisan
and political book, but also an extremely thoughtful and entertaining one. The
reader will learn how unions actually work, rather than how unions ought to
operate, which is the theme of many more learned tomes.

454 **Power, conflict and control in Australian trade unions.**
Edited by Kathryn Cole. Melbourne: Pelican Books, 1982.
309p.

In Australia the opponents of trade unions, which include the mass media have
created the idea of powerful trade unions 'meddling in politics' and 'holding the
nation to ransom' by means of strike action. This collection of essays sets about
to demystify the power ascribed to unions. Contrary to these popular notions the
actions of unions are subject to extensive controls, as the author concludes in her
expository introduction: 'when the formal and informal controls are tallied, and
the power of the unions and their principal opponents assessed, the strengths of
the unions, compared with that of employers, is indeed limited.'

455 **The A.C.T.U.: a short history on the occasion of the 50th
anniversary, 1927-1977.**
James Hagan. Sydney: Reed, 1977. 96p.

A short, factual book which traces Australian unionism from its pioneer days,
records a number of attempts to launch an effective national organization, and
concentrates on the activities of the Australian Council of Trade Unions since its
formation in 1927. In 1981 Hagan published a much more comprehensive study
entitled *The history of the A.C.T.U.* (Melbourne: Longman Cheshire) which
includes an extensive bibliography.

456 **Democracy in trade unions: studies in membership participation and control.**
Mary Dickenson. Brisbane: University of Queensland Press, 1982. 249p. bibliog.

The first study which deals with the internal organization of Australian unions, important because of the influence unions exercise in Australian life. Two union branches are studied in detail: the Port Kembla Branch of the Federated Ironworkers' Association and the Australian Capital Territory Branch of the Administrative and Clerical Officers' Association.

457 **The ironworkers: a history of the Federated Ironworkers' Association of Australia.**
Robert Murray, Kate White. Sydney: Hale & Iremonger, 1982. 341p. bibliog.

The Federated Ironworkers' Association is the main union covering unskilled and semi-skilled workers in the steel industry. The FIA's history is almost a model for the growth of Australian unions. It barely survived the 1890s depression, developed into a strong national organization during the 1920s, was devastated again during the depression of the 1930s, then rebuilt and centralized under militant control from the mid-1930s through the Second World War and the early post-war boom years.

458 **Protecting the protectors.**
Bruce Swanton. Canberra: Australian Institute of Criminology, 1983. 331p.

A survey of the development of police unions in each Australian state, but excluding the Australian Federal Police.

459 **Strikes in Australia: a sociological analysis of industrial conflict.**
Malcolm Waters. Sydney: Allen & Unwin, 1982. 239p. bibliog.

A discussion of industrial conflict from an historical aspect. Easily understood diagrams and tables support the predominantly theoretical text.

460 **Industrial action: patterns of labour conflict.**
Edited by Stephen J. Frenkel. Sydney: Allen & Unwin, 1980. 176p. bibliog.

This book explores industrial action in four key industries – construction, ship-building and ship repair, the waterfront and the telecommunications industry.

461 **Strikes: studies in twentieth century Australian social history.**
Edited by John Iremonger, John Merritt, Graeme Osborne.
Sydney: Angus & Robertson, with the Australian Society for
the Study of Labour History, 1973. 270p.

Strikes, a major feature of life in Australia, have been little studied. The present
book is a collection of eleven case-studies in industrial conflict. The editors' main
aim is to demonstrate that the strike is a complex social phenomenon, rather than
an event with a simple cause and participants neatly divided into 'goodies and
baddies'. Reading the book will lead to a better understanding of Australian
society, including how industrial relations and conflicts relate to political development and community attitudes.

462 **Industrial relations in Australia.**
Braham Dabscheck, John Niland. Sydney: Allen & Unwin,
1981. 360p. bibliogs.

Designed for senior, secondary and tertiary students, but can be read profitably
by general readers with little previous knowledge of the subject. A bibliography is
provided at the end of each chapter to aid the reader who would like to pursue
issues further.

463 **Australian industrial relations.**
D. Plowman, S. Deery, C. Fisher. Sydney: McGraw-Hill, 1980.
rev. ed. 399p. bibliogs.

A clear and thorough study of the framework of Australian industrial relations
against a background of recent events and disputes. A very satisfactory introduction to the Australian system, because it discusses very fully its unique dispute-
settling tribunals such as the Conciliation and Arbitration Commission and the
various state industrial tribunals. The text is supported by a range of helpful
tables and figures. Eminently suited for both students and the interested general
reader.

464 **Industrial relations: an Australian introduction.**
John D. Hill, William A. Howard, Russell D. Lansbury.
Melbourne: Longman Cheshire, 1982. 193p.

A concise overview of industrial relations produced for students of management,
the book is nevertheless suitable as an introductory text for a much wider readership.

465 **Australian labour relations: readings.**
Edited by G. W. Ford, June M. Hearn, Russell D. Lansbury.
Melbourne: Macmillan, 1980. 3rd ed. 595p. bibliog.

The third edition of this classic collection contains key essays on the various
aspects of the subject written by some of its major experts. The book comprises
six parts — industrial conflict, trade unions, management and employer organizations, industrial regulations, industrial democracy and research needs. The focus
is on the more dynamic aspects of industrial relations involving people, processes,
practices and procedures rather than on formal structures.

466 **Collective bargaining and compulsory arbitration in Australia.**
John Niland. Sydney: New South Wales University Press, 1978.
174p. bibliog.

The sytem of compulsory arbitration to settle industrial disputes — with its formal structure of judges, commissions and courts — is unique to Australia. The author argues that collective bargaining as practised overseas has many advantages over the Australian system. A good, straightforward account of the origins of arbitration and its development is given in *Federal arbitration in Australia: an historical outline*, by Bede Healey (Melbourne: Georgian House, 1972).

467 **Radical and working class politics: a study of eastern Australia, 1850-1910.**
Robin Gollan. Melbourne: Melbourne University Press, with the Australian National University, 1960. 226p.

An analysis of the formative period of the Australian trade unions and the Australian Labor Party, as part of a world-wide trend towards social advancement. The author shows how the essential political framework as it exists in Australia today was brought into existence between 1890 and 1910.

468 **Industrial labour and politics: the dynamics of the labour movement in eastern Australia, 1900-1921.**
Ian Turner. Canberra: Australian National University, 1965.
272p. bibliog.

A history of the period in which the labour movement enjoyed considerable political success both through the Australian Labor Party, which formed many state and federal governments, and the activities of the trade unions. The book examines the relation of the industrial and political wings of the movement, the conflicts between Labor politicians and the extra-parliamentary organizations and the part played by left-wing minorities in the movement.

469 **Who are our enemies? Racism and the Australian working class.**
Edited by Ann Curthoys, Andrew Markus. Sydney: Hale & Iremonger, with the Australian Society for the Study of Labour History, 1978. 211p.

An investigation into the history of working-class racial attitudes in Australia. It asks why the working class has experienced racial and ethnic antagonisms and what the effects of these antagonisms have been on labour's industrial and political action.

Natural Resources

470 **The rush that never ended: a history of Australian mining.**
Geoffrey Blainey. Melbourne: Melbourne University Press,
1978. 3rd ed.

First published in 1963, the latest edition is the most comprehensive, up-to-date,
popular history of mining available. Essentially an optimistic and romantic
account, illustrated throughout with the stories of rugged individualistic prospectors, miners and managers, the book fails to consider how beneficial or lasting
episodic mining booms are on the general well-being of the country. After all why
is the Australian landscape littered with abandoned mines and the remains of
once-prosperous boom towns? The latest edition does finish on a grimmer note
than earlier ones, as the postscript records the mining-market crash of the early
seventies and the following recession, as well as the growing opposition of the
conservationist movement. For a different point of view, Blainey's work should
be contrasted with D. Horne's opinions on mining and development in *Money
made us* (q.v.). Blainey has also written other more specialized histories of specific
mining fields. They are: *Mines in the spinifex: the story of Mount Isa mines*
(Sydney: Angus & Robertson, 1960); *The rise of Broken Hill* (Melbourne: Macmillan, 1968); *The peaks of Lyell* (Melbourne: Melbourne University Press, 1955).

471 **Australian mining, minerals and oil.**
John Alexander, Richard Hattersley. Sydney: David Ell Press,
1981. 534p.

This comprehensive reference work has been compiled by two leading financial
writers on all minerals mined in Australia and all listed and major unlisted mining
companies. The company profiles include a history, leases and financial status.
Maps, a glossary of mining and oil terms, and a contact directory are also included.

472 **Energy and the Australian economy.**
Peter J. Brain, Gerard P. Schuyers, with editorial assistance from
Cosima McPhee. Melbourne: Longman Cheshire, 1981. 343p.

Examines the role of energy in the Australian economy in the last three decades
of the 20th century. The examination is based on the results of an econometric
model which is sufficiently detailed to allow for the complexities of alternative
developments of new and non-conventional energy technologies. The authors
point out that although Australia does not have a long-term energy problem and is
likely to be a net energy exporter, it faces problems in the medium term, which
are discussed in detail. The book is a comprehensive and intelligent discussion of
what Australia's energy policy should be now and in the decades to come – it is
not a book for the layman.

473 **Energy in Australia: politics and economics.**
Hugh Saddler. Sydney: Allen & Unwin, 1981. 205p. bibliog.

Australia, a continent which was thought as both barren and 'energy-poor', is,
through recent discoveries, now known to be, except for petroleum, 'energy-
rich'. Saddler provides a comprehensive account of the structure and operations
of the energy industry in Australia. He opens with an analysis of the energy
problem and concludes with a thought-provoking prescription of the policies
needed to overcome the problem. In direct contrast to Bambrick's study (q.v.)
Saddler argues in favour of government intervention and participation, on behalf
of the people, in profitable energy extraction.

474 **Australian minerals and energy policy.**
Susan Bambrick. Canberra: Australian National University
Press, 1979. 240p.

Australia is blessed with rich mineral and energy resources and in a world experiencing energy shortages, Australia is facing the prospect of a resources boom.
How to exploit this favourable position to the nation's best advantage is the
subject of controversy within the Australian community. This book examines
the policy problems with which the mineral and energy sector confronts
Australian governments. Factors discussed include taxation, environment protection, Aboriginal land rights, foreign investment, the development of an integrated
energy policy, the encouragement of local processing of minerals before export
and the role of government. The book consistently argues in favour of the mining
industry and against the concept of higher taxation or the restriction of the
industry relative to other sectors.

475 **Australia's resources future: threats, myths and realities in the
1980s.**
Edited by Peter Hastings, Andrew Farran. Melbourne: Nelson,
with the Australian Institute of International Affairs, 1978.
288p.

Australia is amply endowed with long-term energy sources – coal, natural gas,
uranium and sunshine. The problem discussed is how Australia should go about
sharing this natural wealth with the rest of the world.

476 **Oil search in Australia.**
C. E. B. Conybeare. Canberra: Australian National University Press, 1980. 151p. bibliog.

This book is an authoritative work, written primarily for the layman, which tells of the history, development and recent activities in the search for oil in Australia.

477 **Oil and Australia's future: the economic, social and political aspects.**
Edited by Theo van Dugteren. Sydney: Hodder & Stoughton, 1980. 202p.

These papers read at the 45th Summer School of the Australian Institute of Political Science in Canberra, ACT, in January 1979, identify and discuss the implications of rising oil prices for Australia in the next twenty years.

478 **Black sands: a history of the mineral sand mining industry in eastern Australia.**
I. W. Morley. Brisbane: University of Queensland Press, 1981. 278p.

For over forty years Australia has supplied 90 per cent of the world's rutile and still holds more than 70 per cent of the world's reserves. The total production of rutile, zircon and other minerals from the sands of eastern Australia's coastline was worth over a billion dollars in export earnings. The book provides a detailed geographical, historical, geological corporate and technical description of the industry, as well as the disputes during the last twelve years between the mineral sand producers and the conservationists.

479 **Quarry Australia? Social and environmental perspectives on managing the nation's resources.**
Edited by Robert Birrell, Doug Hill, John Stanley. Melbourne: Oxford University Press. 1982. 366p.

A collection of papers sponsored by the Australian Conservation Society. The contributors argue for the rational management and conservation of Australia's resources in the interests of all Australians.

480 **Australia's continental shelf.**
Edited by J. R. V. Prescott. Melbourne: Nelson, 1979. 198p. bibliog.

An investigation of the characteristics of the continental shelf and the political, legal and economic problems associated with the development of its resources. There is an extensive bibliography and a valuable guide to maps covering the shelf. This collection of essays is of interest to lawyers and geologists, officials and businessmen as well as to the interested general public.

481   A field guide to Australian rocks, minerals & gemstones.
      Wolf Mayer.   Adelaide: Rigby, 1976. 336p.

A very useful, compact reference work intended for a wide readership. It covers
the genesis and identification of rocks and minerals, their physical properties and
the formation of ore deposits and gemstones. Detailed identification tables and
geological maps are supplemented by a glossary and index. The book is especially
useful for an amateur rock-hound or tourist interested in the rock formations of
his surroundings.

482   Gemstones in Australia.
      N. Perry, R. Perry.   Sydney: Reed, 1979. 158p.

A complete guide and description of Australia's precious stones and their
locations; how to mine them and how to recognize them.

483   In search of opal.
      Archie Kalokerinos.   Sydney: Ure Smith, 1967. 137p.

A vivid, first-hand account of a doctor with a passion for opals who struck it rich
on the central Australian opal field of Coober Pedy. The coloured photographs
show the harshness of the environment with which those who mine the sought-
after gemstone have to cope. An authoritative book on the stone and the mining
fields is *A field guide to Australian opals*, by Barrie O'Leary (Adelaide: Rigby,
1977). Another continuously popular book on the subject is Frank Leechman's
The opal book (Sydney: Lansdowne Press, 1982). First published in 1961 it looks
at the stone in a world-wide context.

Agriculture

484 **Australian agriculture: reconciling change and tradition.**
Keith O. Campbell. Melbourne: Longman Cheshire, 1980.
274p.

To overcome the Australian rural-urban schism this book introduces city people
to farmers' attitudes and aspirations, to the social and economic environment in
which they operate, and to current and likely future developments in the rural
industries. It also provides farmers and others connected with the agricultural
industries with an analysis of the problems with which they have to deal. The
book is not concerned with the technological or biological aspects of farming and
is an excellent introduction to Australian farming and farmers for a wide readership.

485 **Australian farming, 1788-1965.**
Samuel Wadham. Melbourne: Cheshire, 1967. 156p.

A layman's history of agriculture in Australia free of jargon, footnotes and
references.

486 **European farming in Australia: an economic history of Australian
farming.**
Bruce R. Davidson. Amsterdam: Elsevier, 1981. 437p.

Although this book gets rather technical in its intensive treatment of farm
profitability, there is useful material on exploration, land legislation, settlement
schemes, transport innovations, marketing arrangements and technological change.
It is a welcome addition to the limited literature on the economic development of
Australian agriculture.

487 **Agriculture in the Australian economy.**
Edited by D. B. Williams. Sydney: Sydney University Press,
1982. rev. ed. 422p.

Like the original 1967 edition, this revised and enlarged text presents a series of
reviews describing the significance of agricultural industries in the Australian
economy. It aims to present an analytical interpretation of the economic forces
that have led to the present situation and to describe the significant changes that
have occurred in recent years. The book is for people involved with agriculture,
geography and trade, but it can also be used by the interested layman.

488 **Australian agriculture: resource development and spatial organization.**
Peter Scott. Budapest: Akadémiai Kiadó, 1981. 136p. bibliog.
(Geography of World Agriculture, 9).

An examination, against a background of recent trends, of the salient features and regional structure of Australian agriculture, the productivity and efficiency of resource use, the complex mosaic of agricultural systems and farming types, and the potential for expanding production and export in the foreseeable future.

489 **The forgotten country.**
Julian Cribb. Melbourne: Australasian Farm Publications, 1982. 183p.

A passionate criticism of Australia's existing agricultural policies. The author, a specialist agricultural journalist, laments the tragic waste of Australia's farming potential and suggests new policies that would revitalize the industry.

490 **The wheat industry in Australia.**
A. R. Callaghan, A. J. Millington. Sydney: Angus & Robertson, 1956. 486p. bibliog.

Australia has always produced a surplus of wheat and is one of the major exporting countries in the world. The book is a comprehensive survey of developments in the wheat industry in Australia from its beginnings to the middle 1950s. While paying attention to the economic aspects of the industry, the authors go into great detail about the technicalities of wheat growing. Another book on the subject, treating it from an economic perspective, is *The Australian wheat-growing industry, 1788-1948* by Edgars Dunsdorfs (Melbourne: Melbourne University Press, 1956). The two books complement each other.

491 **The simple fleece: studies in the Australian wool industry.**
Edited by Alan Barnard. Melbourne: Melbourne University Press, with the Australian National University, 1962. 640p.

A symposium of forty articles on the Australian wool industry. Although written and edited between 1957 and 1960 many of these articles, especially the historical and some of the technical ones, have stood the test of time. The book is divided into the following six main sections: 'The fibre', 'The sheep', 'The land and its uses', 'Production and finance', 'Regional studies' and 'Wool marketing'.

492 **On the wool track.**
C. E. W. Bean. Sydney: Angus & Robertson, 1963. 152p.

In 1909 Bean — later Australia's official historian of the First World War — went to western New South Wales to write a series of articles on the wool industry for the *Sydney Morning Herald*. His experiences resulted in this little volume, which has become a minor classic on the rural life of the inland when Australia really was 'riding on the sheep's back'.

Agriculture

493 **The northern myth: a study of the physical and economic limits to agricultural and pastoral development in tropical Australia.**
B. R. Davidson. Melbourne: Melbourne University Press, 1972. 3rd ed. 298p.

The third edition of this controversial book restates its original conclusions as follows: 'Using the techniques available and the ruling prices of the early 1960s it was possible to demonstrate that any agricultural product which could be produced in northern Australia could be produced at lower costs in the south. In spite of technical developments this is also true of the early 1970s. The dream of a closely settled north, based on family farms or small pastoral holdings, is as remote in 1970 as it was in 1960.' Evidence shows that these words hold for the 1980s as well.

494 **Water and land: two case-studies in irrigation.**
Trevor Langford-Smith, John Rutherford. Canberra: Australian National University Press, 1966. 270p. bibliog.

In a dry continent subject to periodic drought, irrigation offers prospects of stabilized agricultural production. This book appraises Australia's two largest irrigation schemes – the Murrumbidgee Irrigation Area and the whole of the Murray-Darling Basin – and concludes that despite heavy public and private investment over a hundred-year period, irrigation farming has done virtually nothing to achieve such stability. While production has been enhanced for a few million acres of farming land, the rest of the country does not share at all in the national irrigation investment. Various schemes are suggested by means of which benefits could be spread much wider. This is an important book for the specialist rather than the general reader.

495 **Digging stick to rotary hoe: men and machines in rural Australia.**
Frances Wheelhouse. Adelaide: Rigby, 1972. 222p. bibliog.

A history of agricultural machinery in Australia emphasizing the great inventiveness of the men on the land. Their innovative genius and determined efforts placed Australia at the forefront of advances in farming techniques.

496 **The pastoral age: a re-examination.**
G. J. Abbott. Melbourne: Macmillan & Dalgety Australia, 1971. 221p. bibliog.

An argument against the traditional view of Australian history that wool was the catalyst for the social, political and economic transformations of New South Wales before 1850. The author suggests that while wool certainly caused the rapid geographic expansion of the young colony, there were other explanations for the economic growth which accompanied it. He proposes immigration and capital imports as the forces responsible.

497 **Landed enterprise and penal society: a history of farming and grazing in New South Wales before 1821.**
Brian H. Fletcher.   Sydney: Sydney University Press, 1976.
265p. bibliog.
This work shows how the British settlement in New South Wales was transformed from a prison-without-walls to a colony, largely by her farmers and graziers.

Transport

498 Moving goods and people: transport in Australia.
Peter Gilmour. Melbourne: Penguin Books, 1978. 265p. bibliog.

A comprehensive study of the transportation of goods and people on land, in the air and on the sea. The author claims that the haphazard development of Australia's transport services have been at a high cost to the consumer. He suggests some ways in which the development of better transportation services can occur for the rest of this century.

499 Getting around town: a history of urban transport in Australia.
Brian Carroll. Sydney: Cassell, 1980. 176p.

A popular history of urban transport in Australia, supported with many illustrations. Horses and carts, steam and electric trains, trams powered by horses, steam, cables and electricity, ferries, cars, taxis, buses and bicycles are all discussed in detail and there is information also on bridges, transport strikes, petrol rationing and Australian oil finds.

500 The aviators.
William Joy. Sydney: Shakespeare Head Press, 1965. 211p.

To overcome the isolation of its vast interior, Australia recognized the potential of the flying machine at a very early stage. Australians became pioneers in the development of this new invention for commercial purposes. Joy has selected the big names of the heroic years, 1920-38, and records the pilots' daring exploits in detail. Among them are: Kingsford Smith and C.T.P. Ulm, the first to cross the Pacific; Ross and Keith Smith, winners of the 1919 air race from England to Australia; Bert Hinkler, who made the first solo flight to Australia; Hubert Wilkins, who made aerial history in the Antarctic and Arctic, and many others.

501 **Australians in the air.**
Greg Copley. Adelaide: Rigby, 1976. 289p. bibliog.

Australian pioneering efforts in aviation emerged in response to the 'tyranny of distance'. Aviation was the obvious solution to quick communication, both within the vast expanses of the country's interior and with the outside world. This comprehensive book covers the pioneering years of long-distance flights from Europe to Australia, the establishment of regular air services, the exploits of Australian airmen in the two World Wars, the Korean and Vietnamese conflicts, and typically Australian institutions such as the Royal Flying Doctor Service. Many illustrations, both colour and black-and-white, supplement the detailed text.

502 **Australia's two-airline policy.**
Stanley Brogden. Melbourne: Melbourne University Press, 1968. 235p.

In 1952 the government implemented a uniquely Australian 'two-airline policy'. Only two airlines — one government-owned and the other run by private enterprise — were permitted to operate interstate services. The policy has been and still is the subject of bitter political debate. The author describes the colourful early history of Australia's aviation industry, outlines the legal basis of the policy, and evaluates its success. A recent book by Ian Sabey, *Challenge in the skies: the founding of T.A.A.* (Melbourne: Hyland House, 1979), tells the story of the origins of the government-owned airline, Trans-Australia Airlines.

503 **Wings to the world: the story of Qantas, 1945-1966.**
Hudson Fysh. Sydney: Angus & Robertson, 1970. 236p.

This is the last volume of a trilogy on aviation pioneering in Australia by one of the founders of Qantas, Australia's present international airline and the second oldest airline in the world. *Qantas rising: the autobiography of the flying Fysh* was published in 1965, and *Qantas at war* in 1968. Though written as autobiography, the three volumes together virtually amount to a history of the development of international air transport within an Australian context.

504 **Ships and seafarers in Australian waters.**
Max Colwell. Melbourne: Lansdowne Press, 1973. 127p.

A popular, richly illustrated account of Australian shipping from the First Fleet until modern times.

505 **Seaport gateways of Australia.**
James Bird. London: Oxford University Press, 1968. 253p. bibliogs.

Essentially a brief, readable history of the development of the major ports in Australia, starting with some interesting comparisons of the original reasons for selecting each site. The ports discussed include: Sydney with Botany Bay, Melbourne with Geelong, Fremantle, Adelaide, Brisbane, Hobart, Port Pirie, Newcastle, Port Kembla and Whyalla. There are also brief descriptions of lesser ports serving the mining operations in northern and Western Australia, the sugar ports of Queensland, the grain ports of South Australia and the Tasmanian ports. There are also photographs and informative maps, diagrams and statistics.

506 **Australian coastal shipping.**

Barry Pemberton. Melbourne: Melbourne University Press, 1979. 327p. bibliog.

Interstate and intrastate shipping services dominated the Australian transport industry when the rail services were inadequate and road transport was in its infancy. The present book is an historical study of this once-dominant industry. The story is carried up to the present era of container ships and roll-on roll-off craft. Included is a most comprehensive index of more than a thousand ships that have plied the Australian coast since the early 1850s. Many illustrations accompany the text.

507 **North Star to Southern Cross.**

John M. Maber. Prescot, Lancashire, England: Stephenson, 1967. 335p.

This is not a full maritime history of Australia, but provides comprehensive histories of individual shipping companies in the Australian and New Zealand trade from the advent of steam. As far as possible, the book furnishes a detailed fleet list for each company. Some hundred ships mentioned in the text are illustrated.

508 **Redgum & paddlewheels: Australia's inland river trade.**

Peter J. Phillips. Melbourne: Greenhouse, 1980. 165p.

For a brief period between the 1850s and the 1890s Australia's Murray, Darling and Murrumbidgee rivers supported a thriving transport industry. About 300 steamers sailed the river system; today more than 20 are restored and fully operational and they support the expanding tourist traffic. Phillips re-creates the exciting days of river trade with facts and yarns in this thoroughly enjoyable and informative book. He published an earlier book on the same subject in 1974, *River boat days on the Murray, Darling, Murrumbidgee* (Melbourne: Lansdowne Press). Another book of personal reminiscences by a man who spent most of his life on the rivers is *Riverboats and rivermen*, by William Drage and Michael Page (Adelaide: Rigby, 1976).

509 **Railways of Australia.**

O. S. Nock. London: Black, 1971. 284p. bibliog. (Railways of the World, 2).

A comprehensive account of the development and present state of the railway system in Australia. The evolution of an efficient network has been hampered, and still is, by the circumstances which in the 19th century led to each colony using a different gauge for its lines. Only in 1958 was the Railway Standardisation Agreement enacted, which led to the standardization of gauge on the most heavily used lines across state borders.

510 **All stations west: the story of the Sydney-Perth standard gauge railway.**

G. H. Fearnside. Sydney: Haldane, 1970. 167p. bibliog.

The six Australian state railway systems developed as separate entities and built their lines to different gauges. The present book tells of the haphazard colonial developments and the story of the official efforts for the unification of the railway systems and the fruition of those aims in the 4,000 kilometres of standard gauge line linking the east and west coasts of the continent. Crossing Australia in the Indian-Pacific train is one of the great railway journeys in the world. One such crossing is described colourfully by a railway enthusiast Patsy Adam-Smith in *Across Australia by Indian-Pacific* (Melbourne: Nelson, 1971).

511 **Australian steam.**

A. E. Durrant. Sydney: Reed, 1978. 128p. bibliog.

A comprehensive coverage of the steam locomotives of Australia.

512 **Romance of Australian railways.**

Patsy Adam-Smith. Adelaide: Rigby, 1973. 247p. bibliog.

An affectionate book about the Australian railways and the men associated with them by a self-confessed enthusiast.

513 **Romance of Australian trams.**

John Larkins, Bruce Howard. Adelaide: Rigby, 1978. 184p.

A richly illustrated chronicle of the history of Australia's tramway systems from their beginnings to their recent decline. Trams were the favoured means of public transport in cities and towns for many years. In the 1980s only Melbourne has remained faithful to the tram.

514 **A pictorial history of Cobb & Co.: the coaching age in Australia.**

K. A. Austin. Adelaide: Rigby, 1977. 219p. bibliog.

Originally published as *The lights of Cobb & Co.*, this new edition is in a larger format, copiously illustrated in colour and black-and-white and well documented. Austin not only describes the birth, rise and fall of the almost legendary coaching company, but also gives in detail the history of the coaching age in Australia. It lasted for seventy years – from the time when four young Americans led by Freeman Cobb introduced the revolutionary leather-slung Concord coaches, to the unmade Australian goldfields' tracks in 1854.

515 **Australian horse-drawn vehicles.**
Michael Stringer. Adelaide: Rigby, 1980. 280p.

The author traces the history of all forms of horse-drawn vehicles including drays, sulkies, hackney cabs, passenger coaches, military vehicles and so on. The art of coach building is discussed, also included is a rare collection of working drawings used by coach builders in the construction of both private and commercial carriages. It is a delightful book, especially for the aficionado of the subject. A fine selection of over a hundred black-and-white and colour illustrations accompany and explain the text. A very similar book primarily aimed at the growing band of collectors and restorers of horse-drawn vehicles is *Buggies and horse-drawn vehicles in Australia*, by Peter Cuffley (Melbourne: Pioneer Design Studio, 1981).

516 **The roadmakers: a history of main roads in New South Wales.**
Sydney: Department of Main Roads, New South Wales, 1976. 335p.

A detailed record of road construction in New South Wales, Australia's oldest and most populous state.

517 **Outback highways.**
Len Beadell. Adelaide: Rigby, 1979. 237p.

Beadell has written five books telling of his adventures of pioneering road construction in the deserts of central Australia in connection with the Woomera Rocket Range. Here the story of the Gunbarrel Road Construction Party and their twenty-five years of road-making has been brought together in one volume. Beadell's story is amusing and stirring material for armchair travellers of one of the most isolated parts of the world.

518 **The bicycle and the bush: man and machine in rural Australia.**
Jim Fitzpatrick. Melbourne: Oxford University Press, 1980. 250p. bibliog.

The widespread use of the bicycle in rural Australia, especially by itinerant seasonal workers, has not generally been recognized. Fitzpatrick rectifies the record by providing a scholarly study of the role the bicycle played in the bush, and extends the narrative to discuss gruelling overland journeys, the recreational aspects and the impetus cycling gave to the development of tourism. Many interesting photographs and biographical sketches of prominent cyclists round off an original piece of social history.

519 **The camel in Australia.**
Tom L. McKnight. Melbourne: Melbourne University Press,
1969. 154p. bibliog.

Camel transport began in the dry inland regions of Australia in 1881 as a means of supplying fencing contractors, sheep stations, explorers and mining fields. Camels contributed to the opening of the hinterland until the 1920s when they were gradually displaced by motor transport. In 1920 there were over 12,600 camels in Australia, and today there are still many thousands of feral camels roaming the inland. In fact, some have recently been exported to Saudi Arabia! This book is supplemented by the personal experiences of camel-driving by H. M. Barker in his *Camels and the outback* (Adelaide: Rigby, 1965), which provides a fascinating insight into one aspect of the development of transport in Australia.

520 **Bullock teams: the building of a nation.**
Olaf Ruhen. Sydney: Cassell, 1980. 240p.

For a century and a half bullock teams handled most of Australia's commerce and the products of her industry. The teamsters or 'bullockies' — colourful, hard-swearing men — became the stuff of legends and have established themselves as part of Australian folklore. This book, in combination with *Bullockies*, by L. Braden (Adelaide: Rigby, 1968), retell the colourful story of an important segment of Australia's history.

Urban Studies

521 **Australian urban policy: objectives and opinions.**
Max Neutze. Sydney: Allen & Unwin, 1978. 252p. bibliog.
This work and its companion volume *Urban development in Australia* (2nd ed.
1981) provide the standard text on Australian urban studies. Whereas the latter
book traces Australian urban history and provides data on current trends, the
present volume discusses the bases for policy decisions.

522 **Cities unlimited: the sociology of urban development in Australia
and New Zealand.**
Leslie Kilmartin, David C. Thorns. Sydney: Allen & Unwin,
1978. 195p. bibliog. (Studies in Society, 1).
This work represents the new wave of urban sociology which argues that cities
play a vital role in the unequal distribution of scarce and valued resources. In
contrast to the old precepts of urban studies, the book is much concerned with
inequality, social justice and the quality of social interaction.

523 **Cities for sale: property, politics and urban planning in Australia.**
Leonie Sandercock. Melbourne: Melbourne University Press,
1975. 260p. bibliog.
A study of the development of town planning in Adelaide, Melbourne and Sydney
– how these three major cities came to be in their present parlous state. As a
solution for the future, the author argues for 'redistributive' planning – not, by
her own admission, an easy objective to achieve. The major hurdle is that land,
the prime commodity of cities, is controlled by private and not by public interests.
The main thrust of the argument throughout the book is that city planning is, or
should be, for people, not for buildings and definitely not for land.

524 **Ideas for Australian cities.**
Hugh Stretton. Melbourne: Georgian House, 1975. 2nd ed.
367p.
A thoughtful book which investigates the forces that have shaped the urban
planning of Sydney, Melbourne, Adelaide and Canberra. The author suggests
novel directions of reform in order to keep Australian cities amenable for people.

525 **Urbanization: the Australian experience.**
M. I. Logan, J. S. Whitelaw, J. McKay. Melbourne: Shillington
House, 1981. 121p. bibliog.

An examination of some geographical characteristics of Australia's towns and
cities in the context of the national pattern of economic and social development.
The emphasis is on the urban system at the national scale, rather than its component parts.

526 **Australian cities in transition.**
C. A. Maher. Melbourne: Shillington House, 1982. 134p.
bibliog.

A description of the social, demographic, economic and political changes occur-
ring in Australia at the present and how they will affect the projection into the
future of the city and the quality of life of the residents.

527 **The inner suburbs: the evolution of an industrial area.**
Barnard Barrett. Melbourne: Melbourne University Press, 1971.
181p. bibliog.

A study of the inner industrial suburb of Collingwood in Melbourne; how
unplanned urban development, propelled by unscrupulous commercial interests,
affected its rapid growth during the 19th century and created the slum of today.
This legacy is evident in many of the inner suburbs of Australia's large cities.

528 **Beyond the city: case-studies in community structure and
development.**
Edited by Margaret Bowman. Melbourne: Longman Cheshire,
1981. 228p. bibliog.

This collection brings together a selection from the growing number of Australian
community studies. It goes beyond the well-known large seaboard metropolitan
areas, where the majority of Australians reside, to the lesser-known rural communities. Communities studied include company and remote mining towns:
Rylstone, Kandos and Broken Hill in New South Wales; those built during the
mining booms in South Australia, Western Australia and Queensland; Djumdi-
munya, an Aboriginal community in the desert; towns servicing agricultural
hinterlands — Griffith in New South Wales, Nuriootpa in South Australia and
Barcaldine in Queensland; and a major growth centre — the twin towns of Albury
and Wodonga. The essays contribute towards a better appreciation of community
life in Australia.

529 **The vanishing village: a small Australian town in transition.**
Jim Ward, Greg Smith. Melbourne: Quartet, 1978. 202p.

A study of a small unidentified town in Queensland in the process of being
swallowed up by the large metropolis. The authors, two sociologists, present
forty-two virtually unedited transcripts of recorded interviews with the inhabitants. The young and old, businessmen, farmers, labourers and others, say in their
own words what they think about the place and the other residents. This is a
model for many a small town in Australia today, and exposes all the tension and
friction inherent in a fast-changing community.

530 **An Australian new town: life and leadership in a working-class suburb.**
Lois Bryson, Faith Thompson. Melbourne: Penguin Books, 1972. 378p.

A report on the results of a social survey carried out in 1966 of an outer suburb of Melbourne, predominantly working-class in character. An important study as such a great proportion of the Australian population resides in the suburbs, which radiate vast distances from the small city centres which are exclusively devoted to commercial and administrative activities. So characteristic is this phenomenon that Australia has been alluded to as the 'suburban' nation.

Environment

531 Spoils and spoilers: Australians make their environment, 1788-1980.
Geoffrey Bolton. Sydney: Allen & Unwin, 1981. 197p. bibliog.

An historical account of Australians' relationship with their physical environment. It is a sad fact that on their arrival the European settlers completely misunderstood the physical nature of the continent and, in the author's opinion, they still lack a total appreciation of it. The book presents a story of ignorance and exploitation by generations of getters and spenders, although the last twenty years have witnessed the rise of a strong, politically active, environmental movement. Nevertheless Bolton makes the gloomy forecast that 'the economic difficulties of the 1980s and 1990s will embolden governments to encroach upon wilderness areas previously left intact for their scenic value'.

532 Environmental policy in Australia.
Alan Gilpin. Brisbane: University of Queensland Press, 1980. 380p. bibliog.

Over the last decade public concern in Australia has extended to a wide range of environmental issues: pollution, population and its distribution, growth centres and urban rehabilitation, land-use planning, natural resources, nature conservation, forests and parks, industrial location, littering, heritage preservation and environmental education. As a response the federal and state governments have created a number of environment-control bodies such as councils, commissions, authorities or departments, supported by advisory committees. The purpose of the book is to review the achievements and failures of the seven governments and their bureaucracies in environmental protection.

533 The Australian environment: 12 controversial issues.
Alan Gilpin. Melbourne: Sun Books, 1980. 241p. bibliog.

An analysis of twelve notable environmental issues and disputes which have arisen in Australia in recent years. The author, a noted authority on the subject, shows how these arose, what course they took and in what manner they were dealt with or resolved.

Environment

534 **Man and the Australian environment: current issues and viewpoints.**
Edited by Wayne Hanley, Malcolm Cooper. Sydney: McGraw-Hill, 1982. 362p. bibliogs.

A collection of a wide range of works by geographers, soil scientists, resource engineers, political scientists, planners and others to highlight the complexity of the Australian environment. Although written with the needs of secondary and tertiary students in mind, general readers wishing to acquaint themselves with issues affecting the particular environment with which they are associated, or in which they have a special interest, will find plenty of information in these essays.

535 **Environmental management in Australia, 1788-1914: guardians, improvers and profit, an introductory survey.**
J. M. Powell. Melbourne: Oxford University Press, 1976. 191p. bibliog.

During the period under discussion the Australian environment was irrevocably altered for future generations. The profiteers or exploiters, as they are best known, have been the villains. However, Dr. Powell tries to introduce some perspective by shedding light on the less well-known efforts of the guardians and improvers of the environment: the precursors of today's environmentalists.

536 **The politics of pollution.**
Peter Russ, Lindsay Tanner. Melbourne: Visa, 1978. 186p. bibliog.

A scathing, well-documented attack on the Victorian Environment Protection Authority. When it was set up in the early 1970s the authority was intended by the government to play an independent watchdog role over the state's environment. The authors claim that it has failed dismally, arguing that it never had the means to tackle polluters head-on and that it has long since lost the will to do so. To some extent the Victorian experience can serve as a model for the other states, because the newly established pollution-control bodies invariably come up against powerful vested interests.

537 **Australia as human setting.**
Edited by Amos Rapoport. Sydney: Angus & Robertson, 1972. 298p.

A collection of essays on the Australian environment from a wide selection of authoritative writers. On a book of such varied authorship there is a degree of repetition and conflict of views, but as an educational introduction to the Australian environmental problem, its past history, cultural influences, present and future prospects, it has great value. Although written more than ten years ago, few of the problems which existed then have been solved and the issues raised still remain.

538 **Conservation**
Edited by A. B. Costin, H. J. Frith. Melbourne: Penguin Books,
1974. rev. ed. 323p.

This book is a collection of papers discussing the current and potential use of
land, water, vegetation, wildlife, fish, national parks and minerals as well as the
economic and legal aspects of conservation. Although the text is dated in parts,
especially the statistical tables, the basic concern about the consequences of
increasing exploitation of resources is still valid in the Australian context.

539 **Wildlife conservation.**
H. J. Frith. Sydney: Angus & Robertson, 1979. rev. ed. 416p.
bibliog.

A dispassionate, objectively written work on the conservation of wildlife in
Australia. It deals with mammals, birds, reptiles, amphibians and their diverse
habitats. The author surveys what existed, what has been lost, the species faced
with likely extinction, and he makes practical suggestions on conservation.
There are seventeen tables listing native and introduced species of animals, distribution maps and many well-chosen illustrations. An earlier more hot-blooded plea
for conservation was A. J. Marshall's *The great extermination: a guide to Anglo-
Australian cupidity, wickedness and waste* (Melbourne: Heinemann, 1966). The
two books provide a contrast in style while achieving the same object.

540 **Green bans: the birth of Australian environmental politics,
a study in public opinion and participation.**
Richard J. Roddewig. Sydney: Hale & Iremonger, with the
Conservation Foundation (Washington), 1978. 180p.

The more obviously political actions of Australian trade unions in the 1970s
involved strikes or bans against the export of merino sheep, uranium mining, tours
of sporting teams from South Africa and the demolition of historic or otherwise
significant buildings, the latter leading to the celebrated green bans. Australian
law and the constitution make public participation in the protection of the
natural and built environment almost impossible. Development reigns supreme
and with no help from the law the alternative is direct action. The militant
Builders Labourers' green bans to protect the interests of the middle class was an
event unique to Australia. Roddewig, an American land-use attorney who visited
Australia to study this novel phenomenon, has written a lucid, perceptive text,
which owes much to his experience in a very different legal tradition and his
comparative approach.

541 **The south-west book: a Tasmanian wilderness.**
Edited by Helen Gee, Janet Fenton, compiled by Helen Gee,
Janet Fenton, Greg Hodge, artwork directed by Chris Cowles.
Melbourne: Australian Conservation Foundation, 1978. 307p.
bibliog.

The Tasmanian Hydro-Electric Commission's intention to build a dam on the
Franklin-Lower Gordon river has developed into the biggest conservation battle
in Australia. The project which would flood a unique wilderness area has met with
opposition from local and international conservationists and it became an issue in
the 1983 federal election. The book is a comprehensive study of the wilderness
that is south-west Tasmania. The compilers attempt to demonstrate what would
be lost for posterity if the dam project were to go ahead.

542 **A million wild acres: 200 years of man and an Australian forest.**
Eric Rolls. Melbourne: Nelson, 1981. 465p. bibliog.

The author investigates the Pilliga Forest, a vast area of north-western New South
Wales. The subject is vast – no less than man's impact upon the region from the
earliest times to the present. Rolls, a wheat farmer living in the heart of the forest,
is a hunter, conservationist, naturalist and successful poet. These qualities are
combined to produce a magnificent book full of fascinating detail and insight.
Rolls is at his best when he focuses on nature about which he cares deeply. Well-
chosen black-and-white photographs accompany the text.

543 **The coral battleground.**
Judith Wright. Melbourne: Nelson, 1977. 203p.

A study of the politics of conservation by one of Australia's foremost poets, who
was an active participant in the events she describes. The Great Barrier Reef –
2,000 kilometres of spectacular coral reefs, sand cays and islands – is Australia's,
indeed the world's, most precious marine possession. When in the late 1960s the
reef was threatened by limestone mining and oil drilling, a determined campaign
for its preservation was begun by a small group of enthusiasts, which led to an
upsurge of public opinion followed by trade union action. For the time being the
reef, one of the world's natural wonders, was saved from exploitation and possible
large-scale destruction.

544 **A coral island: the story of One Tree Island and its reef.**
Harold Heatwole. Sydney: Collins, 1981. 200p. bibliog.

The Great Barrier Reef stretching along Australia's east coast for some 2,000 kilometres is one of the world's most beautiful landmarks. One Tree Island and its
reef situated in the southern end of the Great Barrier Reef near the Tropic of
Capricorn, have probably been studied in more detail than any other Australian
reef system. The author compiled the book from personal and scientific accounts
made by scientists who worked on the island. The text deals with the geological
and biological past, present and future of the Great Barrier Reef, the building of
One Tree Island and its colonization by plants and animals and the changing cycle
of life above and under water. There are maps, graphs, illustrations, a glossary of
technical terms and a bibliography of publications on the island. A factual but
extraordinarily interesting and readable account for the scientifically inclined
general reader.

545 **The Noosa story: a study in unplanned development.**
Nancy Cato.   Brisbane: Jacaranda, 1982. 2nd ed. 141p.

In recent years the Australian coastline has been despoiled in many places by uncontrolled speculative resort development. The well-known author, Nancy Cato, has lived in one of these mushrooming areas, Noosa Heads, on the south Queensland coast, for fifteen years and has witnessed the destruction of the natural environment by ignorant development. In this matter-of-fact book she details the 'ecological disaster' that has overtaken this once beautiful area.

Science and Technology

546 **Australian pioneer technology: sites and relics . . . towards an industrial archaeology of Australia.**
Judy Birmingham, Ian Jack, Dennis Jeans. Melbourne: Heinemann Educational, 1979. 200p. bibliog.

This book traces the development of technology in Australia in the 19th and early 20th centuries. The authors are mostly concerned with pioneering activity that has left 'evidence in sites and relics'. They range through pastoral, agricultural, mining and manufacturing industries, and look at rusting implements, obsolete machinery, old buildings, mines, vestiges of land-based whaling stations, breweries, tanneries and at the industries based on grapes, hops, sugar cane, tobacco and timber. Omissions, such as pioneer manufacturing in the form of flour milling, brickmaking, pottery building materials and similar endeavours, will be dealt with in a companion volume now in preparation. The present volume is richly illustrated.

547 **Scientists in nineteenth century Australia: a documentary history.**
Edited with introductions by Ann Mozley Moyal. Melbourne: Cassell, 1976. 280p.

As settlement expanded during the 19th century, Australia with its unique animal and plant life became a naturalist's paradise. The author traces the origins of scientific endeavour and achievement during that exciting century. She sketches the character and work of the early scientists and lets them speak for themselves through revealing passages from their letters and reports. This method works well and the book is a pleasure to read.

548 **A century of scientific progress: a history of several aspects of Australian scientific development, with particular reference to New South Wales.**
Sydney: Royal Society of New South Wales, 1968. 478p.

The Royal Societies were established in all the Australian colonies, modelled on the Royal Society of London, to stimulate scientific study. This is the centenary volume of the Royal Society of New South Wales and the articles emphasize the contributions made by pure and applied science to the development of New South Wales.

549 **The Australian Academy of Science: the first twenty-five years.**
Canberra: Australian Academy of Science, 1980, 286p. bibliog.

A narrative account of the main events that led to the formation of the academy and of what it has accomplished up to March 1979.

550 **The Royal Botanic Gardens, Melbourne: a history from 1845 to 1970.**
R. T. M. Pescott. Melbourne: Oxford University Press, 1982. 212p.

A history which follows the development of the gardens from scrubland on the outskirts of the new city of Melbourne into today's magnificent landscaped gardens. The book is divided into chapters covering the period of each director's administration. Among them were the skilled landscape gardener W. R. Guilfoyle, whose plans decreed the basic layout of the gardens today, and the famous botanist, Baron Ferdinand von Mueller. Pescott has written a biography *W. R. Guilfoyle, 1840-1912: the master of landscaping* (Melbourne: Oxford University Press, 1974). Von Mueller's life story is available in *A man on edge: a life of Baron Sir Ferdinand Von Mueller*, by Edward Kynaston (Melbourne: Allen Lane, 1981).

551 **The Chemistry Department of the University of Melbourne: its contribution to Australian science, 1854-1959.**
Joan Radford. Melbourne: Hawthorn Press, 1978. bibliog.

A comprehensive history of the Chemistry Department of the University of Melbourne. The book is also useful as a source of information for the wider development of this discipline in Australia.

552 **The origins of CSIRO: science and the commonwealth government, 1901-1926.**
Sir George Currie, John Graham. Melbourne: Commonwealth Scientific and Industrial Research Organization, 1966. 203p.

This book examines the involvement of the federal government in the application of scientific research to the problems of primary and secondary industry from the time of federation in 1901 to the formation of the Council of Scientific and Industrial Research (CSIR) in 1926. The CSIR was transformed into the Commonwealth Scientific and Industrial Research Organization in 1949, which is Australia's largest research organization today.

Science and Technology

553 **The Noah's Ark syndrome: one hundred years of acclimatization and zoo development in Australia.**
C. F. H. Jenkins. Perth: Zoological Gardens Board, Western Australia, 1977. 147p.

This book outlines the history of the early Acclimatization Societies which were active in all Australian colonies in the second half of the 19th century. Some of their enthusiastic endeavours were misguided by ignorance and contributed to Australia's ecological problems. When the craze for acclimatization declined the societies turned to the establishment of zoological gardens and the book outlines the history of the various state zoos.

554 **Micro invaders.**
Ian Reinecke. Melbourne: Penguin Books, 1982. 272p.

An heretical book about technology. The author identifies the consequences of the introduction of the micro-chip and sceptically examines the rush towards the use of new technology. At all times he places human beings above machines and disputes the claims of supporters of headlong technological innovation that the results of the new technology will be of universal benefit. His book draws on a world-wide experience with technological change with the focus on Australia. A lucid book on the subject dispensing with jargon, eminently suited for laymen.

555 **The phone book: the future of Australia's communications on the line.**
Ian Reinecke, Julianne Schultz. Melbourne: Penguin Books, 1983. 270p. bibliog.

An argument which supports the centralization of high-technology industry in Telecom, the independent publicly funded corporation responsible for tele-communication services in Australia. The book opposes a recent recommendation by an official enquiry that profit-making Telecom functions be transferred to the private business sector.

556 **Sleepers wake! Technology & the future of work.**
Barry Jones. Melbourne: Oxford University Press, 1982. 285p. bibliog.

The author analyses the social impact of job displacement through technological change. It is a controversial book written by a politician, extremely well informed on the subject, who proposes political solutions to the problem. After the March 1983 election Mr. Jones became Minister for Science and Technology in the Labor government.

557 **The Institution of Engineers, Australia: a history of the first fifty years, 1919-1969.**
Arthur Hardie Corbett. Sydney: Institution of Engineers, with Angus & Robertson, 1973. 288p. bibliog.

Issued to celebrate the Golden Jubilee of this important professional association.

558 **Australian inventors.**
Leo Port, Brian Murray. Melbourne: Cassell, 1978. 205p.

A brief, popular history of Australian inventions, which include the stump-jump plough, refrigerators, mechanical shearing, stripper-harvesters, torpedos, thrust bearings, the Owen machine gun and the orbital engine. Illustrations accompany the text.

559 **Venture capital and technological innovation in Australia.**
Sydney: Australian & New Zealand Association for the Advancement of Science (ANZAAS), New South Wales Division, 1982. 158p.

Includes the papers presented at an ANZAAS Symposium in Sydney in February 1982, which discuss ways to overcome the shortage of speculative capital and technological innovation in Australia.

560 **Technology and Australia's future: industry and international competitiveness.**
Peter Stubb. Melbourne: AIDA (Australian Industries Development Association), 1980. 120p. bibliog.

Discusses the relationship between technological innovation and international competitiveness of Australian industry.

561 **Snowy scheme management & administration.**
D. J. Hardman. Sydney: West, 1970. 185p. bibliog.

The Snowy Mountains Hydro-Electric Scheme was the largest single development project ever undertaken in Australia and one of the most complex in the world. This is a comprehensive record of the managerial problems which arose during the long period (over twenty years) of construction and the administrative practices which were pursued. The study reveals a basically efficient organization which can serve as a model for similar large national undertakings.

562 **Struggle for the Snowy: the background of the Snowy Mountains Scheme.**
Lionel Wigmore. Melbourne: Oxford University Press, 1968. 215p. bibliog.

A most comprehensive historical account of the Snowy Mountains Hydro-Electric Scheme, which takes the reader through the events, ideas and struggles that finally led to the full development of Australia's most ambitious civil engineering project. The scheme consisted of building a network of huge dams and miles of pipeline to divert the waters of the Australian Alps to irrigate the dry inland. The project, one of the world's largest undertakings of its kind, was completed in 1972.

563   Snowy Mountains conquest: harnessing the waters of Australia's
      highest mountains.
      Charles Meeking.   Melbourne: Hutchinson, 1968. 192p.

The Snowy Mountains Scheme produces power for New South Wales and Victoria
and irrigates vast tracts of inland Australia. This is a popular account of the long
years of the construction of this immense project by its multinational work force.
An exciting story well told.

564   An end to silence: the building of the overland telegraph line
      from Adelaide to Darwin.
      Peter Taylor.   Sydney: Methuen, 1980. 192p. bibliog.

The completion of the 3,000 kilometres long overland telegraph line in August
1872 — just twenty-three months after work started — across country that had
been traversed only once before, was an epic achievement. This is a popular,
exciting history of the building of the line with many contemporary illustrations.

Population

565 **An issue of people: population and Australian society.**
Robert Birrell, Tanya Birrell. Melbourne: Longman Cheshire, 1981. 277p.

Population has always been an issue in Australia — often it has been a matter of agonizing public debate. Both government and citizens have usually agreed that Australia needs people, indeed has a duty to fill its huge empty spaces. This commitment to population expansion has been reflected in post-war growth when the population nearly doubled from 7.6 million in 1947 to 14.6 million by mid-1980. Most of this increase was due to the deliberate encouragement of immigration. The inflow of people has dramatically reshaped the nation's cultural and ethnic background. The authors examine Australia's post-war immigration programme and the immigrants' economic and social status in Australian society. It is their view that competition for ever-decreasing job opportunities may lead to worsening inter-ethnic relations in the future.

566 **Population, society and environment in Australia: a spatial and temporal view.**
I. H. Burnley. Melbourne: Shillington, 1982. 150p. bibliog.

This is the fourth volume in the 'Studies in Australian Society' series. It discusses the impact of natural environment and economic factors on populaton distribution. Some important themes are immigration and internal migration, the ageing of the population, health inequalities, multiculturalism and trends in Aboriginal population.

567 **Mobility and community change in Australia.**
Edited by I. H. Burnley, R. J. Pryor, D. T. Rowland. Brisbane: University of Queensland Press, 1980. 286p. bibliog.

A collection of research articles from writers of different disciplines on internal migration in Australia. More of historical interest than an indication of the current situation, as much of the statistical evidence relates to the period 1966-71. Population mobility is high in Australia — one in every six Australians over fifteen years of age change their residence each year. With the decline of immigration and fertility rates, population movement within Australia is becoming the dominant cause of change in rural and urban communities.

Population

568 **The empty cradle: fertility control in Australia.**
M. E. Brown. Sydney: New South Wales University Press, 1979.
146p. bibliog.

Traditionally Australians have advocated an increased birth rate to fill the 'empty spaces'. The 'populate or perish' policy has been supported with various social security measures, such as child endowment and family allowances. This pronatalist sentiment, however, has not led to the establishment of large families. This book tries to explain why this has not happened.

Immigration and
Ethnic Groups

569 **Australia's immigrants, 1788-1978.**
Geoffrey Sherington. Sydney: Allen & Unwin, 1980. 189p.
bibliog. (The Australian Experience, no. 1).

A non-technical, general overview of the history of immigration to Australia and
trends in migration. It is an easy-to-read book well suited to the needs of laymen.
A short bibliography points the way to further reading.

570 **The immigrants.**
Wendy Lowenstein, Morag Loh. Melbourne: Penguin Books,
1978. 149p.

A collection of transcripts of tape recordings of interviews with seventeen migrants
whose experience of Australia spans the period from 1890 to the 1970s. Compelling reading, the book shows that some of the contributors are delighted with
their adopted country, whilst the majority are not.

571 **The migrant presence: Australian responses, 1947-1977. Research
report for the National Population Inquiry.**
Jean I. Martin. Sydney: Allen & Unwin, 1978. 261p. bibliog.

A survey of Australian reactions to post-war immigrants in general, with a detailed
examination of these reactions in the areas of education, health and trade
unionism.

572 **Refugees, resources, reunion: Australia's immigration dilemmas.**
Edited by Robert Birrell, Leon Glezer, Colin Hay, Michael
Liffman. Melbourne: VCTA Publishing, 1979. 179p.

A collection of seminar papers which propose different priorities for future immigration policy. No agreement is reached nor are policy prescriptions offered,
rather, the writings reveal and make clear differences of attitude which exist in
the Australian community. The book is useful reading for people uncertain about
the moral and practical implications of immigration issues in Australia.

573 **Immigration into eastern Australia, 1788-1851.**
R. B. Madgwick. Sydney: Sydney University Press, 1969. 2nd
impression, with foreword. 270p. bibliog.

For the first sixty years Australia received the greater part of her population from
the ranks of the convicts and assisted immigrants. This study of the latter group
was first published in 1937 but the arguments and conclusions remain, for the
most part, valid.

574 **The ethnic dimension: papers on ethnicity and pluralism.**
Jean Martin, edited with an introduction by S. Encel. Sydney:
Allen & Unwin, 1981. 186p.

A collection of writings by Jean Martin, who for thirty years was concerned
academically with the study of migration and the role of ethnic minorities in
Australian society.

575 **Community and identity: refugee groups in Adelaide.**
Jean Martin. Canberra: Australian National University Press,
1972. 143p. (Immigrants in Australia, 1).

The first in a series of studies sponsored by the Academy of the Social Sciences in
Australia, designed to examine the contribution of overseas migrants to Australian
economic, social and cultural life. The present study concerns itself with the
Displaced Persons or European refugees who were among the first groups to arrive
in Australia after the Second World War. Many of these minority groups have
developed cohesive and diverse organizations. Professor Martin found that group
organization was not a defensive reaction against Australian pressure towards
assimilation, but a concern to maintain group identity and to preserve national
continuity between past and present.

576 **Refugee settlers: a study of Displaced Persons in Australia.**
Jean I. Martin. Canberra: Australian National University, 1965.
117p.

An early sociological study of the first post-war immigrants to arrive in Australia
– the Displaced Persons or European refugees. Under the Australian immigration
scheme they received assisted passages and guaranteed employment and accommodation. The migrants, for their part, were required to sign a two-year contract
to work where directed. The object of the study was to find out to what extent
these people were assimilated into local society. Assimilation was the official
policy in the early days of post-war immigration – policies of multiculturalism
and officially sponsored ethnicity being of recent vintage.

577　**Future Australians: immigrant children in Perth, Western Australia.**
Ruth Johnston.　Canberra: Australian National University Press, 1972. 290p. bibliog. (Immigrants in Australia, 2).

A research study of second generation settlers, the children of immigrants from Germany, Poland, Britain, with an Australian control group, all resident in Perth, Western Australia. The objective is to discover the degree of assimilation of these children, and Australian attitudes to migrants and how they view the assimilation process.

578　**Immigrants and politics.**
Paul R. Wilson.　Canberra: Australian National University Press, 1973. 175p. bibliog. (Immigrants in Australia, 3).

A study carried out in Brisbane among the two largest groups of post-war migrants – the British and Italians – to find out how they have been affected by the Australian political system.

579　**Migrant crime in Australia.**
Ronald D. Francis.　Brisbane: University of Queensland Press, 1981. 216p. bibliog.

This pioneering introduction to the participation in crime of the overseas-born gives lie to the belief of native-born Australians that migrants are less law abiding. Statistics suggest the opposite.

580　**British immigrants and Australia: a psycho-social inquiry.**
Alan Richardson.　Canberra: Australian National University Press, 1974. 209p. bibliog. (Immigrants in Australia, 4).

By far the greatest number (over 1¼ million) of post-war migrants to settle in Australia were the British. This study shows the process of adjustment to their new country and the reasons why a significant number of them return to Britain.

581　**Scotland and Australia, 1788-1850: emigration, commerce and investment.**
David S. Macmillan.　Oxford, England: Clarendon Press, 1967. 434p. bibliog.

A well-documented account of the contribution of Scotland to the early development of Australia.

582 **From pasta to pavlova: a comparative study of Italian settlers in Sydney and Griffith.**
Rina Huber. Brisbane: University of Queensland Press, 1977. 270p. bibliog.

A sympathetic and informative study, from an anthropological perspective, of the differing circumstances confronting immigrants from one area of Italy. The author has studied eight Trevisani families in Sydney and compared them with the settlement of Trevisani in Griffith, a rural irrigation area in New South Wales. The book shows how the adjustment to their different environments has led to two different life-styles.

583 **Australia through Italian eyes: a study of settlers returning from Australia to Italy.**
Stephanie Lindsay Thompson. Melbourne: Oxford University Press, 1980. 271p. bibliog.

Since the post-war immigration programme began in 1947 about 370,000 Italian migrants have come to Australia and of these some 90,000 or nearly a quarter have left again. The author undertook the research for this book in 1970 in three districts of Italy, where she interviewed 138 farmer-migrants to Australia. Although the book is a sociological document, complete with tables, methodology and questionnaires, the text is interesting and easy to read and it has many informative conclusions about the migrants and the Australian way of life.

584 **Greeks in Australia.**
Edited by Charles Price. Canberra: Australian National University Press, 1975. 228p. (Immigrants in Australia, 5).

Persons of Greek origin make up the second largest non-British population in Australia – some 300,000, including those born in Australia, compared with 450,000 or so of Italian descent. The book presents five studies which investigate the nature and purpose of Greek societies and organizations. They also attempt to explain how Greeks interrelate amongst themselves and with other Australians and their institutions.

585 **After the Odyssey: a study of Greek Australians.**
Gillian Bottomley. Brisbane: University of Queensland Press, 1979. 208p. bibliog.

Greeks are among the most dominant and vocal ethnic groups in Australia. This study concentrates on second generation adults brought up in Australia by Greek parents and explores the significance that Greek institutions and organizations have in their life. The basic concern of the book is to find out whether and how ethnic continuity can be maintained in Australia. With multiculturalism as official government policy this study has implications far beyond the Greek community.

150

586   **German speaking settlers in Australia.**
Josef Vondra. Melbourne: Cavalier Press, 1981. 286p.

An account of German, Austrian and Swiss settlers in Australia from the arrival in South Australia of the first German religious refugees in the late 1830s to the recent immigrants. Vondra concentrates on themes of success and vitality – there are no stories of discrimination or hardship in his book. The author has written a similar book on Greek migrants, *Hellas Australia* (Melbourne: Widescope, 1979).

587   **The French in Australia.**
Anny P. L. Stuer. Canberra: Department of Demography, Institute of Advanced Studies, Australian National University, 1982. 249p. bibliog. (Immigration Monograph Series, 2).

French cultural influence has always been strong in Australia but the French have never settled here in great numbers. There were only some 12,000 French-born settlers in 1976. Though relatively small in number, the French made a notable impact in the gold fields, in wine-making, in the sciences and arts, in commerce and banking and in entertainment. This is a detailed study of French settlement in Australia up to about 1976.

588   **Latvians in Australia: alienation and assimilation.**
Aldis L. Putnins. Canberra: Australian National University Press, 1981. 131p. bibliog.

Latvian migrants were among the first of the post-war arrivals from Europe. By the early 1950s Latvian immigration had practically ceased. The author presents a series of studies of this group of political refugees: their settlement in Australia, mental health, personality characteristics, the extent of assimilation and ethnic identification.

589   **Australian genesis: Jewish convicts and settlers, 1788-1850.**
J. S. Levi, G. F. J. Bergman. Adelaide: Rigby, 1974. 360p. bibliog.

A detailed account of the lives of the Jews who arrived in Australia during the first sixty years of settlement. Eight Jewish convicts landed with the First Fleet and many others followed afterwards. Unlike other European communities Australia had Jewish participation since the early days of its establishment. This may explain the relative absence of discrimination against the Jewish component in Australian society.

590   **Australian Jews of today and the part they have played.**
R. Brasch. Sydney: Cassell, 1977. 235p.

Jews have had an influence in Australian life disproportionate to their numbers. This is a collection of studies of thirty-four Jewish people prominent in modern Australian society.

591 **The diggers from China: the story of Chinese on the goldfields.**
Jean Gittins. Melbourne: Quartet Books, 1981. 148p.

A sensitive account of the thousands of Chinese diggers who joined the Australian gold rushes of the 1850s and after. On the diggings they faced extreme racial prejudice which on several occasions erupted into armed riots. Few of them prospered, many died and most of the survivors returned home.

592 **Fear and hatred: purifying Australia and California, 1850-1901.**
Andrew Markus. Sydney: Hale & Iremonger, 1979. 295p.
bibliog.

A detailed historical narrative of the events and movements which led up to the passing of the Immigration Restriction Act (commonly known as White Australia Policy) by the new federal government in 1901. It compares the Australian with the Californian anti-Chinese movements of the same period. In many ways the racial and immigration attitudes displayed in the 19th century are still prevalent and a reading of this book will help to clarify the immigration debate in Australia today.

593 **The great white walls are built: restrictive immigration to North America and Australasia, 1836-1888.**
Charles A. Price. Canberra: Australian Institute of International Affairs, with Australian National University Press, 1974. 323p.
bibliog.

The discriminatory racial attitude in the second half of the 19th century which led to restrictive immigration policies or the so-called 'White Australia Policy' is shown to have been a particular manifestation of a wider trend. Similar policies were being pursued at the same time in places of much the same character: British Columbia, California, Oregon, New Zealand and more recently the United Kingdom. The book adds a new dimension to understanding the political, social, economic and moral forces in white Anglo-Saxon countries that caused ravage and widespread restrictions on coloured immigration.

594 **Asian migration to Australia: the background to exclusion, 1896-1923.**
A. T. Yarwood. Melbourne: Melbourne University Press, 1967. 210p. bibliog.

A careful, academic study of the control of Asian migration to Australia which makes clear that the White Australia Policy expressed in the Immigration Restriction Act of 1901, was not actuated solely by economic motives and that racial attitudes also played an important role. In 1968, the author published a volume of documents on this subject entitled *Attitudes to non-European immigration* (Cassell).

595 **Non-white immigration and the 'White Australia Policy'.**
H. I. London. Sydney: Sydney University Press, 1970. 318p.
bibliog.

Reflecting an increasing concern with her image in Asia, Australia in 1966 proposed 'dramatic changes' to liberalize her non-European immigration laws popularly known as 'White Australia'. This book makes a comprehensive survey of the background against which change occurred and the accompanying pressures.

596 **Australia and the non-white migrant.**
Edited by Kenneth Rivett for the Immigration Reform Group.
Melbourne: Melbourne University Press, 1975. 327p.

This book presents arguments for further liberalization of non-white migration to Australia. An historical account of changing public attitudes towards the 'White Australia Policy' is included and an examination is made of the massive criticism this policy has attracted overseas.

597 **Alternatives of ethnicity: immigrants and Aborigines in Anglo-Saxon Australia.**
William W. Bostock. Melbourne: Corvus, 1981. 2nd rev. ed.
212p.

A study of how differences in language and culture affects participation in Australian society. It shows clear evidence that the participation of groups such as immigrants and the Aborigines, whose ethnicity differs markedly from the dominant Anglo-Saxon group, is distinctly different.

Australian Aborigines

General

598 **Black Australia: an annotated bibliography and teachers' guide to resources on Aborigines and Torres Straits Islanders.**
Annotated, compiled and edited by Marji Hill, Alex Barlow.
Canberra: Australian Institute of Aboriginal Studies, 1978. 200p.

The purpose of this bibliography is to eliminate prejudice towards and about black Australians. It is an excellent guide for anyone who needs to acquire a deeper understanding of the Aborigines. Regular updating of the work is intended.

599 **The Aboriginal Australians: the first pioneers.**
Catherine H. Berndt, Ronald M. Berndt. Melbourne: Pitman, 1983. 2nd ed. 151p. bibliog.

Intended for secondary school students, this book should attract a much wider readership because it provides a clear, unpretentious and unambiguous 'introduction to traditional Aboriginal culture in the context of past and present: as a background to what is happening now.'

600 **The world of the first Australians.**
R. M. Berndt, C. H. Berndt. Sydney: Ure Smith, 1977. 2nd ed. 602p. bibliog.

A new edition of a text, which like Elkin's *The Australian Aborigines* (see below), has become a standard reference source and a valuable introduction to tradition-oriented Aboriginal cultures. An extensive bibliography directs readers to specialized areas. The authors have written another much more concise book in simple language for the layman, *The first Australians* (Sydney: Ure Smith, 1974. 3rd ed.).

601 **The Australian Aborigines.**
A. P. Elkin. Sydney: Angus & Robertson, 1979. rev. ed. 397p.

In the first edition in 1938 Elkin stated that his aim was to help white Australians understand Aborigines, so that they might begin to appreciate their culture and move towards an awareness of their needs as people. This aim has not changed throughout the many editions of the book. There is a theoretical anthropological approach in the book but this need not concern the general reader. Elkin presents an accurate picture of Aboriginal life and he has revised and expanded his work constantly to include new information. Long regarded as a classic in the field of Aboriginal studies it is still a basic reference text.

602 **The Aborigines.**
R. M. Gibbs. Melbourne: Longman, 1974. 112p. bibliog.

An excellent introduction in simple language to the Australian Aborigines including origins, archaeological research, material culture, social organization and ceremonial life and art. The description of traditional life is supplemented with European contact and race relations. The text is enhanced by an excellent selection of illustrative material.

603 **Australian Aborigines: shadows in a landscape.**
Photography by Laurence Le Guay, text by Suzanne Falkiner.
Sydney: Globe, 1980. 129p.

A fine collection of photographs with minimal text, which conveys a vivid impression of Aboriginal life. The photographs capture the wild beauty of the outback as well as managing to suggest some of the special feeling Aborigines have for the land and its features.

604 **The Australian Aborigines: a portrait of their society.**
Kenneth Maddock. Melbourne: Penguin Books, 1982.
2nd ed. 198p.

When first published in 1972 this book was a useful survey of current thinking about traditional Aboriginal society supplementing the standard texts of Elkin and the Berndts. The new edition has been rewritten and reorganized, the biggest change being the political awareness pervading the book. Maddock raises important questions concerning Aboriginal land rights and relations between black and white.

605 **Kulinma: listening to Aboriginal Australians.**
H. C. Coombs. Canberra: Australian National University Press, 1978. 248p.

A collection of essays, written between 1968 and 1976 by Dr. H. C. Coombs, when he was chairman of the Council for Aboriginal Affairs. Much of the material grew from his personal experience in travelling among, and listening to, Aboriginal people. The book is a comprehensive record of the early years after the federal referendum of 1967 which gave the federal government the power to legislate for Aborigines.

606 **Race politics in Australia: Aborigines, politics and law.**
Colin Tatz. Armidale, New South Wales: University of New
England Publishing Unit, 1979. 118p. bibliog.

A valuable and succinct guide to the major issues in Aboriginal affairs. Professor
Tatz's main theme is that white political systems and institutions have nothing to
offer Aborigines, and have been instruments detrimental to their cause. He
suggests that Aborigines should take action in civil law to secure their rights.

607 **Health business.**
Pam Nathan, Dick Leichleitner Japanangka. Melbourne:
Heinemann Educational, 1983. 216p. bibliog.

An investigation of Aboriginal contact with European health-care delivery in
central Australia and the interaction between traditional Aboriginal health
measures and European practice.

608 **Aboriginal Australian art: a visual perspective.**
Ronald M. Berndt, Catherine H. Berndt, with John E. Stanton.
Sydney: Methuen, 1982. 176p. bibliog.

A book of superb illustrations and stimulating text presenting an overview of
Aboriginal art and showing how it permeates most Aboriginal life. The Berndts
also provide ample evidence for their claim that traditional artists have created
masterpieces of considerable importance to the international world of art.

609 **The Australian Aboriginal heritage: an introduction through the
arts.**
Edited by Ronald M. Berndt, E. S. Phillips. Sydney: Australian
Society for Education Through the Arts, with Ure Smith, 1978.
2nd ed. 320p.

A wide-ranging investigation and description by various authors of the main artistic
driving forces in Aboriginal Australia today — oral literature, visual and represen-
tational art, music and dramatic forms. Both black-and-white and colour illustrations abound in this large volume.

610 **Rock paintings of Aboriginal Australia.**
Elaine Godden, photographed by Jutta Malnic. Sydney: Reed,
1982. 128p. bibliog.

A serious contribution to the understanding of Aboriginal rock painting, with 48
colour plates and numerous black-and-white photographs. The authors obtained
the pictures from personal expeditions to the many thousand-year old rock
galleries scattered throughout Australia. Many galleries were photographed for the
first time with the full approval of the tribal elders.

Black viewpoints

611 Australian dreaming: 40,000 years of Aboriginal history.
Compiled and edited by Jennifer Isaacs. Sydney: Lansdowne
Press, 1980. 304p. bibliog.

A presentation of the Aboriginal world view in the Aborigines' own words. The textual material has been drawn from oral history, song poetry, daily conversation and myths and legends recorded in books compiled by white scholars. Many interesting contributions have been made by Aborigines specifically for this book. The material was checked and edited by the relevant Aboriginal communities. More than 300 magnificent colour photographs illustrate the text.

612 Black viewpoints: the Aboriginal experience.
Edited by Colin Tatz, assisted by Keith McConnochie. Sydney:
Australia and New Zealand Book Company, 1975. 126p.

Fifteen Aborigines present their points of view in this series of lectures to students at Armidale College of Advanced Education. It is an important book and to quote the preface: 'Only by gaining insight into their personal perspectives, into the justifications for their attitudes and actions can we begin to understand the other side of the race relation coin.'

613 Because a white man'll never do it.
Kevin J. Gilbert. Sydney: Angus & Robertson, 1973. 210p.

An important book written by an active participant in recent black activism who is not afraid to evaluate and criticize what the Aborigines have attempted to achieve.

614 A bastard like me.
Charles Perkins. Sydney: Ure Smith, 1975. 199p.

Charles Perkins is an Aborigine who has made a successful career in white society, ranging from a professional soccer player to an assistant secretary in the federal Department of Aboriginal Affairs. The autobiography is compelling reading and a significant contribution to black Australian writing as well as an important first-hand account of the beginnings of black activism in Australia.

**615 The two worlds of Jimmie Barker: the life of an Australian
Aboriginal, 1900-1972.**
As told to Janet Mathews. Canberra: Australian Institute of
Aboriginal Studies, 1977. 218p.

Reconstructed from tape recordings and personal interviews, this is an excellent autobiography by an Aborigine telling in simple language of the transition from semi-nomadic society to that of the missions and reserves. The period covered is 1900-72 and the place is the western districts of New South Wales. It is one of the few authentic revelations of life as actually experienced by an Aboriginal person and is recommended for that reason.

616 **Fringedweller.**
Robert Bropho, son of Nyinda. Sydney: Alternative Publishing Co-operative, 1980. 153p.

The angry story of an Aborigine who neither fitted into the white community nor lived completely as an Aboriginal — a fringe dweller. Bropho is a black activist whose life, apart from activism, is a model of all those Aborigines who live on the edge of the white society.

Race relations

617 **A matter of justice.**
C. D. Rowley. Canberra: Australian National University Press, 1978. 250p.

A much more passionate and angry indictment of white treatment of Aborigines than his earlier scholarly trilogy *Aboriginal policy and practice* (see below). Rowley compares the Aborigines' lot with Solzhenitsyn's *Gulag Archipelago*: 'Scattered over Australia there remains an "archipelago" of tiny islands — groups of Aboriginal families surrounded by the sea of whites — islands to which they have been forced either by law or by economics to withdraw, and from which only the cosmetically favoured few in each generation have escaped by passing as white into the general society.'

618 **Aboriginal policy and practice.**
C. D. Rowley. Canberra: Australian National University Press, 1970-71. 3 vols. (Aborigines in Australian Society, nos. 4, 6, 7).

A scholarly, yet clear and accessible indictment of white Australian indifference to the maltreatment of an inarticulate minority — the original inhabitants of the continent, the Aborigines. The author traces the history of race relations and then focuses on the full-bloods of the interior and the part-Aborigines of the cities and towns. These three volumes are part of the monograph series *Aborigines in Australian Society*, and result from a major research project conducted by the Social Science Research Council of Australia. Volume 1: *The destruction of Aboriginal society*; volume 2: *Outcasts in white society*; volume 3: *The remote Aborigines*.

619 **Aborigines in white Australia: a documentary history of the attitudes affecting official policy and the Australian Aborigine, 1697-1973.**
Selected and edited by Sharman N. Stone. Melbourne: Heinemann Educational, 1974. 253p. bibliog.

An excellent selection of extracts from a variety of sources intended to present and illuminate the history of Australian racism.

620   **White man got no dreaming: essays, 1938-1973.**
      W. E. H. Stanner.   Canberra: Australian National University
      Press, 1979. 389p.

As an anthropologist the author lived with Aborigines, studied their religion and social organization and learned to understand their deep feelings about the tribal lands. These essays have the common theme – treatment of black Australians by white Australians – and demonstrate long experience with the Aborigines. The essays are well written and delightful to read.

621   **Aborigines and colonists: Aborigines and colonial society in New South Wales in the 1830s and 1840s.**
      R. H. W. Reece.   Sydney: Sydney University Press, 1974. 254p. bibliog.

A scholarly book which traces the roots of white racist attitudes in Australia in the years 1830-50 when unrestricted warfare between settlers and Aborigines was the order of the day. The Myall Greek massacre when twenty-eight Aborigines were murdered and the subsequent trials are examined in detail.

622   **Invasion and resistance: Aboriginal-European relations on the North Queensland frontier, 1861-1897.**
      Noel Loos.   Canberra: Australian National University Press, 1982. 325p. bibliog.

The most recent of the 'new wave' studies of white settlement where the Aborigines are portrayed as fighting a series of guerilla against the invading whites. Inevitably the uneven struggle ended in the subjugation of the Aborigines and the conquest of their lands. Loos' study displays originality in that he identifies four frontiers in north Queensland – the pastoral, mining, timber-getting and the maritime – and shows how in each the 'Aboriginal problem' was tackled in different ways.

623   **Black death, white hands.**
      Paul R. Wilson.   Sydney: Allen & Unwin, 1982. 150p.

A study of the condition of the Australian Aborigines living on government-controlled reserves in Queensland. Evidence, based on extensive investigation, shows that the high incidence of crime and self-mutilation on reserves is due to the social and economic deprivation of the inhabitants.

624   **Aboriginal Australians: black response to white dominance, 1788-1980.**
      Richard Broome.   Sydney: Allen & Unwin, 1982. 227p. bibliog.

An overview of Aboriginal-white relationships since Australia was first colonized. This book is based on the scholarly writing of the past decade which has put the original inhabitants of the continent back into the Australian history that they helped to shape. Too often, until recently, history books had excluded the Aboriginal point of view altogether, making the present work a balanced introduction to the subject of race relations in Australia.

Australian Aborigines. Race relations

625 **A nest of hornets: the massacre of the Fraser family at Hornet Bank station, central Queensland 1857, and related events.**
Gordon Reid. Melbourne: Oxford University Press, 1982. 235p. bibliog.

The story of a massacre on the Dawson River in Queensland when the Jiman tribe of Aborigines brutally killed men, women and children; and the even more blood-thirsty retribution exacted by the white community. Reid analyses both causes and consequences of one of the more violent interracial clashes, which also occurred in other parts of the country. It is a sad tale, but it helps account for the development of white racial attitudes which are still prevalent today.

626 **The other side of the frontier: Aboriginal resistance to the European invasion of Australia.**
Henry Reynolds. Melbourne: Penguin Books, 1982. 255p. bibliog.

Until a decade ago Aborigines were merely a footnote in Australian history and historians were chiefly interested in documenting 'the stirring accounts of . . . British enterprise and perseverance'. Along with Charles Rewley, Lyndall Ryan, R. H. W. Reece and Noel Loos, Henry Reynolds belongs to the new historical school which has investigated the violent nature of colonialism in Australia and has accorded the Aborigines an equal role with the white man in the process.

627 **Generations of resistance: the Aboriginal struggle for justice.**
Lorna Lippmann. Melbourne: Longman Cheshire, 1981. 243p. bibliog.

A sympathetic and readable account of the militant resistance movement of Australia's Aboriginal people. This book concentrates on the issues of the 1970s and documents the damage done to Aboriginal culture, health, economy and morale by what is seen as white oppression. Many black-and-white photographs supplement the text and after each chapter a list of recommended books for further reading is provided.

Social Class, Social Groups and Social Change

628 **Australian society: a sociological introduction.**
Edited by A. F. Davies, S. Encel, M. J. Berry. Melbourne:
Longman Cheshire, 1977. 3rd ed. 490p. bibliogs.

A useful collection of studies on Australian society with the notable exception of politics and the media. The coverage is so wide that the book reflects the academic development of sociology in Australia in the mid-1970s.

629 **Social inequality in Australian society.**
John S. Western. Melbourne: Macmillan, 1983. 385p. bibliog.

For generations egalitarianism has been a fond Australian myth. The numerous commissions of inquiry set up in the 1970s by the federal government brought to light a great deal of sociological data pertaining to the structure and functioning of Australian society which proved that social inequalities found in the rest of the world existed in Australia too. The major sources of inequality derive from class, status, power, sex, ethnic origin and age. The book is basically concerned with a discussion of these aspects.

630 **A just society? Essays on equity in Australia.**
Edited by Patrick N. Troy. Sydney: Allen & Unwin, 1981.
247p. bibliog.

A collection of essays which examine the meaning of 'equity' as used in certain academic disciplines – history, law, economics, political science, social theory, and the importance of equity in a number of policy areas – health, public administration, labour relations, women's affairs and, using one case-study, Aboriginal affairs.

631 **Ruling class: ruling culture: studies of conflict, power and hegemony in Australian life.**
R. W. Connell. Cambridge, England: Cambridge University Press,
1977. 250p.

An analysis of class in Australian society from a socialist perspective. Professor Connell's major aim is to show class theory as a useful tool in the understanding of the social situation in the 1970s. He develops the theory by working through some practical cases. The book begins with a critical evaluation of Australian writing on class.

632 **Social stratification in Australia.**
R. A. Wild. Sydney: Allen & Unwin, 1978. 202p. bibliog.
(Studies in Society, 3).

An examination of how Australia's population is differentiated socially within a theoretical framework. The old myth of egalitarianism, as a description of social rights and conditions, is shown never to have existed. Inequality was the order of the day and still persists.

633 **Elites in Australia.**
John Higley, Desley Deacon, Don Smart. London: Routledge, 1979. 317p. bibliog.

An investigation into the question of where power resides in Australia. This book reports on the backgrounds, attitudes and behaviour of national élites in eight major sectors of Australian society: big business, trade unions, federal and state politics, the Commonwealth Public Service, mass media, voluntary associations, major universities and research centres. The authors interviewed 370 men and women who, in their view, made up the national élite in the second half of 1975.

634 **Class and inequality in Australia: sociological perspectives and research.**
Edited by Peter Hiller. Sydney: Harcourt, 1981. 292p.

A collection of readings offering students and lay readers an overview of the range of sociological work in the area of social class and inequality in Australia. The chapters cover both theory and empirical research.

635 **Bradstow: a study of status, class and power in a small Australian town.**
R. A. Wild. Sydney: Angus & Robertson, 1974. 256p. bibliog.

A sociological study of a New South Wales town based on the author's own field observations. He spent two years in the New South Wales town of Bowral and his experiences are as convincing as his statistics. He shows that Australian egalitarianism is a myth in Bradstow: that status, class and political power are closely interwoven and are enjoyed most by a conservative upper class which has imitated English social behaviour ever since the town's foundation in the last century. Wild implies that the conditions in Bradstow are mirrored in many similar towns around Australia. Recommended, this is one book which brings sociological theory to life.

636 **Socialisation in Australia.**
Edited by F. J. Hunt. Melbourne: Australia International Press, 1978. 341p.

A collection of research studies by sixteen social scientists which examine the process of socialization of individuals into Australian society.

637 **The professions in Australia: a critical appraisal.**
Edited by Paul Boreham. Alec Pemberton, Paul Wilson.
Brisbane: University of Queensland Press, 1976. 290p.

A collection of essays appraising the high community status of professional groups in Australia. The authors examine their claims of special skills and complex knowledge to solve personal and social problems, and conclude that future professionals are trained to accept a narrow world-view which leads to a preoccupation with professional status, and a concern with one's privileged position in society to the exclusion of public interest.

638 **Australians at risk.**
Anne Deveson. Sydney: Cassell, 1978. 446p.

In November 1977 the *Final report of the Commission of Human Relationships* was released. Its recommendations, which covered about every aspect of Australian society, caused heated debate in the community, with reactions ranging from horror to enthusiastic approval. In this book Anne Deveson, who was one of the three commissioners, elaborates on a dozen of the major issues covered by the hearings. She has written a short essay on each issue presenting the commissioners' views, then follows it with a selection of the evidence. An appendix lists the recommendations of the commission. The book surveys some of the most sensitive issues confronting Australians – the role of the family, sexuality, rape and abortion, law reform and discrimination against minority and disadvantaged groups.

639 **The family in Australia: social, demographic and psychological aspects.**
Edited by Jerzy Krupinski, Alan Stoller. Sydney: Pergamon, 1978. 2nd ed. 312p. bibliog.

A collection of papers on social, demographic and psychological aspects of the Australian family. Although it contains a mass of data, the papers are introductory in nature and are easily understood by the general reader.

640 **Having families: marriage, parenthood and social pressure in Australia.**
Lyn Richards. Melbourne: Penguin Books, 1978. 329p. bibliog.

A large-scale study of the early years of marriage in Australia, based on a survey of sixty young couples in 1976. They were asked their reasons for marrying and for having children and their views on family size and family roles. Mostly written in a question-and-answer form, the book is lively reading. In a companion volume published in 1979 entitled *Mothers and working mothers* (Melbourne: Penguin Books), the authors look at the question of how and when a mother decides whether or not to work outside the home.

641 **Breaking up: separation and divorce in Australia.**
Ailsa Burns. Melbourne: Nelson, 1980. 206p.

One in four Australian marriages end in the divorce courts and the rate doubled between 1974 and 1978. *Breaking up* is a study of people who have been through the experience of divorce or separation and an analysis of the helping institutions – doctors, priests, marriage counselling services, the legal profession and the courts. Although the book liberally uses quotes from the 335 divorced men and women included in the survey, it remains more an academic than a popular work.

642 **Crosstalk: women, partners and children in the eighties.**
Ian Marshall, Cecelia Morris. Sydney: Fontana/Collins, 1983. 253p.

What have been the effects of the women's liberation movement over the last twenty years? The book attempts to answer this and other questions through intimate interviews with fifty Australian women and men who have lived and matured during this period. All talked frankly about living together and living alone, families and family break-ups, sex, children, freedom and the fear of it, love and the quest for love.

643 **Family violence in Australia.**
Edited by Carol O'Donnell, Jan Craney. Melbourne: Longman Cheshire, 1982. 204p.

A collection of essays on domestic violence in Australia. The contributors discuss spouse abuse, spouse murder, incest and the roles of the police, courts, refuges and counselling services in dealing with this widely spread phenomenon. The book is written from a feminist perspective and shows how many Australian social institutions are based on sexist practices and assumptions.

644 **The half-open door: sixteen modern Australian women look at professional life and achievement.**
Edited by Patricia Grimshaw, Lynne Strahan. Sydney: Hale & Iremonger, 1982. 344p.

A collection of autobiographical pieces by professional women who describe the considerable practical, emotional and psychological obstacles that had to be overcome during their careers. Written with passion and humour the essays are readable and entertaining as well as a valuable piece of 20th-century Australian social history – demonstrating an emerging feminist awareness among educated women.

645 **Nothing to spare: recollections of Australian pioneering women.**
Jan Carter. Melbourne: Penguin Books, 1981. 238p. bibliog.

The recorded reminiscences of women who are now aged between 80 and 100 and lived in Western Australia between 1890 and 1918. The book revives the period as experienced by ordinary women in their own words, and provides entertaining and informative reading. It is a valuable social document on the status of women in Australia at that time.

646 **Australian women: feminist perspectives.**
Edited by Norma Grieve, Patricia Grimshaw. Melbourne:
Oxford University Press, 1981. 333p.

A collection of academic essays which explore the position of women in Australian society from a broad range of perspectives: anthropology, sociology, education, history, psychology, biology and the arts.

647 **Children and families in Australia: contemporary issues and problems.**
Ailsa Burns, Jacqueline Goodnow. Sydney: Allen & Unwin,
1979. 255p. bibliog. (Studies in Society, 5).

Brings together and reviews material on some of the most important social issues facing Australian families: including the impact of television on children, the position of migrant children, the effects on children of working, single and unemployed parents, violence against children, custody, adoption and welfare.

648 **On the side of the child: an Australian perspective of child abuse.**
Peter Boss. Melbourne: Fontana/Collins, 1980. 166p. bibliog.

This study extends beyond the conventional understanding of abuse as merely the physical ill-treatment of children. Boss considers that children who are neglected, ignored or consistently ill-treated physically or mentally, are being abused. His book analyses the causes, the size of the problem, public response to it and possibilities for treatment, prediction and prevention.

649 **Child welfare in Australia: an introduction.**
Cliff Picton, Peter Boss. Sydney: Harcourt, 1981. 162p.

A general description of child welfare services as they operate in Australia at present.

650 **Young Australians.**
Shelley Phillips. Sydney: Harper & Row, 1979. 272p. bibliog.

The author discusses the results of her investigations into the attitudes, beliefs and biases of Australian children in an urban environment. Her study is distinguished by the fact that she uses children, not their parents, as respondents. The sample comprised 2,279 fifth- and sixth-grade students from a random selection of schools in the Sydney area. The age range averaged 10-12 years with roughly equal numbers of boys and girls. Perhaps not surprisingly the results demonstrate that Australian society imitates its American and English counterparts and that adult prejudices and biases are alive and well and flourishing in Australian children.

651 **Children Australia.**
Edited by R. G. Brown. Sydney: Allen & Unwin, with the
Morialta Trust of South Australia, 1980. 282p.

A collection of essays on all aspects of children's lives in contemporary Australia.

652   **Children in Australia: an outline history.**
Sue Fabian, Morag Loh.   Melbourne: Oxford University Press,
1980. 256p. bibliog.

This is one of the several books spawned by the International Year of the Child. It is an outline or preliminary history, as the text is far outweighed by contemporary documents and pictures. There are a series of photographs, cartoons, selections from letters, diaries and fiction as well as newpaper and official reports. The authors allow the collection to speak for itself providing only linking text where necessary. Like the spate of feminist books recently, the present volume is about the history of a majority group in society which hitherto has been submerged under the male-dominated mainstream historiography.

653   **The elderly Australian.**
Bruce Ford.   Melbourne: Penguin Books, 1979. 167p.

The author defines the aged, describes their problems and then concentrates on the various services available to assist them.

654   **Towards an older Australia: readings in social gerontology.**
Edited by Anna L. Howe.   Brisbane: University of Queensland
Press, 1981.

A collection of essays, specially written for this volume, which look to a future in which there will be a greater number and a higher proportion of older to younger people in Australia. They examine the effects of social, economic and political forces on the lives of the aged in Australia.

655   **The aging experience.**
Cherry Russell.   Sydney: Allen & Unwin, 1981. 239p. bibliog.
(Studies in Society, 10).

An in-depth study of how old age is experienced in contemporary Australian society. This book links original survey data to a broad theoretical framework. Working from the premise that old age is a devalued status it examines the implications of this for the personal experience and interpersonal relations of old people. It is not a layman's book, although the case-studies can be read with interest and minimal knowledge of sociological principles.

656   **In the midst of life . . . the Australian response to death.**
Graeme M. Griffin, Des Tobin.   Melbourne: Melbourne
University Press, 1982. 177p.

Australian mortuary customs are discussed from the time of white settlement to the present day.

657 **Australians in poverty.**
Peter Hollingworth: Melbourne: Nelson, 1979. 166p.

According to widely accepted definitions, more than 2 million people are poor in Australia. This book shows in an accessible manner what it means to be poor in Australia. The author also points out how policy inadequacies and misguided planning contribute to the problem.

658 **Poor policies: Australian income security, 1972-77.**
Patricia Tulloch. London: Croom Helm, 1979. 191p. bibliog.

This book examines why and how Australian income security policies perpetuate inequality. Topics such as unemployment, taxation and housing are considered, illustrating the relationship between 'welfare' and 'market' principles, and the difference, if any, between the policies of Liberal and Labor governments. The conclusion: 'During the years 1973-1977 income security policy continued to be dominated by market principles and by allegiance to inequality. Although there were differences in party philosophy and sometimes in strategy, deviation from this basic pattern did not occur under either the Labor or Liberal government.'

659 **People in poverty: a Melbourne survey with supplement.**
Ronald F. Henderson, Alison Harcourt, R. J. A. Harper.
Melbourne: Cheshire for the Institute of Applied Economic and Social Research, University Research, University of Melbourne, 1975. 226p.

First published in 1970, the survey proved the extent of real poverty which exists unrecognized by the complacent affluence of the majority of Australians. Poverty was defined in strictly economic terms as inadequacy of income. Based on carefully collected and analysed statistical material the book is essentially about people. Numerous case-studies illustrate the deprivation and hardship of large numbers of elderly people, migrants, fatherless and low-income families. The supplement to the 1975 edition contains a discussion of poverty research and the changes in policy for the alleviation of poverty that have occurred since the book was first written.

660 **Ads that made Australia: how advertising has shaped our history and lifestyle.**
John Bryden-Brown. Sydney: Doubleday, 1981. 239p.

A light and amusing look at advertising in Australia. The author claims and goes a long way in proving that advertisements have dictated the lifestyle and social attitudes of Australians. This persuasive and entertaining text is backed up by hundreds of illustrations of ads spanning nearly 200 years.

661 **Duck and cabbage tree: a pictorial history of clothes in Australia, 1788-1914.**
Cedric Flower. Sydney: Angus & Robertson, 1968. 157p.

This book consists of more than 200 illustrations linked by minimal text. Another book covering the same period is *Breeches and bustles: an illustrated history of clothes worn in Australia, 1788-1914*, by Elizabeth Scandrett (Melbourne: Pioneer Design Studio, 1978).

662 **A peculiar people: the Australians in Paraguay.**
Gavin Souter. Sydney: Angus & Robertson, 1968. 309p. bibliog.

In July 1893, William Lane with 252 followers − men, women and children − sailed from Sydney to Paraguay to set up a socialist Utopian colony 'New Australia' in which the cherished Australian principles of equality and 'mateship' would at last be fully realized. The well-written book examines this early experiment in communal living, its Australian background, and the reasons for its failure.

663 **Alternative Australia: communities of the future?**
Peter Cock. Melbourne: Quartet Books, 1979. 292p. bibliog.

The first comprehensive account of the alternative movement and communities in Australia. The movement dates from the 1960s protest period and expresses itself in present-day experiments in self-sufficiency and co-operative living. The book is informed by the author's professional training in sociology and his own experiences in communal living. An earlier collection of short pieces on the same theme by a variety of people involved in alternative lifestyles was published in 1975, *The way out: radical alternatives in Australia,* edited by Margaret Smith and David Crossley, assisted by Peter and Sandra Cock (Melbourne: Lansdowne Press).

664 **Race relations in Australia: a history.**
A. T. Yarwood, M. J. Knowling. Sydney: Methuen, 1982. 312p. bibliog.

Aborigines and white Australians are the main protagonists, but immigrant non-Europeans − notably Chinese, Pacific Islanders and Japanese − are discussed beginning with their arrival from the 1840s onwards. An excellent comprehensive introduction to the subject.

665 **Racism: the Australian experience: a study of race prejudice in Australia.**
Edited by F. S. Stevens. Sydney: Australia & New Zealand Book Company, 1972-77. 3 vols.

This heterogeneous collection of topics, authors, styles and degrees of passions on Australian racism provides a broadly based introduction to the subject. Volume 1: *Prejudice and xenophobia* (2nd ed.); volume 2: *Black versus white;* volume 3: *Colonialism and after* (2nd ed.). Volume one deals with prejudice against foreigners and migrant groups in Australia. Volume two addresses itself to Aboriginal/white relations and the last volume is devoted to the manifestations of racial prejudice in Australia's foreign and colonial policies.

Health and Welfare

666 Fair go: welfare issues in Australia.
Ronald Mendelsohn. Melbourne: Penguin Books, 1982. 228p.
bibliog.

A clear exposition of the basic facts behind the complex issues of welfare. The author claims that in the present conservative social environment, welfare is under attack and he has written a counter-attack: it is a reaffirmation of the ideals of caring for others. Mendelsohn also suggests long-term social welfare goals for Australia, which in his opinion should be at the basis of any civilized, democratic society.

667 No charity there: a short history of social welfare in Australia.
Brian Dickey. Melbourne: Nelson, 1980. 252p. bibliog.

An introduction to the development of social welfare in Australia from its foundation in 1788 to the 1970s. This book traces official and community attitudes to people in need and shows how governments and private charities have reacted to their demands and expectations. International surveys show Australia near the bottom of the list of the developed countries in the proportion of GNP committed to welfare. Dickey's summing up is blunt – 'Australian society as it is presently organized ensures that various categories of people become and remain poor. To that extent, most social welfare practices have been residual, for the alternative of major redistribution action is, at least for the foreseeable future, out of the question. The powerless poor have been left behind, and the welfare system in Australia has been made into a support system for the middle classes.'

668 Australian welfare history: critical essays.
Richard Kennedy. Melbourne: Macmillan, 1982. 322p.

A collection of critical and radical essays on the welfare history of Australia.

669 Australian social security today: major developments from 1900 to 1978.
T. H. Kewley. Sydney: Sydney University Press, 1980. 223p.

Supplements the second edition (1973) of the author's standard work *Social security in Australia, 1900-1972*. This book quickly covers the years to 1972 and then concentrates on welfare developments during the 1970s.

670 **The Australian welfare state: growth, crisis and change.**
M. A. Jones. Sydney: Allen & Unwin, 1983. new ed. 355p. bibliog.

Provides an interdisciplinary and integrated overview of the welfare system in Australia, its historical development and the main issues facing it. A comparative, policy-orientated and quantitative approach is taken throughout the text. Extensive use is made of available statistics and many graphs and tables are included.

671 **The condition of the people: social welfare in Australia, 1900-1975.**
Ronald Mendelsohn. Sydney: Allen & Unwin, 1979. 408p. bibliog.

A major, wide-ranging study concerned as much with the economic effect, as of social policy itself. The author, an academic and senior civil servant involved in policy making, concludes that while Australia was something of a social laboratory in the early years of this century, it is no longer a front runner in the social welfare stakes. The northern European countries have outstripped Australia in health care, in education, in income, and generosity of provision of income security. There are chapter bibliographies and an extensive consolidated bibliography for further reading.

672 **Welfare politics in Australia: a study in policy analysis.**
Adam Graycar. Melbourne: Macmillan, 1979. 231p. bibliog.

A discussion of the contrasting social policies of the Labor government, in power from 1972 to 1975 and the Liberal government after 1975, is followed by more technical chapters on planning, policy formulation and implementation, and evaluation. This latter part of the book is most useful for readers who have only a passing familiarity with Australian federalism and the constitutional constraints that frustrate policy makers.

673 **The welfare stakes: strategies for Australian social policy.**
Edited by Ronald F. Henderson. Melbourne: Institute of Applied Economic and Social Research, University of Melbourne, 1981. 256p. bibliog.

A collection of papers and comments delivered at a conference held by the Institute of Applied Economic and Social Research in the University of Melbourne. The authors take issue with a widely held view of welfare as a redistribution downwards from the hardworking middle-class taxpayer to the improvident working man or the receiver of unemployment benefits, and argue that the opposite is true. The most valuable fringe benefits, for instance, go to people already in well-paid jobs. Together the contributors have tried to rethink what is needed to achieve a genuine welfare state in Australia.

674 **Public expenditures and social policy in Australia.**
Edited by R. B. Scotton, Helen Ferber. Melbourne: Longman
Cheshire for the Institute of Applied Economic and Social
Research, 1978-1980. 2 vols.

These volumes arise from extensive studies undertaken by the Institute of Applied
Economics and Social Research on the interaction of Australian public expenditure and social policy in the 1970s. The work provides an opportunity to make an
informed comparison of the effectiveness of the social policies of the reformist
Whitlam Labor government and the conservative Liberal/Country Party government of Malcolm Fraser. It is not a work for light reading but the issues treated
are important ones. Volume 1: *The Whitlam years, 1972-75*; volume 2: *The first
Fraser years, 1976-78.*

675 **Health and Australian society.**
Basil S. Hetzel. Melbourne: Penguin Books, 1980. 3rd ed.

This survey dismisses the myth of the healthy, tanned Australian. By generally
accepted health standards Australians are among the least healthy groups of
people living in developed societies. In this revised edition, the new developments
in health promotion, the finance of health care, the planning of medical manpower
and services are examined.

676 **Community health in Australia.**
Edited by Rex Walpole. Melbourne: Penguin Books, 1979.
226p.

While this collection of essays is mainly directed at practitioners in the field of
community health which emphasizes prevention and rehabilitation, there is much
material on the physical and mental condition of the Australian population. On
closer examination, their health problems stem as much from their bad habits
as from disease. The book also informs on how preventive medicine is practised in
Australia.

677 **Rum regulation and riches.**
Ron Hicks. Sydney: Kelly, 1981. 220p. bibliog.

A history of the Australian health care system. Most of the book is devoted to the
1970s when the policies of succeeding governments caused the system to swing
from compulsory universal health insurance to private insurance. With the
re-election of a Labor government in March 1983, medical insurance seems
destined to swing back again to the universal scheme of the early 1970s.

678 **Psychology in Australia: achievements and prospects.**
Edited by Mary Nixon, Ronald Taft. Sydney: Pergamon, 1977.
318p.

Provides a general picture of the practice of psychology in Australia. It is a factual
record of the past and present (to 1975) and is a guide to present needs and
future possibilities.

679 **Tears often shed: child health and welfare in Australia from 1788.**
Bryan Gandevia. Sydney: Pergamon, 1978. 151p. bibliog.

An introductory history of the health of Australian children from the first settlement of the country to the present.

680 **Drugs: drinking and recreational drug use in Australia.**
F. A. Whitlock. Sydney: Cassell, 1980. 211p.

A radical assessment of drug use and abuse in Australia. The author argues that the effects of legal drugs particularly alcohol and tobacco have far more serious consequences for health and social welfare than all the illegal drugs. According to Professor Whitlock the most successful drug pushers are the hotel proprietors, tobacconists, chemists, doctors, corner-store owners and grocers. He concludes that the lawmakers under the influence of the media have aggravated the drug problem in Australia.

681 **The intruders: refugee doctors in Australia.**
Egon F. Kunz. Canberra: Australian National University Press, 1975. 139p.

Documents the case of refugee doctors who arrived in Australia after the Second World War and found themselves denied the opportunity to practice by both their exclusive local colleagues through the Australian Medical Association and the indifference of the state and commonwealth governments.

682 **The flying doctor story, 1928-78.**
Michael Page. Adelaide: Rigby, 1977. 328p. bibliog.

The Royal Flying Doctor Service is a national institution which provides medical care for people living in the vast and isolated inland regions of Australia. The system originated with the Reverend Dr. John Flynn through the Australian Inland Mission of the Presbyterian Church. The doctors travel by aeroplane from centralized bases and keep in touch with their patients by radio. The book celebrates the 50th anniversary of the service with a detailed history. There are many unique black-and-white photographs.

683 **Australian colonial medicine.**
Jennifer Hagger. Adelaide: Rigby, 1979. 219p. bibliog.

A popular account of illnesses and their treatment in the primitive conditions of colonial Australia. The activities of doctors and nurses, old wives' tales, home remedies, bush treatments and some Aboriginal medicine are included in the entertaining story.

684 **Kill or cure? Lotions, potions, characters and quacks of early Australia.**
Peter J. Phillips. Adelaide: Rigby, 1978. 157p.

A lively account of the charlatans, eccentrics and criminals who took advantage of the shortage of qualified doctors. The gullibility of an uneducated public and Australia's remoteness from the rest of the world, in the second half of the 19th century. An entertaining book which explores an intriguing aspect of Australia's social history in an unpretentious manner.

685 **Goldrush doctors at Ballarat.**
Keith Macrae Bowden. Melbourne: Magenta, 1977. 125p.
bibliog.

This book, a companion volume to the earlier *Doctors and diggers on the Mount Alexander goldfields* (Maryborough, Australia: Bowden, 1974), traces the fortunes of a number of medical practitioners on the Ballarat goldfields between the years 1850 and 1860. Both volumes present a fascinating picture of health and sanitary conditions on the diggings. In short, the conditions were primitive, hospitals at first non-existent and epidemics of fever and dysentery common.

Education

686 **A history of Australian education.**
Alan Barcan. Melbourne: Oxford University Press, 1980. 415p.
The first comprehensive up-to-date history of education in Australia.

687 **Society, schools and progress in Australia.**
P. H. Partridge. Sydney: Pergamon, 1973. rev. ed. 246p.
Although some of the detailed information is outdated, this book is still a useful overview of the social history of Australian education.

688 **Schools for the people: an introduction to the history of state education in Australia.**
B. K. Hyams, B. Bessant. Melbourne: Longman, 1972. 195p. bibliog.
A very useful, short introduction to the main sweeps of educational development in Australia. The book is especially good on the 19th century or the colonial period.

689 **Australian education, 1788-1900: church, state and public education in colonial Australia.**
A. G. Austin. Melbourne: Pitman, 1972. 3rd ed. 300p. bibliog.
The author traces the evolution of a system of universal, public, elementary education in Australia. An important component of the story is an analysis of church-state relations as they affected education.

690 **Pioneers of Australian education. Volume 3: Studies of the development of education in Australia, 1900-50.**
Edited by C. Turney. Sydney: Sydney University Press, 1983. 355p. bibliog.
An examination by various authors of the life and work of fifteen educators in the Australian states during the first half of the 20th century. The book focuses on educational theory and practice with passing attention to legislative and administrative changes.

691   **Federal aid to Australian schools.**
Don Smart. Brisbane: University of Queensland Press, 1978.
152p.

Constitutionally each state in Australia is responsible for its own educational
system. Since federation the federal government has become increasingly involved
in the state-run system. In 1963 it culminated with the introduction of federal
aid. This book puts the growing role of the federal government into historical
perspective, and gives a detailed account of the major initiatives taken by the
commonwealth through specially funded school programmes.

692   **Federal intervention in Australian education.**
Edited by Grant Harman, Don Smart. Melbourne: Georgian
House, 1982. 197p. bibliog.

In this collection of readings federal government involvement in education is
placed in a political and constitutional perspective. Another book on the subject
is *The Commonwealth government and education, 1964-1976; political initiatives
and development*, edited by I. K. F. Birch and D. Smart (Melbourne: Drummond,
1977).

693   **Making the difference: schools, families and social divisions.**
R. W. Connell (and others). Sydney: Allen & Unwin, 1982.
228p. bibliog.

An account of secondary school life in Australia at the present, based on 424
interviews with students, teachers and families in Sydney and Adelaide. According
to the book educational inequality is increasing. On the evidence of the interviews
all the perennial problems like class distinction, sexism and irrelevant curricula
still exist and there are new problems as well: class divisions within families, over-
emphasis on qualifications, teenage consumerism, poverty and many others. The
interesting subject matter and lively style of writing make this book compulsory
reading for anyone with an interest of the present condition of Australian schooling and society.

694   **Marking time: alternatives in Australian schooling.**
Michael Middleton. Sydney: Methuen, 1982. 199p.

An outline of the historical background to Australian education. The argument
that the highly centralized contemporary system has become isolated from the
community it serves, is followed by a model for rebuilding. Included are case
histories of students and alternative schools and a directory of alternative schools
in Australia.

695   **School ties: private schooling in Australia.**
Geoffrey Maslen. Sydney: Methuen, 1982. 280p.

In Australia private schools co-exist with the much larger government school
system. It is a matter of some controversy that the private schools receive government financial support. At the present, private schools are booming; the classrooms are full and the waiting lists are growing. In this well-written study the
author surveys the spectrum of private education and comes up with some controversial yet sympathetic conclusions.

Education

696   **Half a million children: studies of non-governmental education in Australia.**
Edited by John Cleverley. Melbourne: Longman Cheshire, 1978. 282p.

This book gives a partly historical, partly contemporary overview of the diverse institutions that make up the Australian non-government school system. It looks in some detail at Anglican, Catholic and non-Anglican Protestant schools, and at Seventh-day Adventist, Lutheran and Jewish education. It concludes with a section on non-denominational and alternative schools.

697   **Opening up schools: school and community in Australia.**
David Pettit. Melbourne: Penguin Books, 1980. 218p.

The author shows by means of case-studies how some Australian schools have been enriched and stimulated by community involvement, and how through participation parents, students and teachers have co-operated to formulate policy and to negotiate curriculum.

698   **Australian universities: a descriptive sketch.**
David S. Macmillan. Sydney: Sydney University Press for Australian Vice-Chancellors' Committee, 1968. 98p. bibliog.

Although somewhat dated, this is still the only book to collectively present facts on all Australian universities operating in the mid-1960s. Two books may be read as examples of the development of individual universities in the Australian system of higher education. They are: *A centenary history of the University of Melbourne* by Geoffrey Blainey (Melbourne: Melbourne University Press, 1957); and *The University of Adelaide, 1874-1974* by W. G. K. Duncan and Roger Ashley Leonard (Adelaide: Rigby, 1973).

699   **Academia becalmed: Australian tertiary education in the aftermath of expansion.**
Edited by G. S. Harman (and others). Canberra: Australian National University Press, 1980. 260p.

At the beginning of the 1980s tertiary education is becalmed. After a long period of rapid growth it has now entered a state of decline. The 'steady state' phenomenon has arrived. The contributors to the book deal with the crisis facing Australian education and prognosticate the future.

700   **Equal but cheaper: the development of Australian colleges of advanced education.**
E. V. Treyvaud, John McLaren. Melbourne: Melbourne University Press, 1976. 103p. (The Second Century in Australian Education, 15).

To absorb the steadily increasing demand for higher education in the 1960s there arose a three-tier system of colleges of advanced education, teachers' colleges and universities. The new elements were the advanced colleges, supposed to cater for technicians required by an increasingly technological society. The authors dispel some of the myths about the functioning of these colleges, show how they are still determined by the muddled political decisions which brought them into being and suggest that their future depends on a rethinking of the nature of vocationalism in contemporary Australian society.

701   **The future of higher education in Australia.**
Edited by T. Hore, Russell D. Linke, Leo H. T. West. Melbourne: Macmillan, 1978. 291p.

This book consists of twenty-three original contributions on higher education in Australia. The current unfavourable economic climate, declining birth rate, changing student composition, the nature of both curriculum and assessment in secondary schools are examined and future prospects and trends for the next two decades discussed.

702   **The TAFE papers.**
Edited by Don McKenzie, Charles Wilkins. Melbourne: Macmillan, 1979. 135p.

This small volume brings together a number of statements by a variety of people who are directly or indirectly involved in the emergence of technical and further education as an identifiable sector of post-secondary education in Australia.

703   **The great tradition: a history of adult education in Australia.**
Derek Whitelock. Brisbane: University of Queensland Press, 1974. 327p.

The author's definition of 'the great tradition' is the liberal non-vocational attitude to adult learning. Adult Australians have notoriously shied away from this type of education and have preferred technical training and the acquisition of new practical skills. Thus the book is about a great failure rather than a great tradition, but if this is understood it is still interesting reading because of what it reveals about the Australian character.

704   **Australian teachers: from colonial schoolmasters to militant professionals.**
Edited by A. D. Spaull. Melbourne: Macmillan, 1977. 308p.

To overcome the paucity of information on Australian teachers, the editor has culled the material making up the book from academic journals, books and theses. The essays examine teachers' changing status, training, occupational status and their collective voluntary organizations over the last hundred years.

705   **Sociology of education: Australian and New Zealand studies.**
Edited by R. K. Browne, L. E. Foster. Melbourne: Macmillan, 1983. 3rd ed. 450p.

A collection of sociological studies on education in Australia.

Crime and Social Deviance

706 **The Australian criminal justice system.**
Duncan Chappell, Paul Wilson. Sydney: Butterworth, 1977. 2nd
ed. 528p.

The second edition of this comprehensive collection of readings on Australian
criminology differs from the first edition (1972) in context, layout and
quality of articles – very few of these articles appeared in the earlier edition.
Therefore the earlier edition is still relevant and should be read in conjunction
with the new volume.

707 **Social deviance in Australia.**
Edited by Anne R. Edwards, Paul R. Wilson. Melbourne:
Cheshire, 1975. 294p.

A collection of readings on the disapproved forms of deviance from approved
social behaviour in Australia. They include prostitution, incest, chronic drunken-
ness, homosexuality, suicide, dropping out from tertiary education, physical
illness and involvement in traffic accidents. The omissions are crime and
delinquency, but information on these is readily available elsewhere.

708 **Two faces of deviance: crimes of the powerless and the powerful.**
Edited by Paul R. Wilson, John Braithwaite. Brisbane:
University of Queensland Press, 1978. 309p.

This book questions conventional beliefs about crime and criminals. The central
theme is that it is not the traditional law-breakers, the thieves, prostitutes and
muggers who are the most flagrant rule breakers in Australian society, but the rule
makers themselves – the politicians, bureaucrats, business and professional men –
who, because of their privileged and powerful positions, are virtually immune
from prosecution. This volume is the first collection of Australian evidence in
support of this proposition. It is a radical critique of Australian society.

709 **Delinquency in Australia: a critical appraisal.**
Edited by Paul R. Wilson. Brisbane: University of Queensland
Press, 1977. 269p.

A collection of readings by a wide range of specialists in this field, which survey
the social problem of juvenile delinquency in Australia.

178

710 **Women and crime.**
Edited by Satyanshee K. Mukherjee, Jocelynne A. Scutt.
Sydney: Australian Institute of Criminology, with Allen &
Unwin, 1981. 200p.

A serious contribution to the subject of female crime in Australia, which refutes
with cold, hard statistics the growing popular belief that, due to the changing
status of women through the efforts of the feminist movement, the female crime
rate has been rising. The book provides evidence that there has been no such
increase since the turn of the century, although at different periods there have
been alternate increases and decreases.

711 **Drug traffic: narcotics and organized crime in Australia.**
Alfred W. McCoy. Sydney: Harper & Row, 1980. 455p. bibliog.

A wide-ranging study of the corrupting influence of crime and criminals on all
levels of Australian society. The author concentrates on the drug problem and
using historical evidence shows that Australians' addictive drug problems date
back at least a hundred years. In the 1970s organized heroin traffic had become
big business while criminal influence extended into the highest police and political
circles.

712 **Crimes that shocked Australia.**
Alan Sharpe. Sydney: Currawong, 1982. 328p. bibliog.

An account for popular consumption of 50 crimes committed throughout Australia's history. Illustrations accompany the text.

713 **The prison struggle: changing Australia's penal system.**
George Zdenkowski, David Brown. Melbourne: Penguin Books,
1982. 440p.

A radical critique of Australian prison reform since 1970, a period which has
witnessed systematic brutality and violation of human rights in prisons.

714 **Wilful obstruction: the frustration of prison reform.**
Tony Vinson. Sydney: Methuen, 1982. 232p.

A torrid, personal account of the author's term as chairman of the New South
Wales Corrective Services Commission from 1979 to 1981. The commission,
seen as a radical innovation at the time, was set up to implement the recommendations of the Nagle Royal Commission into New South Wales prisons. How
Vinson's and the commission's work was constantly obstructed by the prison
officers, and a number of riots and other disturbances by prisoners, is the
theme of this thought-provoking book.

715 **The Kelly outbreak, 1878-1880: the geographical dimension of social banditry.**
John McQuilton. Melbourne: Melbourne University Press, 1979. 250p. bibliog.

Ned Kelly is the most notorious of the bush rangers and somewhat of a folk hero. There has been endless scholarly debate whether he was a 'thieving murderous thug' or the victim of an unjust social system driven to lawlessness. McQuilton is the first writer to set the story in its proper political, economical and geographic perspective. He sets out to discover why the Kelly gang turned into bandits and why their contemporaries declined to turn them over to the police, despite the lucrative reward offered. There is an exhaustive bibliography of Kellyana, and illustrations and maps accompany the text.

716 **The bushrangers.**
Wiliam Joy, Tom Prior. London: Muller, 1971. 208p.

A popular account of the exploits of the bushrangers. Bushranging is a term evolved in Australia to denote the robbery of individuals or institutions by a person or gang who used the 'bush', or the wild scrub country, as the base for their operations. Their crimes included stock-stealing, housebreaking, arson and murder. They lasted from the early days of settlement to the late 19th century. Some of the bushrangers, like Ned Kelly, became folk figures. The book is illustrated.

Sport and Recreation

General

717 **Sport in history: the making of modern sporting history.**
Edited by Richard Cashman, Michael McKernan. Brisbane:
University of Queensland Press, 1979. 368p. bibliog.

Nine of the seventeen essays in this collection, which originated in a scholarly
gathering in 1977, relate to Australian themes. Although of uneven standard, the
essays are well worth reading as there has been surprisingly little serious study of
Australian sports history or sociology. There is of course a large body of literature
on various sports which is merely chronological and anecdotal. The papers from
the second sports history conference held in 1979 have also been published as
Sport: money, morality and the media, edited by R. Cashman and M. McKernan
(Sydney: New South Wales University Press, 1982).

718 **The proud Australians: more than a century of sport.**
Bruce Howard. Adelaide: Rigby, 1978. 208p.

The Australian passion for sport and recreation is portrayed by hundreds of illustrations ranging from colonial days to the present.

719 **Sunny memories: Australians at the seaside.**
Lana Wells. Melbourne: Greenhouse, 1982. 184p.

Most Australians reside on or near the coast with its overabundance of superb
beaches. They also revel in a warm climate enabling them to enjoy the hedonistic
pleasures of the seaside for more than six months of the year. This large book
presents an account of Australians' preoccupations with the seaside in both words
and pictures.

720 **Their chastity was not too rigid: leisure times in early Australia.**
J. W. C. Cumes. Melbourne: Longman Cheshire Reed, 1979.
378p.

The first book to be entirely devoted to the leisure activities of the early settlers
from 1788 to the gold rush days in the 1850s.

Sport and Recreation. General

721 Australia at the Olympics.
Andrew Dettre. Sydney: Hamlyn, 1980. 109p.

Australia is one of the three nations which has participated in each of the modern games since they commenced in 1896, the others are Greece and Great Britain. Australian sportsmen and women have a very good record of achievement having won 186 medals, 64 of them gold up to and including the 1980 Moscow Games. This book produced just before those games provides a concise record of performances at all modern Olympics including those of the Australians.

722 The champions.
R. S. Whitington. Melbourne: Macmillan, 1976. 135p.

Twenty-four Australian sportsmen and women were selected by the author as the most outstanding performers in their particular discipline. He discusses their achievements and performances in a lively manner, as he knew many of them well and watched them perform in his capacity as both sportsman and sports writer.

723 The encyclopaedia of Australian sports.
Malcolm Andrews. Sydney: Golden Press, 1979. 248p.

An alphabetical listing of nearly 700 entries of past and present sporting personalities, race horses, greyhounds, clubs, events and specific sports. It is a mine of information for anyone with an interest in the Australian sports scene. Many portraits and action photographs illustrate the text. A similar book which can be used in conjunction with Andrews's is *Encyclopaedia of Australian sport,* by Jim Shepherd (Adelaide: Rigby, 1980).

724 Ampol Australian sporting records.
Edited by John Blanch. Melbourne: Budget Books, 1981. 6th ed. 552p.

A popular large-format reference book crammed with facts, pictures and statistics of more than eighty sports in which Australians compete.

725 Sport in Australia: selected readings in physical activity.
T. D. Jaques, G. R. Pavia. Sydney: McGraw-Hill, 1976. 171p. bibliog.

A collection of essays of varying standard on the sociology of Australian sport — a much neglected subject in a sport-obsessed society.

726 The best of the last ten years in Australian sport.
Edited by David Lord. Adelaide: Frost, 1978. 224p.

The best performers and their achievements in thirty different sports are highlighted in articles written by twenty-six Australian sports journalists.

727   Outdoor recreation – Australian perspectives.
Edited by David Mercer. Melbourne: Sorrett, 1981. 171p.

The introduction says: 'This book of original essays is intended to be read along with its earlier companion volume *Leisure and recreation in Australia* (Melbourne: Sorrett, 1977). It presents a selection of recent writings, ideas and policy discussions in the still relatively young field of Australian outdoor recreation research.'

728   Australian coins, notes & medals.
Bill Myatt, Tom Hanley. Sydney: Horwitz Grahame Books, 1982. rev. ed. 262p. bibliog.

A definitive book about Australian numismatics suitable for beginners and advanced collectors.

Individual sports and pastimes

729   First Tuesday in November: the story of the Melbourne Cup.
D. L. Bernstein. Melbourne: Heinemann, 1969. 327p. bibliog.

Horse racing and betting are popular Australian pastimes and the Melbourne Cup run on the first Tuesday in November is the premier race of the year. On this day Melbourne has a public holiday and all of Australia comes to a standstill for a fateful few minutes while the race is on. People who do not bet throughout the year will have a 'flutter' on the cup. The book is a richly illustrated story of the running of the race and the social life associated with it, since the running of the first Cup race in 1861. A chronological account of each Cup race up to and including 1981 is available in Bill Ahrens's *A century of winners: the saga of 121 Melbourne Cups* (Brisbane, Australia: Boolarong, 1982).

730   The surfing life.
Midget Farrelly as told to Craig McGregor. New York: Arco, 1967. 192p.

'You go into oblivion. Suddenly all your life is there in this long, long stretched-out wave, everything that has been on your mind has become material . . . Nothing matters any longer but you and the board and the wave and this instant of time . . . . . . ' The extract from the first chapter demonstrates former world surfboard riding champion Farrelly's absorption in his sport. The rest of the book includes instructions on how to ride a board, as well as the hazards of the sport, and the author's surfing experiences both in Australia and overseas.

731 **Surfing subcultures of Australia & New Zealand.**
Kent Pearson. Brisbane: University of Queensland Press, 1979.
213p. bibliog.

A sociological examination of the lifestyle of the subculture of 'surfies'. The author contrasts these individualistic board riders with their counterparts – the members of surf life-saving clubs. He finds that each group has its own set of values and enjoys life in the wild blue water for different reasons. In the course of the book the reader learns about the history of the sport and gains an insight into the Australian mentality, as the popular media have imprinted the 'surfie' stereotype on Australians at large.

732 **Australian surfing and surf life saving.**
Jack Wilson. Adelaide: Rigby, 1979. 111p.

Because most Australians live within easy reach of the coast, they surf in greater numbers, proportionately, than any nation on earth. They have built a unique life-saving system and a great variety of beach and surf contests in which the various life-saving clubs compete. This volume provides in anecdotal style, the history of board and body surfing, and of surf life saving. There is also information on notable surfing personalities, resuscitation methods, and surfing hazards including dangerous marine creatures.

733 **Yachting in Australia: yesterday, today, tomorrow.**
Lou d'Alpuget. Melbourne: Hutchinson, 1980. 330p.

This definitive book on the subject combines an exhaustive up-to-date history of sailing in all states with a detailed record of Australian participation in international competition. The well-illustrated volume provides thorough, accurate and entertaining reading.

734 **Australians on the road.**
Pedr Davis. Adelaide: Rigby, 1979. 232p.

In a land of huge distances and relatively affluent inhabitants the motor car from its earliest days was regarded as an indispensable means of individual transport. Motoring writer, Pedr Davis, covers all aspects of Australia's motoring history. He includes stories of pioneers, adventurers who criss-crossed the continent, daredevil drivers and optimistic manufacturers. The text is complemented with hundreds of photographs. It is a book for anyone who is interested in cars.

735 **Australia's greatest motor race – the complete history.**
Bill Tuckey, Ray Berghouse. Sydney: Lansdowne, 1981. 240p.

The book traces the history of this annual touring car endurance race from its beginnings as the Armstrong 500 at Phillip Island, Victoria in 1960 through to the 1980 Hardie Ferodo, with an appropriately titled chapter on each annual event. The 1,000 kilometre race has captured the imagination of the Australian public. In addition to the thousands who make the annual pilgrimage to the mountain, there are millions watching the spectacle on television. In recent years it has been transmitted also to overseas viewers, because of international participation in the race. The first of an intended series of annuals was published by the same team to cover the 1981 race *James Hardie 1000, 1981/82: Australia's greatest motor race* (Sydney: Lansdowne, 1981).

736 **An illustrated history of Australian tennis.**
R. S. Whitington. Melbourne: Macmillan, 1975. 126p.

Australians have excelled at many sports, but perhaps their greatest achievements on an international scale have been in tennis. At times they have completely dominated Wimbledon and the Davis Cup. The author presents a chronicle of Australian tennis performances in a lively manner as, over forty years, he has watched the finest tennis players and witnessed many of the best tennis matches in his capacity as sports journalist.

737 **Great players of Australian tennis.**
Paul Metzler. Sydney: Harper & Row, 1979. 202p.

A well-set-out book, full of sepia photographs, which presents a concise history of the game in Australia.

738 **An illustrated history of Australian cricket.**
R. S. Whitington. Melbourne: Currey O'Neil, 1982. rev. and re-illustrated ed. 176p.

It was only natural that cricket, the peculiarly English game, should be taken up by the Australian colonists. This handsomely produced book provides a pictorial record of the game from its beginnings in 1803 to the present. The text focuses on the game itself with occasional hints at the social significance of cricket. Treatment of this important aspect of Australian cricket still awaits its historian.

739 **The great Australian book of cricket stories.**
Edited by Ken Piesse. Melbourne: Currey O'Neil, 1982. 403p. bibliog.

A collection of tales, jokes and snippets from various sources about Australian cricket. This is a book for browsing by the cricket enthusiast.

740 **The wildest tests.**
Ray Robinson. Sydney: Cassell, 1979. rev. ed. 221p.

An expanded version of the 1972 edition, the book looks at eighteen international cricket matches which have been halted by riots and disturbances.

741 **The Datsun book of Australian test cricket, 1877-1981.**
R. S. Whitington. Melbourne: Five Mile Press, 1981. 413p.

A detailed record of every international cricket match or test played in Australia.

742 **Bodyline umpire.**
R. S. Whitington, George Hele. Adelaide: Rigby, 1974. 225p.

Hele was umpire at the notorious 'bodyline' series of test matches played between England and Australia during 1932-33. The book resurrects the bitter controversy of those days which nearly resulted in the end of Anglo-Australian cricket.

Sport and Recreation. Individual sports and pastimes

743 **The game they play in heaven: Australian rugby from the inside.**
Steve Finane. Sydney: McGraw-Hill, 1979. 168p.

An 'insider's' story by an Australian international representative, which sheds some light on how Australians play the game of rugby.

744 **Australian football.**
Sydney: Murray Books, 1979. (Murray's Sports series). 143p.

This short book introduces the layman to Australian Rules football, the origin of the sport and its development. It proffers advice on good play and the rules as well as statistics of the code in Victoria, South Australia and Western Australia.

745 **How to play football Australian style.**
Edited by Jim Main. Melbourne: Currey O'Neil, 1981. 121p.

A popular book for fans and players with advice from seventeen 'greats' on play in all positions, and on specific skills. Rules of the game and numerous black-and-white action shots are included.

746 **The book of VFL finals.**
Foreword by Tom Hafey, compiled by Graeme Atkinson.
Melbourne: Five Mile Press, 1981. rev. ed.

A factual record of the Victorian Football League's finals series dating back to 1847. There is information on competing teams, attendance figures, goal-kickers, best players with descriptions of the major matches in each series plus a comprehensive appendix of statistics. It is illustrated with many action photographs.

747 **Up where Cazaly? The great Australian game.**
Leonie Sandercock, Ian Turner. London: Granada, 1981. 272p.
bibliog.

Australian Rules football is a fast, spectacular game between teams of eighteen players. Invented locally it is the dominant football code in four of the six Australian states. This book unlike most Australian sports writing is not merely an anecdotal and statistical account of the play itself. The authors attempt to trace the origins and development of the code giving consideration to the economic and social influences on it. Finally they speculate on the game's present development, give reasons for that development and consider its ultimate consequences. The focus is on Melbourne, where the game attracts crowds of up to 3 million people annually.

748 **Australian golf: the first 100 years.**
Terry Smith. Sydney: Lester-Townsend, 1982. 203p.

A large-format, richly illustrated history of golf and golfers in Australia.

749 **Lords of the ring.**
Peter Corris. Sydney: Cassell, 1980. 200p. bibliog.

A history of boxing in Australia – this book is not a mere recitation of fights and fighters, but tries to explain why, and with whom, professional fist fighting was popular in Australia for almost two hundred years, and why it lost popularity; who controlled boxing and how. Photographs support the text.

750 **Australian chess – into the eighties.**
Edited by Ian Rogers, illustrated by Ron Tandberg, photographs by Haydn Barber. Melbourne: Sun Books, 1981. 168p.

This book is essentially about the Australian championship in Adelaide in January 1980, which was won by the author. As it contains 50 extensively annotated games with notes by 12 of Australia's leading chess players, it is a good indication of the standard of Australian chess. Several players have been recognized as International masters, including the author, but as yet there are no Grandmasters, although Robert Jamieson achieved his first norm at the 1982 Chess Olympiad in Lucerne.

751 **Freshwater fishing in Australia.**
Gordon Wood. Sydney: Reed, 1982. 124p.

When not affected by drought, Australia for a dry continent, offers remarkably good inland fishing. This is a guide to how, where and what to fish. It provides up-to-date information on both the established and the newly emerging fishing grounds, the species of fish, the times to fish and the methods most likely to succeed.

752 **Trout fishing in Australia.**
Dan Gilmour. Adelaide: Rigby, 1977. 165p.

The author draws on a vast experience to describe where trout are to be found in Australia, how they behave and how they may be caught. Much of this information is presented through amusing accounts of trout fishing exploits by Gilmour himself. A very readable and fascinating fishing and outdoors book.

753 **The sandgropers' trail: an angling safari from Perth to the Kimberley.**
Philip Bodeker. Sydney: Reed, 1971. 236p.

The author took his family on a fishing trip lasting six months up and down the Western Australian coast. The book describing their experiences, is not merely another fishing tale, but introduces the reader to the wild and beautiful scenery of the north-west, its bird and animal life and the colourful characters whom the family met. Photographs illustrate the story.

Food and Drink

754 **One continuous picnic: a history of eating in Australia.**
Michael Symons. Adelaide: Duck Press, 1982. 278p. bibliog.

An original book which brings together the story of Australia's agriculture, food business, cooking and restaurants. Anyone familiar with Australian cuisine will agree with the author's opinion that 'Traditionally the country has treated food as merely something to fill up on and people have largely ignored quality, freshness and a real knowledge of food. We have always had plenty of food so we haven't starved but we don't know where it really comes from or how to cook it.'

755 **The tradition of Australian cooking.**
Anne Gollan. Canberra: Australian National University Press, 1978. 211p. bibliog.

This is not just a recipe book although it contains over 400 recipes, hints and remedies, as well as hundreds of illustrations of early household gadgets. It is in fact an historical account of the part food and cooking has played in Australian society.

756 **A taste of Australia in food and pictures.**
Peter Taylor. Sydney: Pan Books, 1980. 127p.

An attempt to define Australian regional culinary style as the adaptation of English cooking. Similar popular books, which also include recipes, are *A taste of the past: early Australian cooking*, by Joyce Allen and Valerie McKenzie (Sydney: Reed, 1977); and *Australian colonial cookery*, by Penelope Vigar (Adelaide: Rigby, 1977).

757 **Beer, glorious beer.**
Cyril Pearl. Melbourne: Nelson, 1969. 173p.

Australian annual per capita beer consumption is one of the highest in the world. This is a light-hearted book about Australian beer-drinking habits, drinking places and folklore associated with the brew.

758   **Australian complete book of wine.**
Compiled by Len Evans.   Sydney: Summit Books, 1976. rev. ed.
500p.

Although not well-known overseas Australian wines compare favourably with the
international product. This large illustrated book presents an encyclopaedic
survey of the country's wine-making industry and includes 200 pages of detailed
tasting notes. South Australia, where wine-making was pioneered by German
settlers, produces about 66 per cent of Australia's wine, including the highest
quality examples. The industry in that state is surveyed in *Wines and wineries of
South Australia*, by Mike Potter (Adelaide: Rigby, 1978). Another classic area is
the Hunter Valley in New South Wales. It is surveyed in *The wines and history of
the Hunter Valley*, by James Halliday and Ray Jarratt (Sydney: McGraw-Hill,
1979).

759   **Classic wines of Australia.**
Max Lake.   Brisbane: Jacaranda, 1966. 134p.

A book intended for the lover of Australian wine, by a well-known personality
and educated palate, Dr. Max Lake, who makes his own highly regarded wine at
Lake's Folly in the Hunter Valley region of New South Wales.

Art

760 **Artists and galleries of Australia and New Zealand.**
Max Germaine. Sydney: Lansdowne Editions, 1979. 646p.

'A comprehensive biographical dictionary and who's who of living Australian and New Zealand painters, sculptors, printmakers, art personalities, galleries, institutions, bodies and awards in the field of visual arts specially written for use by students, galleries, collectors, educational establishments, libraries, valuers, art dealers and insurers.' This reference work is invaluable to anyone interested in the Australian art scene.

761 **Australian National Gallery: an introduction.**
Edited by James Mollison, Laura Murray. Canberra: Australian National Gallery, 1982. 290p.

Published to mark the opening of the new gallery in Canberra, the national capital, in October 1982. In a lavishly illustrated survey the authors outline the history of the gallery project from federation in 1901, the siting and design of the building on the shores of Lake Burley Griffin, the nature of the collections and the patterns of coherence the gallery is attempting to establish.

762 **European vision and the South Pacific, 1768-1850: a study in the history of art and ideas.**
Bernard Smith. London: Oxford University Press, 1960. 287p. 171 plates. bibliog.

This book is concerned with the European interpretation of the Pacific. It considers the work of artists attached to scientific voyages in the 17th and 18th centuries. Because their work was required to be scientifically exact in depicting the scenery, native life, flora and fauna and geology, the artists were impelled to abandon the more generalized, subjective style of European art. The result was a new range of styles and subject matter. Although beginning with voyages prior to the discovery of the east coast of Australia, the greater part of the book is concerned with the beginnings of Australian art until 1850.

763   **The art of Australia.**
Robert Hughes.   Melbourne: Penguin Books, 1970. rev. ed.
331p.

An appraisal of Australian painting from the beginnings of settlement to 1964.
The author has a highly individualistic approach, which can stimulate as well as
exasperate the reader. Perhaps it is best read in conjunction with B. Smith's
Australian painting (see below).

764   **Australian painting, 1788-1970.**
Bernard Smith.   Melbourne: Oxford University Press, 1971.
2nd ed. 483p.

This is the second edition of a book which has become a basic text on Australian
painting. It has been written not for the specialist, but for those seeking a useful
and comprehensive introduction to the subject and should be valuable to artists,
teachers, scholars and the general reader. The text is accompanied by 440 illustrations.

765   **Place, taste and tradition: a study of Australian art since 1788.**
Bernard Smith.   Melbourne: Oxford University Press, 1979.
2nd rev. ed. 304p. bibliog.

This pioneering work has been out of print since 1945. The author evaluates the
development of Australian art within its social, political and cultural context,
at the same time analysing the overseas influences on local art and artists. It is
the first book since William Moore's *The story of Australian art* (Sydney: Angus
& Robertson, 1934), to treat Australian art comprehensively. The book's influence
was and still is enormous. It remains essential reading on the subject.

766   **Documents on art and taste in Australia: the colonial period,
1770-1914.**
Edited by Bernard Smith.   Melbourne: Oxford University Press,
1975. 299p. bibliog.

An annotated critical anthology of writings by, or about, artists who lived and
worked in Australia between 1770 and 1914. Collectively they provide an illuminating insight into the development of Australian art.

767   **The development of Australian sculpture, 1788-1975.**
Graeme Sturgeon.   London: Thames & Hudson, 1978. 256p.

This is the first comprehensive and up-to-date history of Australian sculpture and
sculptors. The scholarly yet readable text is accompanied by many illustrations.

768 Australian sculptors.
Ken Scarlett. Melbourne: Nelson, 1980. 730p.

This massive reference book contains biographical information on some 450 Australian sculptors. It is not a history and can be seen as complementary to G. Sturgeon's *Development of Australian sculpture* (see above). In addition to personal details the author presents full information on awards, prizes, commissions and public collections in which sculptors are represented.

769 Rebels and precursors: the revolutionary years of Australian art.
Richard Haese. Melbourne: Allen Lane, 1981. 324p.

An important study of the modernist rebellion in Australian painting in the 1940s. The book is a perceptive, painstaking and absorbing analysis of the period 1938-47, covering both the life of art and the lives of the artists, both the social context and private struggle. The author even unfolds and explains the conflicting ideologies of the period. Reproductions of all the important paintings of the period as well as portraits of the other personalities involved in the struggle against the artistic establishment are included.

770 The years of hope: Australian art and criticism, 1959-1968.
Gary Catalono. Melbourne: Oxford University Press, 1981. 215p.

There is not an overabundance of histories of Australian art. This study by a young critic is therefore interesting for its observations and judgements on an interesting period in contemporary Australian art. The book is attractively presented and well illustrated.

771 Australian watercolour painters, 1780-1980: including an alphabetical listing of over 1200 painters.
Jean Campbell. Adelaide: Rigby, 1983. 351p. bibliog.

A detailed, critical examination of the work of all major exponents of watercolour in Australia over the last 200 years. It is an essential record of a much neglected subject.

772 The black swan of tresspass: the emergence of modernist painting in Australia to 1944.
Humphrey McQueen. Sydney: Alternative Publishing Cooperative, 1979. 178p. bibliog.

An opinionated, stimulating and idea-provoking work on Australian art by this well-known author of the intellectual Left.

773 **Australian women artists, 1840-1940.**
Janine Burke. Melbourne: Greenhouse Publications, 1980.
188p.

The first published history of Australian women artists features the lives and art of 44 women who worked and exhibited in Australia and Europe from the mid-19th to the mid-20th century. Painters, watercolourists, pastellists, print-makers and book illustrators are included and a large selection of their works illustrates the text.

774 **Artists of the Australian gold rush.**
Alan McCulloch. Melbourne: Lansdowne, 1977. 214p. bibliog.

This book introduces readers to 54 artists who were active during the gold rush decade of the 1850s and many fine reproductions of their work, which ranged from drawings for the popular market to oil paintings.

775 **The golden age of Australian painting: impressionism and the Heidelberg School.**
Alan McCulloch. Melbourne: Lansdowne, 1977. 2nd ed. 196p.
bibliog.

The Heidelberg School was the first art movement to consciously illustrate national life, consequently Australians have always had great affection for this group of Victorian artists. The book contains 110 illustrations of paintings in colour and 38 in monochrome accompanied by an appreciative and readable text.

776 **The Australian landscape and its artists.**
Elwyn Lynn. Sydney: Bay Books, 1977. 159p.

A selection of a hundred paintings spanning 143 years devoted to the Australian landscape. An individual text is given to each of the fifty artists included and there is a short general introduction.

777 **Masterpieces of Australian painting.**
James Gleeson. Melbourne: Lansdowne, 1969. 222p.
(Australian Art Library).

An individual selection of reproductions of Australian paintings. The selection attempts to include an example of the work of each artist now recognized as having made a definite contribution to Australian painting. It is chiefly a picture book with a note of appreciation and analysis accompanying each colour plate.

778 **The potters' art: an Australian collection.**
Edited by Janet Mansfield, photographs by Douglas Thompson.
Sydney: Cassell, 1981. 94p.

A useful overview of the contemporary professional potter in Australia, the book describes the work and lifestyle of 27 potters.

779 **Australian pottery of the 19th and early 20th century.**
Marjory Graham, photography by Donald Graham. Sydney:
David Ell, 1979. 176p. bibliog.

A pioneering work on the history of pottery in each Australian state and the major potters and their wares. Primarily aimed at the collector and the social historian the book has much to offer the general reader interested in the beginnings and development of Australian craftsmanship. Some 200 illustrations enhance the text. The author has published a companion volume entitled *Australian glass of the 19th & early 20th century* (Sydney: David Ell, 1981).

780 **The inked-in image: a social and historical survey of Australian comic art.**
Jane Lindesay. Melbourne: Hutchinson, 1980. 236p.

It is said that the graphic humour of a nation reveals much about the nature of its inhabitants. This is certainly true of Lindesay's collection of Australian black-and-white comic art which relates how Australia's cartoonists over the years evolved an indigenous humour which exposed national attitudes, characteristics and social behaviour. Other similar collections of cartoons have been published by Jonathan King, *The other side of the coin: a cartoon history of Australia* (Sydney: Cassell, 1979. rev. ed.); *Stop laughing, this is serious: a social history of Australia in cartoons* (Sydney: Cassell, 1980. rev. ed.); and by Peter Coleman and Les Tanner, *Cartoons of Australian history* (Melbourne: Nelson, 1973).

781 **The loaded line: Australian political caricature, 1788-1901.**
Marguerite Mahood. Melbourne: Melbourne University Press,
1973. 306p. bibliog.

A well-written, amusing study of the evolution of the political cartoon in Australia during the colonial period. Through the caricatures the book shows how the common man reacted to contemporary political events. It also provides an outline of Australian political, social and press history and an informed account of the ways in which cartoons have been reproduced over the past 200 years.

782 **Panel by panel: a history of Australian comics.**
John Ryan. Sydney: Cassell, 1979. 223p.

The first ever survey of comic strips in Australia, this is a history of the newspaper strips as well as the once flourishing local comic book industry. An interesting, profusely illustrated account of an important aspect of popular culture in Australia.

783 **Silver and grey: fifty years of Australian photography, 1900-1950.**
Edited and with text by Gael Newton. Sydney: Angus &
Robertson, 1980. 120p.

Presents the work of 35 creative photographers who were active from 1900 to 1950. The subjects covered are varied – from the pictorial landscapes and portraits of the 1900s to the 1930s, to the urban, industrial, documentary, fashion and architectural studies of the 1940s to the 1950s. Short biographies of the photographers are included.

784 **The story of the camera in Australia.**
Jack Cato. Melbourne: Institute of Australian Photography,
1977. 2nd ed. 187p.

This history of photography in Australia is primarily a text but there are also
some 150 illustrations, ranging from early daguerreotypes through newspaper
shots to portraiture.

785 **Pioneer crafts of early Australia.**
Murray Walker. Melbourne: Macmillan and the Crafts Council
of Australia, 1978. 172p. bibliog.

A survey of the extraordinary range of skills which evolved during the early days
of settlement in a country where the alternative to 'making do' was doing without.
Early settlers 'made do' with the material to hand — the timber, the clay, the
rocks. With simple, often handmade tools they produced a range of articles,
functional, utilitarian and recreational — all devised with the aim of sustaining
and enhancing their isolated lives.

786 **A guide to collecting Australiana.**
Juliana Hooper, Toby Hooper. Melbourne: Macmillan, 1978.
117p. bibliog.

One of several books for the collector of Australiana, it ranges through books,
prints, furniture, silver, pottery, photographs, postcards, signs, bottles and glass-
ware and assorted bric-à-brac. Some other useful guidebooks are *Collecting
Australia's past* by Douglass Baglin and Frances Wheelhouse (Sydney: Cassell,
1981); *First fleet to Federation: Australia's antiques*, by Caroline Simpson and
others (Sydney: Golden Press, 1977); *The Australian antique buyer's companion*,
by Peter Cook (Sydney: Reed, 1981).

Performing Arts

787 **The Performing Arts Year Book of Australia.**
Sydney: Showcast, 1976- . annual.

Each annual volume presents, with a few exceptions, a reliable record of what happened in Australia in all branches of theatre, film, television, radio, drama, opera, dance, and music of all kinds from highbrow to low. It lists casts of all productions, all indexed and lavishly illustrated. It is a true vade-mecum of the entertainment industry in Australia.

788 **Theatre in Australia.**
John West. Sydney: Cassell, 1978. 260p.

This large-format volume is a panoramic, popular history of players and productions in Australian theatre since the beginnings to the mid-1970s. It is not a history of the drama itself. There are many illustrations of theatres, performances, stage settings and playbills, which are interesting for their own sake.

789 **Theatre comes to Australia.**
Eric Irwin. Brisbane: University of Queensland Press, 1971. 260p. bibliog.

The author claims that the period from 1826 to 1838 saw the birth of the first true Australian theatre. Meticulously researched and historically accurate, the book is also most readable and entertaining, because it is written in a delightfully simple and engaging manner. It should appeal to a wide audience.

790 **Curtain call.**
Nancy Bridges. Sydney: Cassell, 1980. 139p.

A generously illustrated, nostalgic tale of forty years of Australian vaudeville and variety theatre told by a former stage performer.

791 **A family of brothers: the Taits and J. C. Williamson; a theatre history.**
Viola Tait. Melbourne: Heinemann, 1971. 303p.

The story of five brothers who for half a century ran the world's largest theatre chain − J. C. Williamson's. It is a valuable history of commercial theatre in Australia in the 20th century, as the firm of J. C. Williamson dominated the theatrical scene for that period. After the book's completion the firm merged with another − Edgley and Dawe and ceased to exist.

792 **It don't seem a day too much.**
Claude Kingston. Adelaide: Rigby, 1971. 208p.

For over fifty years the author worked in various capacities for the J. C. Williamson organization, the famous Australian theatrical firm. In these reminiscences he discloses many stories about the theatrical celebrities J. C. Williamson brought to Australia from overseas. The book is an entertaining piece of Australian theatre history.

793 **Opera and ballet in Australia.**
John Cargher. Sydney: Cassell, 1977. 352p.

A very personal view of the major theatrical arts in Australia by the well-known host of two national radio programmes of classical music. As in his radio broadcasts, Cargher's approach is irreverent and humorous. He is the popularizer *par excellence*. The book has been criticized for inaccuracies and lack of objectivity, but it certainly provides entertaining reading.

794 **The Australian opera: the first twenty years.**
Sydney: Friends of the Australian Opera, 1977. 78p.

Consisting mainly of photographs the book also lists year-by-year operas performed since 1956 by the national company together with producers, designers and conductors involved with the productions.

795 **Singers of Australia from Melba to Sutherland.**
Barbara Mackenzie, Findlay Mackenzie. Melbourne: Lansdowne, 1967. 309p. bibliog.

Although written some years ago, this book still provides useful historical information on the lives and careers of the seventy singers included.

796 **Ballet in Australia: the second act, 1940-1980.**
Edward H. Pask. Melbourne: Oxford University Press, 1982. 317p. bibliog.

Although this is not the definitive book on the subject, which still remains to be written, this is a useful blend of chronology and personal recollections of performances witnessed. Together with his previous volume *Enter the colonies dancing: a history of dance in Australia, 1835-1940* published in 1979, the two books provide the only comprehensive record of Australian dance history. Both books are profusely illustrated.

797 **Australia's music: themes of a new society.**
Roger Covell. Melbourne: Sun Books, 1967. 356p.

When it appeared in 1967 it was the first serious attempt to present a history of music in Australia set in a social context. In the absence of any other major work on the subject in the intervening years, Covell's work still stands as the best introduction to the development and sources of Australian music up to the mid-1960s.

798 **Australian composition in the twentieth century.**
Edited by F. Callaway, David Tunley. Melbourne: Oxford University Press, 1978. 248p.

Twenty-two composers are included in this indispensable, though somewhat dated, reference work. It is a useful guide to the biographies and work of the most important composers of creative music in contemporary Australia. Some chapters are completely accessible to the general reader, though others require at least a basic musical training. The book includes lists of works, bibliographies, discographies and indexes. An earlier book of similar content is James Murdoch's *Australia's contemporary composers* (Melbourne: Macmillan, 1972).

799 **The Australian jazz explosion.**
Mike Williams, photographs by Jane March. Sydney: Angus & Robertson, 1981. 171p.

A collection of transcribed interviews rather than an interpretative work, thirty-two subjects in the book expound freely their musical values and reminisce about their lives in jazz. The results are entertaining and enlightening as the jazz scene in Australia possesses many witty and outrageous personalities. Many excellent photographs aptly illustrate the text.

800 **Black roots, white flowers: a history of jazz in Australia.**
Andrew Bisset. Sydney: Golden Press, 1979. 182p.

An illustrated pioneering history strong on the personalities, places, periods and styles of Australian jazz. The author's essential conclusion is that there is a recognizable Australian style of jazz, distinguished by a 'spirited, uninhibited, uncontrived, guileless excitement'.

801 **Rocklens.**
Photographed by Bob King, edited and annotated by Glenn A. Baker. Sydney: Cassell, 1981. 146p.

A presentation of the Australian rock scene through the excellent photographs of Bob King. More than 600 visual images, with captions and annotations by G. A. Baker, a young rock expert, depict the performers, both local and overseas, the faces, the locations and the incidents.

802 **Playing for Australia: a story about ABC orchestras and music in Australia.**
Charles Buttrose. Sydney: Australian Broadcasting Commission and Macmillan, 1982. 186p.

Since its formation in 1932, the Australian Broadcasting Commission has been sponsoring classical music and has been responsible for creating orchestras that now serve Australia's six states. At present there are close to a million attendances at ABC concerts and recitals each year. The author, former assistant general manager of the ABC with special responsibility for orchestras has written an informed and entertaining account of the important role of the ABC in the nation's musical life.

803 **Festival: the story of the Adelaide Festival of Arts.**
Derek Whitelock, assisted by Doug Loan. Adelaide: Adelaide Festival Centre Trust, 1980. 217p.

The week-long Festival of Arts has been held every two years since 1960 and is the best known event of its kind in Australia. It features both local and overseas artists and encompasses most art forms. The book commemorates the first twenty years of the festival.

Architecture

804   **The walls around us.**
Robin Boyd, with a new preface and epilogue by Trevor Howells.
Sydney: Angus & Robertson, 1982. new ed. 142p.

When it was first published in 1962 this concise and entertaining history of Australian architecture was acclaimed not only by the young for whom it was written, but also by adults. Boyd makes it easy for the uninitiated to recognize the various styles from Georgian to Skyscraper Gothic and made clear the distinctions in style between the different states and explained the social and climatic reasons for them. Two decades later the text is still fresh and relevant, and Trevor Howells brings the work up to date in an epilogue and supplements Boyd's drawings with new photographs of most of the buildings and styles discussed in the work.

805   **The Australian ugliness.**
Robin Boyd, afterword by Harry Seidler. Melbourne: Penguin Books, 1980. 2nd rev. ed. 268p.

Harry Seidler points out in the new afterword that this classic analysis of Australian architecture and urban planning is as relevant today as in the 1960s when Robin Boyd first wrote the book. In true Boyd style, he not only examines the ugliness of the physical and built environment, but also expounds on the national character which has produced such unsightliness. Like his other books, *The Australian ugliness* is lively, well informed and original. It should provide entertaining reading for a wide audience.

806   **Australia's home: why Australians built the way they did.**
Robin Boyd: Melbourne: Penguin Books, 1978. 2nd ed. 316p.

Boyd's treatise on the origins and development of Australian domestic architecture, first published in 1952, has attained the status of a classic. He deals primarily with what he first recognized and called 'the vernacular in domestic building' — the small houses of which Australia has more in ratio to its population than any other country. The book is not merely an architectural treatise, although it deals with that subject with originality and authority, but an excellent social history of the domestic habits of ordinary Australians. The reader will find the book rich in entertaining information and quiet humour.

807 **Australian housing in the seventies.**

Howard Tanner. Sydney: Ure Smith, 1976. 144p.

This book surveys the full range of housing in Australia. The Australian dream of an individual house set on a spacious suburban block has produced cities that are much larger in area than similarly populated centres overseas. Recently there has been a trend towards higher density living such as home units and town houses. These are also fully illustrated and explained.

808 **Architecture in Australia: a history.**

J. M. Freeland. Melbourne: Cheshire, 1968; Penguin Books, 1972. 328p.

Illustrated by more than 230 photographs of significant buildings, the work provides interesting social insights as well as a comprehensive account of the history of Australian architecture. Professor Freeland has also published a much more specialized book on the development of the profession in the country *The making of a profession: a history of the growth and work of the architectural institutes in Australia* (Sydney: Angus & Robertson, 1971).

809 **The Australian pub.**

J. M. Freeland. Melbourne: Sun Books, 1977. rev. ed. 192p. bibliog.

Since first settlement the Australian pub or hotel has been a most socially significant and colourful feature of Australian society. In pioneering times the public houses were often the first buildings to be erected and in those struggling years the pubs provided the settlers with an anaesthetic to despair. Freeland's book examines the historical and social implications of pubs in Australia, but being an architect his viewpoint is mainly architectural. Many photographs illustrate different styles of pub architecture. It is a fascinating and often amusing book.

810 **Architects of Australia.**

Edited by H. Tanner, photography by Richard Stringer. Melbourne: Macmillan, 1981. 144p. bibliog.

Presents a broad perspective of Australian architecture over a period of more than 150 years through the work of 18 architects considered to have been the leading proponents of architectural style of their time. The text is well supplemented with contemporary photographs and carefully chosen historical pictures including many charming architectural drawings.

811 **Australian architecture, 1901-51: sources of modernism.**

Donald Leslie Johnson. Sydney: Sydney University Press, 1980. 234p. bibliog.

Examines the rise of modernism in Australian architecture through the work of two immigrant practitioners: Walter Burley Griffin, the American designer of Canberra, who worked in Australia from 1913 to 1934, and the Viennese architect Harry Seidler who arrived in Australia in 1948. The illustrations are well chosen and include both photographs and line drawings of plans. The author has also published an important monograph on Griffin, *The architecture of Walter Burley Griffin* (Melbourne: Macmillan, 1977).

Architecture

812   **Historic buildings of Australia: vol. 2.**
Australian Council of National Trusts.   Sydney: Cassell, 1981.
272p.

The latest in a series of large-format, lavishly illustrated volumes sponsored by the Australian Council of National Trusts which celebrate Australia's cultural heritage through the built environment. The first volume in the series, *Historic homesteads of Australia*, was published in 1969. This was followed by *Historic public buildings of Australia* in 1971; *Historic houses of Australia* in 1974; *Historic homesteads of Australia, 2* in 1976; *Historic places of Australia, 1* in 1978 and *Historic places of Australia, 2* in 1979. Selected chapters from each of these are reproduced in *Historic buildings of Australia, 1* published in 1977 and the present book.

813   **Australian colonial architecture.**
Philip Cox, Clive Lucas, selected photographs by Wesley Stacey.
Melbourne: Lansdowne Editions, 1978. 280p. bibliog.

The period treated between 1788 and 1850 is regarded as colonial. It was provincial British architecture that was established in Australia during the first sixty years of settlement, created by the British settlers, enriched sometimes by their experiences in India and other exotic places, and adapted to suit local materials and climatic conditions. The informative and authoritative text covers the whole of the continent and is accompanied by over 500 illustrations of existing buildings and those long demolished.

814   **The early Australian architects and their work.**
Morton Herman.   Sydney: Angus & Robertson, 1970. 2nd rev.
ed. 248p. bibliog.

A pioneering book based on long and careful research which presents a detailed account of colonial building in Australia from 1788 to 1845 and 127 of the author's drawings, many in colour, illustrate the book.

815   **The architecture of Victorian Sydney.**
Morton Herman.   Sydney: Angus & Robertson, 1964. 2nd ed.
192p. bibliog.

A comprehensive photographic survey of the buildings of Sydney's Victorian age.

816   **Fine houses of Sydney.**
Robert Irving, John Kinstler, Max Dupain.   Sydney: Methuen,
1982. 197p.

A fine book describing in text and pictures twenty-one distinctive examples of Sydney's architecture.

817 **The Sydney Opera House.**

Vincent Smith. Sydney: Hamlyn, 1974. 160p.

Joern Utzon's Opera House, one of the most exciting edifices of this century, caused heated controversy during the period of its construction. This book examines in hindsight the heated clashes between architects, builders, politicians and critics, as well as providing a photographic record of the construction period. Two other books were published dealing with the in-fighting at the height of the controversy: *The Sydney Opera House affair*, by Michael Baume (Melbourne: Nelson, 1967); and *The other Taj Mahal: what happened to the Sydney Opera House*, by John Yeomans (London: Longman, 1968).

818 **Early colonial houses of New South Wales.**

Rachel Roxburgh, photography by Douglass Baglin. Sydney: Lansdowne Press, 1974. 503p. bibliog.

A loving, detailed study of some fifty houses dating from the early years of settlement. The book is lavishly illustrated with photographs and drawings. It is a mine of information not only on the houses but also on the intimate personal history of their inhabitants reflecting on the social history of the period.

819 **Victorian heritage: ornamental cast iron in architecture.**

E. Graeme Robertson. Melbourne: Georgian House, 1960. 229p.

A mainly photographic survey of the history, design and patterns of ornamental cast iron in the state of Victoria. Cast iron decorating was more widely used in Australia than perhaps anywhere else in the world and led to the emergence of a distinctive Australian style. Robertson's *Sydney lace: ornamental cast iron in architecture in Sydney* (Melbourne: Georgian House, 1962) and *Adelaide lace* (Adelaide: Rigby, 1973) are companion volumes which extend the story to New South Wales and South Australia, while *Ornamental cast iron in Melbourne* is 'designed as a sequel to *Victorian heritage*'. There are also detailed studies by the same author of two Melbourne inner suburbs: *Carlton* (Adelaide: Rigby, 1974); and *Parkville* (Melbourne: Georgian House, 1975).

820 **Historic buildings of Victoria.**

Edited by David Saunders. Brisbane: Jacaranda, 1966. 278p.

Ten short prefatory essays relate the mainly photographic content of buildings to the historical development of Victoria.

821 **Building a city: 100 years of Melbourne architecture.**

Granville Wilson, Peter Sands. Melbourne: Oxford University Press, 1981. 201p. bibliog.

A history of Melbourne architecture to the late 1930s. The excellent photographs are directly related to the text.

822 **Early Melbourne architecture, 1840 to 1888.**
Compiled and edited by Maie Casey (and others). Melbourne:
Oxford University Press, 1963. 2nd ed. 184p.
A book of photographs with a very short introduction and marginal comments.

823 **Building Queensland's heritage.**
Janet Hogan. Melbourne: Richmond Hill, 1978. 157p.
A book sponsored by the Queensland National Trust which describes the state's significant buildings of architectural interest, it also provides a visual guide for readers interested in Australia's past.

824 **Early buildings of southern Tasmania.**
E. Graeme Robertson. Melbourne: Georgian House, 1970.
2 vols. bibliog.
A comprehensive, superbly produced photographic study of the built environment in Australia's small island state. The northern part of Tasmania was covered in collaboration with Edith N. Craig in *Early houses of northern Tasmania* (Melbourne: Georgian House, 1964. 2 vols.). An abridged more accessible volume was published in 1966.

825 **Early Adelaide architecture, 1836-1886.**
E. J. R. Morgan, S. H. Gilbert. Melbourne: Oxford University Press, 1969. 169p.
A photographic record with brief factual commentary on extant buildings in 1969 in the inner Adelaide area.

826 **Western towns and buildings.**
Edited by Margaret Pitt Morison, John White. Perth: University of Western Australia Press, 1979. 345p. bibliog.
A pioneering, comprehensive study of the architecture and urban development in Western Australia produced on the occasion of the 150th anniversary celebrations of white settlement in Australia's biggest state.

827 **The Australian homestead.**
Philip Cox, Wesley Stacey. Melbourne: Lansdowne, 1972. 318p. bibliog.
A survey of thirty-four homesteads 'chosen as representative of the main streams of architectural development, as magnificent and historic buildings and because their gardens and outbuildings reflect the true homestead environment.' The houses are so arranged that the book traces the development of domestic architecture through the Georgian, Regency and Victorian periods to the Second World War. During this era the Australian economy rested mainly on the export of fine wool. This condition is fully reflected in the magnificence of these palatial buildings. Architectural history and social commentary is finely balanced throughout the book.

828   **The homestead: a Riverina anthology.**
Peter Freeman.   Melbourne: Oxford University Press, 1982.
304p. bibliog.

The Riverina is an extensive highly productive agricultural district in southern
New South Wales. Freeman devotes the first four chapters to a historical account
of the Riverina and the techniques used in building the homesteads. He then
examines in detail thirty selected homesteads, grouped under the pastoral districts
in which they are situated. There are detailed maps showing exact locations of the
buildings and the account of each station is accompanied by well-chosen illustrations, which include drawings, maps, fine modern black-and-white photos,
portraits of past owners and historical photos or engravings. It is a thoroughly
satisfying and professional volume. It is a companion volume to *The woolshed: a
Riverina anthology* (Melbourne: Oxford Univesity Press, 1980).

829   **Australian woolsheds.**
Edited and photographed by Harry Sowden.   Melbourne: Cassell,
1972. 251p. bibliog.

Sowden claims that woolsheds represent a truly Australian vernacular architecture
because, for nearly a century the country's economy depended on its exports of
wool – the country rode on the sheep's back. The many perceptive photographs
capture the aura of a bygone age and the introductory essay on the history of
wool-growing in Australia adds much interest to the book.

830   **Rude timber buildings in Australia.**
Philip Cox, John Freeland, photographs by Wesley Stacey.
London: Thames & Hudson, 1969.

The authors chronicle the rise and flowering of the use of timber in building construction in Australia which is now sadly in decline. They argue that being uncomplicated buildings built by ordinary people in a straightforward fashion and using
materials readily to hand, timber buildings 'often have a character and honesty
that are rare and often missing from their more erudite architectural betters.' The
134 beautiful photographs of timber homesteads, huts, woolsheds, granaries,
barns, churches, schools and ordinary houses amply illustrate this thesis.

831   **The Australian verandah.**
Photographs by Douglass Baglin, text by Peter Moffitt.   Sydney:
Ure Smith, 1976. 128p.

The verandah, in all its varied forms, is one of the most distinctive architectural
feature of Australian buildings. It was a necessity in a continent of harsh extremes
of climate to shelter people from sun and rain and protect buildings from extreme
heat. Baglin's photos capture the uniqueness of the verandah in what is essentially
a pictorial record with brief descriptive captions.

The Media

832 **Australia's media monopolies.**
Humphrey McQueen. Melbourne: Visa Books, 1981. 218p.
bibliog.
An analysis of the Australian media from the Marxist point of view, this book
draws conclusions, similar to those of non-Marxist critics, which identify the
Australian media with the interests of big business. The author investigates the
concerns of the four monopolies which control the Australian media: the
Murdoch, Fairfax, Packer and Herald and Weekly Times groups. The book was
first published in 1977 and is the only study of the entire media in Australia.

833 **The mass media in Australia.**
J. S. Western, Colin A. Hughes. Brisbane: University of
Queensland Press, 1983. 209p. bibliog.
The first edition of this book, published in 1971, provided an early insight, based
on the computer analysis of a survey into the extent to which Australians used
their mass media. The second edition shows that between 1966 and 1979 when
the two surveys were conducted, television had become the principal source of
information for shaping political attitudes, while the importance of the daily
newspapers had declined.

834 **Politics and the media.**
H. Rosenbloom. Melbourne: Scribe, 1976. rev. ed. 1978. 160p.
A concise analysis of the role of the media in Australian politics by a journalist
who between 1973 and 1975 was press secretary in two successive Labor governments. He examines the structural features of the major media, their internal
politics, vulnerability to political manipulation and political influence.

835 **The press in Australia.**
Henry Mayer. Melbourne: Lansdowne Press, 1964. 281p.
bibliog.
When published in 1964 this was the most thoroughly researched analysis of
Australian newspapers ever written. It is still essential reading on many aspects of
the press as many of the arguments are still valid. It is updated by Professor
Mayer's more recent writings such as his chapter on the media in *Australian
politics: a fifth reader* (q.v.).

836 **The politics of the press.**
Patricia Edgar. Melbourne: Sun Books, 1979. 224p.

Dr. Edgar examines the ownership of the press in Australia. Through interviews with journalists, editors, executives and proprietors she focuses attention on what she sees as the shortcomings of the nation's major newspapers and illustrates how bias operates. The central chapter is a detailed content analysis of the 1975 election coverage by a number of newspapers.

837 **Fixing the news: critical perspectives on the Australian media.**
Edited by Keith Windschuttle, Elizabeth Windschuttle. Sydney: Cassell, 1981. 321p.

A collection of articles from the *New Journalist*. Since 1972 this radical journal has maintained consistent criticism of the news media in Australia and of government actions affecting the media. The articles present evidence of bias in the press and investigate the power of the owners and the influence of political conservatives. The journalists themselves are criticized for perpetuating the methods used by the media. Possibilities for reform are considered. An essential book for anyone interested in the operation of the mass media in Australia.

838 **Outside interference: the politics of Australian broadcasting.**
Richard Harding. Melbourne: Sun Books, 1979. 219p.

Richard Harding was a member of the publicly funded Australian Broadcasting Commission from 1975 to 1978. Here he documents his experiences and personal observations of political intervention in Australian broadcasting through the government's control of funding and appointment of commissioners to the commission.

839 **Broadcast and be damned: the A.B.C.'s first two decades.**
Alan Thomas. Melbourne: Melbourne University Press, 1980. 230p. bibliog.

A history of the Australian Broadcasting Commission from its establishment as a statutory, publicly funded authority in 1932 to 1948 based on the ABC's own records. The author's thesis is that during those first two decades the commission was totally integrated into the Australian Establishment's conservative value system, even though the commission itself continued to pine for the values and independence of the British Broadcasting Corporation, which had been its model.

840 **The ABC — Aunt Sally and sacred cow.**
Clement Semmler. Melbourne: Melbourne University Press, 1981. 232p.

The author worked in the Australian Broadcasting Commission for thirty-five years until his retirement as deputy general manager in 1977. In the book he reflects on the nature and role of the ABC in the nation's cultural life.

841 **Small screen, big business: the great Australian TV robbery.**
Susan Kippax, John P. Murray. Sydney: Angus & Robertson,
1979. 81p. bibliog.

Extensive field research into the structure of the present broadcasting system in
Australia and a comparison of it with those of other western countries lead the
authors to the conclusion, that poor TV programmes are typical of nations
dominated by networks depending on advertising for revenue. This compact
booklet includes suggestions for reform which would lead to greater diversity in
TV broadcasting in Australia.

842 **Turning on, turning off: Australian television in the eighties.**
Sandra Hall. Sydney: Cassell, 1981. 105p.

An excellent, easy to read general survey of programme content, the key issues
facing Australian TV and a short consideration of future trends. Strongly
recommended as an introductory text. Another useful book by the author is
Supertoy: 20 years of Australian television (Melbourne: Sun Books, 1976).

843 **Radio power: a history of 3ZZ access radio.**
Joan Dugdale. Melbourne: Hyland, 1979. 252p.

This book is about the rise and fall of the Australian Broadcasting Commission's
multi-lingual ethnic access radio station 3ZZ in Melbourne 1974-77. Being a
genuine experiment in open access broadcasting, much controversial material went
on the air and official complaints were lodged about the 'divisiveness' of the
programmes. The government shut down the station in 1977 and ethnic radio
became the responsibility of the Special Broadcasting Service. The new ethnic
station is not permitted to broadcast any 'controversial' material and the ethnic
communities are not directly involved in the management of its operations.

844 **The magic spark: the story of the first fifty years of radio in
Australia.**
R. R. Walker. Melbourne: Hawthorn Press, 1973. 192p.

To celebrate the golden jubilee of radio in Australia, the author wrote this
popular history of commercial broadcasting, making only passing reference to the
Australian Broadcasting Commission, the government sponsored system. The
book is useful on the beginnings of broadcasting in Australia.

845 **Australia's commercial media.**
Bill Bonney, Helen Wilson. Melbourne: Macmillan, 1983. 331p.

This book describes the structure of the Australian media industries, with special
emphasis on the central role of advertising and marketing. Despite its ubiquitous
presence in Australian culture the advertising industry has been little studied. This
book fills the gap.

846 **History of magazine publishing in Australia.**
Frank S. Greenop. Sydney: Murray, 1947. 300p.

A detailed historical account of periodical publications in Australia from 1803 to 1947. Assessment is made of the literary content and significance of the periodicals. Some reference is also made to newspapers.

847 **Cross currents: magazines and newspapers in Australian literature.**
Edited by Bruce Bennett. Melbourne: Longman Cheshire, 1981. 269p.

A collection of essays on the contribution of literary periodicals and newspapers to Australian literature. All the important titles are treated in some depth.

Magazines and Periodicals

848 **Bulletin.**

Sydney: Australian Consolidated Press, 1880- . weekly.

Australia's longest running periodical, the *Bulletin* has many of the features of the popular news magazine, such as *Time, Newsweek* and *Spiegel*. It caters for readers who want to be better informed about what is currently happening around Australia. It concentrates on three main areas of politics/economics, the arts, and business and investment, and also covers such day-to-day topics as food, hobbies, fashion, sport, etc. There is a high degree of humour in the form of cartoons and regular columns by a team of satirists. Letters to the editor are featured prominently and advertisements are carried. The *Bulletin* in 1890 had the astonishing circulation of 80,000; now, a century later, it is just about reaching that figure again. A history of the *Bulletin* was published in 1979 to celebrate its centenary, it is *The journalistic javelin: an illustrated history of the Bulletin*, by Patricia Rolfe (Sydney: Wildcat Press, 1979). More than 500 cartoons from the magazine are a notable feature of the book.

849 **Australian Women's Weekly.**

Sydney: Australian Consolidated Press, 1933- . weekly, monthly since 1983.

Australia's most popular magazine. Nearly 4 million people, both women and men, read it every week although the contents are pitched at women. Not surprisingly, because of its huge circulation advertisements comprise some 50 per cent of each issue. In the eyes of the advertisers the average Australian woman retains a very traditional female image. To quote, 'she is unsophisticated, home-centred, concerned with keeping herself and her family attractive, well-fed and healthy and shows no interest in the areas of traditional male decision making.' The same commentator who made a contents analysis of the *Weekly* in late 1979, concludes that, although the magazine probably presents a more liberated image of woman today compared to ten years ago, this image consists of a woman . . . 'slim, attractive, energetically enjoying stimulating and fulfilling paid employment while simultaneously maintaining a clean, attractive, efficiently run household, containing pleasant well-mothered children, with a contented (if somewhat nebulous) well-wifed husband as an optional extra.' A lively and profusely illustrated history of the magazine by Denis O'Brien entitled *The Weekly* was published in 1982.

850 **Current Affairs Bulletin.**
Sydney: Department of Adult Education, University of Sydney,
1947- . monthly.

Every issue of CAB consists of two or three articles on current events by experts
in a particular field. Articles are not confined to Australia; they range over
national and international affairs, politics, science, culture, education and
economics. CAB mirrors the interests and preoccupations of well-informed
Australians and at the same time it attempts to stimulate thought and discussion
on current topics which should concern all Australians. It enjoys a wide distribution throughout the country.

851 **Australian Quarterly.**
Sydney: Australian Institute of Political Science, 1929- .
quarterly.

A very useful publication for anyone interested in Australian public affairs,
especially politics and government and the economy. The journal has always
attracted writers of the highest calibre, many of them directly involved with the
matters under discussion. The articles are rarely over-technical or jargon-ridden,
because the institute sees as one of its main objectives the education of a wide
public. Opposing viewpoints are encouraged. Each issue of the journal contains an
excellent chronicle of the political events of the previous three months.

852 **Meanjin.**
Melbourne: University of Melbourne, 1940- . quarterly.

One of the better-known of Australia's 'little magazines', although mainly literary
in emphasis *Meanjin* has always concerned itself with the wider cultural scene and
comments on contemporary socio-political issues. It presents a rich and unique
record of the development of liberal, left-of-centre ideas in Australia over the last
forty years. The circulation is small at about 2,500 copies per issue.

853 **Quadrant.**
Sydney: Australian Association for Cultural Freedom, 1956- .
monthly.

A general cultural magazine with a conservative bias, combining controversy,
politics and literature. Although its public affairs comment is usually slanted, the
literary contributions in the form of poetry, short stories and reviews are consistently of a high standard. Its circulation of about 3,500, and monthly frequency
puts it half-way between the little magazines and the popular media.

Magazines and Periodicals

854 **Overland.**
Melbourne: Overland, 1954- . quarterly.

A magazine of the democratic Left, Overland's editorial policy states 'temper democratic, bias Australian'. The editor sees this commitment serviced by promoting the best prose and fiction, together with critical writing on general culture and current affairs. Each issue contains a mixture of new and established writers; social-realists being featured more than in other literary magazines. As *Overland* is neither academic nor popular but rather the expression of a community which includes its editors, its subscribers and its contributors, understandably it has a small circulation and has been criticized for its introversion.

855 **Arena.**
Melbourne: Arena Publications, 1963- . 4 times a year.

A Marxist journal of criticism and discussion, *Arena* includes articles on Australian history, literature and current affairs among others of non-Australian content. *Arena* is interesting for its interpretation of Australian affairs which differs greatly from mainstream discussions of the same issues. It can at times be heavy going, because of the authors' strict adherence to Marxist dialectic and terminology.

856 **Nation Review.**
Melbourne: Squall Echo, 1969- . monthly.

Referred to as 'The Ferret' ('lean and nosey as a ferret') by its producers and readers, the now defunct *Nation Review* has had a chequered career. It was established in Melbourne in 1969 as the *Sunday Review*, a national weekly newspaper, and was intended as an alternative to the more conservative and conventional press. Committed to change and scathing about existing social, political and economic conditions, it took up all the causes of permissiveness and consistently supported the Left in politics, a unique position to take in the generally conservative Australian press. Over the years many of Australia's best writers contributed to the *Review* and developed its own intellectual vernacular – tough and bawdy. Definitely worth reading for an alternative point of view of current affairs.

857 **Journal of Australian Studies.**
Melbourne: Victorian Historical Association, 1977- . twice yearly.

The journal provides a medium for the publication of the results of a variety of research into specifically Australian aspects of life – past and present. Inevitably since the journal is published by an historical society an historical flavour predominates, but the editors hope to attract contributions from a wide range of disciplines, including Australian history, geography, archaeology, politics, sociology, literature, economics, etc. Each issue carries useful book reviews and shorter book notes.

858   **Australian Book Review.**
Melbourne: Peter Isaacson Publications, 1978- . 10 times a year.

The official journal of the National Book Council, an association of booksellers, attempts to provide comprehensive reviews of new Australian books in all fields, including literature, history, politics, economics, sociology, science, technology, the arts, hobbies and sports. It inherits its title from an earlier book review journal which appeared between 1961 and 1973. Indispensable for professionals in the book world, such as librarians and booksellers as well as all people interested in keeping up-to-date with new Australian writing.

859   **Australian Journal of Politics and History.**
Brisbane: University of Queensland Press, 1955- . 3 times a year.

A scholarly journal which provides a reliable source of information for overseas readers seeking to acquaint themselves with Australian development or Australian attitudes and policies towards contemporary national and international issues. Political chronicles of the federal and state governments of Australia and New Guinea are especially informative. They provide detailed summaries of public affairs for the periods falling between issues of the journal. Each issue contains an extensive book review section and book notes by specialists in their respective fields.

860   **Australian Literary Studies.**
Brisbane: English Department, University of Queensland, 1963- . twice yearly.

A scholarly journal exclusively devoted to the study of Australian literature intended for the initiated rather than the layman, whose interests would be satisfied by the general cultural journals like *Meanjin, Quadrant, Overland* and *Southerly*. *Australian Literary Studies* carries historical and critical articles, bibliographies and biographical information, interviews, reviews and lists of research in progress. An annual bibliography of studies in Australian literature appears in the May issue. From time to time special issues are published on a particular theme, such as an individual author and recent or new writing.

861   **Australian Outlook.**
Melbourne: Australian Institute of International Affairs, 1947- . 3 times a year.

As the institute is precluded by its rules from expressing a collective opinion on any aspect of international affairs, *Australian Outlook* provides a forum for independent opinion on the subject. The journal has the twofold objective of serving students of international relations as well as its own members, many of whom are academics. Geographically the journal concentrates on Australasia and South-East Asia, but it publishes articles on areas beyond this region by Australian and overseas scholars who have worked in Australian institutions. In this way an Australian perspective on international affairs is maintained.

Magazines and Periodicals

862 **Art and Australia.**
Sydney: Ure Smith, 1963- . quarterly.

The quality magazine of the Australian art scene carries articles on all the fine arts, covers exhibitions and often has biographical information on artists. Profusely illustrated in both colour and black-and-white. There is an art directory in each issue which lists in detail all recent exhibitions, gallery acquisitions, prices paid for them, recent art auctions, competitions and prizewinners. In short, *Art and Australia* is an excellently produced and informative publication for anyone interested in any aspect of the fine arts in Australia.

863 **Theatre Australia.**
Sydney: Theatre Publications, 1976- . monthly.

Carries material on all the performing arts including theatre, ballet, opera and concerts. All current productions are reviewed as well as selected films, books and records. There are articles of general theatrical interest and on specific topics. Many black-and-white photographs accompany the text.

864 **Cinema Papers.**
Melbourne: Cinema Papers, 1974- . bimonthly.

Up to the mid-twenties there was a flourishing Australian film industry which then declined due to American influence. Local film-making enjoyed a rebirth in the 1970s, which also saw the publication of *Cinema Papers*. It covers the local cinema and television industry in great depth and includes interviews with well-known foreign directors, reviews of overseas films and festivals, and an international production round-up. There is a detailed local production survey listing every feature film, short and documentary being produced for cinema or television. Censorship listings are given in full, as are box office grosses by current releases in Australia and overseas. All in all an exhaustive and interesting magazine for the Australian film buff, as well as a mine of information for the serious student of the local film and television industry. The same publishers issue the *Australian Motion Picture Yearbook*, a valuable guide to the year's events.

865 **Rydge's.**
Sydney: Rydge Publications, 1928- . monthly.

Rydge's is one of Australia's longest established business and investment magazines. Articles on taxation, advertising and personnel practices are regular features and emphasis is placed on investment recommendations, stock exchange reports and recent legal decisions of commercial importance. There are regular reports of political developments likely to affect business. It has a circulation of about 50,000 copies per issue. Rydge's has recently acquired two rivals, the weekly *Business Review* and the fortnightly *Australian Business.*

214

866 **Weekly Business Review.**
Melbourne: The Age and the Australian Financial Review, 1981- .
weekly.

The magazine appears every Saturday morning and can be regarded as the
weekend edition of the *Australian Financial Review* (q.v.). *Business Review* has a
colour magazine format and 'sums up the week's events, breaks new stories and
spots the coming trends.'

867 **Australian Business.**
Sydney: Australian Consolidated Press, 1980- . fortnightly.

This magazine is a sister publication of *The Bulletin* (q.v.). Like the *Weekly
Business Review* (q.v.) it is slanted towards big business. Both are of interest to
overseas businessmen trading with Australian firms, investing in this country or
intending to undertake business ventures here.

868 **Search.**
Sydney: Australian & New Zealand Association for the
Advancement of Science, 1970- . 10 times a year.

The object of the association is, 'to foster communication between scientists
of all disciplines, and between scientists and the general public including young
people, especially in Australia, New Zealand and neighbouring countries.' The
emphasis is on interdisciplinary studies. The journal is an indispensable source
of up-to-date information on the state of science and technology and the role
it plays in Australian society.

869 **Australian Natural History.**
Sydney: Australian Museum, 1921- . quarterly.

The unique wildlife of Australia is believed to have resulted from the geographic
isolation of the continent. Thus more than 500 recognized species of eucalypts,
popularly known as 'gum-trees', dominate the scene throughout the various
climatic zones. Nearly half the native mammals are marsupials – animals which
produce their young imperfectly formed and suckle them in pouches. They
include the kangaroo family, the koala, wombat, possum and others. There are
300 species of lizard, 140 species of snake and two species of crocodile, and there
is the platypus, an amphibious monotreme with fur, duck-like bill and webbed
feet. It lays eggs and suckles its young. *Australian Natural History* carries informative articles in layman's language on this unique flora and fauna. Many colour
photographs, black-and-white illustrations, diagrams, charts and maps are
included in every issue. For those interested in more detailed information, lists of
further reading are provided at the end of most articles.

870 **Habitat Australia.**
Melbourne: Australian Conservation Foundation, 1973- .
bimonthly.

The magazine of the Australian Conservation Foundation which is active in the
preservation of the Australian environment and its unique flora and fauna. Carries
many photographs and book reviews as well as articles of general interest and
news of particular conservation projects in all parts of the continent.

Magazines and Periodicals

871 **Wildlife in Australia.**
   Brisbane: Wildlife Preservation Society of Queensland, 1963- .
   quarterly.

'The Wildlife Preservation Society of Queensland is a non-profitmaking scientific and educational organization centred in Brisbane. Through its official quarterly publication *Wildlife in Australia*, it seeks to increase and disseminate knowledge of Australia's natural history, and in this way foster greater understanding of the urgent problems of conservation.' To achieve a wider impact, articles are written in layman's language. Every issue contains illustrations, many of them in colour. The journal is recommended to anyone interested in Australia's unique flora and fauna and its preservation.

Newspapers

872 **The Age.**
   Melbourne: David Syme, 1854- . daily.

Published in Melbourne, the capital of Victoria, Australia's second most populous state. It rivals the *Sydney Morning Herald* for the title of Australia's most prestigious daily newspaper. The similarities between the two papers are numerous. Both represent Australia's best in authoritative reporting, penetrating analyses and interesting features. Both achieve their largest circulation within their respective states, but are read widely and are very influential throughout the country. The *Age's* involvement in controversial issues with outspoken editorial policies and its small 'l' liberal attitudes make it the least conservative of all the mass circulation dailies. The circulation was about 240,000 in mid 1983. On the occasion of its 125th anniversary in 1979 a selection of extracts and pictures was published under the title *125 years of the Age* (Melbourne: Nelson), edited by Geoffrey Hutton and Les Tanner. Another collection of excerpts was published in 1980 entitled *The best of The Age, 1979-80,* edited by Peter Cole-Adams (Melbourne: Nelson).

873 **The Sydney Morning Herald.**
   Sydney: John Fairfax, 18 April 1831- . daily.

The nation's oldest metropolitan daily was founded on April 18, 1831. This and the Melbourne *Age* are the leading quality newspapers in Australia. The *Herald* is a serious, dignified and sometimes a trifle dull newspaper. It has a good coverage of foreign news and analyses of national and New South Wales state politics. Because of its appeal to the middle class, the *Herald* excels in economic, financial and business reporting. It encourages comment and feedback and at least half the editorial page is devoted to letters to the editor. To compete for the popular audience crime and disasters are featured. In the weekend an excellent literary supplement is noted for book reviews and art criticism of a high standard. Around 250,000 *Heralds* are sold each day. A history of 150 years of the *Herald* was published by Melbourne University Press in 1981. It is *Company of Heralds* by Gavin Souter.

874 **Canberra Times.**
Canberra: Federal Capital Press & John Fairfax, 1926- . daily.

Although published in the federal capital where the national parliament sits and covering in detail political events as well as international news, it is essentially a local product serving the needs of the local population of about 250,000. Because it can draw on talented guest columnists and writers from the many institutions situated in the capital, the *Canberra Times* features good interpretative articles on many topics of current interest. The weekend issues have excellent literary and arts pages. Its circulation is about 60,000.

875 **The Australian.**
Sydney: Nationwide News, 1964- . daily.

Australia's only attempt at a truly national newspaper began in 1964. Printed in Sydney, Melbourne and Brisbane it is on sale early in Canberra, Adelaide, Hobart and Perth. The publisher of *The Australian* is Rupert Murdoch, the Australian equivalent of Beaverbrook, who recently took a controlling interest in the London *Times* and already owns Britain's biggest daily *The Sun* and *The News of the World*. In the USA he owns the *New York Post, New York Magazine* and the *Village Voice*. *The Australian* has been accused of bias, and in December 1975 the paper's journalists took the unprecedented action of a two-day-strike accusing the publisher of 'news fabrication' and electoral bias in the ongoing federal election, to which there were countercharges by Murdoch that they had 'cut bias out of journalists' biased stories'. The paper's circulation in early 1983 was 110,000.

876 **National Times.**
Sydney: John Fairfax, 1971- . weekly.

A national weekly offering background investigative articles on politics and economics. Pitched at the affluent middle class it also devotes much space to consumer-orientated material on wine, food and fashion; films, theatre and other performing arts, motoring and travel, and money matters and investment advice. It attracts more than 100,000 readers per issue.

877 **Australian Financial Review.**
Sydney: John Fairfax, 1971- . weekly.

Published for the business community, the paper enjoys a good reputation for its authoritative, well-written interpretations of current developments in politics, government, industry, commerce and investment; coverage is local and international. It is the Australian equivalent of *The Wall Street Journal* or the Canadian *Financial Post*. Circulation is around 60,000. See also *Weekly Business Review* (q.v.)

878 **Courier-Mail.**
Brisbane: Queensland Newspapers, 1933- . daily.

The main daily of Queensland's capital city, Brisbane. Like all the smaller state capitals' newspapers it concentrates on local events and presents a parochial view of national affairs. Its circulation in early 1983 was 235,000.

879 **Advertiser.**
Adelaide: Advertiser Newspapers, 1858- . daily.

Published in Adelaide, capital of South Australia, it has a circulation of 225,000 and is chiefly a chronicle of state events.

880 **West Australian.**
Perth: West Australian Newspapers, 1833- . daily.

The *West Australian* published in Australia's largest and remotest state has a circulation of about 250,000.

881 **The Mercury.**
Hobart, Tasmania: Davies Brothers, 1854- . daily.

Published in Hobart, the capital of Tasmania, Australia's island state, it is of local interest only and has a circulation of about 56,000.

882 **Northern Territory News.**
Darwin: Northern Territory News Services, 1952- . daily.

The Northern Territory with a population of only about 120,000 recently achieved semi-statehood. The *News* is read by about 20,000 people.

Films

883 **Australian Motion Picture Yearbook, 1883.**
Edited by Peter Beilby, Ross Lansell. Melbourne: Four Seasons-Cinema Papers, 1983.

Since the first edition appeared in 1980, the *Yearbook* has become a most useful collection of information about the Australian film industry. It contains general articles on various aspects of film-making and a useful listing of names, addresses, organizations and statistics. Indispensable for the film buff.

884 **History and heartburn: the saga of Australian film, 1896-1978.**
Eric Reade. Sydney: Harper & Row, 1979. 353p.

Although Reade's books, of which this is the latest and most comprehensive, provide a detailed chronological record of film-making in Australia, they are short on critical evaluation. This large-format book contains many illustrations and is useful as a reference for basic source materials.

885 **Australian film, 1900-1977: a guide to feature film production.**
Andrew Pike, Ross Cooper. Melbourne: Oxford University Press, with the Australian Film Institute, 1980. 448p. bibliog.

A chronological history of every feature film produced in Australia and released before the end of 1977. Each of the 488 entries contains details of the production team and cast, a synopsis of the plot and notes on the shooting, marketing and popular and critical reaction. Over 400 illustrations, some in colour, and an index complement the text.

886 **The pictures that moved: a picture history of the Australian cinema, 1896-1929.**
Joan Long, Martin Long. Melbourne: Hutchinson, 1982. 185p.

By the late 1920s a staggering 2.5 million Australians out of a total population of some 6 million attended the movies and about 94 per cent of the films shown were American. Yet Australia had made about 60 feature films before Hollywood came into being and by the time sound arrived, had produced 200 more. The book is based on 250 stills from two documentaries Joan Long produced for Film Australia – *The passionate industry* and *The pictures that moved*, which portray vividly the variety of early Australian film-making.

887 **Australian film: the inside story.**
Ken G. Hall. Sydney: Summit, 1980.

Memoirs of one of Australia's most prolific and successful film-makers, who produced 18 features between 1934 and 1946, 2,500 newsreels and numerous shorts. While focusing on his own career he illuminates the fascinating history of film-making in Australia. Hall is opinionated, if sincere, on the recent new wave of films, and readers should look for more objective assessments of this period elsewhere.

888 **The last new wave: the Australian film revival.**
David Stratton. Sydney: Angus & Robertson, 1980. 337p.

A record of facts and opinions, the result of lengthy interviews with film-makers, about the resurgence of the Australian film industry during the 1970s. The author, who was the director of the Sydney Film Festival from 1966 to 1982, traces the industry's fluctuating fortunes through the biographies of directors and an examination of critical responses to their work. There is a useful index of full production details of the films discussed.

889 **The new Australian cinema.**
Edited by Scott Murray, Peter Beilby. Melbourne: Nelson, 1980. 207p.

A critical anthology about the revival of the Australian feature film industry during the 1970s. The writers examine the many genres evident in recent cinema, including 'social realism', 'comedy', 'horror and suspense', 'fantasy', 'personal relationships and sexuality', 'children's films'.

890 **Government and film in Australia.**
Ina Bertrand, Diane Collins. Sydney: Currency Press and the Australian Film Institute, 1981. 200p. bibliog.

The history of government involvement in the film industry in Australia dates back to the early years of the century. Government has legislated on such aspects of the industry as control of premises used for film exhibition, regulation of the content of entertainment in the interests of 'good manners and decorum of the public peace', censorship, entertainment tax, customs tariffs on imported films, quotas for Australian films, films in education, documentary film production and film lending libraries. Likewise the new wave of film-making which has recently gained Australia a respected place in international cinema resulted from government assistance to feature film production.

891 **Film censorship in Australia.**
Ina Bertrand. Brisbane: University of Queensland Press, 1978. 227p.

A documentary record of the long story of control over the content of films shown in Australia, which has been concerned not only with the traditional trio of sex, violence and horror, but with such subjects as blasphemy, cruelty to animals, the use of slang, offending Australia's allies in wartime, showing foreign nationals in a bad light and depicting scenes of low habits of life.

Literature

892 **Australian literature: a reference guide.**
Fred Lock, Alan Lawson.   Melbourne: Oxford University Press,
1980. 2nd ed. 120p.

An annotated guide to reference books and sources of information. Indispensable
for the serious student of Australian literature.

893 **The literature of Australia.**
Edited by Geoffrey Dutton.   Melbourne: Penguin Books, 1976.
rev. ed. 612p. bibliog.

Since it was first published in 1964, this book has become very popular in its
field. The revised edition has important new chapters on contemporary novelists,
poets and playwrights, as well as original material which has been updated. A
good book for the newcomer to Australian literature.

894 **The Oxford history of Australian literature.**
Edited by Leonie Kramer, with contributions by Adrian Mitchell
(and others).   Melbourne: Oxford University Press, 1981. 509p.
bibliog.

The most recent general survey of the history of Australian literature. This book
is broken down topically, different authors contributing on different genres:
Adrian Mitchell writes on fiction, Terry Sturm on drama and Vivian Smith on
poetry. There is also an excellent bibliography compiled by Joy Hooton.

895 **A history of Australian literature.**
H. M. Green.   Sydney: Angus & Robertson, 1961. 1469p.
2 vols.

This standard comprehensive treatise ends in 1950, but an updated revised edition
is soon to be published.

896   **Australian writers.**
L. J. Blake.   Adelaide: Rigby, 1968. 268p. bibliog.

This book is 'not a history of Australian literature; it is a survey of Australian writing' from 1788 to 1966. It is divided into four sections: the historians, the biographers, the novelists and the poets. Each section surveys the authors and their works in chronological order. There are evaluative, brief descriptions of the works. This is a useful book for the non-specialist readers who are interested in selective reading about Australia.

897   **Creative writing in Australia: a selective survey.**
John K. Ewers.   Melbourne: Georgian House, 1966. rev. ed.
230p. bibliog.

The aim of this handbook is to present the main trends shown in the growth of Australian literature, together with evaluations of those writers who have significantly contributed to that growth. A readable book suitable for the interested layman.

898   **An introduction to Australian literature.**
Edited by C. D. Narasimhaiah.   Brisbane: Wiley, 1982. 201p.

This collection of essays was first published in 1980 in Mysore, India, as a special issue of *The Literary Criterion* subtitled 'The flowering of Australian literature'. The contributors are all top-rank Australian men of letters and their contributions wide ranging. It is a useful introductory work for all people interested in acquiring some knowledge of Australian literature.

899   **Australian literature: a conspectus.**
G. A. Wilkes.   Sydney: Angus & Robertson, 1969. 143p. bibliog.

A short introductory survey of Australian literature. The author has divided its development into three periods: the colonial (to 1880), the nationalist (1880-1920) and the modern (from 1920). Wilkes' critical insight allows him to select a few significant writers within each period and examine them in some detail. The main thesis of the work is Australian literature seen as a product both of the extension of European civilization and of the development of an indigenous culture.

900   **Australia's writers.**
Graeme Kinross Smith.   Melbourne: Nelson, 1980. 342p.
bibliog.

A presentation of fifty-four Australian writers, many of whom have been interviewed by the author; others he has met on their home ground. The many illustrations, especially recent photographs of people, places and buildings complement the text. There is a select bibliography for each author for those who want to read some of their work. A very useful book for quick reference and easy browsing.

Literature

901 **Writing about Australia.**
Rohan Rivett. Sydney: Angus & Robertson, 1969. 84p.
(Foundation for Australian Studies, no. 1).

A critical but rather restricted assessment of modern Australian non-fiction writing: the war books produced by the Australian war correspondents who achieved international reputations in this field; some landmarks in Australian historical writing; travel accounts; and the subject of biography. A useful book for readers interested in these categories of writing about Australia in books published before 1969.

902 **Red letter days: notes from inside an era.**
Jack Beasley. Sydney: Australasian Book Society, 1979. 198p.

A highly readable account of the Australasian Book Society with some sketches of prominent left-wing writers, whose works the society published. The author was secretary of the society.

903 **The literature of Western Australia.**
Edited by Bruce Bennett. Perth: University of Western
Australia Press, 1979. 304p.

One of a series of books published in connection with Western Australia's 150th anniversary, this volume surveys the state's literature in all its forms, ranging from diaries, letters and journals through the novel, the short story, poetry, drama, children's books to literary journalism.

904 **The Stenhouse circle: literary life in mid-nineteenth century Sydney.**
Ann-Mari Jordens. Melbourne: Melbourne University Press,
1979. 186p.

Nicol Drysdale Stenhouse was Australia's first and probably only important 19th-century literary patron. He dominated the intellectual life of the New South Wales colony after his emigration in the 1840s. His splendid collection of books which he freely made available to the leading literary figures of the colony, eventually formed the nucleus of Sydney University Library. The book illuminates the intellectual life of 19th-century Sydney and is an important chapter in the cultural history of Australia.

905 **The Australian tradition: studies in a colonial culture.**
A. A. Phillips, with an introduction by H. P. Heseltine.
Melbourne: Longman Cheshire, 1980. 156p.

This is a re-issue of the 1966 edition with a new introduction by Harry Heseltine. First published in book form in 1958, the essays represent a milestone in the development of critical analysis of Australian literature and culture. Phillips castigated the cultural cringe of Australians – their deference to English precepts – and demonstrated the worth of a distinctive, national Australian literature. In 1980 another collection of Phillips' radio broadcasts, newspaper reviews and critical articles appeared, entitled *Responses: selected writings* (Australian International Press). This book extends and supplements the earlier work.

906 **Social patterns in Australian literature.**
T. Inglis Moore. Sydney: Angus & Robertson, 1971. 350p.
bibliog.

A wide-ranging study of national characteristics as revealed in Australian imaginative literature. The literary evidence indicates that the major patterns were largely formed during the first half of the 19th century. Since the Second World War, however, the original strong influence of the country has been modified by the stronger influences exerted by Australia's highly urbanized and industrialized society.

907 **Australian cultural elites: intellectual traditions in Sydney and Melbourne.**
John Docker. Sydney: Angus & Robertson, 1974. 182p. bibliog.

Melbourne and Sydney, the two largest cities in the country, have always been rivals on the popular plane. Docker extends the rivalry to the differing intellectual traditions of each city and demonstrates how these have produced contrary concerns among their intellectuals: a different style of politics and differing forms of artistic expression.

908 **Dream and disillusion: a search for Australian cultural identity.**
David Walker. Canberra: Australian National University Press, 1976. 279p. bibliog.

A study of four writers who in the first forty years of this century were working in pursuit of a truly Australian culture. Frederick Sinclaire, Vance Palmer, Frank Wilmot and Louis Esson were born around the early 1880s, knew each other and lived in Melbourne for a large part of their lives and they shared a common aim to found an indigenous culture. The book is informative reading for its incisive analysis of the intellectual climate in Australia during the period of their pre-eminence.

909 **The Penguin book of Australian short stories.**
Edited and introduced by Harry Heseltine. Melbourne: Penguin Books, 1976. 290p.

A well-chosen collection of Australian short stories with a very good, short introductory essay.

910 **Bards, bohemians, and bookmen: essays in Australian literature.**
Edited by Leon Cantrell. Brisbane: University of Queensland Press, 1976. 350p.

A collection of essays of literary criticism suitable for the more advanced reader.

911 **Native companions: essays and comments on Australian literature, 1936-1966.**
A. D. Hope. Sydney: Angus & Robertson, 1974. 287p.

A collection of literary criticism by one of Australia's leading poets. His gift for language and clarity of judgement combine in a memorable book of essays and reviews. Recommended for laymen as well as the *cognoscenti*.

225

912   **The Australian experience: critical essays on Australian novels.**
Edited by W. S. Ramson.   Canberra: Australian National
University, 1974. 344p.

The seventeen essays examine a selection of well-known Australian novels, any of
which can be profitably read by newcomers to Australian literature.

913   **Twentieth century Australian literary criticism.**
Edited by Clement Semmler.   Melbourne: Oxford University
Press, 1967. 370p.

A collection of the more important writing about Australian literature by Australian critics during this century.

914   **Literature and the Aborigine in Australia, 1770-1975.**
J. J. Healy.   Brisbane: University of Queensland Press, 1978.
305p. bibliog.

A well-documented study on how white Australians have tried to 'come to
grips' with the Aborigines as depicted in works of the imagination since the time
of settlement of the continent. The book has much to offer readers interested in
literature as well as in Aborigines from a sociological point of view.

915   **Obscenity, blasphemy, sedition: 100 years of censorship in
Australia.**
Peter Coleman.   Sydney: Angus & Robertson, 1974. rev. ed.
141p.

This book was first published in 1961 when the censorship issue was very much
alive. Today the war against literary censorship, with its great battles over *Ulysses,
Lady Chatterley's lover, Portnoy's complaint* and *The little red schoolbook*, is
practically over, although minor skirmishes still break out from time to time. This
is a lucid and balanced account of the rise and gradual decline of government
censorship of books, magazines and newspapers in Australia.

916   **Collins book of Australian poetry.**
Chosen by Rodney Hall.   Sydney: Collins, 1981. 458p.

An anthology of Australian poetry which includes some Aboriginal song words
as well as poems by migrants which have been written in English or translated
from their native languages. An accomplished poet himself, Hall believes poetry to
be a living organ of language. Most of the poems in his collection fulfil that
criterion. There are short biographical notes of all the poets and an introduction.

917   **Preoccupations in Australian poetry.**
Judith Wright.   Melbourne: Melbourne University Press, 1965.
217p.

A series of related but separate essays by one of Australia's leading poets. She
examines the most accomplished practitioners of the art and attempts to show the
difficulties they have faced in acclimatizing and adapting the European poetic
traditions and methods to a wholly new and different environment.

918 **The landscape of Australian poetry.**
Brian Elliott. Melbourne: Cheshire, 1967. 346p.

A study of Australian poetry concerned with the Australian landscape, which white men have always found hard to come to grips with, because of its uniqueness and harsh difference from the soft European image.

919 **The Penguin Book of Australian verse.**
Introduced and edited by Harry Heseltine. Melbourne: Penguin Books, 1972. 483p.

A fine selection of Australian poetry since the arrival of the English in 1788. Heseltine has edited a volume of more recent poetry complementing the earlier volume *The Penguin book of modern Australian verse*, 1981. Both books have short but informative introductions, good as overviews of the subject.

920 **Contemporary Australian drama: perspectives since 1955.**
Edited by Peter Holloway. Sydney: Currency Press, 1981. 438p. bibliog.

A collection of dramatic criticism by academics, journalists and a few professional theatre people covering the 25 years since Ray Lawler's enormously successful play *The summer of the seventeenth doll* which was performed in London and later filmed by Hollywood. It marked a new era in Australian playwriting and theatre.

921 **A history of Australian drama.**
Leslie Rees. Sydney: Angus & Robertson, 1978. 2 vols.

This is the only comprehensive review of Australian drama. Indispensable for students it is also an excellent book for the general reader. There is a selection of black-and-white illustrations in both volumes. Volume 1: *The making of Australian drama from the 1830s to the late 1960s*; volume 2: *Australian drama in the 1970s: an historical and critical survey*.

922 **Five plays for stage, radio and television.**
Edited with an introduction by Arlene Sykes. Brisbane: University of Queensland Press, 1977. 279p. bibliog.

A representative sample of five Australian plays written between the 1920s and 1970s. There is a very useful introduction to Australian drama and some interesting extracts from letters and interviews relating to the playwrights. The plays are: *The drovers*, by Louis Esson; *The one day of the year*, by Alan Seymour; *What if you died tomorrow*, by David Williamson; *The golden lover*, by Douglas Stewart; *Lindsay's boy*, by Ted Roberts.

923 **Contemporary Australian playwrights.**
Edited by Jennifer Palmer. Adelaide: Adelaide University Union Press, 1979. 192p.

An edited series of interviews, originally broadcast on ABC radio, with nine playwrights and critic-publisher Katharine Brisbane.

Literature

924 **After *The Doll*: Australian drama since 1955.**
Peter Fitzpatrick. Melbourne: Arnold, 1979. 200p. bibliog.

A critical study of plays and playwrights and their place in an evolving dramatic tradition. It is the best survey of recent Australian drama. The book contains a bibliography of all plays discussed in the text and a select list of recent criticism.

925 **Innocence and experience: essays on contemporary Australian children's writers.**
Walter McVitty. Melbourne: Nelson, 1981. 277p.

Australian children's book authors have achieved international recognition. In this collection of essays McVitty describes the output of eight contemporary writers who have made major contributions to the genre: Mavis Thorpe Clarke, Joan Phipson, Eleanor Spence, Patricia Wrightson, Hesba Fay Brinsmead, David Martin, Ivan Southall and David Thiele. The book is illustrated with photographs of the authors and with illustrations from many of the books described. There is a comprehensive bibliography with each essay and every author has written a short account of the influences and beliefs which have shaped his or her work.

926 **A history of Australian children's literature, 1841-1970.**
Henry Maurice Saxby. Sydney: Wentworth Press, 1969-71. 2 vols.

A standard account of the subject. Confined mainly to works of fiction, either published in Australia, by Australians or overseas visitors, or published overseas but set in Australia. Occasional illustrations from the books discussed are included. Contains a chronological bibliography. A comprehensive, author bibliography is Marcie Muir's *Bibliography of Australian children's books* (Melbourne: Hutchinson, 1970. 2 vols.).

927 **Complete book of Australian folklore.**
Compiled and annotated by Bill Scott. Sydney: Ure Smith, 1976. 429p.

For a young country Australia has a strongly developed and unique folklore heritage. This big, lavishly illustrated book, using contemporary writings, looks at the history that shaped the Australian tradition, songs, tall stories, poems and ballads. Although there is an index, not as complete as it should be, which allows for quick reference, it is really a volume for browsing.

928 **A dictionary of Australian folklore: lore, legends and popular allusions.**
W. Fearn-Wannan. Sydney: Lansdowne Press, 1981. 582p.

This large reference work can be described as both a 'folk treasury' and a dictionary of Australian popular allusions. So, if readers of Australiana come across words or phrases like bunyip, 'The Bushman's Bible', the Black Stump, Never-Never, cultural cringe, Our Glad, Mr. Rylah's teenage daughter or wowsers, or want to know more about local and interstate rivalries, or axe men or bullock drivers, this is the book to consult. Thus it is both a work of reference and a delightful browsing medium. There are many illustrations.

929 **The big book of Australian folk song.**
Ron Edwards, with illustrations by the author. Adelaide: Rigby,
1976. 507p. bibliog.

A collection of more than 300 songs with music, words and notes on derivation.
Arrangement is by title. There is a comprehensive index listing all known variations
of every song collected in Australia to date – some 1,800 in all. Publications in
which the songs have appeared are also listed.

Language

930 **The Australian language.**
Sidney J. Baker. Sydney: Currawong, 1978. new ed. 517p.

Republished in several new editions since 1945, this popular reference work traces the origins of distinctively Australian slang terms and classifies some of their origins by listing those that derive from the countryman, the underworld and soldiers at war. Although it is not collated into a dictionary as such and is now somewhat dated, the book remains vastly stimulating and entertaining reading.

931 **The English language in Australia and New Zealand.**
G. W. Turner. London: Longman, 1972. 2nd ed. 241p. bibliog.

A study of the English language as spoken and written in Australia and the modifications imposed upon it by isolation and environmental differences. The author has also edited a handbook for English usage in Australia with contributions from eleven specialists entitled *Good Australian English and good New Zealand English* (Sydney: Reed Education, 1972).

932 **The Australian language: a look at what we say and how we say.**
Bill Hornadge. Sydney: Cassell, 1980. 303p.

An entertaining account of Australian English with seemingly never-ending examples of slang expressions laced with anecdotes of their origins.

933 **A dictionary of Australian colloquialisms.**
G. A. Wilkes. Sydney: Sydney University Press, 1978; Fontana/ Collins, 1980. 370p.

Professor Wilkes has compiled a scholarly work of definitions of common and uncommon Australian words and sayings together with comprehensive references to origins and works in which they have been used. As well as being a work of reference for people new to Australian English the book provides for some diverting leisure-time reading.

934 **Morris's dictionary of Australian words, names and phrases.**
Edward E. Morris. Melbourne: Currey O'Neil, 1982. new ed.

First published in 1898 as *Austral English*, this was the pioneering work of Australian English and as such retains an historical interest.

935 **The Macquarie dictionary.**
Editor-in-chief A. Delbridge. Sydney: Macquarie Library, 1981.
2049p.

There are thousands of words and expressions beyond slang, that are either peculiar to Australia or which have meanings in Australia quite different from their meaning in other English-speaking countries. The Macquarie, 10 years in the making, bases its definitions, its pronunciations and its view of the English language as used in Australia. The Australian meaning of the word, if it is the most common meaning the word has in Australia, is given first. It is a comprehensive and scholarly dictionary. A compact and portable *Concise Macquarie dictionary* has also been published.

936 **Linguistics in Australia since 1958.**
G. W. Turner. Sydney: Sydney University Press for the
Australian Academy of the Humanities, 1976. 17p.

A useful survey of the development and state of linguistics in Australian tertiary learning institutions.

Libraries and Museums

937 **Australian libraries.**
Peter Biskup, Doreen M. Goodman. London: Bingley, 1982.
3rd ed. 221p. bibliog.

This book begins with a history of Australian libraries from their colonial beginnings to the present day. Separate chapters are devoted to state libraries, public libraries, the National Library of Australia, school libraries, libraries in tertiary institutions, special libraries, library associations, archival and manuscript depositories, librarianship education and library automation. The new edition brings the reader up to date with the latest developments and advances in Australian librarianship.

938 **Design for diversity: library services for higher education and research in Australia.**
Edited by Harrison Bryan, Gordon Greenwood. Brisbane: University of Queensland Press, 1977. 790p. bibliog.

A major survey of library services in Australia. The volume includes topics such as planning, resources, service, education, management, buildings and policy formation. The approach is historical. Although some of the authors' projections have already been overtaken by events, the book will be a standard reference for years to come.

939 **A book collector's notes on items relating to the discovery of Australia, the first settlement and the early coastal exploration of the continent.**
Rodney Davidson. Melbourne: Cassell, 1970. 138p. bibliog.

The author is an avid collector of Australiana. He describes the major Australian libraries and the great private collections, mentions the important bibliographies, discusses the booksellers' catalogues, lists other literature of interest to the collector and devotes the bulk of the book to a discussion of the rare and important early imprints paying attention to prices. The interested reader can also consult two earlier volumes on Australian book collecting. *Across the years: the lure of early Australian books*, edited by Charles Barrett (Melbourne: Seward, 1948); and *The art of book collecting in Australia*, by George Mackaness (Sydney: Angus & Robertson, 1956).

940   **Australia's national collections.**
Clem Lloyd, Peter Sekuless.   Sydney: Cassell, 1980. 320p.
bibliog.

A guide to where-to-see-what in the main national collections with some material on how they came into existence and developed. Institutions covered are: the Australian War Memorial and the National Library of Australia — both in Canberra, the six state galleries, universities, regional libraries and galleries, some local historical societies and National Trust houses. The book is profusely illustrated.

941   **Collections of a century: the history of the first hundred years of the National Museum of Victoria.**
R. T. M. Pescott.   Melbourne: National Museum of Victoria, 1954. 186p.

The centenary history of the National Museum of Victoria which houses collections of natural history.

942   **The Science Museum of Victoria: a history of its first hundred years.**
Warren Perry.   Melbourne: Science Museum of Victoria, 1972. 203p. bibliog.

The Science Museum of Victoria is Australia's oldest museum of applied science. Written to appeal to the intelligent layman the book is a detailed history of the development of the museum and on a broader scale illustrates changing official and public attitudes to science and technology.

Reference Works

943 Australia Handbook.

Australian Information Service. Canberra: Australian Government Publishing Service, 1941- . annual.

The handbook is an annual publication with a wide distribution throughout the world. It has been prepared by the Australian Information Service with the assistance of Australian government departments, associated organizations and other authorities. The publication presents in a concise manner, the story of Australia – its people, history, geography, wildlife, and its economic and cultural development. Excellent for quick reference on all aspects of Australia, it is illustrated and contains a number of basic statistical tables.

944 The Australian encyclopaedia.

Sydney: Grolier Society of Australia, 1977. 3rd ed. 6 vols.

This basic reference work gives 'a comprehensive picture of Australia and its people, both past and present.' The third edition is in 6 volumes and is a masterpiece of compression. There are more than 6,000 articles in about 2,400,000 words by 300 distinguished contributors. The only valid criticism is that there is no index to the work and that the cross referencing is inadequate. The second edition which was published in 1953 had 10 volumes including an index volume and is still useful for information on topics excluded from the latest edition.

945 Australia in figures.

W. G. Coppell. Melbourne: Penguin Books, 1981. rev. and enlarged ed. 200p.

A new updated edition of this popular statistical reference book full of concisely presented economic, political and social information much of it in graphic form supported by parallel commentaries.

946 Who's Who in Australia.

Melbourne: Herald & Weekly Times, 1906- . triennial.

Contains more than 2,000 career summaries of living men and women of prominence and achievement based on information supplied by the subjects. Also included are details of etiquette such as the table of precedence and official dress, lists of overseas diplomats in Australia and its representatives abroad, commonwealth and state ministries and judges of the commonwealth courts.

947 **1,000 famous Australians.**
Adelaide: Rigby, 1978. 368p.

Biographies of one thousand famous Australians from 1788 to the present. To qualify for inclusion, one must have been born in, or have spent considerable time in Australia. Distinction may have been achieved nationally or within a professional circle. The entries are divided into sections, such as 'The pioneers', 'The sporting arena', 'The innovators'. Some biographies are accompanied by a photograph and there is an index of names.

948 **Australian dictionary of biography.**
General editor Douglas Pike. Melbourne: Melbourne University Press, 1966- . 8 vols to date.

Biographies of over 6,000 people will be included in this standard reference source when the projected 12-volume work is completed. So far 8 volumes have been published. The first two volumes cover the period 1788-1850. Volumes 3-6 cover 1851-90. The period 1891-1939 is partly completed. Sources of biographical information are included at the end of each entry.

949 **Dictionary of Australian biography.**
Percival Serle. Sydney: Angus & Robertson, 1949. 2 vols.

Includes men and a few women who died before the end of 1942. Even when the *Australian dictionary of biography* is completed, this work will continue to provide a valuable historical perspective.

950 **Press, radio and T.V. guide: Australia, New Zealand and the Pacific Islands.**
Sydney: Country Press, 1914- . Latest edition, 24th, 1981.

Information is listed separately for each country. Newspapers are arranged geographically and serials by subject category. Also contains an alphabetical listing of members of the press, radio, television, advertising and associated professions.

951 **Annals of Australian literature.**
Grahame Johnston. Melbourne: Oxford University Press, 1970. 147p.

A listing of the principal publications of each year from 1789 to 1969 together with an index of authors with their works. Literature is interpreted broadly and is not restricted to poetry, fiction and drama. Additional information included is births and deaths of authors, foundation dates of newspapers and periodicals, books and visits by notable writers from abroad, and writings in languages other than English.

952 **Who's who of Australian women.**
Compiled by Andrea Lofthouse, based on research by Vivienne Smith. Sydney: Methuen, 1982. 504p.

The first who's who of living women who have excelled in their field of endeavour. There is a useful index of 38 categories, which guide the reader to the major involvements of the 1,430 women included in the book.

Reference Works

953 **Australian technology directory, 1981.**
Canberra: Technology Media Services, 1981. 193p.

A comprehensive guide to technology organizations, services and facilities in Australia.

954 **Roots and branches: ancestry for Australians.**
Errol Lea-Scarlett. Sydney: Collins, 1979. 232p.

A standard type of handbook for tracing Australian family history. It is comprehensive and straightforward and lists all the main sources necessary for genealogical research.

955 **Australian protocol and procedures.**
Sir Asher Joel. Sydney: Angus & Robertson, 1982. 371p.

The author covers all of Australia's public and private institutions and the accepted way of dealing with them. Packed with useful information it is intended as a sort of everyman's guide to living in an ordered and polite society.

956 **The Australian dictionary of acronyms and abbreviations.**
Compiled by David J. Jones. Leura, New South Wales, Australia: Second Back Row Press, 1981. 2nd rev. ed. 220p.

A useful, standard dictionary of the thousands of abbreviations, acronyms and initialisms which are in use in Australia.

957 **Directory of Australian associations, 1981/82.**
Researched and edited by B. Chan. Brisbane: Australasia Reference Research Publications, 1981. 2nd ed. 471p.

A comprehensive listing of nearly 8,000 associations and organizations active in varying fields of Australian affairs. Excluded from the directory are alumni associations, most student organizations, local community and ratepayers' associations, social clubs, sports clubs, local church groups, very small labour unions and other similar groups. The directory is arranged alphabetically by name with a subject index which classifies each entry by the service offered or by principal types of activity. Included also is an abbreviations' index and an alphabetical list of publications issued by the bodies.

958 **Australian official publications.**
Edited by D. H. Borchardt. Melbourne: Longman Cheshire, 1979. 365p.

This is the only book which attempts to present a comprehensive overview of the vast mass of documents produced by government agencies in Australia. Besides assisting readers to identify what categories of publications are being issued, the book explains how they can be traced and how to find them in libraries.

959 **Australian bibliography: a guide to printed sources of information.**
D. H. Borchardt. Sydney: Pergamon, 1976. 270p.

This is a selective and evaluative bibliography of bibliographies relating to Australian subjects. In the author's words: 'selection has . . . been exercised on the basis of quality, general usefulness and relevance within the field of bibliography proper.' There is a list of works referred to in the text numbering 638 items and a very useful subject index.

960 **Bookmark: an annual diary and directory for readers and writers, libraries and librarians, publishers and booksellers.**
Melbourne: Australian Library Promotion Council, 1973- .
annual.

An excellent guide for all people involved with books and publishing. The diary pages note births, deaths etc. of authors, and other events connected with literature.

961 **Australian Books in Print.**
Sydney: Thorpe, 1956- . annual. 1983 ed., 606p.

Besides listing Australian books available for sale, this standard work includes useful lists of associations active in the book world, literary societies and literary prizes and awards, with details of how to apply for them. In addition there are detailed listings of Australian publishers and their addresses and Australian representatives of overseas publishers. Not included are publications of associations and other non-commercial organizations and most government publications. The hard copy appears annually and a complete update is available monthly on microfiche.

962 **Guides to Australian Information Sources.**
Sydney: Pergamon Press, 1983- .

A new series of bibliographic essays designed to extend *Australian bibliography*, by D. H. Borchardt which was last issued in its third edition in 1979. Volumes published in 1983 were *A guide to sources of information on the arts in Australia*, by Ray Choate; and *A guide to Australian economic and social statistics*, by A. J. Hagger. The books are essential for in-depth research in Australian studies and useful to all people needing to find out what has been written about a specific subject of interest. Further volumes in other subject fields are in active preparation.

963 **Guide to Australian reference books: humanities.**
Compiled by Wilma Radford. Sydney: Library Association of Australia, 1983. 81p.

A useful compilation of books for ready reference. Humanities includes philosophy, psychology, religion, language, literature, architecture, town planning, fine arts, applied arts, photography, music, performing arts, recreation and sports. Entries are briefly annotated as to scope and there is an integrated author, title and subject index.

Reference Works

964 **The Business Who's Who of Australia.**
   Sydney: Riddell, 1964- . annual.

A standard directory used to identify and locate Australian businesses. There are several other company directories and each one varies as to the basis of selection for inclusion in its lists and the amount of information provided. Examples are *Australian Key Business directory* (Melbourne: Dun & Bradstreet, 1973-); *Largest 1000 Companies in Australia* (Sydney: Financial Analysis & Publications, 1979-); *Jobson's Year Book of Public Companies in Australia and New Zealand* (Melbourne: Jobson's Publications, 1928 -). A companion to the latter, restricted to mining and oil companies, is *Jobson's Mining Year Book* (Melbourne: Dun & Bradstreet, 1957-).

Index

The index is a single alphabetical sequence of authors (personal and corporate), titles of publications and subjects. Index entries refer both to the main items and to other works mentioned in the notes to each item. Title entries are in italics. Numeration refers to the items as numbered.

247

259

262

263

Map of Australia

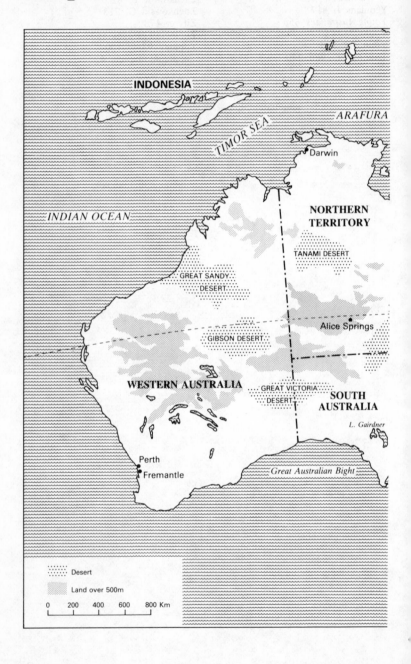

This map shows the
more important towns and other features.

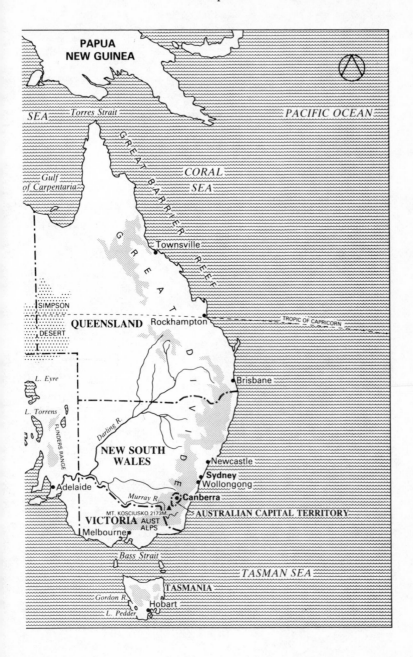

PAPUA
NEW GUINEA

SEA   Torres Strait

PACIFIC OCEAN

*Gulf
of Carpentaria*

*CORAL
SEA*

GREAT BARRIER REEF

GREAT

● Townsville

SIMPSON

QUEENSLAND   Rockhampton

TROPIC OF CAPRICORN

L. Eyre

L. Torrens

DESERT

Darling R.

● Brisbane

FLINDERS RANGE

NEW SOUTH
WALES

● Newcastle

Sydney
Wollongong

● Adelaide

Murray R.   ●**Canberra**

MT. KOSCIUSKO 2173M.   AUSTRALIAN CAPITAL TERRITORY

VICTORIA   AUST
ALPS

Melbourne

Bass Strait

TASMAN SEA

TASMANIA

Gordon R.
L. Pedder   Hobart

The
GOLFER'S
HANDBOOK

Published by Sellers Publishing, Inc.
P.O. Box 818
Portland, Maine 04104
For ordering information:
(800) 625-3386 toll free
(207) 772-6814 fax
Visit our Web site: www.rsvp.com
E-mail: rsp@rsvp.com

ISBN-13: 978-1-56906-998-1
Library of Congress Control Number: 2007935163

1 3 5 7 9 10 8 6 4 2

Conceived, designed, and produced by
Quid Publishing
Level 4 Sheridan House
114 Western Road
Hove BN3 1DD
England
www.quidpublishing.com

Illustrations: Matt Pagett and Steven Bannister
Design: Ali Walper and Lindsey Johns
Printed and bound in China

NOTE
Every effort has been made to ensure that all information contained in this book
is correct and compatible with national standards at the time of publication.
This book is not intended to replace manufacturers' instructions in the use of their products
— always follow their safety guidelines. The author, publisher and copyright holder assume
no responsibility for any injury, loss or damage caused or sustained as a consequence
of the use and application of the contents of this book.

The

GOLFER'S HANDBOOK

Tips, Wit, and
Wisdom to Inform
and Entertain

Tony Dear

SELLERS
PUBLISHING

CONTENTS

Find the grip that feels
most comfortable
to you — see
page 19

The Little White Ball
— see page 16

INTRODUCTION

Oh happy days, a golf book. Like the world needs yet another one of these. At my local book store, there are a couple of long aisles devoted to "Sport" (or rather "Sports" because I now live in the States), and a couple more just for golf. There are more books about golf, in fact, than there are on baseball, basketball, and American football combined.

On a recent trip back home to the UK, I noticed that, here too, the golf section in most high-street book stores was sufficiently large to have broken away from the wider "Sports" shelves. I suppose anything's possible in today's world; but I still couldn't help being surprised by the sight of golf books outnumbering soccer ones. I guess that this means there is still a huge appetite not just for the game of golf, but also for everything written about it — which can only be a good thing for its future. So, to add to that vast array of golfing literature, here are some of my own thoughts on the game, some the product of idle musings, others the result of hours of painstaking research. I hope you enjoy them all.

IT'S ALL GOOD

The aim of this book is simple: To entertain as well as to inform. There are plenty of tips, drills, and useful instructions aimed at improving your all-round game, but the underlying message is that golf is a fun, gratifying, and ultimately fulfilling activity regardless of how many strokes it takes you to get around the course. Sure, a round full of triple-bogeys will certainly be frustrating, but I hope even after a round of 121 you can still take some positives home with you, such as the fact that you got a bit of sun and holed a putt to break 122.

Even though none of us may amount to anything much on the golf course, I think golfers who learn to appreciate their surroundings, the fresh air, the exercise, and banter, who recognize that their level of proficiency has no bearing on their worth as a human being and don't take the game too seriously, can claim to have golf figured out. They may have never shot a course record between them, but they had as much fun as the guy who did.

Well, that's a nice idea, but who am I kidding? Once golf bites, the game frequently becomes an all-

The joy that comes from holing a putt to beat 100 for the first time is like no other.

consuming burden rather than the harmless pursuit it should be. I know a dozen people for whom golf is a millstone around their neck. The joy they once derived from the game has all but disappeared.

Fortunately, with the help of work, two kids, and a newfound interest in hiking, I have managed to control my own addiction in recent years, though I remember well the days when golf was the point at which life began and ended. Partly through my imitation of that notorious grinder Nick Faldo, and partly because I was a moody teenager, I used to zero in on my target and virtually forget the people with whom I was paired. The really sad part about this is that, although I was quite good for a while, I was never good enough to justify blanking my playing partners. But then, how good do you have to be to justify ignoring your playing partners? I'm pretty sure the level at which it's okay to be rude doesn't exist.

The great Bobby Jones once said "there's golf and then there's tournament golf." I understand what he was getting at, but ultimately both are supposed to be fun. And if you happen to bank a massive check playing the second, then good for you — and it's your turn to buy the drinks!

A game of golf is a great opportunity to get out in the sunshine, meet new people with a similar passion, and wear bad shorts.

OUR ROUND

Should we ever be paired together, by all means do whatever you can within the rules to shoot your best score. But for heaven's sake, let's try to make the most of our time away from the real world. I hope you like to talk, laugh, and, if it's a social game, play ready golf. Please don't waste time pacing off the yardage or reading your putt from every angle. Leave all that stuff to the pros. And let's judge the success of our round not by how many over or under par we finish, but by how keen we are to do it all again.

GOLF: WHAT'S THE POINT?

It's easy to ridicule golf, and golfers; it really is terribly simple to poke fun at us and our game. Consider the fact that until recently our choice of wardrobe made us look truly ludicrous, and we spend thousands on equipment that's unlikely to make much difference and that could be better spent on, oh I don't know, a hundred and one more useful things.

We go out in the snow, talk about the game as if it's the most important thing in the world, and participate with the sort of passion and vigor that our family, friends, and careers would surely benefit from. Our shelves droop under the weight of hundreds of "must read" volumes, most of which we never read. And, at the root of it all, the fact remains that instead of dreaming up plans to make the world a better place we are consumed with thoughts of our next round and how we're going to hit a little white ball around a big field into a small hole.

Of course, when it's put like that the game seems incredibly trivial. Using a similar rationale, one could make any sport or game sound totally inconsequential. No normal person would miss snooker, darts, tennis, or fishing, for instance, if they suddenly disappeared. Take away the fact it gives hundreds of millions of people from every part of society and every corner of the planet (apart from America) something to get excited about every weekend and you could even say the same of soccer; it's just a bunch of kids kicking a ball into a net. Big deal.

REASONS FOR OUR MADNESS

Tragically, many unfortunate people never get further than the cover and therefore fail to discover the worlds we golfers, anglers, soccer players, and even fans of squash inhabit; but the fact that we golfers are so consumed by our sport can undoubtedly be a good thing. The golf course is an appropriate place to release stress (just don't release it in the direction of your playing partners). Eighteen holes provide a good opportunity for calm, coherent thought. And no one can deny the benefits of walking five miles, socializing with friends, satisfying our need for competition, or simply having an interest that maybe no one else in the family truly understands.

BIG BUSINESS

In addition to that, golf's impact on the economy is immense. In 2005, America's golf-related revenue was $76 billion, making it bigger than the movie industry. Directly and indirectly, it creates roughly two million jobs in the States, and while I don't have the figures for the rest of the world, I do know golf does many economies no harm whatsoever.

It also teaches kids, and a fair few adults besides, the value of sportsmanship, integrity, honesty, companionship, and all the other ideals that banal politicians persistently bring up, but which I certainly hope the game instills in my kids.

THE BOTTOM LINE

I suppose the biggest justification for playing golf, however, is that it's just plain fun.

Snow, rain, wind, heat. We don't care.

Some 18 years ago, my mates and I played our own US Masters — not the United States Masters you understand, but the Utterly S**t Masters. The venue was Hollingbury Park in Brighton, England, and a privileged field of ten was invited to compete for the coveted brown jacket I had picked up at a thrift store. (The Masters' version is green, of course, but we thought brown more appropriate.) The runner-up, meanwhile, would become the proud owner of an old, crooked tankard from the same thrift store, bearing the inscription "For Frank and Betty on their 40th Wedding Anniversary."

The weather on the day of the tournament was glorious, and with the sun slowly disappearing everyone that had already finished ringed the 18th green as the final group putted out. After Joe, cigarette dangling from his lips and thick, Cossack military trench-coat buttoned all the way from his shins to his neck, holed the last putt of the day we retired to the Half Moon, which, as luck would have it, was owned by the winner's dad.

Over beer and sandwiches, we awarded the jacket and agreed this should become an annual event (alas, university, weddings, babies, and jobs have all decided otherwise). By the end of the evening, somewhat the worse for wear, we were raising a glass to the canny Scotsmen who invented the game — I'll never forget it.

THE BIG DOG

Golf club manufacturers aren't stupid. They know how pumped up we get from smashing a big, looping drive straight past our pals' balls. Consequently, they invest millions and millions of dollars into producing ever larger, shinier, more powerful drivers to satisfy the caveman in every golfer.

Twenty years ago, drivers were more or less judged by looks alone. Persimmon woods were very beautiful — lovingly carved, shaped, whipped, and varnished — but beyond their appearance there wasn't much to get excited about. I had a persimmon Mizuno driver that was so attractive I didn't want to ever chip or scratch it by hitting a golf ball, so I kept it hidden in the garage, bringing it out only on very special occasions. It was very nice to look at and all, but so technologically inferior to modern drivers that an annotated drawing would have had just one line, pointing to the clubhead, with the caption, "Nice-looking clubhead." My, how times change.

SPACE-AGE DRIVERS

These days, annotated diagrams of drivers look like a map of the New York Subway. The most popular driver on the market not only boasts an all-titanium deep-face head, but four little weighted screws that can be moved around four different holes in the sole of the club to promote certain types of shots — more weight near the heel (nearer the shaft) for a draw, more near the toe for a fade. It has Inverted Cone Technology (to my mind this whole business of referring to even the smallest innovation as "Such and Such" technology is very tedious), a very low Center of Gravity,

enhanced gear effect and, get this, an eMOI of 5800.

"An eMOI of 5800!" I hear you gasp. "They can't be serious."

Knowing what an eMOI is, and whether or not one of 5800 is better than one of 6000, really doesn't matter, of course. What does is that the combination of space-age materials and technical expertise behind these new clubs enables you to smack your golf ball further than you ever did in the dark ages. Major developments to the ball (see page 16) and, to a lesser degree, the shaft (see page 85) in your club make significant contributions to longer drives, but the driver now looks so sleek and dangerous we assume it must be all the driver head's doing. The gold, red, blue, green, or yellow graphite shaft in your driver does at least look somewhat more hi-tech than the simple steel rod of yesteryear, but your ball is still round and white with little dimples on it.

Your driver head has changed almost beyond recognition, especially if you purchased one of those square-headed Nike or Callaway clubs, which promised to hit the ball straighter than anything had before, and probably did.

Even a club as advanced as the r7 Superquad may be obsolete by the time this book is published.

LOFT

It's no good having all this technology at your disposal if you purchase the wrong club, and by the wrong club I mean one with insufficient loft. A few years back, one of the ways men compared their masculinity against that of other men was by comparing driver lofts — the lower the better.

So, a guy with a 7° club was quite a bit manlier (he probably earned more, could bench press more, and was certainly better in bed) than a guy with an 11° driver. The thinking was that the wimp who needed 11° of loft was so puny he couldn't get the ball up in the air without a good deal of help from his equipment, whereas the guy with just 7° was so big and powerful and created so much clubhead speed that he had a hard time keeping his ball below outer space.

What happened, of course, was that anyone with a 7° driver who wasn't a regular winner on one of the professional golf tours or in the major championships spent years pounding his ball into the ground, at least never hitting it above knee height (I probably did this for five years before seeing the light), and playing his next shot from a good distance behind the 11° guy. "Didn't quite get that one," we'd say. "But when I do, watch out."

At the turn of the century, research found that, because of the way the ball was developing, everyone besides a few genuine bombers like Tiger Woods and John Daly needed more loft if they wanted to maximize the distance they hit the ball.

The average golfer with a swingspeed of 90 m.p.h. needs a driver with a good 11°, maybe 12°, of loft. Anything less and you probably aren't hitting your tees shots as far as you could. Friends who did go to the trouble of getting the most suitable driver for their swing and swingspeed may now be busting it past you, making golf considerably less fun than it should be.

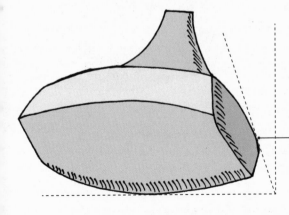

Always use a driver with the right amount of loft for your swingspeed and angle of attack. A typical 15–18 handicapper should have at least 10°, or even as much as 12°.

A clubhead's loft is the angle at which the face is set back from vertical.

THE SCIENCE OF IRONS

Iron clubheads may not have seen quite as many changes as drivers or putters in recent years — they're still the same basic shape and size — but they haven't exactly stood still either. Thinner faces, alloy face inserts, heel/toe tungsten inserts, urethane cavity inserts, and wider soles have all made modern irons so much easier to hit than what grandpa used.

Keeping abreast of new iron launches ten years back wasn't difficult. The manufacturers realized that distance was the be-all-and-end-all for most golfers so most of their R&D budgets were plowed into drivers and balls. Now you just need to blink a couple of times and TaylorMade, Callaway, or Mizuno have changed their entire iron inventory. It really doesn't take long for any club, irons included, to start looking a bit dated.

CAVITY-BACKS OR MUSCLE-BACKS?

Until 1961 when Ping introduced the first perimeter-weighted irons, clubheads were very basic-looking chunks of metal only slightly wider in the sole than at the top and possessing absolutely no game-improvement features whatsoever. They were so unforgiving that if you thinned a shot on a cold, frosty morning, you would still be feeling the rattle in your hands and arms four holes later.

Thankfully, other manufacturers, following Ping's lead, soon started moving the club's weight from the middle to the outside of the head, thus increasing its resistance to twist following off-center strikes. The game became an awful lot easier as a result because badly struck shots were now ending up somewhere near the green instead of squirting off sideways into the bushes.

Cavity-backs have come a long way since those early days and now have so many bells and whistles it's a wonder they don't swing themselves. Just check out what TaylorMade's r7 CGB has going on: a thin 17-4 stainless steel face; "Distance-Enhancing Inverted Cone Technology" (the inverted cone is milled directly onto the inner side of the clubface and increases ball velocity); a hollow top-line that allows discretionary weight to be placed more effectively around the clubhead's perimeter; and toe/heel tungsten weights that further enhance the club's stability. Basically, if you can't hit a ball high, far, and straight with one of these you must be useless.

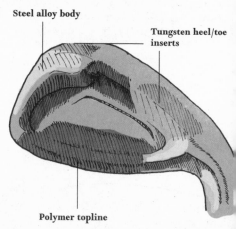

Steel alloy body

Tungsten heel/toe inserts

Polymer topline

Grandpa wouldn't recognize a modern cavity-back iron like the TaylorMade r7 CGB or Cobra VF1 (above).

Not surprisingly, cavity-backs account for well over 80 percent of iron sales and I'm telling you here and now to buy them. They are available at virtually all price points so you will have no trouble finding the right set for you.

The alternative is the blade, which has progressed significantly from the days when you could shave or cut bread with it, but which remains the domain of highly skilled golfers (bear in mind though that far more pros use cavity-backs than blades). Blades have come on so much, in fact, they even go by a new name — muscle-backs — but they're still the callous, ruthless, pitiless clubs they always were; only slightly more tolerant of your imperfect strikes than they were years ago.

So why would anyone use them? Because good players are able to shape shots better, and when you do catch it flush there might not be a better feeling in the universe.

CAST OR FORGED

The vast majority (but not all) of cavity-back heads are made using the investment-cast process in which molten metal (usually stainless steel with a little chromium and nickel) is poured into clubhead-shaped ceramic/sand molds, then cooled. Blades/muscle-backs are forged (again, not all of them) from softer carbon steel in a manner not too dissimilar to how the village blacksmith used to work, the difference being that forged golf clubs are now squeezed into shape by a highly technical machine called a press rather than hammered into submission on the anvil.

Forged clubheads are supposed to feel a bit softer than cast heads and there's still a market for them despite the fact

various studies have shown few golfers, not even tour pros, can feel the difference. Unless, that is, in their wallet — as they are quite a bit more expensive too.

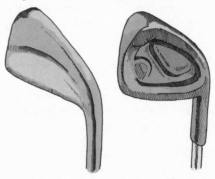

A muscle-back and a cavity-back iron. The one on the right is for you and me. The one on the left is for Tiger and his pals on the pro tours.

Your set

Most sets come with eights irons — from a 3-iron with about 20° of loft, to a pitching wedge with 48° — although some manufacturers, most notably Adams, don't bother with 3-, 4-, and sometimes even 5-irons, replacing them with hybrid clubs (see page 24) that are considerably easier to get off the ground and high in the air than standard long irons. I would recommend anyone with a handicap of, say, 12 and above seriously considering this hybrid/iron mix. After all, why bother buying long irons that you're never going to use; or, if you do use them, will land you in trouble?

WEDGES

Necessity is the mother of invention so it was inevitable the old pitching wedge–sand wedge combo would one day be updated. The gap between the typical 48° pitching wedge and 56° sand wedge needed filling, and 56° wasn't quite enough loft for an almost vertical lob shot that lands on the green like a balloon.

So the 52° gap or approach wedge and 60° lob wedge were born and suddenly golfers were hitting a vast array of short-game shorts they hadn't been able to before without manipulating the clubhead somehow.

This standard four-wedge set soon became obsolete itself though with extra lofts, bounce angles, and finishes (chrome, rust, beryllium copper, black, gun-metal, oil can, satin) being added all the time. The result is a staggering choice of wedges, apt really to make a right-side-of-the-brain dreamer like myself a bit confused. And they don't even have names any more — often, wedges are simply known by their lofts.

HOW MANY SHOULD YOU HAVE?
I've survived with three — a 48° pitching wedge with 8° of bounce, a 56° sand wedge with 12° of bounce, and a 60° lob wedge with 6° of bounce — for years without ever really thinking I could do with an X° wedge with Y° of bounce. I tried a 52°

A pro might want all four wedges for specific shots, but the average golfer should get by with lofts of 48° (PW), 56° (SW), and 60° (LW). By not adding a fourth, you can keep a 5-wood or hybrid that you'll find much more useful.

wedge for a while, but found I missed the lofted wood I'd had to forego.

I'm fairly certain that most mid-to-high handicappers could get by with a similar set-up, maybe selecting wedges with more bounce if their course has soft, fluffy sand and moist, lush turf, or less bounce if they play at a links where the lies are much tighter and the bunker sand much firmer.

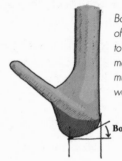

Bounce is the angle of the sole in relation to the ground and it makes bunker shots so much easier than they were back in the day.

Bounce angle

WHAT IS BOUNCE?
In 1931, after taking a flight with Howard Hughes during which Hughes explained that an aeroplane's battle with drag was similar to that of a pitching wedge's with sand, then three-time major champion Gene Sarazen began messing about with his wedge. He soldered metal onto the bottom — making the club's trailing edge rest on the ground with the leading edge raised slightly — to enable the club to splash through the sand rather than dig into it. The metal on the sole gave the club "bounce," the angle between the sole and the ground. It changed bunker technique forever.

THE PERFECT PUTTER

Your putter sees a lot of action, hitting almost 50 percent of the shots you ever play. So it makes sense to find one that works and, when you do, to guard it with your life.

Despite the fact so many of their shots are used up on the green, most golfers practice their putting about as frequently as Haley's Comet passes by. And even though improving their putting is just about the easiest way to lower their scores (Jack Nicklaus once said that while few golfers could ever attain his level of ball-striking, anyone could become as good a putter as him), most will splurge thousands on new drivers, irons, shirts, balls, and green fees before they spend so much as a penny on a new putter.

Part of the reason as I see it, is that golfers don't want to spend any cash on any item that could be replaced, though not terribly effectively, by an empty coke can tied to the end of a stick. And nor do they feel the need to practice a part of the game that looks so innocuous, is really quite dull, and which can't put them in any trees or lakes unless they're really, really bad.

But I think the main reason why the driving range gets busy while the putting green is empty, and why golfers don't take the time to get fitted properly for a putter is because they are so darned expensive. I don't know when they became so pricey, but I do know that if I ever found a spare bundle of notes lying about, I wouldn't be spending them on a putter.

We really should be paying more attention to our putting though. There's very little I can tell you about choosing a putter, however, other than to go for whatever you think will help you hole the most putts. It may be short, long, have a face insert or tiny grooves, be center-shafted or heel-shafted, blade or mallet.

For some reason blade putters are now the type that used to be called heel/toe weighted putters, while genuine blades have all but disappeared. Mallets, on the other hand, used to look like, er, mallets but today put you in mind of Transformers (the hi-tech kids' toy, not the device that transfers electrical energy from one circuit to another through inductively coupled electrical conductors). Which style you choose is all down to personal preference. For the record, I like a nice Ping-Anser-style blade, with a 36 in-long shaft and can't abide the wacky, extra-terrestrial mallets. You'd have to pay me to use one of those.

The putter on the left won't eat you, but it might help if you rarely find the middle of the putterface. Many modern blades retain the popular Ping-Anser shape (right) and have sufficient heel/toe weighting to stabilize poor strikes.

THE LITTLE WHITE BALL

The golf ball is in big trouble. It's going too far... for the pros, anyway. These days, great players from the past, most notably Jack Nicklaus and Arnold Palmer, are up in arms about the distance modern tour pros are hitting it. The classic tracks they used to find demanding are now mere pitch-and-putt courses that require no more than a driver, a bunch of wedges, and a putter — or so they say.

BETTER BALLS, LONGER HOLES

Tiger Woods went round 72 holes at Hoylake in the 2006 Open Championship hitting his driver only once, and that got him into trouble. The rest of the time he used a 2-iron off the tee, taking advantage of the bone-hard fairways. He won by two with a score of 18 under par. Seems the oldies have a point.

It certainly is the case that without a stout wind or knee-deep rough, Hoylake, the Old Course at St Andrews, Muirfield, Sunningdale, Merion, the National Golf Links, and a host of other great courses around the world no longer test the best. So they either stop hosting

professional tournaments altogether, or get lengthened, and lengthened, and lengthened...

This is regrettable, certainly. I used to love watching the European Open on the Old Course at Sunningdale in Surrey, but by the mid-1990s the course had become obsolete as a tournament venue. And without crossing the old London Road or stealing a few acres from the adjacent New Course, that's how it's going to stay.

At the same time, if people watch the pros on TV playing 7,500-yard courses, then they demand the same. This is utter madness, of course, as most golfers can't

Does it Really Matter which Ball You Use?

OK, I'm sorry, I'm just ranting now. The point of this page was to give you some hints as to what sort of ball is best for you. Well, let me start by saying that if you can't break 100, it really doesn't matter, so I suggest you stop forking out your hard-earned cash for Pro-V1s and instead buy Top-Flites from the supermarket. With all due respect, you are not hitting it hard enough to gain any advantage from all the hi-tech stuff going on in the modern

ball. Only when you start driving it a decent distance and are knocking on 79's door should you concern yourself with what type of ball you're playing and consider using a fancy three- or four-piece ball such as the Pro-V1, HX Tour, or Nike One Platinum. Only at this level will you begin to appreciate the extra distance, stable ball flight, piercing trajectory, and responsive feel around the greens that justify these balls' price tags.

break 80, or even 90, from the middle tees, so hitting off the back tees makes scores that are perfectly high enough already, thank you very much, even higher. What's worse is that longer courses require more land, which costs more money, which bumps green fees up. Longer courses also take longer to play, which is part of the reason why many people are leaving the game and why fewer and fewer are choosing to take it up.

IN PRAISE OF BETTER BALLS

Many would argue those are all perfectly sound reasons to stop any further improvements to the ball, or even roll it back a few years. I say, just hold on a minute there, cowboy.

The fact is, handicaps are not coming down. The average golfer had a hard time breaking 100 twenty years ago, and still does, even with the multilayer, urethane-covered ball. The 6,500-yarder we've been playing for years still provides as much sport as most of us can handle. However, even though our scores aren't coming down, we've become accustomed to hitting our Titleist Pro-V1s and Callaway HX Tours. To go back to a lighter, less aerodynamic ball would be hard to swallow.

So, what do we do? Well, allow me to throw a couple of suggestions out there:

+ Roll the ball back by all means, but only for the fraction of players for whom Merion and Sunningdale, and so on are now too short — in other words, the pros.
+ Keep the ball as it is and cut fairways longer, so shots don't run as far.

What's Inside?

The rise of the solid, multilayered, urethane-covered ball led to the demise of the wound ball because the former provides a combination of distance, durability, and feel that balata balls never could. Today's balls fly on a shallower, more parabolic trajectory than soft-wound balls.

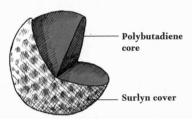

Polybutadiene core

Surlyn cover

Today's two-piece ball

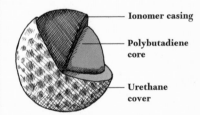

Ionomer casing

Polybutadiene core

Urethane cover

Today's multilayered ball

+ Make the rough longer so there is actually a penalty for finding it.
+ Stagger fairway bunkers a good distance up the hole so no matter how far you hit it off the tee there's a bunker waiting for you if you stray offline. And make those bunkers deep.

⚜ THE GRIP

To play golf at a level where you can score in the 80s, 70s, and maybe even the 60s, you've first got to learn how to hold the club correctly. For the beginner, the recommended grip feels uncomfortable, but a few minutes' practice every day will make it feel natural in no time. I suggest you do it, because without a decent grip you are making an already hard game harder.

As someone who has taught the game for a living, I'm confident I could predict the shape of your shots by observing how you hold the club. Actually, there's a fairly simple formula involved here: a weak grip tends to fade or slice the ball; a strong one draws or hooks it.

WEAK VERSUS STRONG

So what is a weak grip exactly, what is strong, and what's in-between? Contrary to what you might be thinking, a weak grip doesn't mean you're holding the club too lightly and a strong one doesn't mean your hold is too tight.

No, a weak grip is one in which you can see too much of the palm of the top hand, or too much of the back of the bottom hand. Assuming the leading edge of the clubface was perpendicular to the target line as you addressed the ball (and was therefore "square" to the target), the clubface is more than likely to be open, or facing to the right, when you strike the ball because your forearms will have a hard time rotating properly and bringing the clubface back to square. This imparts left-to-right sidespin on the ball, making it curve to the right. Conversely, a strong grip promotes too much forearm rotation and causes the clubface at impact to be closed, or pointing to the left of your target. And that means a low, slinging hook, probably heading for trouble.

For a weak or strong grip to be successful (and there certainly have been players who have done well with what appear to be poor grips), you must therefore manipulate the forearms and hands in order to hit the ball with a square clubface — hold off the release if you favor a strong grip, or exaggerate it with a weak grip. That is why the great teacher, Harvey Penick said that if you have a bad grip, you need a bad swing to compensate.

Unless you're blessed with the talent of Jose Maria Olazabal (weak), or Fred Couples, Paul Azinger, Bernhard Langer, John Daly, and so on (strong), then holding off or exaggerating the release with any degree of consistency just isn't going to happen. Your clubface will rarely be square to the target line and you'll be fighting a hook or a slice all day. And that's no fun.

A neutral grip, neither weak nor strong, is therefore to be encouraged. Just feel like the back of your top hand and palm of the bottom hand face the target. If you want to make your grip slightly stronger, and many people do as it encourages a slight draw and consequently a few more yards, simply turn both hands clockwise slightly (right-handers).

Now, grip the club lightly — about four on a scale of one to ten — in the fingers of each hand rather than across the palms, and smile as your ball flies straight for a change.

CONNECTING THE HANDS

No one ever played good golf with their hands separated on the club. The question is, how are you going to bring them together? There are three basic methods, known as: Baseball, Vardon, and Interlocking.

+ Baseball: All ten fingers in contact with the club, but the little finger of the bottom hand presses against the index finger of the top hand.
+ Vardon (or Overlapping): Named after the great Jersey-born player Harry Vardon who didn't invent it but did make it famous, this grip moves the little finger of the bottom hand so it settles in the groove between the index and middle fingers of the top hand.
+ Interlocking: Achieved simply by twisting the index finger of the top hand and the little finger of the bottom around each other.

Just go with whichever grip feels most comfortable to you.

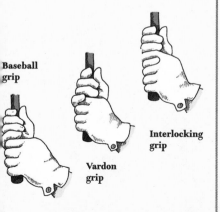

Baseball grip

Vardon grip

Interlocking grip

Gripping Advice

On the Thursday of the 1987 Open Championship at Muirfield in Scotland, well-known teacher John Jacobs was giving a free clinic to members of an awed public in the huge exhibition tent. Jacobs, a genial Yorkshireman credited with improving the games of several great players, was talking about grips and I was leaning on his every word having suspected for a long time that my dodgy hold on the club may have been to blame for years of less than stellar golf.

As he left the stage to much applause, I barged through, desperate to catch him. "Mr Jacobs, Mr Jacobs, I'm rubbish at golf, can you help?" Okay, those might not have been the actual words, but that's pretty much how I felt. "Certainly son," he beamed. "Show me your grip." Before I had even put my bottom hand on the club, he said, "Ah, so you're a slicer."

His swift analysis and correct assessment (I did indeed suffer from an unholy slice) were stunning. I mean, I was quite literally stunned. How could he possibly know which way my ball flew from the position of my left hand? The man had obviously sold his soul to the devil in return for the knowledge of good and evil, or at least the difference between a good and bad golf grip. "Just turn your top hand clockwise so the 'V' formed between your thumb and index finger points to your right shoulder," he said. Lesson over. I was drawing the ball within a week.

LINING IT ALL UP

The grip got two pages all to itself and both alignment and posture warrant at least that, if not more; but if you're as hooked on the game as I am, I'm sure you already have a library stacked with books showing you how to stand to the ball. So let's keep it brief...

No doubt about it, most bad shots are caused by errors in the set-up. Jack Nicklaus used to say if you addressed the ball correctly, you were 75 percent of the way to hitting a good shot, or was it 85 percent, or 95 percent... In any case, the point is that only by aligning yourself and the clubface correctly will you hit the ball in the desired direction, and only by adopting the correct posture will you create a solid base, help maintain your balance to the end of the swing and facilitate a wide, smooth swing.

SQUARE
The word "square" is used so often when talking about body and clubface alignment, it definitely pays to know what it means. Your body is square to the target if your feet, knees, hips, and shoulders are aligned parallel left of it, by which I mean if you stand two and a half feet from the ball you should ideally align your body two and a half feet left of the hole (provided the hole is your target of course). Your clubface is square to your body if it points in the same direction, wherever that may be, and it's square to the target if the leading edge is perpendicular (at right angles) to an imaginary line linking the two.

If all that sounds a trifle complex, it can be summed up simply by imagining you're standing on the inner rail of a train track with the ball on the outer rail. The target is at a point in the distance on the outer rail.

Doesn't that make it all a lot easier to understand? For a straight shot your body is aligned straight down the inner rail while the clubface points at the target on the outer rail. If you wanted to fade the ball (left to right), you'd start by bringing your left foot and left side away from the rail slightly, thus aligning your feet and shoulders to the left of the target (see page 93). To hit a draw, you'd align your feet and shoulders across the tracks (see page 92). The clubface, however, remains pointed at the target in both instances.

If your body is aligned square to the target and you want your clubface to be square as well and therefore hit a straight shot at the target (never a bad option), this is what it should look like.

PERFECT POSTURE

Watch all the great players and you won't see two swings alike. But rewind the tape, look a little closer, and you'll notice they all start from a fairly similar position. Yes, some players appear slightly taller and more erect than others, while some may look a little stiffer, but, with very few exceptions, professionals get the various elements of their posture right.

There are more elaborate, scientific-sounding procedures for guaranteeing you stand to the ball correctly, but I think it can be summed up with the following: knees flexed; bum out; back straight; chin up. Your feet should be slightly wider than shoulder-width apart when hitting a driver, and inch closer together as the club gets shorter.

Develop good posture and you will look like a soccer goalkeeper getting ready to save a penalty, though he may have a little more flex in the knees than you require. What is more, not only will you strike the ball better, but you're unlikely to suffer as many back complaints as golfers whose posture is faulty.

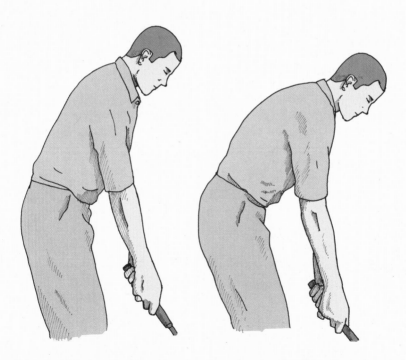

The golfer on the left looks relaxed but athletic, he is primed ready to fire. The golfer on the right is slouching, has a rounded back and is not in a good position to make a balanced and powerful swing.

BALL POSITION

Positioning the ball incorrectly a fraction either side of where it should be could mean the difference between the lake and a very makeable putt for birdie. It's difficult and probably futile ranking the different parts of your set-up in order of importance, but many teachers consider the importance of ball position second only to the grip.

Position the ball correctly and your clubhead will approach impact at an appropriate angle of descent, reach the bottom of its arc a split second after making contact (taking a shallow divot, squeezing the ball off the turf, and creating a little backspin) and hit the ball squarely. Put it too far forward, however, and your shoulders will be open to your target (aligned to the left) and the clubhead will have started moving inside the target line when it contacts the ball which will almost certainly start left. The club will also have bottomed out already so you may hit it fat too. That's a lot of things

going wrong! Likewise, if it's too far back in your stance, your shoulders will be slightly closed (aligned right) and a push, or block, becomes likely.

DIFFERENT THEORIES

For 20 years I, like most golfers, positioned the ball in relation to my feet. But I recently came across what might be a better method for guaranteeing the right position; playing it opposite various points on my left side. (Not having known about this until now clearly explains why I never won the Open.) This makes sense because the person who pushes his or her feet unnaturally far apart (I've seen guys with legs spread so wide a fat pig could get through) and plays the ball off the left heel will probably start with their

Driver — Opposite the outside of your left shoulder (which for most people is about the same place as the inside of the front foot).

Fairway wood or hybrid off the ground — Opposite your left armpit (about two inches behind where it was for the driver).

Long and medium irons — Opposite your left ear (two inches further back still).

Short irons or wedges — Opposite your left cheek (just forward of center).

hands too far behind the ball. And that doesn't work.

Most golfers agree the ball should come back as the club gets shorter, but while many think it should move back half an inch or so for every club until it reaches the middle of the stance with the 9-iron or pitching wedge, others prefer playing all their iron shots with the ball very slightly forward of center. That doesn't work for me because it creates slightly too steep an attack with the long irons.

And then there's nine-time major champion Ben Hogan who played the ball an inch or so inside his left heel for every shot he played. It was just his right foot that moved — closer to the left, and across the line (see below), as the club got shorter.

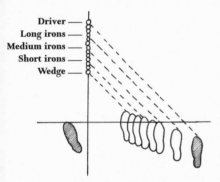

Driver —
Long irons —
Medium irons —
Short irons —
Wedge —

You'll notice Hogan's stance was closed for the woods and long irons in relation to his target. He did this because it helped establish an image of the preferred path of the clubhead — approaching the ball from the inside — and to clear the right side of his body in the backswing. The only time his stance was perfectly square was with the mid-irons. With the short irons he opened his stance to promote a high, accurate fade that stopped quickly after pitching.

Sport, Game, or Just "a Good Walk Spoiled?"

Mark Twain obviously never felt the thrill of coming up the 18th needing a par to win. He never hit a perfect drive high against a perfect blue sky that stayed in the air seemingly forever and dropped to Earth 280 yards ahead of him. And he never played a British links course on a summer's day and finished as a huge, red sun finally dipped below the horizon. If he had, he would never have uttered such foolish nonsense — "a good walk spoiled," indeed. We'll reject Twain's musings, but the question of golf being a sport or game remains.

Thirty years ago, before Tiger Woods came along, and when a number of players actually hit shots while taking a drag on a cigar or cigarette, few would have regarded it as sport; a good smoke spoiled maybe.

In the modern age, however, following the example set by Woods, players are building Popeye forearms and bionic legs. They're working out several times a week to build the stamina they need to survive three practice rounds, four tournament rounds, the crush of media requests, and countless international corporate outings. Of course it's a sport. And if you ever saw Seve Ballesteros or Lee Trevino play, you'd say it was an art too.

🏌 HYBRIDS

Nothing says equipment boom or helps out high-handicap golfers quite like the hybrid. The driver has certainly had its share of attention in the last decade, and some putters now have what look like claws or fangs sticking out their backs. But improvements to these clubs make existing shots slightly easier. A hybrid is so versatile and so easy to hit, it gives you shots you never had before.

Call me strange, but the shot that always used to instill fear in me wasn't escaping a greenside bunker from a plugged lie, the fairway bunker shot, the lob shot to a tight pin, the drive to a precariously narrow fairway, or even the tee shot over water; no, it was a 3-wood off the turf. I'm not talking about a 3-wood off a significant slope or into a strong wind, merely a straightforward shot of 210–220 yards, say, off a perfectly level lie with no wind, water, or woodpeckers to upset me.

But no more do I dread this distance, or lay up with a 6-iron and wedge on — pretty low I know, but if you saw some of my 3-wood shots... Now I just uncork my 18° hybrid, make a nice easy swing and watch the ball fly high, land soft, and cosy up to the hole. Well, to be honest that's only happened about four times, but that is four times more than it ever happened with a 3-wood.

WHAT'S A HYBRID?

A hybrid looks like a small-headed wood, but plays as easily as a mid-iron thanks to the position of the center of gravity (CG). Because of a hybrid's dimensions, the CG is positioned much lower and further back in the head than in long irons, which results in a much higher trajectory than a shot played

The first time I saw someone chip with a hybrid I did a double-take. The first time I tried it, I too became a believer.

with an iron of the same loft. So you can hit a 210–220-yard shot with a club that's as easy to hit and that produces the same sort of trajectory as a 5-iron. It's great out of the rough and you can chip with it too.

Hybrid — Long-Iron Equivalents

A 17° hybrid has roughly the same loft as a 2-iron, while a 20° hybrid is the equivalent of a 3-iron.

23° — 4-iron
26° — 5-iron
29° — 6-iron
32° — 7-iron

NB These are the figures for Callaway's Big Bertha Heavenwood Hybrids and may not be the same as other manufacturers' clubs. Adams' IDEA Pro, for instance, comes in five lofts: 16°, 18°, 20°, 23°, and 26°.

It looks like a small wood but plays like a 5-iron. Give the person who came up with that concept a medal.

1ST TEE NERVES

Unless they're coming down the stretch knowing they have a chance to take home a pro-store gift certificate for winning the monthly medal, there is nowhere amateur golfers are more jittery than on the 1st tee.

I'll never forget the day my mate John succumbed to nerves on the opening hole at Southport and Ainsdale GC in Lancashire. He'll forgive me for saying this, but John is not Ryder Cup material. So it's not surprising that, as he stood on the tee of this intimidating 204-yard par 3, called "Trial," with the wind blowing in his face and four elderly members looking on, he became more than a little self-conscious.

He shouldn't have done it, but John interrupted his pre-shot routine to take one last look at the small but intimidating gallery assembled behind him. He addressed his ball thinking only of how he could avoid embarrassing himself. Clearly, he was not "in the zone."

John's swing is fairly quick at the best of times, but on this occasion it was barely perceptible. The foot-long, six-inch-deep divot he carved out of the ground definitely was, though. Thanks to the size of this great clod of earth, John's clubhead was barely moving by the time it reached the ball, which barely toppled off the tee. His face a swelling purple, John turned to me for direction, clearly at a loss over what to do. In the end, I think he just pocketed his ball, told me to meet him on the 2nd tee and ran off.

Overcoming Fear

John's primary emotion as he lined up to hit was fear. All he could think about were the distinguished gentlemen lining the tee, and what they might do should he duff it. When you're playing your best you forget about who's watching, swing mechanics, and what the consequences might be — you are absorbed by the process rather than overcome with fear.

John needed to take a few deep breaths and focus on slowing his heartbeat. At the same time, he should have been visualizing exactly where he wanted his ball to go, and then gone through his pre-shot routine (see page 94) without ever losing the mental image of a successful outcome. Of course, he didn't want to spend two or three minutes doing all that, nor did he want to stand over the ball wondering just how bad his shot might turn out.

Probably easier said than done, but just block the people watching out of your mind. And really, in the big scheme of things, who cares about your shot? It matters not one bit if you make a hole-in-one or hit it backward. Just hit it and go find it.

THE SWING

In March 1916, Ernest Jones was badly injured in a battle by German artillery near Loos in France. He had 16 pieces of metal removed from his head, right forearm, and right leg, which was subsequently amputated below the knee. Four months later, walking with the aid of an artificial limb, he shot 83 at Royal Norwich in Norfolk, England. A few weeks after that he had a 72 at Clacton in Essex.

That Ernest Jones should overcome such an obvious and restricting disability as this to shoot the scores he did and later become one of the best teachers of his day (and perhaps in the history of the game) suggests that more than anyone perhaps, Jones understood the secret to good golf. So what was his secret? Swing the clubhead.

Yes indeed, swing the clubhead. Don't go looking for variations, explanations, elaborations, or additions. Letting the clubhead swing, you see, creates far more centrifugal force (and consequently distance) than you'll ever get with a series of technically correct but swingspeed-sapping positions that you piece together.

The perfect golf swing should not feel like a series of set positions, but one continuous, flowing motion. It's the only way you'll ever generate clubhead speed.

TEACHING THE SWING

Today's teachers don't dismiss tempo and centrifugal force altogether, but they seem far more concerned with angles and the positions of the clubhead and body before and during the swing. With all due respect, these teachers have to pay the staff they employ at their numerous "academies" around the world somehow and they aren't going to do that by issuing one simple three-word instruction to every player they meet. People might catch on, after all.

Of course, you also need to be holding the club correctly, exhibiting sound posture, and have the ball positioned between your feet in just the right spot to hit the ball sweetly, and it would be wrong to suggest stockpiles of instruction books, magazine articles, videos, DVDs, downloads, and so on actually make the average Joe worse at golf than he otherwise could be. But for

most normal people (people with jobs, kids, and insufficient free time in which to practice eight hours a day), too much knowledge can be a bad thing.

FORCE VERSUS POWER

Jones emphasized the application of force over power. Everyone has power, he said, some more than others, but not everyone can apply that power correctly to a stationary golf ball. If they could, Phil Pfister of Charleston, West Virginia, currently the world's strongest man, would be the best golfer in the world, or at least the longest hitter of a golf ball. He's neither.

Jones asserted the only way to ensure all your power is directed forcefully into the back of the ball at the exact moment of impact is by forgetting mechanics, swinging the clubhead, and allowing the wrists, elbows, shoulders, hips, legs, knees, ankles, and toes to move naturally as they do when you are walking, and for them to follow the lead of the hands. "All other motions are admirable as followers," he said, "but disastrous as leaders."

Jones was constantly asked by people he met what the problem with their swing was. "Nothing," he would reply. "You do not have a swing."

Keep it Simple

I'll bet there are times when you do swing the club beautifully, gracefully even. When? Immediately after having sliced one into the trees. You storm over to your bag, pick out another ball, tee it up and hit it without a single thought as to how you're doing it. Beginners first need to familiarize themselves with the correct grip, posture, and ball position. But players who have been playing a while and have all that stuff down need to forget about swing planes, supernating wrists, and the like, and just swing their clubhead.

THE BALL IN FLIGHT

John Jacobs was the first teacher to discuss ball flight laws — why the ball behaves the way it does — in any great depth, back in the early '70s. His theories went largely uncontested until the turn of this century when science and technology had to stick their oar in and muddy the waters.

Type "golf shot's initial direction" into any search engine and you will get a plethora of matches. Inevitably, on the first few pages of results you find several sites that agree unreservedly with what Jacob's called "golf's geometry." In his book *Practical Golf*, Jacobs discussed "golf's four vital impact elements" — clubhead path, clubface angle, angle of descent, and clubhead speed — at great length, concluding, among other things, that the path of your clubhead dictates the direction in which your ball starts. Subsequent curvature — hooking to the left or slicing to the right — is caused, he added, by the angle of the clubface at impact in relation to its path.

Jacobs taught that a straight pull to the left is caused by an out-to-in swingpath with the clubface square to that path (in other words, closed to the target). A pull-hook (starts left, curves further left) occurs when the clubface is closed in relation to the out-to-in path and a pull-slice (starts left, slices right) is the result of a face that is open to that clubhead path.

Knowing all this made it easy to work out why a block-push (straight right), hook (starts right, curves way left) or push-slice (starts right, goes further right) happens. And it also allowed me to decipher how I hit the ball straight at my target, or why it might curve left or right after starting out on the intended line. I learned this lesson young, have lived by it since, and even taught it to others.

JACOBS' CHALLENGERS

Unfortunately, as is so often the case, that's not quite the whole truth, and a handful of the results for that Web search we carried out earlier will take you to sites that refute Jacobs' theories. One of them even goes as far as to call his ball flight laws the "Ball Flight Lies."

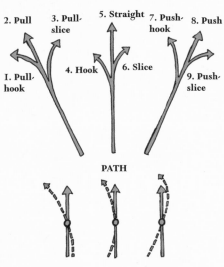

BALL FLIGHT

2. Pull 3. Pull-slice 5. Straight 7. Push-hook 8. Push
1. Pull-hook 4. Hook 6. Slice 9. Push-slice

PATH

FACE

Closed →	Pull-hook	Hook	Push-hook
Square →	Pull	Straight	Push
Open →	Pull-slice	Slice	Push-slice

I've hit every one of these shots several thousand times each. It definitely pays to know how swingpath and face angle affect a shot.

The authors of these sites insist that the clubface angle has a far greater effect on initial direction than its path, saying the ball starts on a line more or less perpendicular to the clubface regardless of its path. Your clubhead may be moving from out-to-in, they say, but the ball can still start true.

WHO'S RIGHT?

I've done more than enough research to tell you I haven't really got a clue. But after 20 years of hitting every kind of shot under the sun, and testing it out on the range countless times by hitting intentional hooks, slices, pulls, and blocks, I'm sticking with Jacobs. And Jack Nicklaus is a firm believer too, at least he was when he wrote the following in 2001: "The out-to-in path produces pulled shots when the clubface alignment matches it, or a left-to-right slice when the clubface is open to it at impact." Seems pretty unambiguous to me.

Also, I'm not sure I understand how the clubface theory explains how a ball could start left and slice back to the center — a very common shot. Your ball starts left of the target if the face is closed at impact, they say; but if the face is closed, and slice spin is caused by an open face, how does the ball slice back? Perhaps I'm missing something here.

However, because this theory has numerous backers who I assume are challenging Jacobs' assertions based on evidence from slow-mo cameras and the like, far be it from me to discount it.

I'm sure there is a degree of truth in what both camps say. Perhaps the faster the club is moving, the greater effect the clubhead's path has on the ball's initial direction — or that may be garbage. Anyway, I'm sure it won't be long before mathematicians come up with a scary formula to explain it all.

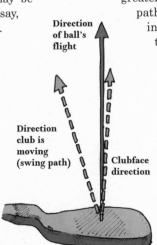

Direction of ball's flight

Direction club is moving (swing path)

Clubface direction

An alternative theory to Jacobs' Ball Flight Laws.

THE IMPORTANCE OF STRATEGY

There seem to be a lot of "most important lessons" in this book. And here's another. Good strategy, or course management, can save you plenty of strokes without you changing a thing in your set-up or swing. You don't even have to practice. All you have to do, in fact, is make better decisions; hit the shots you know you can handle and avoid those you'll never pull off in a million years.

Imagine you're on the tee of a straight, 330-yard par 4 with a narrow fairway bordered on the left by trees and on the right by a lake. The green is small, quick, and the pin cut on the right side, just over a deep bunker. You are playing a strokeplay medal round (for matchplay strategy see page 99) so what your opponent or partner gets up to really doesn't matter, nor does the hole's Stroke Index. Which club and what type of shot do you hit?

Weekend golfers will haul the driver out long before they even get to the tee — after all it's a 330-yard hole, so it must be a driver, right? Well, hold on just a minute there tiger; the driver may be the club that gets you

nearest to the green, but you probably can't actually reach it and there's a bit of trouble short of the putting surface in the shape of some shaggy mounds and that deep bunker. Plus, your driver is the

2
Par 4

° 345 ° 316 ° 349 ° 250 ° 327

If you have a yardage book that shows the layout of the hole you are about to play, take the time to study it closely (while your opponent's hitting so as not to waste time) and devise a sound strategy for the hole taking your strengths into account and the places you really must avoid.

club that can curve the ball the most, so with the trees and water lurking on either side of the fairway, it could land you in a spot of bother. So why risk it?

Okay, so the driver's back in the bag. How about a 3-wood? Hmm, most amateurs hit their 3-wood every bit as waywardly as the driver so, again, probably not a great choice. In that case, how about a hybrid? Now you're talking. Say you hit a 17° hybrid 200 yards off a tee. That will leave you about 120–5 yards to the hole, assuming this course measures its holes to the center of the green. That's a nice, full 9-iron — a shot you've hit a thousand times before.

So, a hybrid it is then, but what's your line? Well, the pin is tucked behind the bunker on the right so that would suggest going left off the tee to leave yourself a clear line for your approach... but hang on, there are trees over on that side. Good point, we'll veer back toward the center of the fairway because having to hit a 9-iron over a bunker isn't as bad stymieing yourself behind a sturdy silver birch. So you play a 17° hybrid to the center of the fairway, a 9-iron slightly behind the hole and two-putt for a par.

If you normally hit a driver and take six you'll have saved yourself two shots with just a moment's deliberation back on the tee. Sensible course management like this really can be the only difference between 105 and 97, 94 and 86, or a sleeve of golf balls and the keys to a new sports car (or, more realistically, a new driver).

START AT THE HOLE
AND WORK BACKWARD

Always ask yourself: "which part of the green gives me the easiest putt?" Followed by: "from which part of the fairway is it easiest to find that part of the green?" And then lastly: "which club do I need to hit off the tee to put me in that spot in the fairway from which I can find the desired part of the green?" "Oh" you may ask, "can't I just slash away with my driver and be done with it?" If you like, but don't come running to me when you make a double bogey.

Other Considerations

If you're playing a par 5 with bunkers and water up by the green, which you can't possibly reach in two, think seriously about where you want to leave your second shot. If you're more comfortable hitting a 110-yard pitching wedge than a 25-yard lob over water and sand, doesn't it make sense to hit your second to a spot 110 yards short of the green rather than get as close to it as possible?

Always aim to leave yourself an uphill putt, especially if you know the greens are fast. Downhill putts, particularly quick ones, can be very tricky.

If you're in a deep bunker, ask yourself if you've ever got out of one that deep before. If not, swallow your pride and come out sideways. Your attempts to quite literally dig yourself out of trouble might amuse your partners, but you won't be laughing.

It's probably not a good idea to attempt a 240-yard carry over a deep gorge if the furthest you've ever carried a ball is 220 yards.

AT A STRETCH

The swing gurus can harp on about swing planes, swing speed, and swing paths until the cows come home, but if you're not flexible enough to turn, resist, pivot, and flex then you're going to have a hard time making a balanced and powerful swing.

I'm no physiotherapist but I do know that as we age our bodies inevitably weaken, become more prone to injuries, and get increasingly less flexible.

Golfers on the US Champions Tour still hit it 280 yards off the tee and shoot very impressive scores partly because of improved equipment and partly because the prize money is so great there's plenty of incentive to keep on keeping on. The biggest factor, however, is undoubtedly the high level of fitness and agility these over-50s maintain thanks to regular aerobic workouts and dedicated stretching.

Sadly, putting a club behind our backs, holding each end and twisting a couple of times, or swinging two clubs together on the 1st tee for 30 seconds, just isn't going to be enough. So, to remain flexible and able to swing hard at the ball without pain into your 40s, 50s, and beyond, I suggest you commit to a program of stretching exercises and perform them at least three or four times a week, but preferably every day.

I'm not laying down the law here, just gently nudging you toward the exercise mat or a comfy bit of carpet and encouraging you to do something that, in time, can actually become quite addictive and that will indubitably have a positive effect on your well-being and, far more importantly, your golf.

MY ROUTINE

Having recognized the need for daily stretches — I'm not getting any younger, and I've experienced bouts of pretty severe back pain for going on three years now, and my golf swing was actually beginning to hurt — I visited a physiotherapist and borrowed some DVDs from the local library. Going on what the physio told me and what I learned from the DVDs, I put together my own 20-minute routine that I try to complete every day, ideally in the mornings.

If all that sounds a bit keen, bear in mind that it is only 20 minutes. I don't follow it to the letter, and I certainly don't get outfitted in some lime green get-fit outfit, or for that matter the latest hi-tech athletic clothing; I just slip into some shorts and an old T-shirt. But there's no question it helps. Don't get me wrong, I still can't do the splits, but I can get the club pretty high above my head, transfer my weight correctly, hit a ball fairly hard, and maintain my balance.

As is the case with anything remotely medical you really need to take account of your own abilities; what suits one person will just as likely have another in spasms for a month. However, there are thousands of books, DVDs, and Web sites (just search for "golf stretches") out there with countless stretches for people of all ages, physiques, and flexibility. Perhaps you could visit a physio like I did, and benefit from some advice that is tailored to your needs.

I merely scratch the surface with my little collection, but it does a job so I'm in no hurry to add any more. So, to get

I Hamstring Stretch 1 — Basically, I make an upturned "V" with my body, placing my palms face down on the floor and keeping the soles of my feet grounded too.

Hamstring Stretch 2 — Lying on the floor, I raise one leg to 90° keeping it straight. Pointing my toes at my face, I find a point where I feel some discomfort in my hamstring, and hold this position for 20 seconds before swapping legs.

Knees to the Side — On my back, I raise my knees, together, off the ground, then move them to one side, and turn my head the other way for an extra "twist," before stretching the other way.

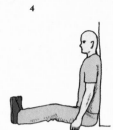

4 Against a Wall — I simply sit with my back flush against a wall, and I mean flush. I then push my backside up against the wall until I can feel my whole spine pushing against it, and remain in this position for a minute.

5 Shoulder Stretch — Placing one arm across my chest, I place my other hand on the elbow of the outstretched arm and pull my arm in toward my chest until I can feel a slight stretch. I hold the position before repeating the stretch on the other arm.

6 Upper Leg Stretch — Adopting a shoulder-width stance, and holding onto something for support with my left hand, I bring my right foot straight up behind me and grab it with my right hand. I then pull my foot up until I can feel a slight stretch on the front of my thigh. Then I relax, switch, and do the other leg.

you thinking along the right lines, here are just a few of my stretches. (Forgive me for not giving them proper names like "Supine Half Curl With Lateral Oblique Lunge" — I find all that stuff quite meaningless.)

BAGS, SHOES, AND GLOVES

What you carry your clubs in may not be as crucial to your score and enjoyment of the game as the clubs themselves, but it's still important in its own way; as are your choice of footwear and hand-wear. Golf, like most pursuits, is considerably more fun when you're comfortable.

THE CARRY/STAND BAG

Today's young golfers must wonder how those of us getting on in years ever managed to haul our clubs round 18 holes. The bags of my youth were significantly heavier, had a paucity of pockets, and no legs so I couldn't just let it fall off my shoulder and have it stand to attention next to my ball.

As a young golfer I had to bend over to put my bag on the ground, and back over again to take out the club of my choice, and back over yet again to pick the bag back up and return it to my shoulder. No wonder I and a good many of my contemporaries now face a life of back pain, medication, and physical therapy.

I am staggered every time I read this, but a top of the range carry/stand bag today, such as the Sun Mountain Swift, weighs less than 3 lb! The strap on my

1985 backbreaker probably weighed more than that, and the Swift has got legs! Honestly, 3 lb... with legs!

If that weren't reason enough to roll your eyes and commence a lengthy diatribe about how much tougher life used to be, modern bags have triangular non-slip foot pads "to resist sinking into the grass and sliding on slick surfaces," two back straps that criss-cross and thereby reduce the pressure on the shoulder on which you habitually carry your bag and even a pen holder. Thank goodness kids today don't have to carry a pencil in their pockets, that's all I can say.

And, of course, bags now come in a veritable palette of colors. In addition to all the usual colors, the Swift is available in russet, cactus, and Baltic (red, green, and blue to you and me), while Ogio's Vaporlite comes in juice, petrol, garnet, flame, and even chiaro — go look it up.

CART BAGS

For golfers who can no longer carry their clubs and play with the help of a motorized cart, weight and legs aren't so much of an issue. Sure, the heavier your bag the sooner your motorized cart's battery is going to pack up, but it's no big deal if your bag weighs a few more pounds than it could. And if you travel by cart, what the hell, get a 10 lb tour bag with room enough for your entire wardrobe and a couple of pets.

This bag can hold your clubs, your raingear, about 30 golf balls, an umbrella, your snacks, your gloves, keys, wallet, and sunscreen, and still weigh less than my old bag, empty. And it can probably do your laundry too.

A modern golf shoe is stylish, comfortable, and grips the ground like glue.

SHOES

It goes without saying that golf's technological revolution has had a major influence on shoes as well. Kilties, the strange, leather flaps on top of the shoe whose purpose was never made clear to me (it surely can't have been style) have thankfully been consigned to the dim and distant past, though a few manufacturers won't banish them altogether and still offer kiltied pairs, mostly in their women's ranges.

Thanks to vastly improved chassis design, better sole grips (rubber cleats now that metal spikes have also been cast out) and foam or gel-molded uppers, the stability, balance, and comfort of a golf shoe can't be compared with yesterday's stiff, poorly balanced shoes. Actually, they can: today's shoes are great; those from a generation ago were rubbish.

Modern shoes can get pretty costly though, especially if you're looking at Footjoy Classics and other top-of-the-range shoes; however, there are plenty of good-value shoes to be had. I get by with a pair of old GreenJoys, but if I were in the market for a new pair I'd probably opt for the Adidas Tour 360.

GLOVES

Two years ago, I purchased a glove boasting anatomical relief pads said to increase comfort and decrease friction, a pre-rotated finger design to promote the natural motion of my fingers and strategic index-to-hand motion and web interface zones to... well, who knows what they were for?

Shortly after buying this, I discovered it was illegal for use in competition largely because it was simply too advanced and put users of other, less futuristic gloves at a serious disadvantage. At least, that's how I read the ruling.

I can't help thinking the game's rules makers (the United States Golf Association in the US and the Royal and Ancient Golf Club everywhere else) were a little premature in this instance, because I'm as wayward and inconsistent as I ever was prior to purchasing it. Somehow I'm just not reaping the benefits of those strategic web interface zones.

My advice is not to waste too much time worrying about your choice of glove. To put it simply, leather gloves might cost a bit more than synthetic micro-fiber all-weather gloves, but won't be turning anyone into Tiger Woods.

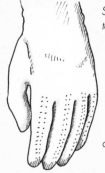

Some players prefer not to wear a glove, but I think that's because they grew up playing without one and just got used to it. If they ever tried one on, they'd probably discover a whole new world of grip and control.

WARMING UP RIGHT

The practice ground is perhaps my favorite place to go when attending a professional tournament. Here you'll see all the top players in fairly relaxed mode hitting far more shots than you'll ever see them hit out on the course.

But the range is worth finding for another reason. Observe closely and you'll learn a very important lesson; the warm-up isn't a time for reckless swings with the driver, but a structured session that hardly ever changes from day to day.

While the typical golfer's warm-up may involve nothing more arduous than a sprint from the car to the 1st tee and a few superficial stretches that really just make him feel a bit dizzy, the pros' systematic approach to warming up sees them arrive at the range an hour or so before their tee-time.

After several minutes' of proper, effective stretching, a pro will invariably pull out the sand wedge and hit a few pitches. It's a slow start that allows the muscles to get used to the idea they are wanted for another round of golf. Having loosened up a bit, the pro will begin working through the clubs, eventually reaching the driver, but probably only hitting four or five shots.

Many pros hit the same number of balls with each club — three fades, three draws, three high, three low, and three regular shots with a pitching wedge, then an 8-iron, then a 6, and so on. It's also common to see them work their way back up through the bag after hitting the driver, finishing with a short iron so they can establish a rhythm for the day.

The pro will head to the short-game area maybe half an hour before tee-time and hit a number of chips, pitches, lobs, and bunker shots. At Tee minus 15 minutes, the pro will stop at the practice putting green. Just as it was on the range, the task here is not to practice, but rather build a smooth tempo and also get a feel for the speed of the surfaces. Then a finish with a few short, easy putts, will help give

The pro's warm-up is relaxed, not hurried; hitting balls for 30 minutes or so establishing a rhythm for the day, and ending up on the practice putting green.

a very strong mental picture of the ball dropping into the hole.

The root cause of many amateurs' weaknesses out on the course can be found in their warm-ups. So here is a direct comparison between the structured routine a pro will run through, and the haphazard five minutes that many amateurs make do with. Which do you recognize?

PRO'S WARM-UP

+ Arrives an hour before tee-time
+ Several effective stretches
+ Starts with sand wedge
+ Hits 30–40 shots in total
+ Spends 15 minutes on short-game
+ Hits a couple of chip shots on the 1st tee perhaps
+ Spends 15 minutes putting
+ Starts feeling relaxed and loose

AMATEUR'S WARM-UP

+ Arrives five minutes before tee-time
+ Touches toes a couple of times
+ Starts with driver
+ Hits as many shots as will fit into two minutes
+ Hits a couple of chips and a couple of putts on the 1st tee perhaps
+ Starts feeling stressed and stiff

TEN-MINUTE WARM-UP

If other activities prevent you from arriving an hour before you start, at least do a few decent stretches (see pages 32–3), hit a few chips and putts on or around the putting green, and make a few smooth swings with the club you will be hitting off the 1st tee, trying to clip a few blades of grass and focusing on tempo and balance.

GOLFING MATTERS

Go Easy on Your Greenskeeper

We watch the Masters on TV and want greens just like Augusta's. We see European Tour players taking on 7,500-yard courses and want the course we play on lengthened. We watch the Players Championship from the TPC of Sawgrass with its exciting, if a little gimmicky, island green and wonder when we're going to get ours.

Moves to recreate these conditions are often reckless and ill-conceived, however. What we tend to forget is that Augusta National (home of the Masters) has an almost limitless budget, a greenskeeping staff of dozens, it closes for half the year, it probably hosts a fifth the number of rounds that most courses do (or a tenth in the case of municipals), and the weather in Georgia is normally pretty good. Everything that your course isn't, hasn't, or doesn't in fact.

Extending courses is counter-productive because 99 percent of golfers have no business playing any course over 7,000 yards. They couldn't reach many of the par 4s let alone par 5s and rounds would become that bit longer at a time when people's recreational time is getting shorter. Plus building new tees is really expensive, which, as we've seen before, means higher green fees and higher membership subscriptions.

As for Sawgrass and its island green; do you really want to lose half a dozen balls at a single hole?

PICKING A PRO

Tiger Woods has one. Jack Nicklaus had one in the prime of his career. Nick Faldo went from under-achieving journeyman to multi-major winner after finding the right man for him. Tom Watson, Arnold Palmer, Bobby Jones, Seve Ballesteros, Greg Norman, and Annika Sorenstam all have had or still have one. Could it be that you need a teacher too?

While it's true certain players don't benefit from formal coaching, I am almost willing to bet my house you would become a more competent golfer by taking lessons, especially if you haven't been playing long.

Beginners need to learn the fundamentals before proceeding to the full swing, while seasoned players require if not constant observation then at least occasional confirmation that their set-up is sound. Nicklaus used to start each season with a lesson from his man Jack Grout just to make sure his basics had survived the winter. And if it's good enough for the Golden Bear, it is most assuredly good enough for the rest of us.

SO WHO YOU GONNA CALL?

It's probably okay for total beginners to phone the nearest course, range, golf center, or academy (incidentally, when did places where you learn golf start calling themselves "Academies," and the guys that run these places "Deans"? I mean, it's not ballet or military exercises we're learning here) and ask for the least expensive pro to take them out and show them the ropes. It's likely you'll get a 17-year-old apprentice, but he should be able to get you holding the club and standing to the ball correctly at least.

If you build a good rapport with Junior and are confident he can take you to the next stage by all means stick with him. I've seen enough nightmare situations though — I was responsible for plenty myself during my time as an overly eager young teacher — to suggest you find someone with a little more experience to take over from here. What you definitely, absolutely, positively do not want is a young chap who thinks he knows it all (something I've definitely been guilty of in the past) teaching you to swing like Tiger Woods. If you had Woods's physical attributes then perhaps you could swing like him; but you don't, so you can't.

Group classes are a good option for beginners. You learn the basics but pay a fraction of the cost of individual lessons.

EXPERIENCE

Find a pro who has seen it all before — every swing and every body type — and who can take what ability you have and maximize your potential.

The Lesson from Hell

I recount the following story knowing full well that ten years previously the young teacher could have been me and the pupil any one of the poor, defenseless souls who came to me for lessons.

One bright, sunny day a few summers ago, I was at the driving range when I became aware of a lesson going on in the bay next to mine. A very young assistant pro was instructing a middle-aged woman whom I suspect hadn't been playing for more than a month.

I couldn't help listening in and was astonished to hear the pro talk about swing planes, resistance, and leverage. The woman clearly felt some discomfort every time she tried to keep her right knee bent while reaching for the roof with her hands. She grimaced when trying to maintain her body angles throughout the swing.

According to the textbook, the pro was right all along. But according to the feedback he should have picked up from his charge's expressions, my guess is that this lesson did nothing to encourage her to come back.

Unless you're playing scratch, a good teacher won't ask you to pronate your forearms or resist the turn of the upper body against relatively static hips. A good teacher will keep it simple and appropriate for your level. A good teacher will notice your belly sticking over your trouser belt or your troublesome back, and will have asked about your six-day-a-week job and how little time you have to practice. A good teacher will ask what it is you hope to achieve from your lessons, and will be able to tell you whether your aspirations are realistic. And rather than take you on the two-year swing-building odyssey that Faldo embarked upon with David Leadbetter, your wise old hand will offer suggestions as to how you can make your faulty, but impossibly deep-rooted, swing still work for you.

BOTTOM LINE

One point worth remembering is that your pro has every right to expect some effort on your part. No matter how good any pro is, if you aren't going to practice what you're told, you may as well not bother showing up.

Ask questions, be clear about what is being suggested, and practice whatever you learn. But if it's obvious your pro is asking something of your body that it clearly isn't capable of, I suggest that you look elsewhere.

A veteran pro can work with what little you've got and still make you a strong player.

THE FUNDAMENTALS OF PUTTING

There's a well-known story about a kid who, watching golf for the first time, asks his father watching with him why the players always try to miss their first putt and then knock the second putt in. And I suppose until you learn just how testing putting can be, the question is a fair one.

On the face of it, tapping a small ball toward a hole three times as wide, across a carefully maintained surface with a tool devised by one of the world's top metallurgists really shouldn't be as difficult as we make it. And it certainly shouldn't cause uncontrollable psychological and muscular twitches — the yips (see page 98) — in otherwise normal, healthy human beings.

I believe thinking that putting is easy actually helps make it so. A reliance on expensive putters and convoluted training aids just seems to make it more complicated than it need be.

No two putters (the people, not the clubs) are alike. If you watched Bernhard Langer circa 1990, Chris DiMarco, and Phil Mickelson putting, and didn't know any better, you might not think they were all trying to achieve the same thing. Some crouch, some stand tall. Some use a conventional reverse overlap grip, while an increasing number don't. And some allow the putterhead to move back and through on a smaller version of their full swing arc, while others move it straight back and through. But as with the full swing, good results start with a set of fixed fundamentals that you really must adhere to if you want to get the ball in the hole sooner rather than later.

GRIP AND SET-UP
✦ First, get comfortable and spread your weight evenly between both feet.
✦ Grip the putter how you like (see below), but generally your palms should face each other. Grip the club lightly. With the standard reverse overlap method, the putter grip should rest in the palm of your left hand and the shaft point straight up your left arm so it appears to be an extension of the forearm.

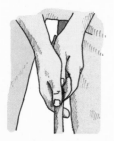

Reverse Overlap. Index finger of left hand rests on middle fingers of right hand. Both thumbs on top.

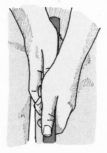

Cross-handed. Left hand below right, again thumbs on top.

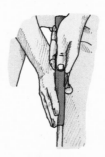

The Claw.

The Claw Mk II.

- I've seen good putters whose feet were open or closed to the target line, but everyone's shoulders are square.
- Some good putters have their eyes inside the target line, but no good putter ever positioned them outside the line. Most position their eye directly over the ball, or try to.
- Position the ball forward of center; how much is up to you. I've seen some put it opposite their left big toe, but I don't know of any good putters who position the ball behind center.

THE STROKE

Only your shoulders, arms, and hands should move; while your knees, waist, and head remain totally still. (Envisage the "Y" formed by the putter and your arms remaining fixed throughout.) The backswing and follow-through should be roughly the same length — accelerate the putterhead through the ball.

The speed and tempo of the stroke should remain constant for all putts. All that changes is the length of stroke: the longer the putt, the further the putterhead moves back and through.

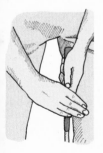

The Claw Mk III.

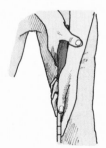

Bernhard Langer resorted to this after numerous bouts of the yips. Hey, whatever works, right?

HIT DOWN TO HIT UP

This concept is touched upon in "Ball Position," again in "Backspin," and a number of other places, but it is still worthy of its own entry. It is, after all, so very, very important.

At first it may sound strange, and indeed in many other sports, if you want the ball to go up, you hit the ball, well... up. In this game the clubhead of a short or medium

Ball first, ground second.

iron (the driver should be rising as it contacts the ball sitting on a tee, and long irons should ideally sweep the ball off the ground without taking much of a divot) should be moving downward when it strikes the ball. This creates the backspin that helps the ball climb steeply into the air and stop quickly on the green.

By positioning the ball correctly, somewhere between the center of your stance and opposite your left heel (see page 22) and then transferring your weight properly on to the instep of your back foot in the backswing and forward on to the front foot in the downswing (nearly all your weight should be on your front foot with your waist facing the target at the end of your swing), you should strike the ball moments before the club reaches the low point on its swing arc.

WHAT TO WEAR

You won't believe me, but at the start of the 20th century, golfers were extremely well dressed. They still looked pretty spiffy well into the 1930s and 40s. So when did it all go wrong?

First, a little history. A hundred years ago, the golfer's wardrobe consisted of collared shirts, ties, and tweedy jackets. When standards began dropping (that may be harsh; let's say dipping) in the 1920s, golfers soon realized they could hit the ball further simply by removing their starchy outer garments, and that wearing something with a bit of color wasn't illegal. Slowly, the white, long-sleeved shirt was replaced by short-sleeved, soft-collared T-shirts and jackets by either cardigans or sweaters.

Smart, formal, dapper even. Shame he couldn't get his hands above his head without ripping a sleeve.

EXPRESS YOURSELF

Sartorially, golfers began parting ways in the 1940s and 50s. Virtually identical up to that point, many players remained elegant while others began to express their inner dazzle. So while Sam Snead and Ben Hogan preferred understated class, Jimmy Demaret would take trips to New York to shop for vividly colored shirts and slacks.

Next, while Arnold Palmer, Jack Nicklaus, and Gary Player were keeping it simple (although Player did once slip on a pair of trousers with one black leg and one white leg), Demaret's garishly saddled shoes were being filled by Doug Sanders, the Peacock, who missed a tiny putt on the 18th green at St Andrews in the 1970 Open Championship that would have won him the title. He lost the next day in a play-off with Nicklaus and, with all due respect, I'm glad he did. I mean, can you imagine someone wearing tight, plum-colored trousers and a bright pinky-orange cardigan holding aloft the Claret Jug? The very idea...

IT ONLY GETS WORSE

Of course, the less said about the rest of the '70s the better, although it's worth pointing out the style-free fashions of the decade sealed golf's reputation for poor dress sense seemingly forever.

The '80s and '90s saw only minor improvements. Yes, the orange-and-green checked, flared trousers Tom Watson wore when winning the 1977 Open (held up by a ghastly white belt, which has somehow made an unwelcome return to the game) had been replaced by more restrained khakis. But these were shapeless and, worse, pleated. Shirts became horribly baggy with sleeves coming down a few inches lower than the elbow. Not only could you play golf in them, you could camp out in them too.

THE LINDBERG EXPLOSION

At the start of this century, Sweden's Jesper Parnevik spurned the baggy look in favor of tighter, shorter-sleeved, shirts and flat-front trousers designed by

On the right golfer, short-sleeved, figure-hugging shirts work well.

Stockholm's J. Lindberg. Parnevik had the frame suited to closer-fitting clothes and for the first time in 30 years a professional golfer looked cool. But now every Tom, Dick, Justin, Sergio, and Mikko is out there with the drain-pipe orange trousers, obligatory white belt and tight shirts. And while it shows some progress, seeing the occasional fat bloke in figure-hugging attire is less than appetizing.

But it's not just the big-boned who should stay clear. Old, bad, and infrequent golfers should reject it too. The Lindberg Look is strictly for the young, slim professional — the rest of us just look silly.

KEEP IT SIMPLE

My policy, for as long as I can remember, has been to mimic what I wear to work on the golf course. That means bland khakis (and the occasional slightly more elaborate pair of slacks), unfussy shirts, and black or brown shoes. If you really want to wear more decorative clothing, like England's Ian Poulter for instance, then you had better have the game to back it

up. I'd say you need to be playing off five or better to justify the attention a Lindberg print will get you, and get down to scratch before wrapping a white belt around a pair of neon trousers won't outshine your game.

Mock Turtles

Not an indie-rock band from Manchester, Lewis Carroll's fictional character, or even a Victorian soup. Golf's version of the mock turtle is, in fact, a sweater that resembles a polo-neck and which Tiger Woods made popular a few years back. Comfortable, stylish, warm, and not too dressy, it works as well on the high street as it does the golf course. It still doesn't quite suit the guy whose belly droops over his belt, though. But then, what does?

The mock turtle looks good especially on a certain Tiger Woods.

⚓ ON THE SLOPES

A lot of instruction books put shots from sloping lies in the "Trouble Shots" chapter; but they really needn't be any trouble at all.

These shots are all about balance. Make a few minor adjustments to your address position, and a short, compact swing and you'll do fine.

WHEN YOU'RE HITTING UPHILL:
+ Take more club. Hitting uphill means a longer shot, effectively. The steeper the slope the more club you need.
+ Tilt your right shoulder down a little and flex your right knee slightly more than usual. This prevents too steep an attack on the ball.
+ Play the ball in the middle of your stance and aim a little right as the tendency is to pull the shot.
+ Don't let your weight hang back on your back foot. Push it forward on to the front foot as normal.

WHEN YOU'RE HITTING DOWNHILL:
+ Take less club, as shooting downhill effectively shortens the shot.
+ Tilt your left shoulder down a little and straighten your right leg a touch.
+ Play the ball an inch back of center, and aim slightly left of your target as the ball has a tendency to fade.

+ Again, let your weight move on to your front foot and feel like the club moves down the slope after impact.

WHEN THE BALL IS ABOVE YOUR FEET:
+ Aim right as the slope will encourage a pull or hooked shot.
+ The ball is closer to you so grip well down the handle.
+ Play the ball in the center or an inch back of center.
+ Push your weight forward slightly as it will want to fall back down the slope on to your heels.

WHEN THE BALL IS BELOW YOUR FEET:
+ Aim left of your target as this shot will want to move left to right in the air.
+ Put a little more flex in your knees and tilt a little more from the hips.
+ Grip the club at the top of the handle.
+ Again, play the ball in the center or slightly to the right of center.
+ Place a bit more weight on your heels.

Sloping lies call for a few alterations to your usual set-up and a shorter swing to help you keep your balance.

HEROES

Golf is so hard to master, amateurs can't help but look on wide-eyed when they see the world's best crack a driver down the fairway.

I'm at an age now where I don't really have heroes, at least not in the sense that I want to be Tiger Woods when I grow up. I no longer idolize but respect such players. I could happily watch Woods on the practice ground all day, and who wouldn't admire the work he does for his charitable foundation and learning center? But I don't have a huge Tiger poster on my bedroom wall, a Tiger headcover, or a Tiger screensaver.

That said, I must admit to keeping a Seve Ballesteros scrapbook when I was younger. It couldn't have lasted more than a couple of months and was randomly cobbled together — just a few photos and clippings — but it kept me busy for a while and helped strengthen my love for the game. Today, Woods is similarly revered by kids around the world, and it's only to be hoped that such a great role model should help cement the next generation's love for the game.

I wouldn't mind it a bit if my kid chose Tiger Woods for a hero.

Uniqueness

Far too many golf courses are guilty of marketing misinformation and near hysterical hype when promoting their layouts. I mean, just how many "unique" golf courses can there be? And exactly which championships has your "Championship Course" hosted lately?

This "problem" is out of control in the US and getting worse in the UK. I recently read of a new course in England that not only claimed to be unique but also entirely natural despite having been "created" by one of the world's top course architects. How do you create something entirely natural?

I understand these courses are trying to attract business, and that's not a crime; but the truth of the matter is that too many of these "unique" courses have very little to distinguish them from dozens of others.

No golf course is unique, not even the Old Course at St Andrews. It's a links course, a very special links course, but still one of over 200 of its type in the world. The closest I've seen to unique was a nine-hole course somewhere in South Australia whose name I forget. It was laid out over a wide expanse of dirt, its greens small squares of bitumen that softened in the midday sun, and into which I sank. If this is unique, then I'm not sure that uniqueness is something worth shouting about.

PLAY A LINKS

Britain and Ireland are fortunate to have a virtual monopoly on links courses. If you've never experienced their very particular charms and challenges then I urge you to stop whatever you're doing (reading this book presumably), get on the phone, and make a tee-time at a links course — any one will do.

It might look bleak and fairly uninviting to begin with, but if you haven't played a links before you'll understand what all the fuss is about by the time you reach the 3rd tee.

What is a Links?

Some say a river estuary, or firth, must be close or that there should be nine holes out to a distant point and nine back to the clubhouse. Others maintain it must be nearby the sea with views of the water from most, if not all, the holes.

There are just too many exceptions to these rules for me though. The bottom line really is coastal sand dunes on which fine fescue grasses grow, but which sustain very few trees. Low-lying bushes, principally gorse, are common, however, and the ground is usually undulating, the turf firm and fast thanks to its exceptional drainage and the bunkers deep enough to prevent the fine sand being blown away. And, because most of them are very old, links courses are almost entirely natural with none of the artificial frills such as ponds, lakes, fountains, waterfalls, and flowerbeds so common on modern courses. Also,

you can expect a handful of blind shots where the drive or approach shot has to clear a dune.

Are links courses bleak? Certainly, on a gray winter's day, they can be downright desolate. Are they unfair? Sure they are, you can hit a perfect drive only to watch it rebound off a small mound into the rough. Are they quirky? Absolutely, some links holes are just plain weird. But these are all the reasons why we love them so much.

What a Links Definitely is Not

Because of the global appeal of the Open Championship and the popularity of golf trips to Britain and Ireland, links courses are practically revered around the world. So it's no great surprise marketers who don't really have a clue what a links course is apply the term to virtually any course with a few mounds, a bit of wind, and a lack of trees.

It doesn't matter how many fake mounds a course has though, how much wind blows through it, or how few trees there are; if it's not on or near the coast, doesn't play over undulating sand dunes, and its turf is soft and lush, then it doesn't make the list.

How to Play Links Golf

I'm really not the man to be telling you how to play a links as I've had precious little success on them. The best I've ever shot over the dunes, in fact, was 75 at Southport and Ainsdale many, many moons ago. If, like me, you're used to playing an inland parkland course with its broad-leafed grass, tree-lined fairways, and artificial water hazards, then playing a links course is the equivalent of moving from the French Open to Wimbledon. It's a totally different form of the game that requires a whole new approach.

You need to take advantage if you're teeing off downwind, and you need to know how not to fight the wind when it's in your face. A few adjustments might well be necessary when putting too (see page 100).

Fairway lies tend to be very tight and firm, and if you make contact with the ball slightly before hitting the turf and take a shallow divot you should create sufficient backspin to hold the equally firm greens. With irons, you should play the ball in the middle of your stance — hands ahead, shaft angled forward — and feel like you squeeze the ball off the turf.

Off such tight lies, and also in the bunkers, you will need a sand wedge with very little bounce. Indeed, it might be better to use your lob wedge out of the sand. Play the ball a little further back in your stance than normal and come down quite steeply and slightly closer to the ball than you would at an inland course where the sand is typically light and fluffy. It is much finer and denser at a links so if you enter too far behind the ball the club will probably skim across the surface and you'll blade the shot straight into the 6 ft revetted wall in front of you.

Finally, if your ball bounces at a funny, unexpected angle off a bump in the fairway and rolls into a bunker, don't say that every book and magazine article you've ever read about links courses didn't warn you.

If you're unlucky enough to encounter a bunker face like this I would highly recommend coming out backward.

HOLE·IN·ONE

Don't think for a second I'm going to give you any tips on how to make a hole-in-one, except perhaps to "hit it straight at the hole with the right club." You see, despite hitting the pin, the rim, and the flag itself on any number of occasions, an "ace" has eluded me all these years.

Walter, a native of Japan but now living in Honolulu, was in no hurry to celebrate his hole-in-one. Despite it being the first of his life and coming at an age when he was unlikely to make another, he quietly picked his ball out of the hole, put it in his pocket, and started off for the next tee.

"For Heaven's sake Walter," I lamented. "You just made a hole-in-one. Aren't you going to at least tip your cap to an imaginary gallery?"

Walter looked at me sternly and, because of the language barrier, lifted his finger to his lips and uttered something that needed no English on his part or Japanese on mine for me to understand: "Shhhh," he said, shaking his head.

As Walter strode off, his friend Toshio, the eldest of the three retired Japanese bankers with whom I had been grouped, walked over and explained. "When you're playing in England, are you meant to buy everyone in the clubhouse a drink after a hole-in-one?"

"Absolutely," I said.

"Well, this is the busiest course in the world; and there are a lot of people in the clubhouse."

I could see the course was packed, but I hadn't the faintest idea that Ala Wai GC — a couple of miles from Waikiki Beach — was the busiest course in the world. Now that I did, I knew where Walter was coming from.

But on reflection, I doubt very much that I could have been so reticent and maintained my composure quite like Walter. I suspect, in fact, I might have done something really silly like climb a tree, dive into a pond, or do some ridiculous Chi Chi Rodriguez-style dance with the flagstick.

AS GOOD AS IT GETS

I've come close to making an ace several times, but the blessed ball has never dropped. A few days after the round with my new retired Japanese banker buddies I was at a course with one of those only-in-Hawaii-type par 3s: mountains covered in lush jungle to my right, turquoise ocean to my left, and a 200-yard-wide inlet between the tee and green in which waves crashed against the rocks. To say it was postcard material doesn't do it justice, and a hole-in-one at this hole, of all holes, would surely rank very high on one's list of memorable lifetime achievements.

My ball came within two inches of giving me dinner conversation material for years to come. Okay, it would have become dull at some point, but like any golfer, I could have embellished the story to include a couple of whales breaching in the bay below, and perhaps a brutal tempest moving in off the ocean.

My ball came so close to going in that a guy standing on his villa balcony some 50 yards to the right of the green threw his hands in the air and screamed "Yeeeeeeooooowwwwhhhhh" as it rolled toward the hole, caught the lip, and spun out.

You know, I pay my taxes, I repair two pitch marks on most greens that I come to, and I even feed the ducks occasionally on cold winter days. I deserve a hole-in-one. And when I read about a Californian woman who claims to have made 16 in 2007 alone I can't help but feel just a little snubbed.

After an ace on a hole like this, I might retire my clubs to the attic forever. Apart from winning a major, could the game get much sweeter?

WATCH TIGER WOODS

He's still got a little way to go to reach Jack Nicklaus' record of 18 pro major championships but, assuming he remains healthy, it's only a matter of time before he does. Surely he's the finest player ever, and until you see him play you have no idea how hard and how purely a golf ball can be struck.

At the 2000 Open Championship, played on the Old Course at St Andrews, I had the good fortune to follow Woods for all 18 holes of his second round, inside the ropes — a privilege afforded members of the press. His 66 looked utterly routine. He never missed a shot and by the end of play he led by three. By the time he was handed the Claret Jug on Sunday evening, he was eight shots ahead of second place.

Watching Woods play is a seminal moment in a golf fan's life. To a non-golfer that will sound absurd, but I think it's a shame they can't appreciate just how brilliant Woods is. You can always remember the time(s) you saw him play and most of the shots he hit. I suppose it must have been the same watching Sobers or DiMaggio swing a bat, Pele kick a football, Ali land a punch, Schumacher round a bend, Hinault or Armstrong climb L'Alpe D'Huez, Spitz win Gold, Red Rum negotiate Beecher's Brook, or Sampras fire a cross-court forehand.

The crack of impact when Woods hits a driver is unlike any sound you will have heard on a golf course before. Unless the sky is blue and the sun behind you, it's unlikely you'll be able to follow the flight of his ball, for a few holes at least while your eyes adjust. You mouth crude words when you see how high and how far he hits his irons and you shake your head at his delicate touch around the greens. His putting? Let's just say don't ever bet on him missing, no matter how far away he is.

I would suggest a few things to look out for that might help you with your own game. But apart from his textbook address position and how still he keeps his head when putting, I'm not sure any connection can be made between his game and ours. Just take whatever opportunity you get to watch him and go home satisfied you saw the best golfer that ever lived.

Tiger Woods in full flight is an awesome sight.

MAKING LISTS

Pick up a copy of any major golf publication and you can't help but notice that the world of golf is rankings mad.

The charm of St Enodoc in Rock, Cornwall, England is almost too much to bear.

The cynic in me says a large part of the reason these rankings exist is to stimulate advertising revenue, and give each issue a snappy cover line; and while there's more than a grain of truth in that, they also provoke a lot of feisty debate in the clubhouse bar — my top three, by the way, are the Brancaster, the Bunker Bar at Bandon Dunes, and the modest but perfectly appointed bar in the men's locker room at Bay Hill in Florida, where I once spent an afternoon sipping cocktails and playing cards with my partners from the morning. For what it's worth, here are my ten favorite courses:

+ St Enodoc, England
+ West Lancashire, England
+ Narin and Portnoo, Ireland
+ Kingston Heath, Australia
+ Black Mesa, USA
+ North Berwick, Scotland
+ Old Course, St Andrews, Scotland
+ Royal Portrush, Ireland
+ Bandon Dunes, USA
+ Walton Heath (Old), England

DAWN OR DUSK?

If, like me, you're at your physical and mental best well after midday, playing golf shortly after dawn is all too rare a treat. But as all golfers know, it's easier to be up at 6 a.m. for a tee-time than at 9 a.m. to go to work.

If circumstances were different — no family, no job, a body that functioned properly before mid-morning, and so on — I'd play all my golf between the hours of 5:00 and 8:30 a.m. This is a magical time when the rising sun hasn't yet grown uncomfortably hot and the early morning light gives the colors of the grass, trees, flowers, and sky an intensity you just don't get later in the day. The fresh, cool dew cleans the air, the greenstaff are whirring into action, and, without taking up where Robert Browning left off, the birds are singing, and all is right with the world.

If you've never played golf at this time of day, I suggest you try it at least once this summer. However, if that's really not for you, if you have a hard time waking up, showering, breakfasting, and driving to the course before sun-up then don't worry, late summer evenings are almost as good. The course is emptying, the

light equally sublime, and by the time you walk in off the 18th green, the bar's open.

Golf at dawn, a real treat.

CELEBRATING THE RIGHT WAY

Hole a 15ft putt on the last green to win the club championship and it's likely you're going to react. But you don't want your win to be remembered only for the ludicrous celebration you unloaded as the putt dropped.

At the 1990 US Open at Medinah in Chicago, 45-year-old Hale Irwin had a monster putt on the 72nd green to take the clubhouse lead. The ball took forever to cross the wickedly fast putting surface but eventually toppled in, whereupon Irwin set off on a mad dash around the gallery whooping, hollering and high-fiving.

After holing a curly birdie putt on the final green, which he himself later admitted never looked like it was going in, Seve Ballesteros won the 1984 Open Championship at St Andrews, and went into his famous 360° conquering matador routine.

Both celebrations were a touch excessive perhaps but, given the context, entirely justified. Irwin hadn't won a major for 11 years and became the oldest winner of the US Open. Seve's second Claret Jug came at his favorite course after beating two of his biggest rivals in Bernhard Langer and Tom Watson. Plus, he always was a bit of a showboat.

For heaven's sake calm down. You're embarrassing yourself.

Celebratory Don'ts in Club Competitions

+ Do not doff your cap — no one's looking.
+ Do not throw your ball to the gallery — no one's there to catch it.
+ Do not throw your hat into the air — save that for graduation day.
+ Do not stand still with both arms raised for more than three seconds.
+ Do not jump up and down, run to the cup (run anywhere for that matter), blow any kisses, look at your partners with a sort of "Take that!" gesture, point at the hole, dive into any ponds, moonwalk, or wave the flag around in the air.
+ On no account start crying.

You may be something of an exhibitionist yourself, but I'm afraid your win just doesn't warrant such excess. In most individual club competitions, anything more than a single fist pump and a whispered "Yes!" is generally considered vulgar. If you're playing in a team competition, however, and you hole the putt that wins the overall match, by all means pump your fist twice, maybe three times, and embrace your teammates. No, on second thoughts, just shake their hands and, if you must, slap their backs. Whatever you do though, do it after having shaken your opponent's hand.

THE BASIC PITCH

On and around the green is where club golfers can make quick inroads into their handicap. The 50–80-yard pitch shot is a stock short-game shot that club golfers will need five or six times a round, possibly more. So it would be to your very great advantage were you to master it.

LOFTED PITCH

Most of the distance between the ball and the hole is covered in the air. If contact is pure, you're playing from a nice firm lie and hitting a high-spinning ball, it should bounce one or twice before stopping abruptly.

✦ Use your sand wedge or lob wedge (60°) and play the ball roughly midway between your feet or perhaps an inch or two back of that. Your hands should be ahead of the ball with the shaft angled forward slightly.

✦ Grip down the club a little and stand closer to the ball than normal with your feet closer together. Open your stance slightly and press a little more weight onto the front foot.

✦ With soft, supple arms — definitely not stiff and rigid — and allowing your wrists to hinge naturally, hit down making contact with the ball first then the ground. There should be a small but pronounced shift of weight, so finish on your front foot with your waist facing the target.

✦ To gauge how long your swing should be and how hard you need to hit the ball in order for it to travel the desired distance, I'm afraid you will have to practice.

RUNNING PITCH

To hit a slightly lower, flatter shot that runs more along the ground (useful if the hole is cut at the back of the green and you're near the front), use a pitching wedge or 9-iron. Bear in mind if you have a bad lie and can't generate much backspin, the running shot with a less-lofted club is the better option. If the pin is at the front but you have a bad lie and can't play the more lofted pitch, accept the fact that 20–30 ft. past the hole may be the best you can do.

Play the ball in the center of your stance, hands forward, to promote the necessary downward strike. Swing back allowing your wrists to break a little and keep your head still. Finish facing the target.

READING THE GREENS

I could give you a few pointers on what to look for when reading greens, but when it comes to actually judging how hard to hit the putt and on what line it should start, I'm afraid you're on your own.

The best green-readers have a sixth sense that allows them to visualize how much a putt will break when hit at a certain speed. It's partly innate, but you can certainly become a better judge of speed, and therefore line, with experience and practice. But even with this skill, you still need to consider the effect certain conditions will have on your putt. I reckon most people instinctively pick up on the following factors, but it doesn't hurt to say them again:

Begin analyzing your putt as you approach the green. There is a lot you can learn from a distance.

+ The shorter the grass, the quicker the putt, of course.
+ Early morning dew, or indeed any moisture, will slow a putt.
+ The darker the shade of green, the slower the putt.
+ The coarser the grass, the slower the putt.
+ Greens will probably be slightly slower late in the day than they were in the morning.

It pays to start reading the green as you approach it. I've heard it said the best place to get a good indication of a green's contours is from 20 yards away. Note any significant slopes, the color of the grass, firmness of the ground, and wind (yes, wind affects putts). Feed all this into your on-board computer, hit return, and you should be left with a very clear picture of your ball rolling into the hole.

There is another more scientific way to read the line of your putt than by simply bending down and looking at it.

A handful of pros do it today, and several greats from the past did it. However, Tiger doesn't and nor do I; not because Tiger doesn't, you understand, but because I don't really know how to.

PLUMB-BOBBING

To plumb-bob correctly, you need to discover which is your dominant eye. The simplest way is to form a circle with your thumb and index finger and stretch out your arm. Position the circle so there is a distant object in the center. Then close each eye in turn and whichever eye you can still see the object with, or the one that moves it the least, is your dominant eye.

Now stand a few feet behind your ball, on a direct line with the hole. Hold your putter up at arm's length and let it hang vertically. Look with your dominant eye and hold the putter so the shaft cuts through the ball. Whichever side of the shaft the ball appears on is the direction in which the putt will break. Whether this actually shows you something new, or simply confirms a line that you had already assessed intuitively depends on who you listen to. Plenty of people believe in it; but, like I say, I don't do it.

PLAY MORE BREAK

Amateurs tend to miss breaking putts on the low side of the hole. We're often told to aim at the apex of a putt — the point at which the curve is greatest. But if we aim at that point the ball will most likely already be below it by the time it draws level. Because they travel faster immediately after impact, putts move fairly straight early on and curve back to the hole as they lose momentum. But a putt will break some before it reaches what we think is the apex. And that means if you aim at the apex your putt starts on the wrong line. It's difficult to say exactly how much more break amateurs should play, but rest assured you need to play more break.

If you know what you're doing and don't waste any time you should at least try plumb-bobbing. It could confirm your initial thoughts on which way the putt might break.

A Word About Grain

Ten years ago in Harare, before Mugabe wrecked the place, I played on greens with so much grain (the tendency of grass to grow in a certain direction) that reading putts was next to impossible. I would see a considerable right-to-left break but my playing partner, a local, would insist the putt broke left to right. Never quite able to trust his advice, I would stroke my ball and watch in shock as it turned uphill, away from the hole. In northern Europe, and Britain in particular, greens don't really have grain. There's not as much sun so growth isn't as rapid and, of much greater significance, the turf is totally different.

In America, however, grain is common in the south on Bermudagrass greens, although clubs rotate mowing patterns so no single pattern is ever truly established. And when you hear TV commentators mention grain at a PGA Tour event put your hands over your ears and shout "I can't hear you," because when the green is mowed as short as it is at big-time golf events, it is too short for grain to have any effect.

⛳ MASTERS TICKETS

When Dorothy and friends emerge from the forest toward the end of their arduous journey along the Yellow Brick Road and catch sight of the Emerald City, they halt and gaze upon it in wonderment. "It's beautiful, isn't it?" Dorothy gushes. "Just like I knew it would be!"

Most people watching the Masters from Augusta National for the first time know exactly how Dorothy feels. I first saw it in 1985 and can remember gawking at the screen for several seconds trying to take it all in. To a British lad whose few experiences of golf to that point had involved bone-chilling rain, muddy fairways, and dodgy greens, Augusta's lush acres looked almost surreal. It was simply too sublime for words.

I vowed to go there one day, ideally as a player, but if necessary in the role of caddie, reporter, waiter, greenskeeper, or patron (at Augusta, spectators are not referred to as fans and together they do not form a crowd: they are patrons, and many patrons make a gallery); anything if it meant getting to see this fantasyland.

I've still to make my Masters debut, more's the pity. And now, nearing 40 with my best playing days so far behind me I can barely remember them, my chances of being invited to join the rather select field are fading somewhat. And given my woeful lack of stamina, I doubt I'll ever carry a 50lb bag up and down its taxing slopes either.

I thought I might make it as a reporter a few years back, but at the last minute my editor decided he was going instead. Now, as a humble, lowly freelancer, I'm more likely to see the inside of the Queen's handbag.

Professionally (can you imagine being paid to do your job at Augusta National!) that leaves greenskeeping and waiting tables. I've mown the lawn a few times and pulled my share of pints but, in the words of Homer Simpson, I suspect this particular employer wants people "that are good."

So as a patron it is then. But the club's waiting list for tournament-day tickets, which first opened in 1972, closed for a second time a few

Can there be a more beautiful hole than the 12th at Augusta? If I ever make it to the Masters, this is where you'll find me.

years ago. Thus, getting tickets directly from the club is not happening any time soon. Some patrons do sell their badges to brokers, but these brokers certainly know their value so don't expect to find one for much less than $900.

PRACTICE ROUNDS

With so few tournament-day tickets available, your best chance of getting inside Augusta during the Masters might be for a practice round. I'll take it because, frankly, I prefer practice days. The players are more relaxed, play more shots, hit balls on the range a bit longer, seem more willing to sign autographs, it's cheaper, and you still get to see the whole course. Plus I'd rather watch the actual tournament on TV because you're far less likely to miss anything important.

+ To get tickets direct from the club at face value, visit the official Masters Web site ticket information page (http://masters.org/en_US/about/ticket.html) and follow the instructions.
+ You'll find a number of reputable brokers on the Internet (just Google "Masters tickets") selling tickets for Monday at about $200. The price usually goes up to about $300 for Tuesday and $400 for Wednesday, the day of the par-3 tournament.
+ Your last chance may be a tout, or scalper. They are legal in the state of Georgia, but must be licensed and at least 1,500 ft. from the entrance to the venue.

 # SUNSCREEN

You might not think it necessary on a cold rainy day, but the summer sun can get quite potent; and if you're lucky enough to play your golf in, say, Arizona or the Med, you're definitely going to need some.

Cancer Research UK estimates the number of people in the United Kingdom who develop skin cancer every year at 70,000, of which roughly 5,000 are golfers, while there are more than a million new cases of skin cancer a year in the States. Common sense is a great weapon in the fight against it (complete most of your round before 11am or start after 3pm if possible), but if you don't have any, remember to:

+ Wear tightly woven fabrics, a wide-brimmed hat that shades the face, neck, and ears, and golf-specific sunglasses that protect the eyes against cataracts and macular degeneration.
+ Protect lips with a lip-balm that has an SPF of at least 15.
+ Use only "broad spectrum" sunscreens (they block out both UVA and UVB rays) with an SPF of at least 15. SPF 30 sunscreens usually cost way more but give only 3 percent added protection. Apply generously 15–20 minutes before going outside and again at the turn.
+ Sand and water reflect UV rays so keep it in the fairway.

For me, the driving range is not so much a place to practice as a bolthole; somewhere I can exit the chaotic world of work, child-rearing, and home improvements and enjoy some "alone time" — just me, my Cleveland TA-7s, and a big, muddy field.

I don't go nearly enough. But when I do, I feel like I've returned to the world of my early 20s when things like trajectory and swingplane were really important. Here, my mind is not consumed with house or college payments, but five-yard draws and distance control.

JUST HOW BENEFICIAL IS IT?

Two buckets of balls is probably better for your game than two buckets of fried chicken, but it's important to realize that conditions at most ranges with artificial turf mats do not accurately reflect those you face on the course. Strike a typical mat a couple of inches behind the ball and the club skids off the surface into the ball. Thus, a swing that would most likely have caused you to hit the ball fat will probably hit it thin and you'll get a more satisfactory result, or at least, a very different result from the one you would have got off grass.

Better mats with silicone gel inserts (which not only give better feedback but also do a good job of preventing golfer's elbow, carpel tunnel syndrome, and other wrist and forearm injuries) are on the way. But they're not cheap, so don't hold your breath waiting for them at your local range.

In addition, range balls are, by and large, completely rubbish. Hollow, hard as nails or made entirely of rubber with small chunks missing, they don't fly nearly as far as your Titleists, nor as consistently.

USE YOUR TIME EFFECTIVELY

Though great entertainment, hitting your driver as hard as you can with no specific target is worse than useless. Work on what you learned at a recent lesson instead, without cutting corners. Carry out your pro's instructions to the letter and you should see some rapid improvements. Always, always, always hit at a target and focus on the fundamentals of grip, posture, ball position, and alignment. Do not treat it as an aerobic workout by whizzing through a hundred shots in ten minutes. Take your time and think about every shot as if you were playing it in competition.

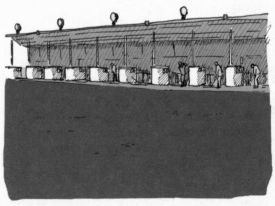

A golfer's home away from home.

THE DRINKS CART

It seems strange to me, because every golfer I know likes a snack every few holes, but I've never seen a drinks cart anywhere other than the States.

The first time most non-American golfers are confronted by the American drinks cart they are often bowled over and spend a good five minutes rummaging through all the cabinets, cupboards, refrigerators, and trays trying to decide what to buy.

For me, early morning tee-times (few) usually mean coffee and a muffin. Playing around lunchtime (far more often unless it's too hot) calls for beer and a sandwich. Any other time, I'll probably have a chocolate bar, an apple, and who knows, maybe even a sneaky Bushmills.

As for tipping, remember if you are on an American resort course your fellow golfers will probably be fairly affluent. So don't waste time working out what 10 or 15 percent of $10.34 is; just hand the attendant an extra $5 and move on.

HOW TO WATCH A TOURNAMENT ON TV

Set the channel and hide the remote; you need to be prepared to make the most of a major championship on TV.

For me the experience starts a few days before the event with a good read of all the newspaper previews. I'll rip an illustrated course map out of one of the magazines, and load my refrigerator with drinks and snacks. There's no need for the remote control as the channel remains unchanged, but I might pull the easy chair a little closer to the television.

Now resident in the US, I have a friend around for a "British Open Breakfast" at 6 a.m. on the morning of the fourth round. Whatever he thinks of a full English breakfast, it's all about ritual: making your preparations; the buzz of anticipation; and, best of all, watching the action unfold.

Four days of Open Championship coverage, plus preview shows and highlights. It's what TV was invented for.

DEALING WITH A SLICE

You golf therefore you slice. I'm not sure I could ever enjoy the game if I knew beyond any doubt that the next shot I was going to hit would curve viciously and uncontrollably to the right, and the one after that, and the one... Good job you can deal with it fairly easily. It'll take some effort, mind.

A slice is that oh-so-predictable shot that drives golfers absolutely nuts. A simple grip change helped me (see page 19) but that's not to say my banana shot doesn't reappear from time to time. Now I know why it happens though, and what I have to do to put it right, or should I say left.

FIXES

We know that left-to-right sidespin, or clockwise spin, is caused by a clubhead cutting across the ball — making a glancing blow — with a face that's open relative to the path of the clubhead. The more glancing the blow, the more spin is imparted. The wickedest of all slices therefore occurs when the clubhead approaches impact on an out-to-in path with a face that's open in relation to that path.

There are dozens of swingpath fixes for you to try, but the simplest and most effective drill I know for being rid of the over-the-top move every slicer is guilty of is simply to place two balls on either side of the one you're hitting. The three balls should form a diagonal line going from low left to high right (as shown). You can only avoid the outer balls and strike the middle ball solidly with an in-to-out swing path. It's helpful when using the swingpath drill to start with small, slow swings and build up gradually to a full swing.

There are also many plausible reasons for your clubface being open at the point of impact, but I think it safer to focus on just three; too weak a grip, too tight a grip, and improper forearm rotation. And since improper forearm rotation is caused primarily by too tight or too weak a grip, let's concentrate on... grip.

First, let's make sure your grip is neutral or, better still, a touch strong. A good way to know how weak or strong your grip is, is to count the number of knuckles you see on each hand as you look down. If you have a weak grip you

With an out-to-in swingpath you'll probably clatter all three balls. Only with an in-to-out swing can you hit the middle ball alone.

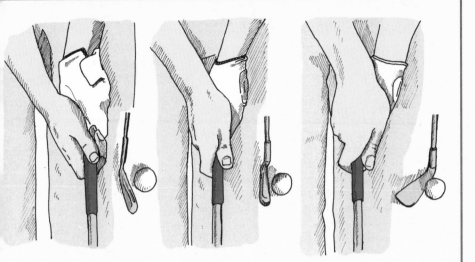

can see only one knuckle of your left (top) hand and are probably hitting weak slices. Move that hand clockwise so you can see three or all four. Conversely, you may be able to see two or three knuckles on your right hand. You need to move it clockwise again so that only one is visible.

If you think the tight grip you have now is correct, holding it with the correct amount of pressure is going to feel very loose; but just try it. See how it eases tension in your forearms and shoulders? In fact, do you feel how it relaxes the whole body? Now you can really swing the clubhead (see pages 26–7), whip those hands, wrists, and forearms through impact, and get a much better feel for where the clubhead is and where the face is pointing.

It is also worth remembering that a clubhead with a little offset will definitely help you trim your slice. A club is offset when the face is set back from the neck (hosel). The greater the offset, the easier it is for the slicer to square the clubface in time for impact.

It is very important to be able to feel the clubhead. People who use clubs that are too light tend to hit weak slices, or block fades because they have no feeling for where the clubhead is and can't instinctively rotate the forearms sufficiently to square the face.

Finally, remember that the harder you hit the ball with a clubface that isn't square, the more sidespin you'll impart. So if you really are having a hard time squaring the face, take a club or two more than you think you need and swing with a slightly slower tempo.

PRACTICE MAKES BIRDIE PUTTS

It's often said that a good putter is a match for anyone, which is true unless he or she takes eight to reach the green. With this in mind, it's well worth practicing your putting, and using a few drills to make it a bit more enjoyable.

LONG PUTTS

Any time you're 20 ft. or more from the hole, the speed of the putt becomes your primary focus. Many people three-putt from this range because they leave their first effort a long way short or drill it several feet past the hole, even though their line is usually pretty good, never more than a foot or so either side of the hole. By focusing on speed, you should therefore guarantee leaving your first putt within tap-in range of the hole.

The dustbin-lid drill simply involves imagining that the hole is the size of a dustbin lid. It's an oldie and most golfers will be familiar with it, but I make no apology for including it here because it works. If your lid is anything like mine — about three feet in diameter — and your lag putt finishes within its circumference, you should have little trouble with your next putt.

Another good trick for improving your long putting is to putt balls from a variety of distances. Putt toward the edge of the putting green, attempting to bring the ball to a stop as close to the edge as possible. This is another simple but effective drill you've probably come across before, but have you actually tried it? I mean really tried it? Commit half an hour to it once or twice a week and you are almost certain to develop a better feel for speed.

SHORT PUTTS

The only time that missing a three-foot putt isn't infuriating is when it's for a 12.

You can, and will, become a much more potent golfer if you can make sure you never miss from three feet.

The stroke for long putts may bring the putter inside the target line on the backstroke, but for short putts it should move straight back and through. A really good way to develop this movement is to create a corridor of tees (below) behind and in front of your ball that prevents the putterhead from moving on the wrong path.

A final, if potentially infuriating drill is to try to hole 100 consecutive putts, from just a couple of feet. If you miss then you have to start again, whether it was your first putt or your last. This should help you keep your concentration on the greens around the course. To break the monotony, move around the hole taking no more than five putts from the same spot at any one time.

Putting down a corridor of tees. Tiger uses it a lot, and he's the best short putter who ever played the game.

Imagining a hole this size works wonders for you confidence. Aim to get long putts inside a larger target and you'll hole one every now and again.

MASTERING THE CHIP

This is a shot you've just got to have. You simply cannot get by without it. Failing to get up and down from just off the putting surface can really hurt your score and turn what should have been a great round into a distinctly average one.

Amateurs miss a lot of greens. Miss them by a lot and a solid pitch shot might be needed. But often you'll miss the putting surface by just a few yards and have a clear line to the hole. At times like these, let the standard chip-and-run come to your rescue. But, before we start, what's the difference between a chip shot and a pitch shot? Basically, a chip shot is shorter, lower, and more apt to run rather than spin to a quick stop.

The chip is usually played from just off the green and from a lie that doesn't require a lot of chopping with a sand or lob wedge. The best results are achieved when your ball lands on the green as early as possible and runs like a putt the rest of the way to the hole.

BASIC TECHNIQUE
It really couldn't be simpler but, like all shots, you'll only improve with practice. Experiment a little to see how hard you need to hit the ball, how it reacts from

different lies, how the conditions of the green affect the roll of the ball, and what trajectory suits the demands of the shot.

+ From a good lie to the side of the green, and with nothing between you and the hole 20 yards away, try a 6-iron, 7-iron, or 8-iron.
+ Read the green as you would a putt and pick a spot where you want the ball to land.
+ Play the ball slightly back of center and lean forward slightly (a little more weight on your front foot than back).
+ Your hands should be ahead of the clubhead at address and that is where they must be at impact. This really is of paramount importance, and it means the swing is generated mainly in the shoulders with only a little wrist action. Don't let your shoulders, arms, and wrists become wooden, as you'll lose all feel, but grip the club lightly and allow for a slight wrist hinge if

I

Take a narrow, open stance, with your hands and weight slightly ahead of the ball.

2

Make a simple up and down movement of the shoulders, with perhaps a slight flex of the wrists.

the distance of the shot requires it — absolutely no scooping with the bottom hand though.

✦ The ball should fly quite low. Aim for it to land on the green early and run to the hole.

CHIPPING DRILLS

Here are two of my favorite drills:

To ensure absolutely no scooping with the bottom hand, place a ball a few inches behind the ball you're hitting (to the right as you look down). Now just hit shots trying to avoid the back ball. Soon you will develop the downward strike required and make crisp, clean contact.

To develop good distance control, place four or five clubs on the ground about five feet apart, like rungs on a ladder. Hit shots with different clubs trying to land the ball between the spaces, then try it with the same club. You will learn the different trajectories you get with each club and how the ball reacts once it lands (the lower the trajectory the more it will run). Do this often enough and you will develop a feeling for which club is required to hit the chip shot you face.

3

Make a downward strike on the ball, crisp contact, a little run… and you just saved your par.

GOLFING MATTERS

Smell the Flowers (Just Do It Quickly)

It was the one and only Walter Hagen who encouraged golfers not to hurry, not to worry, and, because we're here only for a short time, to smell the flowers along the way.

And I couldn't agree more — just as long as we don't hold up a group on the tee while sniffing the rhododendrons at the side of the fairway. After all, what is the use of being surrounded by all that nature if you're not going to stop and have a look at it every so often? No other sport allows participants to spend so much time amongst the flora and fauna while not actually performing.

To be honest, I'm not a huge fan of flowers on golf courses. They're okay in their place and Augusta National's look very nice, but I prefer the gorse and heather of links and heathland courses. There's nothing better than gorse when it is giving off its sweet almond aroma.

BEATING THE BUNKERS

In its rightful place, on the shores of a turquoise ocean, sand is great; however, the moment you put it in a big hole in the ground next to the putting surface it becomes bad, very bad. Pros may not regard greenside bunkers as hazards any more, but they still put the fear of God into amateurs; however, there's no need to worry, there are solutions...

If you don't like bunkers now, you should have been around in the old days when the sand was never raked. You should have played in the 1953 and 1962 US Opens at Oakmont CC in Pennsylvania when special rakes were used to create deep furrows from which creating backspin was almost impossible. You should have played before clubs everywhere decided to make the sand in their bunkers of uniform depth and texture. You should have been around when bunker play was really difficult!

Players who grumble at inconsistencies in bunkers today don't know how easy they've got it. Strong? Maybe, but bunkers are supposed to be hazards. You're supposed to be penalized for finding one. Unless you're gifted at sand play, you're meant to lose a stroke. So, instead of moaning about how the sand in this

Hit the sand an inch or two behind the ball, depending on how firm it is.

bunker is a little firmer than the sand in that last one, perhaps you should make more of an effort to avoid them in the first place. That to one side, let's assume you've found the sand, and get onto the important work of getting the ball out.

SIMPLE GREENSIDE EXPLOSION

There are two important don'ts to remember here: first, don't try to clip your ball off the sand without moving a single grain; second, don't take a ton of sand hoping your ball will be in there somewhere. So here's what you do:

- Aim your feet and body a little to the left of your target.
- Open the face of your sand wedge (many players actually prefer to play out of the sand with a lob wedge), then grip the club normally (do not grip the club then open the face). This puts extra loft on the club helping you get the ball out quickly.
- Play the ball a little forward of center (do not allow the club to touch the sand at address as this results in a two-shot penalty) and flex your knees quite a bit.
- Visualize a spot in the sand about an inch or two behind your ball.
- Make a fairly normal swing with perhaps a little more wrist action than normal and thud into the sand at that spot behind the ball.
- Let the clubhead come out of the sand a few inches ahead of where the ball

The dreaded poached egg. You won't get any backspin and you'll have far less control than you would from a good lie, but fear not; you can still get the ball out easily enough.

was, with the feeling that the clubface remains facing the sky — do not roll your wrists over.

+ Make a full, balanced follow-through.

Right now this all probably sounds a bit complex; but follow the instructions, practice them, and get used to the feeling of splashing in and out of the sand with an open clubface.

THE PLUGGED LIE

When the sand is damp, or your shot's angle of descent is almost vertical, it's likely your ball will bury itself in the sand. If you find your ball half submerged, abandon all thoughts of applying any backspin and stopping it near the hole, unless the hole happens to be on the other side of the green. From this lie, the ball will tend to run a lot so try to land it well short of the cup.

Instead of opening up your stance and the clubface as you would with a good lie, you need to square both up to the hole and push a little more weight onto your front foot. Play the ball in the center of your stance and make a steep, aggressive swing coming down into the sand, again about an inch behind the ball.

FAIRWAY BUNKERS

Fairway bunker shots elicit a unique pitch of fear for most high handicappers.

But again, they aren't that tough if you just make a few simple alterations to your set-up:

+ Stand square to your target.
+ Grip down the handle of your club an inch or two.
+ Play the ball in the middle of your stance.
+ Make a short, compact swing and maintain your height. You shouldn't disturb too much sand.

The 60-Yard Bunker Shot

You'll often hear this is the toughest shot in the game, but by taking a pitching wedge instead of your sand iron you can actually make this shot relatively straightforward. Use a slightly open stance, a slightly open clubface, come into the sand an inch behind the ball, and there you go.

If the bunker lip is too high it may just be a sand wedge back onto the fairway. But if there is no lip, there's no reason why you can't take the club the yardage calls for, or maybe one more, and knock it on the green.

THE CLUB PRO

How the lot of most club pros has changed over the last half century. No longer do they smoke Woodbines alone in a cold back office or bow to members who regard them more as club servants.

Your club pro: smart, polite, good-humored, and incredibly hard-working.

Today's pro is not the crusty old codger of yesteryear but generally a young athlete with good business acumen whose role has shifted gradually from teacher and club repairer to entrepreneur and administrator.

Sure, the pro can still beat you with both arms tied behind someone else's back, but he's probably too busy checking his stock inventory, ordering, running club and society tournaments, managing staff, shopfitting, and clubfitting to have enough time to actually play the game.

Years ago, golf pros used to play tournaments during the week and head back to their clubs at weekends to change grips, give the odd lesson, and listen to members moan about the condition of the course or give them a breakdown of their round, shot by dismal shot.

The job today is certainly more invigorating than that — especially if you can swing a teaching gig in Dubai, the States, or Continental Europe — but youngsters thinking about a life in the pro-store should ask themselves whether they can handle a working week of 80-plus hours, very few of which actually involve playing golf.

ARE YOU BEING SERVED?

My few short years as an assistant came between the thankless days of the tournament player/club pro and those of the modern incarnation with business diploma and launch monitor equipment. In the summers, my day would start at about 7:30 a.m., be spent mostly in the store selling chocolate bars and cans of soft drinks, and finish whenever the last golfer went out, usually about 8 p.m. In the winter, my hours were cut in half and so was my pay. It was hard work for little money, but I respected my boss and was good mates with the other assistants. I loved every second.

MINIATURE GOLF

Although I never quite get down on all fours to read a putt or go through my usual pre-putt routine, miniature golf is still serious business. Once, during a game with my son, I found myself becoming a "Competitive Dad," accusing him of rules infractions and considering my options at the Windmill Hole.

This particular windmill's sails rotated a little faster than I'm used to and three times I failed to get past, falling further behind my son who placed his ball one inch from the cup at the start of every hole and scored a very impressive 18.

This story might seem out of place in a book about "proper" golf, but my dad and granddad used to take me to a miniature golf course. And every time we finished, I couldn't wait to go back.

I'm not saying that miniature golf necessarily fuelled my passion for the bigger game, but it certainly didn't delay it. And, unlikely though it sounds, I may well have picked up a few putting tips while negotiating a six-foot tall, orange T-Rex.

Don't even think about going round the side; that's as bad as laying up at a 450-yard par 5.

I've known several golfers who spent more time in the 19th hole than on the course.

THE 19TH HOLE

Your day at the golf course doesn't end until you've enjoyed a drink or two with your playing partners. Our time is short nowadays. When the three or four hours of recreation time you're allowed every quarter have elapsed you may need to shoot off home and do something really important like mow the lawn.

Even if it's a quick beer, by staying on after your game you are effectively saying you enjoyed your partners' company and would like to do it again some time. By heading straight home the moment your round is over, you miss out on a fundamental part of becoming a golfer. But remember…

+ Don't drink if you're driving.
+ Don't start talking about your round, not with me anyway.
+ Offer to buy the first round.
+ Pay up on any lost bets.
+ Don't push your luck. You've still got those jobs at home to do, remember?

THE GOOD PUTTER

I won't give you his name because at some point over the next 400 words or so I might get emotional and call him something I shouldn't. The guy I'm talking about had a golf swing that made your great-grandmother's look powerful. But I never beat him, because with a putter in his hands he was pure gold.

The old boy might not look dangerous, but watch out. He could be deadly with a putter.

I won't tell you the name of the course, but as soon as I start writing about this demon putter, plenty of readers will instantly know who I mean, as his fame with the flat stick has spread far and wide. All I will say is that he was quite a bit older than me and couldn't hit a drive within 20 yards of mine.

The first time I played him was in the first round of a matchplay competition. On the 1st tee, he awkwardly shuffled his body into the desired position, spent at least 15 seconds getting comfortable, and finally lurched the club away from the ball, which flew 200 yards tops.

After the same shuffling routine preceding his approach shot and another unconvincing strike, his ball managed to crawl up on to the edge of the green, not remotely within birdie range.

As he pulled his gruesome-looking putter from his dirty, shapeless bag — an unsightly mass of broken zips and torn pockets — he hunched over his ball in the most ungainly fashion, all the time shuffling his feet and jostling the putterhead.

As his ball rolled smoothly into the hole from 40 ft. or so, I got my first indication of how this guy managed to maintain such a low single-digit handicap and how he was the current course record holder.

I was very much mistaken if I thought this first putt was a fluke because it happened again and again. He didn't birdie every hole, but he certainly had his share, and finished me off on the 14th green. I'd been guilty of judging this golfer by his appearance and wrongly interpreting his nuts-and-bolts putter and awkward style.

The fact was that he had used the same putter all his life, and performed exactly the same shuffles before every single putt he ever hit. He was totally "in the zone" and I don't think I have ever played with or against anyone else who could putt quite like him. You have to admire it really, but at the time, boy, was it demoralizing!

THE DARK ART OF GAMESMANSHIP

Gamesmanship is the use of aggressive, often dubious, tactics such as psychological intimidation or disruption of concentration to gain an advantage over one's opponent. That's enough for many people to regard it as cheating.

However, it happens all the time and while I don't resort to it myself (I rarely play in anything of consequence any more, so what's the point?) I know that by not doing it and letting my opponent know how I feel about it, I'm simply playing into the hands of a player who does. The fact is, a cheeky remark about someone's backswing or tricking your opponent into playing the wrong club isn't breaking the rules. You may be messing with your rival's head, but it's not illegal.

Some say offenders show a shocking disregard for the game's etiquette and should therefore be disqualified (since January 1, 2004, tournament committees have been allowed to disqualify a player for a "serious breach of etiquette") but it's difficult to prove any intent in most cases. And anyway, it's far less bothersome than someone jangling the change in their pocket, or talking loudly on their cellphone during your backswing

— both instances where disqualification is probably justified.

While I'd like to reiterate I don't really approve of gamesmanship, here are five effective moves I might employ if I were ever to change my mind:

+ Hit my driver a really long way then act like I miss-hit it.
+ En route to my drive, which I know is really long, take a look at my opponent's ball as I walk by. Stop and act like it's mine then appear surprised when it's pointed out to me that in fact mine is 30 yards further on.
+ The second my opponent hits a tee shot, I would walk off the tee quickly as if it really doesn't matter where the ball ends up.
+ If my opponent walks fast, I should walk really slowly; or if my opponent is slow, I should do everything quickly. It's enough to disturb anyone's routine.
+ Any remark about your opponent's technique usually has a negative effect on their swing as they can't stop thinking about what you said. "When did you start doing that thing with your legs/hands/head/elbows/feet?" usually works... or at least, so I'm told.

"Not my ball? Where's mine then? All the way up there? Really? Good Lord."

THE SHANK

I remember one practice session that went something like this; warm-up, shank, shank, shank, pack up. I reckon the best way to deal with a dose of the shanks is not to deal with them at all. Just put the clubs away, go home, and forget they ever happened.

The sight of the ball darting off sideways can have a profound effect on a golfer. Stunned, the brain doesn't quite know how to cope, processing a range of emotions that starts with shock and passes through embarrassment, bemusement, and anger before ending with fear (am I going to do that again?), all within a couple of seconds.

Your teacher can tell you why the hosel made contact with the ball, but may not be able to explain the intangible sensation — one of golf's greatest mysteries — that makes it so difficult to regain any sort of rhythm once the darned things show up.

TECHNICAL REASONS FOR A SHANK

Some think an open clubface is to blame, others a closed clubface. I'm not sure it's the face we need to be concerned with so much as the path of the clubhead — to the inside coming back and rerouting to an extreme out-to-in path on the way down.

The golfer is usually standing too close to the ball, bending over too much, or has his or her weight back on the heels at address, which causes the body to move toward the ball slightly in the downswing and thus push the club on to the out-to-in swingpath.

STOP THEM

Like I said earlier, the best plan might be to pack up and come back tomorrow. But what if you're in the middle of a round?

First, think of something else, quick! Tie your shoelaces, clean your clubs, or peel a banana while remembering some good shots you've hit; and finally try these:

+ Clip the grass with a few practice swings focusing on re-establishing your tempo.
+ Stand about half an inch further from the ball.
+ Ensure your weight is on the balls of your feet.
+ Picture the toe making contact with the ball, or
+ Imagine hitting the bottom right corner of the ball.

If you can't stop shanking it in the middle of a round, try envisaging the ball divided into four quarters and aim for the one at the bottom right.

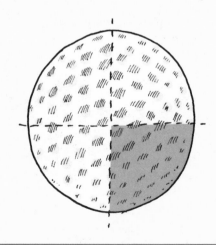

TAKING A DECENT PHOTO

Golfers take pictures of the great holes they play, or holes on which they make a miraculous birdie. Unfortunately, most of our pictures are appalling; and of the thousands I've taken on courses around the world, I'd say about four are any good.

It's easy to take a bad picture of a golf course. Take it as you're walking off the green looking backward, or on the tee looking forward with a lens that makes the flag on a 150-yard hole appear several miles away, and take it when the sun is high in the sky.

The great images of courses we see in books and magazines are usually the result of much forward planning. Professional photographers walk the course before shooting it to get an idea of picture-worthy holes and good locations from which to shoot them. They're up at dawn and back late in the evening when the sun is low and the light is softer — giving the hole an entirely different character to the harsh midday sun.

More often than not, they have a step ladder (or sometimes even a helicopter) to give them a bit of elevation. It's not essential, but the most memorable pictures often seem to have been taken from above the hole.

But all this is not to say that the amateur snapper can't take a perfectly decent picture with an inexpensive camera. With today's digital cameras you can shoot as many images as you like, discarding the ones that don't work and keeping those that do — all without spending a single cent. So go ahead, take hundreds — without holding up play, of course — the more pictures you take the quicker you'll realize what clearly doesn't work and what might.

A bit of elevation and dramatic light bring a scene to life. You can also see how the sky fills the top third, with the tree and the pin positioned roughly on the left and right thirds.

Putting a bunker, some rough or flowers in the foreground adds interest — a great swathe of green fairway can be very dull. Avoid looking toward the sun as this risks the appearance of blotches of color known as flare. If you really want to shoot in this direction, obscure the sun behind branches or leaves. Also, while a cloudless day is better than a gray one, a few fluffy white clouds are always nice.

Finally, imagine dividing the frame into a grid of thirds. Instead of placing the subject right in the middle of the frame, where it can look pretty dull, try setting the important elements roughly on these lines of thirds. Almost invariably, this will add a bit of life to what would otherwise be a boring shot.

⛳ MAKING THE BALL BITE

Amateurs have long regarded backspin as golf's Holy Grail. The ability to hit a ball in such a way that it pitches on the green then rolls backward marks, for many, the difference between a competent golfer and a hopeless hacker.

Every shot has some degree of backspin, just not always enough for the ball to land on the green and check up. But you don't necessarily want your ball to check anyway, as it's difficult to predict or control how far it will come back. Instead, you want it to take one hop and come to an abrupt but controlled halt, preferably close to the pin.

THE PHYSICS

There are numerous explanations for how backspin is created. Some say it's all down to a club's loft, while others claim that face grooves grip the ball. Friction generated by the downward strike of the steel face on a dimpled, rubber cover also gets a mention.

Actually, they're all correct and this combination of loft, grooves, and friction explains how a motionless ball can start rotating at roughly 10,000 revolutions a minute within half a millisecond of being struck. Loft is by far the biggest contributor — the more oblique (angled) the strike, the more backspin you get — with grooves, the top edges of which grip the ball as it compresses and travels up the face, a distant second (the fact that grooveless faces perform almost as well as those with grooves in dry conditions proves how little effect the currently permitted channels have on the amount of spin produced). But while all that's incredibly interesting, the question of how you get a ball to behave like it's tied firmly to the end of a piece of string remains.

THE TECHNIQUE

There really is no great secret to it, and that's the truth. Professionals aren't magicians, nor do they have any special equipment. The clubs and balls they use are essentially the same as yours, assuming you hit a high-spinning ball such as a Titleist Pro-V1 or Nike One Platinum. (A hard, two-piece Surlyn ball like the Pinnacle Gold FX Long might be good for long-drive contests, but you'll have a job stopping it on the green unless you've got the swingspeed of Tiger Woods.) So how do they do it?

They, or rather their caddie, keep their clubs clean. Grooves affect the amount of backspin you get less than you think. But it certainly helps if you keep them clean, and you'll have a job creating backspin with a clubface like this.

They strike the ball a fraction of a second before the clubs hits the ground (see pages 22 and 41). After impact, the clubhead cuts down a little into the turf, taking a divot.

They swing fast. Sure, this is an area where the pros have an advantage, but most amateur golfers possess sufficient swingspeed to create backspin. They just need to hit the ball cleanly.

You should also be aware that it is much easier to create backspin from a good lie on a firm fairway than from a less than perfect lie in long, wet grass. Satisfy all these criteria and there's no reason why your ball shouldn't behave itself on the green and settle down quickly. But like I said, you don't really want a lot of backspin, no matter how cool it looks. You just want your ball to take one hop and stop.

 # THANK YOU...

Having made only one acceptance speech in my life, and that a fair few years ago, I'm probably not as well qualified as say, Tiger Woods, to tell you what to say in your moment of victory.

However, I will say this: the safest approach is to make it instantly forgettable. After all, the only two Open Championship winners' speeches I can remember are memorable for all the wrong reasons. In 1995, John Daly accepted the Claret Jug from the secretary of the R&A, in front of the R&A clubhouse, wearing a grotesque green windshirt with his sponsor's logo slapped across the front. No one's asking you to put a blazer on John, just remove the gaudy billboard.

Then there was Nick Faldo's effort at Muirfield in 1992. After thanking the press, with whom he enjoyed a less than cordial relationship, from the heart of his bottom, he finished with an excruciatingly regrettable rendition of "My Way."

Commiserate with the runner-up and thank the greenskeeper, organizers, and everyone else. Then call it a day.

⚑ LAUNCH IT

I swear some people would rather hit the ball 320 yards than shoot 68. It seems strange to me, but if having your ball travel further is all important then stop slashing wildly and learn the secrets of effortless power.

First things first; your gear needs to play its part. Have your driver fitted properly. A club with the right amount of loft and correct shaft flex, plus a suitable choice of ball, will ensure optimum launch angle and low spin rate — just what we're looking for. Also, the soles of your shoes need to be clean, with the cleats in good condition. And your grips and glove (if you wear one) need to be clean and tacky. You also need to use extra-long tees.

Now soften your grip and lose any tension in your elbows and shoulders. It's natural to associate power with a tight grip, but this prevents the forearms rolling. Also, turn your right foot out so that it points to 2 o'clock rather than 12. This helps you bring the club up and down on the inside and ensures a full hip and shoulder turn, which, among other things, leads to an increase in clubhead speed. Lastly, focus on maintaining good tempo and striking the ball flush.

Training

Flexibility (see pages 32–3) and strength in the abdominal area — the technical term used by many is "core" — are all important. Your core, the engine of your swing, needs to be strong and elastic to store up and release energy quickly. A couple of good Web sites I visit occasionally for appropriate exercises are www.beginnertriathlete.com — which sounds a little scary, but has got a sensible and effective plan for your abs — and the Mayo Clinic's site at www.mayoclinic.com. Both have search tools — just type in "core strengthening" and you should be directed to the appropriate pages. But remember to consult your doctor before starting any exercise routine.

Turning the right foot out a little lets you make a bigger hip and shoulder turn.

The right hand rolls over the left. The palm now faces behind the golfer, not up to the sky. This can only happen with a light grip and an absence of tension in the arms and shoulders. Note too the head is still behind where the ball was teed. This is a powerful release.

YOU ARE WHAT YOU EAT

Anyone tuning in to the Masters and seeing some of the plumper players waddling around might think that a good diet wasn't a particularly high priority for golfers. And for the likes of you and me it probably isn't. But that's not to say we can't all make some improvements.

I'm not suggesting anything radical here. But it would be foolish not to take advantage of research carried out into biomechanics and nutrition in recent years. A few minor modifications to your diet might not only help you feel better, it might help you play better too.

Actually, much of what the nutritionists are telling us we've known for decades; since we tore our first chunk out of a thick steak, or wolfed down our first doughnut, in fact. But the message is clear and we'd do well to remember it; large quantities of sugar and saturated fat really won't keep us in peak physical condition and allow us to perform at our best.

Take breakfast, which I think we all now know is by far the most important meal of the day. Occasionally it's a large bacon sandwich on crusty white bread with a steaming cup of coffee or tea, but most of the time it's little more than a snatched cereal bar — neither is ideal.

The former might be filling (and taste heavenly), but all that bleached flour, bacon fat, and caffeine plays havoc with the metabolism, raising blood sugar levels and leaving us hungry again by the time we reach the turn. Likewise, the cereal bar isn't going to satisfy our hunger for long and will result in numerous unscheduled snack breaks.

The ideal golfer's breakfast, according to a couple of well-qualified nutritionists I know, consists of oatmeal or porridge, fruit juice, yogurt, boiled eggs, and toast made with whole-wheat or multigrain bread. A nice cup of tea, ideally without sugar, is fine too. Start the day like this and you should feel pleasantly sated until the cheeseburger, fries, and cola you order at the end of your round.

ON-COURSE SNACKING

According to my sources, a 180 lb man should drink a litre of cool (not ice cold) water during a round of golf. And you should maintain blood sugar levels with fruit (any), snack bars (a multigrain one rather than a chocolate bar), or nuts such as walnuts, pecans, cashews, and almonds. Sadly, for those of us with a taste for such things, beer and hot dogs are simply not the choice of champions.

Though my snack habits have improved of late, I don't currently have any of the above in my bag.

A ROUND WITH DAD

It may not seem like it at the time, especially when you're young and would rather be out with your friends but, apart from getting married and having kids, playing golf with your dad is just about the most special thing in the world. I wish I could still do it.

Cancer took my dad when still a relatively young man. He was first a cricketer then a golfer and he showed me how to play both. We played our first proper round of golf together shortly after my 14th birthday. I shot 101, a score that didn't really compare favorably with Seve's, the only standard that mattered, but was, Dad assured me, a pretty decent effort for a first-timer.

From then until the day he died, five years later, I guess we played only 30 more rounds together. Most of them I remember as if they happened only yesterday.

The one that really sticks in the memory though, for reasons both good and bad, was at a wonderful seaside course in Cornwall, England, called Mullion. Perhaps I remember this particular round so well because of Mullion's fantastic location on the cliffs of the Lizard Peninsula. Or maybe it's because Dad, a solid but unspectacular 13-handicapper, played the round of his life. Or maybe I still regret the childish manner in which I reacted to being so comprehensively beaten by my old dad.

The sun was shining, the wind whipped across the hills and valleys, and whitecaps crashed against the rocks below. It was the sort of day courses like Mullion were built for. And while I played like a fool, Dad reeled off par after par. He finished with a very tidy 73 while I was somewhere in the mid-80s.

But instead of draping an arm round his shoulder and congratulating him on such a great round, I believe I stormed off the 18th green, locked myself in the car and opened a bag of crisps. My petulance would have impressed a Hollywood "It" girl, but it still bothers me 20 years later. Not to worry though; I suspect the courses in Heaven look a lot like Mullion, so one day we'll have a rematch, only this time I'll beat him.

FIX A GAME WITH YOUR DAD
Working on the assumption that every "rule" should carry with it some profound nugget of wisdom, I offer this advice; regardless of how well you get on with your father, irrespective of how good or bad at golf he is, notwithstanding the fact you haven't played with him in five years, get out for a round with your dad as soon as possible. And use the three or four hours you have together to tell him everything you've been meaning to tell him.

PROUD FATHER
One of my fondest memories of Dad is of his turning up at the award ceremony for the 1987 Haywards Heath GC Junior Club Championship, which I happened to win by seven shots!

Dad had been in the hospital for weeks but his doctors thought him stable enough to come home for a few days. His first day out coincided with the tournament and as soon as he felt comfortable, he drove up to the course to see how I'd done. Somewhere between the car park and the clubhouse, someone told him I'd shot 71 and was looking a likely winner with only two or three groups remaining.

I will never forget the smile on his face as he shook my hand (Dad was a bit Victorian and not one for hugging, backslapping, or any other flagrant displays of affection). The man was virtually on death's doorstep but his joy was as evident as the disease that ravaged his body. Surgery, radiation, chemotherapy, and all the rest of it had literally made him half the man he had been just a few months before, but he summoned the energy from somewhere to celebrate.

After being handed the trophy and an oversize Sony Walkman with no rewind button, I waited for the thunderous applause to die down then thanked the organizers, the greenstaff, and my playing partners (see page 75). But I can't remember if I thanked my dad or not. God, I hope I did.

The golf course is the perfect place to tell your dad how much he means to you, or about how you lost your job, and just got married in Las Vegas, and how you need to borrow a couple of grand... anything really.

HOW TO HIT THE LOB SHOT

Made a lot easier in recent years by the introduction of 60° and 64° wedges, the lob rises and drops almost vertically and therefore runs very little after it lands. Phil Mickelson has perfected this spectacular shot, making an almost full backswing but hitting the ball no more than 20–30 yards.

The lob is a very useful shot to have if the hole is cut just the other side of a bunker or water hazard, where you will need to hit the ball high and limit the amount of roll.

If he were to make poor contact, Mickelson would skin the ball 100 yards over the ropes and into the shrubbery beyond. His lobs almost take his nose off, however, shooting straight up and plummeting to the ground usually no more than a foot or two from the hole.

It's very important to remember this is a difficult shot, requiring exceptional hand–eye co-ordination, and one that Mickelson attempts only when he needs to; when there is a bunker, some water, or a mound between him and the hole, and he needs to loft the ball over the trouble before stopping it quickly.

It's also worth mentioning that this shot is made a lot easier if the ball is lying on a fairly soft bit of ground. The quality of the contact needed for playing a lob off a very tight lie is beyond most club golfers — and don't even think about playing it out of a divot.

+ Assess how high the shot needs to go, how hard you need to hit it, and where you want the ball to land.
+ You're probably attempting a lob because there is something nasty between you and the hole, so make sure you clear it.
+ Play the ball forward of center, with your hands level with the ball.
+ Establish a wide, balanced base with a little more knee flex than usual. Aim left of the target.
+ Your weight should be evenly distributed between your feet.
+ Allow for just a little wrist hinge.
+ Keep your head very still and your eyes on the back of the ball.
+ Accelerate the clubhead through the ball and finish with your weight mostly on your front foot.

MAGNIFICENT MUNICIPALS

The publicly owned golf course may be a little ragged at the edges and its greens might not putt as smoothly as those at private courses. But given the price of a round, who's complaining?

Every Friday afternoon a four-ball of college students would duck out of sociology lessons and drive up to Tilgate Forest GC, a fantastic municipal course in the UK. There, the game of choice was usually a Texas Scramble as three of the four were total hacks who weren't welcome at any other golf facility and who didn't much fancy keeping their own scorecard.

A round at Tilgate might take these intrepid class-skippers anything from two and a half to five hours depending on who was in front of them; two and a half if the course was quiet, five if they got lumped behind a group with no clue what "expected pace of play" meant. Most of the time it was five because Tilgate, like most municipals, was extremely busy and attracted a number of golfers for whom etiquette was something that other people did.

From bad golf to bad manners, from people failing to hit their tee shot past the forward tees and having to drop their trousers, to kids running out from the bushes and nicking golf balls, it all goes on at the municipal. Here's a sample of some of the more interesting things I have witnessed:

✦ A middle-aged man who hit his tee shot between his legs after predicting a gentle fade that would keep his ball short of the fairway bunkers. Everyone who saw it collapsed in stitches, except the guy who hit the shot. He looked bemused and checked his club, convinced it was somehow responsible.

✦ A nervous-looking man who hit a shank off the 1st tee that went through the windscreen of a Jaguar XJS owned by one of his playing partners.

✦ A young man dressed in nothing but a pair of skimpy, electric-blue shorts and a pair of sunglasses who told me to go forth and multiply before he hid his club somewhere about my person, after I had politely enquired if my group might be allowed to play through his.

✦ An eight-ball that spent at least three minutes running round the green screaming and high-fiving after one of them holed a chip shot.

"Munis," you've got to love 'em.

Municipals are not known for the excellence of their greens.

HOW GREEN ARE THE GREENS?

A 2006 survey by the Scottish Golf Environment Group (SGEG) found that 51 percent of courses applied less than 80 kg of potassium fertilizer per hectare to their greens; but what does that really mean?

Rest assured these figures mean as little to me as they probably do to you. I haven't the faintest idea just how much potassium fertilizer would be considered excessive; but I do know that the question of the environment is important enough to warrant such a survey, and that courses monitor their environmental impact closely enough to be able to answer it. Both of these facts are welcome developments from the days when some courses would unthinkingly dump bags of fertilizer on anything that grew.

The SGEG isn't alone, of course. Groups researching the impact of golf on the environment have been popping up wherever golf is played for 20 years or more. Thanks to their influence, and a growing preference among golfers for "minimalist" courses, the world has seen a definite shift away from the over-fertilized and over-watered layouts of the 1980s and '90s.

It was these sorts of developments that gave golf a wretched reputation among environmentalists and indeed the wider public. And like its enduring reputation for bad clothing (see pages 42–3), golf has found it hard to shake its poor image despite the numerous environmentally friendly initiatives now in place around the world.

A 2002 University of London survey backs this perception up with numbers, showing that 80 percent of the golfers who were surveyed believed that courses were good for the environment, while only 36 percent of non-golfers agreed.

Golf faces some serious challenges regarding irrigation, but thankfully the days of wanton over-consumption are becoming a thing of the past.

In the States, where many courses, especially those in the Southwest, use vast quantities of water every day (some courses are replacing the grass on their greens and tees with synthetic turf to cut costs) the figures are similar. Only 30 percent of non-golfers in America believe that the game is beneficial to the environment.

As a golfer I suppose I'm biased, but I think that many of these negative judgments are based, at least in part, on the images of the past. Perhaps people should visit the truly organic Askernish GC on South Uist, or the wonderfully "un-manicured" Temple GC in Berkshire, to see how far the game has progressed since the substance-abusing, hose-happy days of the 1980s. And besides, if the land is up for development anyway, would you really rather have yet another concrete shopping mall and vast parking lot? Sure, golf still has some way to go, but it's at least heading in the right direction.

THE GOLFING GODS

Happy to give me a birdie on the forgettable 17th, they heckle me on my backswing at the tee of the heroic 18th. Capricious, fickle, and frequently vindictive, the golfing gods have been having fun at my expense for 20 years.

I know the golf gods exist because I've seen things happen on golf courses that really shouldn't. I've seen balls skim across water and cosy up against the flag. I've seen balls destined for the woods ricochet off overhead power lines back on to the fairway. I've seen thinned shots hit halfway up the pin at 100 miles an hour, but drop into the hole. Yes, I've seen countless shots happen that couldn't possibly have occurred without some outside agency or other being involved.

The trouble is, however, none of these outrageous strokes of good fortune ever happen to me. The luckiest I've ever been on a golf course was when I lost control of a cart that slid down a muddy embankment, but stopped just short of the river at the bottom.

I'm pretty sure that playing golf while believing that the game's gods have got it in for me does my game no good whatsoever. But much of the time, I can't help myself.

GOLFERS OF THE WORLD UNITE

Global golf travel has many attractions, not least of which is playing with some pretty exotic characters in some unfamiliar places.

Until you get on a plane bound for some far-flung corner of the planet, your experiences of this game will remain fairly bland — at least, not nearly as far-fetched as they could be. Some sunny resort at home or abroad is as far as many will venture, but for those with a touch of wanderlust that's just a little too predictable.

My globe-trotting days may well be behind me, at least for the time being, now that I've got a family to think about. But the memories of past trips, and the people I played with, keep me going until I can venture off once more into the unknown. Here are just a few of the weird and wonderful individuals I've met playing golf:

+ a bushman in the Outback who lived the life of Crocodile Dundee (apart from the bit where he goes to New York);
+ a student in South Africa who played barefoot, and was still a scratch golfer;
+ a Hindu preacher in Indonesia;
+ a billionaire in Hong Kong;
+ the 11-time winner of Costa Rica's national championship;
+ and a Zimbabwean farmer who gripped the club with his left hand below his right, but still played to his three handicap.

GET YOURSELF FITTED

Listen very carefully, I shall say this only once: you must have your golf clubs custom-fitted to your specific body type and swing characteristics if you're ever going to fulfill your potential.

Of course it's in their interests to say this, but professional clubfitters — not the cowboys who build you a set of clubs based on their best guess — insist that poor-quality clubs that have been custom-built will work better for you than a top-quality set that hasn't. The whole point of custom-fitting is to ensure your good swings are justly rewarded, and that you no longer have to manipulate your swing to compensate for clubs that are not suited to you.

A static fit is a good start, but now you need to hit balls, ideally with a launch monitor analyzing your every move.

Two Ways to Get Fitted

There are two methods for fitting a golfer: static and dynamic. A static fit can be completed at most club manufacturers' or golf retailers' Web sites. Your height, hand size, and one or two other measurements are taken, and your current clubs' specifications and resulting ball flight assessed. The static fit is a good starting point, certainly better than no information at all, but to be fitted as comprehensively as possible you need to add a dynamic fitting. This is where a launch monitor records your swing speed, the ball's launch angle, its spin rate, and the resulting carry.

Who Can Do It?

Most club professionals are certified clubfitters (manufacturers license the pro to fit their clubs). Sometimes a fitting, which normally takes up to an hour, is free, and if there is a small charge the pro will probably reimburse it if you buy the clubs from him or her.

Independent clubfitters (try the International Professional Association of Clubfitters at www.ipac.com) are usually well-qualified and affiliated with a retail facility, but don't necessarily teach or play the game for money. They perhaps give the most thorough fittings — this is, after all, what they do — and will give you a list of your specifications at the end of the session. You will have to pay a little more for this than you would a club pro, but you can then take your specs to a vendor to order the clubs.

A demo day is a really good opportunity for you to try out some new clubs.

Retail stores are a better place to have clubs custom-fitted than they were ten years ago, but they still have their limitations as the fitting tends only to be static. If they do have a launch monitor the staff are sometimes clueless as to how it actually works: "Have you tried turning it off and on again?"

Club demo days allow you to hit new models with a wide range of specifications but usually without a launch monitor present. So you don't get a scientific evaluation of your shots — spin rate, ball speed, and so on. Although for some people that stuff doesn't really matter as much as gauging how a club feels and simply seeing the results.

If you really want to push the boat out, visit the fitting studio at a manufacturer's headquarters. I went to Callaway's Performance Lab once and was blown away by the rate at which technology had clearly advanced since I was last fitted. The process was also extremely good fun; like playing a games console, only ten times better.

The Shaft is All-Important

If you don't think the shaft has much effect on your golf, try hitting Tiger Woods' clubs (actually, he probably wouldn't let you). If your swing is anything like mine, you wouldn't get the ball much more than 20 ft. off the ground, even with an 8-iron. The shafts are way too stiff for the likes of you and me and they load and unload (bend and bend back) very little or too late for the average amateur to square the clubface. Shots therefore tend to fly low and to the right. A session with a launch monitor and a decent fitter are essential if you want to identify the shaft that works best for you.

As you can see, the launch monitor processes an awful lot of information — clubhead speed, launch angle, spin rate, and so on. But it can't tell you to stop wearing yellow trousers.

Sole/Face Tape

A launch monitor provides information that assists the fitter in optimizing clubface loft and shaft flex. The lie of the club (the angle of the shaft to the ground at address) is another very important aspect that also needs to be considered.

If your clubs are too flat at address the shaft will naturally be more upright at impact and the toe will contact the ground with the heel raised. The shot will fly to the right of your intended target. Likewise, if your clubs are too upright you will tend to hit it left.

You can record the lie of your clubs by hitting balls off a lie board with impact tape stuck to the sole of your iron. If the resulting mark appears toward the toe, the lie is too flat; in the middle means it is just right; while near the heel means the club is too upright.

The mark left when the sole hit the lie board is in the middle of the tape, which means the owner of this club cannot blame the lie for a wayward shot.

KEEPING SCORE

Shoot a ten-under-par 62 but fail to sign your scorecard or fill it out correctly, and instead of winning the tournament you could be disqualified. So how about a few quick reminders to help you avoid that horrible situation?

We all know the story. Argentine Roberto De Vicenzo makes a three at the 71st hole at the 1968 Masters but playing partner, Tommy Aaron, puts him down for a par 4 by mistake. After finishing with what he thinks is a round of 65 that should at least earn him a berth in a play-off, it is discovered De Vicenzo has signed his card before noticing Aaron's error. The four stands and a 65 becomes a 66 — one too many for the play-off.

In the heat of battle at a major championship, with his focus elsewhere, it's almost understandable, albeit regrettable, for a player to miss slight inaccuracies such as that which De Vicenzo overlooked. But there is no excuse for you and me, after playing a comparatively insignificant club event, to get it wrong. There's no great pressure, you probably won't already be thinking about your round tomorrow, and how you're going to win the tournament, and you won't be expected in the media tent for a press conference. You have plenty of time and all you have to do is make sure the score your partner has you down for on each hole matches the score you put in the "Marker's Score" column on your partner's card (and that this score is correct, of course). You don't even have to add it all up and write in the total — let the officials do that.

Filling in a scorecard is very simple, but mistakes are often made. Just ensure that the scores for each hole are correct, and that you have signed your card before handing it in.

TURN IN A CORRECT SCORECARD

It's so important that it's worth going over the basics:

+ Fill in all the info at the top of the card (your name, handicap, date, and so on).
+ Exchange cards with another member of your group.
+ Write that player's scores in "Player's Score," yours go in "Marker's Score."
+ At the end of the round, make absolutely sure the numbers you have down for yourself under "Marker's Score" are the same as those your partner wrote down on your card, under "Player's Score." Say the scores out loud if need be.
+ Only when the scorecards tally and you are confident everything is in order, should you sign your partner's card (under "Marker's Signature") and give it back, then sign your own ("Player's Signature") and hand it in.

GO BACK AND START YOUNGER

For most, the golf swing does not come naturally. It's an unfamiliar action that requires great flexibility. So you want to start swinging a golf club and ingraining the movements before it's too late.

L et me rephrase that (because it's never too late to take up golf); while your body is still sufficiently pliant to perform the motion without too much pain.

Some people do pick up a club for the first time the day after retiring, thinking that a few holes in the sunshine with friends every day might be a good way to spend their twilight years. But contorting hands and limbs in a manner as yet untried, in order to propel a ball high into the air, will not come easily to an arthritic man who's had both hips replaced.

As far as I know, the only major champion who picked up a club for the first time after his 20th birthday was America's Larry Nelson. He started at 21 and eagled the first hole he ever played! Exceptions like Nelson aside, you really need to start at an age when your body is supple and athletic. If you have kids who want to be the next Tiger Woods, take them to a pitch-and-putt course, a driving range, or even a miniature golf course

where they can have a good time. Don't buy any equipment just yet. Let them decide they are definitely interested in golf before you go wasting your money. Then, when it's clear they really are taken with the game, take them along to a local course and introduce them to the pro. A decent pro should have experience teaching kids and make these early experiences enjoyable. And if you live near a professional tour venue, there's no better way to fuel a kid's fascination than by taking him or her to watch their heroes.

When it's time for your kid's first set, don't just cut down your old irons; the clubheads are probably too heavy for a youngster. Invest in some proper junior clubs instead. And please, please don't push your children; let them discover for themselves what a fun, challenging, and enriching game golf is. If you try to force them into it, the chances are that they will just end up resenting it.

Find a pro who makes lessons fun. Yelling at a bunch of kids to keep their heads down is not terribly encouraging and will put them off in no time at all.

⚓ A DAY AT THE OPEN

Since the first championship was held in 1860, when just eight professionals entered, the Open has grown somewhat. A far cry from the days in which Willie Park picked up the first of his four victories, in 2007, winner Padraig Harrington beat 155 other golfers to the £750,000 top prize and the famous Claret Jug. It's a huge event and one of Britain's greatest. If you get the chance, you have to go.

I'm sure some American readers will choke on their corn dogs and spray latte through their noses when I say this; the Open Championship is the greatest tournament in the world.

Golf fans in the States (which is where I now live, so I'm expecting more than a little comeback) understandably perceive the Masters and their own national Open as being greater, but in my daydreams I'm always holing out on the 18th green at St Andrews to win by a stroke and be crowned Champion Golfer for the Year.

A day at the Open is a memorable occasion. The exhibition tent is well worth a visit and I like to spend a good hour watching players warm up at the practice ground before sitting in front of the huge TV screen in the tented village with a burger and beer. But, of course, you've got to head out to the course at some point.

I worked out long ago that trying to follow groups including Tiger Woods, Ernie Els, John Daly, or old favorites such as Seve Ballesteros and Jack Nicklaus was a total waste of time. You have to be extremely fit and get a bit lucky to see so much as half a dozen shots without standing on tip-toes and craning your neck, or having some four-year-old

kid on it's parent's shoulders accidentally kick you in the face.

Instead I might follow a group of lesser-known players so I can at least see the course (following a group the whole way round can mean a hike of between six and ten miles depending on how often you get lost and how many visits you make to the beer tent or toilet).

More often than not though, I'll find an empty seat among the 17,000 or so available in the grandstands and watch every player come through. There I can sit back and watch the world's best golfers playing one of the game's greatest courses for its biggest prize. Apart from the occasional fool shouting "Go in the hole," "You the man," or any number of equally moronic utterances, it really couldn't get much better.

When Italy's Costantino Rocca holed his monster putt on the 18th green at St Andrews in 1995 to force a play-off with John Daly, I was watching from a grandstand. As the guy who sat next to me jumped up to celebrate he knocked my glasses clean off my face. By the time I located them all the commotion had died down.

THE RULES OF THE GAME

The current R&A rulebook (you can find a pdf at www.randa.org) is 208 pages long. Some of the pages are filled with ads admittedly, but we are talking about one exhaustive set of guidelines and instructions here. As it says in the foreword, the book is the result of four years' work and consultation between the R&A and USGA. It would take at least that long for me to read the thing and commit its finer points to memory.

Unbelievably there are 40 pages of decisions and definitions before you even get to Rule 1. There are 34 rules in all (28 of which have been revised for the 2008–2011 edition) with all sorts of clauses and sub-clauses. There are three appendices (the first of which has three parts), ten rules on amateur status, a section on gambling, and a 24-page index. Frankly, it's terrifying.

When I worked in the pro store, I had a pretty good grasp of the rules. But now, 16 years on, I'd say I am only slightly more familiar with them than your average weekend golfer. Basic rules such as what to do when your ball is in an unplayable lie, where to drop after finding a water or lateral water hazard, and the procedure one should follow after hitting out of bounds are still etched on my mind, I suppose because I now refer to them more often than I'd like. But rules like 25-1a: "Interference by an abnormal ground condition" just don't roll off the tongue quite as easily as they once did.

I won't go into details about any specific rules, for that I would recommend *Golf*

You've got the weekend to learn it. There will questions...

Rules Explained by Peter Dobereiner and Bill Elliott, or the light-hearted *Do I get a Drop?* by Doug Anderson. Instead I thought it might be more fun to tell you the story of the respected club veteran who I saw break the rules many times in a single round.

He had been at the club for decades, was one of "the boys," and may even have been on a committee or two. At the 18th, his drive came to rest a few feet in front of a tree. His backswing was impeded and in trying to advance the ball, he missed it altogether. Quickly, all in one non-stop motion in fact, he took another swipe and got his ball up near the green. After a chip and a putt he was in for five. When we came to signing our cards, however, he queried the five, saying he had made a par 4. "But didn't you..." I stopped abruptly; a junior accusing one of the most respected men in the club of cheating would not go down well.

I bring this up because, despite the fact it happened 21 years ago, I can still see him, clear as crystal, chopping twice at his ball by the tree. Cheating stinks and the stench never goes away.

PLAYING WITH THE PROS

If you're fortunate enough to play in a pro-am you need to know the drill in order to avoid upsetting your pro, and looking a total fool.

I once played in a pro-am with a well-known Australian player. My four partners and I had chosen him at a draw party the previous evening hoping that not only would he give us a few great tips, but also foster a fun and relaxed atmosphere with the genial, easy-going manner of your typical Aussie.

He didn't say a word for eight holes. As invited guests, we hadn't paid a penny for the privilege of being there, but let me tell you, I for one was beginning to feel a little cheated.

An amusing incident on the 9th tee, which will have to wait for another day I'm afraid, and another on the 13th cracked the ice, however, and by the 18th we were all getting along famously.

Curious why "Our Pro" had blanked us for eight holes I asked his caddy if there had been a problem. "You should see some of the morons we get," he said. "He doesn't really enjoy these things, because even though we're working he's expected to laugh at every lame joke and offer advice all the time. It just took him nine holes to realize you lot were okay."

"Our Pro" was, of course, no different from the vast majority of the other pros with whom you could one day be paired. So despite shelling out big bucks, and therefore having every right to expect your pro to join in the fun, remember this is the last practice round before the tournament starts; they might not be the life and soul of the five-ball.

Your pro is already in the hole for three, so what on earth are you doing lining up a putt for a seven?

TIPS FOR PRO-AM PARTICIPANTS

It's mostly common sense really, but here are a few pointers to help you get the most out of your encounter with a pro.

- Look smart and show up on the tee five minutes before the pro.
- Greet the pro with a handshake and a smile. By all means say what a pleasure it is to meet him or her, but nothing too gushing, mind.
- For goodness sake don't worry about how badly you play. I guarantee you, the pro has seen worse.
- Unless you really are a stand-up comedian, do not act like one.
- Once your pro has made a birdie and you have no way of improving on that, you must pick your ball up.

PLAYING WITH THE BOSS

When it comes to playing with the boss protocol is far stricter in the States than the UK, for example; but wherever you are playing in the world, it's worth having a think about what you and your boss can expect from the day.

Imagine you're an office junior and have just received an invitation to play golf with your CEO, the infamous Gordon Gekko. You've only ever seen him twice, certainly never spoken to him, and now you have an invite — issued by his PA of course — to spend four hours in his company. He's an intimidating man and you're anxious about making a good impression as you realize this round could make or break your career.

You prepare the night before, choosing your outfit carefully and cleaning your clubs and shoes. You arrive at the course well ahead of time and are either warming up on the range as Mr Gekko arrives or sitting in the lounge with his favorite tipple waiting for him. On-course dialog is entirely at his discretion, but however it goes, it never gets chummy.

Do you beat him? No hard and fast rules on that. You decide to gauge his demeanor, asking yourself how he'd react if you took him to the cleaners. Would he be impressed or find it disrespectful and make your life a living hell?

Although Gekko is a work of fiction and didn't play golf (racquetball was his game), this type of scenario isn't uncommon in the States, where frequent magazine articles spell out exactly what's expected of the employee.

PLAYING FOR REAL

In my experience, workers needn't be quite so apprehensive or pay quite as much attention to the details. That said, your boss won't be terribly impressed

if you disregard the preferred code of behavior altogether. So it can't hurt to:

+ Turn up before your boss.
+ Look presentable.
+ Remember that your boss isn't your best mate. Keep the language as clean as your shoes, and for that matter make sure your shoes are clean.
+ Silence your cellphone.
+ Try hard to win without being unpleasantly competitive.
+ Offer to pay for everything. Your boss probably won't accept your offer, but it doesn't mean it isn't appreciated.

My friend John, a marketing executive, concurs with the above, but adds he would book a lesson for a few days before the round. He'd then have a bit of time to practice what he learned.

Unless you know your boss very well, keep the banter clean and don't talk about the office unless your boss brings it up.

HOW TO CURVE THE BALL... INTENTIONALLY

Shaping shots to the left or right is a dying art. That's not to say today's golfers can't do it, they just don't need to very often.

Golf shots fly straighter today than they used to, not necessarily because today's golfers are any better than the golfers of the 1960s, say (they aren't), but because today's equipment is. Low-spinning golf balls and light titanium drivers, in which manufacturers can add or remove weight to specific areas of the clubhead to affect a certain type of shot, have seen a reduction in the amount of sidespin that a golfer can create.

That's no bad thing when you're faced with a narrow, tree-lined par 4 where you must find the fairway. But because pulls and pushes — affected by the golfer's swingpath not the ball's specifications — still happen every bit as often as they used to, what do you do when you miss the fairway, get stuck behind a tree, and need to curl one round the branches to find the green?

While unintentional sidespin is less of a problem than it used to be, golfers needing to hook or slice a shot on purpose can still do it with a few alterations to their set-up and, in the case of a hook, some quick wrists or, for a slice, quiet wrists that prevent the release of the clubhead.

THE INTENTIONAL DRAW/HOOK

The laws that determine the flight of a golf ball (see page 28) tell us that a hook — a shot that starts to the right of your target and curves back to the left — occurs when the clubface is closed in relation to that swingpath. So, to hit a big, slinging hook round a tree, align your feet, hips, and shoulders well to the

right of it but the clubface at the target. The clubface is now closed in relation to your stance and should therefore be closed to the path of your swing. Now, when you swing back normally along the line of your feet and hit the ball with this closed clubface the ball will miss the tree to the right and hook back toward your target. At least that's the theory.

✦ To encourage more hook spin, feel like your wrists are rolling over through impact, and the toe of the clubhead

Aim to the right of the target

Target line

To hit a big hook, aim your body well to the right of your target, but the clubface at it. Your aim lines converge. And roll the wrists a little more than usual.

beats the heel back to the ball. Feel like the inside of your left forearm and the top of your right forearm face the sky. The feeling is not unlike a top-spin forehand in tennis (admittedly just with the right hand).

✦ The more you want to hook the ball, the further right of the target you aim your body and the more you roll the wrists. So, if you just need a small draw, keep the clubface looking at the target but aim your body only slightly to the right. As always, grip the club lightly.

THE INTENTIONAL FADE/SLICE

If you missed the fairway to the right, chances are you'll have to hit a big slice that starts well to the left of the trees then cuts back toward your target. By now you've probably worked out that to hit this slice you do the opposite to what you would when hitting a hook, but just in case:

✦ Aim your feet, hips, and shoulders well to the left of the obstacle.
✦ Aim the clubhead at the target.
✦ Swing along the line of your feet and hold off the release of the clubhead. The heel of the clubhead must beat the toe to the ball. Feel like your forearms remain well separated.
✦ The more slice-spin you want, the more your aim lines (clubface and body) should diverge.

JUST FEEL IT

At a clinic several years ago, I asked Welshman Ian Woosnam how he hit such a delightful little draw. He thought

Keep your clubface facing the target for a fade but aim your body well left. Your aim lines diverge. Hold off the release a little.

about it for a few seconds. "Er, I don't really know to be honest," he replied. "I just do." At a similar event with Colin Montgomerie a few years later, I asked the big Scot how he managed to hit his powerful fade time and time again. He didn't really know either.

The lesson is that both Woosnam and Montgomerie are "feel" players. They just feel the shot they need to play. Montgomerie said he didn't set up any differently for a fade than he would do for the very occasional draw that he hit, but that if he did mean to hit a draw he probably felt his hands and wrists needed to be a little bit more active through the ball.

YOUR PRE·SHOT ROUTINE

Humans often perform certain actions better if we aren't conscious of what we're doing. Whatever the sport, the best players are able to exist in an unthinking moment, putting everything into motion without mental distractions.

After practicing for months and months, Olympic figure skaters execute their routines not by desperately trying to remember the difference between a double axel and a triple salchow, but by simply allowing their mind and body do what they have been trained to do. Likewise, golfers swing at their free-flowing, rhythmical best when they minimize conscious thought and let the subconscious take over.

Your routine must be the same for every shot. Try aligning the clubface to the target first, then your body in response to the clubface. And waggle the club, shuffle your feet, flex your knees, anything, to avoid getting "stuck" over the ball.

A pre-shot routine is a very good way to do this, and you'll notice every single professional golfer bar none has one and carries it out for every single shot they play. By enacting exactly the same routine every time we can remove unhelpful technical clutter from our heads and arrive at the ball tension-free and able to swing the club with the freedom, balance, and speed of which we are capable.

UNIVERSAL ELEMENTS
Your routine can include whatever movements and actions you like. But remember; it will only be any good if you repeat exactly the same movements before every shot.

Having selected a club and decided what sort of shot to play, a typical pro will stand a few yards behind the ball, picking a target and picturing a good result. Then he or she will move alongside the ball and align the clubface before moving into position. Once in position, the pro eases the tension in the forearms by lightening the grip and waggling the club. Then the initial move away from the ball is smooth and fluid rather than jerky and erratic.

A routine such as this will help switch off your mind, and promote a fluid swing, stopping the demons in your head from distracting you at the top of your swing with thoughts of what went wrong the last time you played this hole.

ETIQUETTE

Call me a joy-killing, party-pooping, sport-spoiling wet blanket, but part of the reason our sport is so special is because we have a set of behavioral guidelines that the vast majority of players actually adhere to.

This is not some pointless code; without it, the condition of our courses would suffer, and playing golf would not be so safe and enjoyable... and these days a serious breach of etiquette could result in disqualification from a competition.

✦ Most important is a regard for other players' safety. Never hit until the group in front of you is well out of range. Don't make practice swings close to other players, and if there is even the slightest possibility your ball will hit another player then shout "Fore."

✦ It doesn't matter how badly you want to win, you should show your playing partners respect by standing well away from them as they play their shots; ensuring your cellphone is silenced; not walking on or casting a shadow over their putting lines, or standing directly behind the hole while they are putting. And after you've putted out,

Ask your playing partners if they would like you to tend the flag.

Repair pitch marks by inserting your repair tool at the back of the mark and pushing the turf toward its center. Tap down gently with your putter. Do not lever turf up to fill the dent, or twist the repair tool.

stick around until your partners have finished; don't rush off to the next tee.

✦ Your group should keep pace with the group ahead; or if a gap opens up between you and those in front, and the group behind catches up, you should invite them to play through. Maintain your pace by being ready to play when it's your turn; placing your bag so you don't have to walk to the front of the green after finishing; and walking briskly, filling in your scorecard as you go. Also, if your ball may be lost, play a provisional and call the group behind through as you look for the original.

✦ Finally, look after the course: be careful not to take divots with practice swings; replace your divots; rake bunkers; repair pitch marks; don't stand your bag on the green or too close to the teeing area; and remove and replace the flag carefully.

EYE·BALLING

Back when there were no yardage charts, laser rangefinders, or digital GPS-enabled distance-measuring devices, golfers used to estimate the distance left to the hole with, imagine this, their own two eyes.

Despite the relentless advance of technology, there's a lot to be said for relying on your eyes today. For a start, standing at your ball, looking at the flag and deciding that it's roughly 147 yards away is an awful lot cheaper than doing it with any of the latest gadgets, or for that matter a yardage planner booklet, which are becoming ever more expensive.

The advantage of using hi-tech instruments to measure your yardage is of course superior accuracy. I don't care how long you've been eye-balling, a gadget that picks up high-frequency, low-power radio signals from four GPS satellites orbiting the Earth and deduces its own position and then the flag's using a mathematical principle called trilateration is probably going to beat your best guess, at least more often than not. As far as I can see, that's where the benefits end, however. There is an argument, which the manufacturers push relentlessly, that says such gadgets and gizmos speed up play, but I'm not convinced. They'll certainly lop a chunk of time off your round if you're in the habit of pacing out the yardage to the hole on every shot, but who does that?

If, however, you are in the market for one of these things, then consider some of a GPS system's advantages over a rangefinder:

+ A funky color screen.
+ You can input all your stats, keeping tabs on your strengths and weaknesses.

+ You will know your exact elapsed playing time (although you could do this with your watch).
+ You can measure your shots and know the distance you hit each club enabling the device to recommend clubs.
+ You do not need a direct line of sight to the hole to know the distance remaining.
+ The initial purchase can be cheaper than for a rangefinder.
+ They are often lighter and usually less bulky than rangefinders.
+ They are quicker than a rangefinder. Just look at the screen and pick your club.

You can't order pizza with it but it gives pretty accurate yardages.

But, of course, the laser rangefinder has its advantages too:

+ No annual subscription fees.
+ No downloading course information from manufacturer's database.
+ Provided you can keep your hand still, it can actually be more accurate.

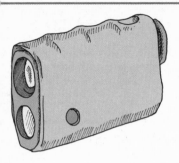

There is an enormous range of rangefinders on the market.

The choice between GPS and laser is not cut and dried. Each has its advocates, and there are decent arguments in favor of both. Myself, I'm staying out of it. My eyes (well, if I'm honest my contact lenses) still work well enough for me to know it's an 8-iron.

GPS units and laser rangefinders can tell you the shot is 134 yards, not the 130 you estimated. But for how many of us does that really make a difference to the club we choose and the type of shot we play?

 ## HATS OFF

On a top shelf in the darkest corner of my closet are 63 baseball caps I've bought, been given, or picked up on various golf trips. Some of them are so gaudy it's unlikely they'll ever see the light of day, but there are a handful that get an airing once every so often.

Thanks to Tiger Woods' choice of headwear, the baseball cap is now very much part of the golfer's uniform. Shallow-fronted and narrow-brimmed is the style of choice for most of today's young studs, but among the sport's older participants you still see the odd over-size front, mesh back and wide brim; a style that should, in my opinion, be accompanied by a piece of straw dangling from the golfer's mouth.

Other acceptable styles, albeit ones that only certain individuals might be able to pull off, include; the pork-pie hat, bucket hat, flat cap, coconut hat, ivy cap, army hat, the fleece cap, and even the visor, whose popularity I have never really been able to understand.

Hats that I don't much care for, besides the aforementioned visor, include Panamas and those circular-brimmed straw hats that Greg Norman used to wear. The only person for whom that design ever looked good was Greg Norman, and then only just.

THE YIPS AND HOW TO SHAKE THEM

What a miserable existence it would be knowing that no matter how brilliant your drive and approach shots were, you were still going to double-bogey the hole after making four involuntary stabs at the ball with your putter. To everyone with the yips; my heart goes out to you.

Most people my age associate the yips with Bernhard Langer, the incredible German professional who has overcome them a number of times with a series of different putters and grips, not to mention perseverance and hard work. One of the earliest reported cases, however, was six-time Open champion Harry Vardon who would address the ball and "watch for the right hand to jump."

For years it was assumed the problem was purely psychological. But recent research has identified another culprit. Not only are fear and performance anxiety (what most golfers term "choking") to blame but also focal dystonia, a neurological disorder often described as an occupational cramp and characterized by involuntary movements or spasms. Fine, but how does this new-found knowledge help you get rid of the darn things?

Yips Tips

Considering how many Web sites, magazine articles, and books are devoted to the subject, my paltry suggestions on how to get rid of the yips might seem a tad simplistic, but here goes:

✦ You need to stop worrying so much. No 17-handicapper should get the yips. What's the worst that can happen if you miss a few putts — you'll become an 18-handicapper?

✦ You've got to try something different than what you've been doing for so long. Try a new grip, a belly or broomhandle putter, or putt left-handed. Try a new grip on a left-handed broomhandle — you get the point; do something unusual.

✦ If none of that works then you might also want look into Emotional Freedom Techniques (www.emofree.com). This might sound a bit new-age — EFT is a needle-free version of acupuncture that claims to provide relief from pain, disease, and emotional issues — and I wouldn't mention it at all if it weren't for studies showing that, to date, EFT has had a 100 percent success rate with yippers.

✦ Finally, read Hank Haney's *Fix the Yips Forever*.

Crazy though it might seem, big bucks and big brains are coming together in the search for a yips cure. However, there are a number of relatively simple cures before you resort to this.

THE THRILL OF MATCHPLAY

In the genteel game of golf, it doesn't hurt to throw down the gauntlet of head-to-head competition every once in a while; bring it on...

Matchplay is golf at its sportiest, as much a battle of wits as ability. If you've got a grudge against someone, it's far more satisfying to beat them 6&5 than by six shots in a medal round.

MATCHPLAY MOVES
There's so much psychology tied up in matchplay that it's worth running through a few tips that might give you the mental edge. This isn't gamesmanship, just cunning tactics.

The Ryder Cup is matchplay at its pulsating best, and always fantastic entertainment. I'm so hooked on the game that I get excited about the Madeira Island Open, so you can imagine what the Ryder Cup does for me.

+ Don't start out trying to match your opponent shot for shot. Play the course. If it's really tight coming down the stretch you might then take more notice of what your opponent is doing.
+ If it's close, hit your tee shot shorter than your opponent's and stiff your approach shot first, thus putting all the pressure on them.
+ Concede a few two/three-footers early on, but make your foe putt out on the later holes. That will deprive your rival of any confidence-building short putts early on, and also introduce an element of doubt as to why you made him or her hole this one but gave the others.
+ Always expect your opponent to play a brilliant shot or hole a long putt so you won't be upset when it happens. If it lips out, count it as a bonus.
+ Always speak positively about yourself and believe what you say.
+ Never give up when you're down, and never go easy when you're up.

Foolish Words

I remember a school match in which I went four down after four. As my opponent and I walked to the 5th tee, we started talking. He mentioned he was useless at matchplay and that, before today, had never won a single game.

I'm no Jack Nicklaus when it comes to tactics, but I didn't need to be to take advantage of his pessimism and distrust of his own game. Not surprisingly, he crumbled when I started playing a bit better and I beat him 3&2.

⚓ PLAYING IN THE WIND

You've played a sheltered inland course all your life but you're off to Scotland for some links golf. The first course you play is Royal Dornoch, and while the view from the 1st tee is pretty special, the gale blowing in off the North Sea could be a problem.

The wind at a coastal course seems very different to that which you might face in the sheltered suburbs. For a start it smells of salt, but more than that, it's cold and probably strong enough to render your yardage planner all but meaningless.

For the first-time visitor to a links, the wind can be totally overwhelming. You can fight it all day and always, always come off second best. Downwind, your ball flies much lower than expected, pitches well short of the green, and still seems to pick up speed as it vanishes over the back. Into the wind you'll lose your hat and, just as bad, your ball will balloon into the air before dropping to the ground halfway to the hole.

To put it simply, you've got to expect higher scores in strong winds. It's inevitable. However, there are a few measures you can take to limit the damage, and even make the wind work for you.

HEAD ON

If you're on the tee using a driver, tee the ball a little lower, move it back an inch in your stance, grip the club a little lighter, and focus on making a smooth swing. Solid contact is much more important than swing speed. Try to hit the ball hard and you'll most likely impart too much backspin and the ball will rise and fall like a paper plane. Just aim to "sweep" through the ball, rather than "hit" it.

You can apply a similar method to your iron approach shots. Take more club, grip down the handle a little, play the ball back in your stance, and make an easy swing. Abbreviate your follow-through and above all don't impart too much backspin by hitting the ball hard. That just sends the ball too high and it lands well short of the green.

When hitting into the wind I picture Ernie Els' smooth rhythm. Although his clubhead is moving very fast, the acceleration in his swing seems very gentle and unhurried.

DOWNWIND

Playing downwind is a bittersweet combination of longer drives coupled with impossible-to-stop approach shots. Tee the ball higher with the driver, position it half an inch forward in your stance, get the feeling you're swinging up on the ball, and launch it high into the sky where it can catch a free ride.

When approaching the green, just make your best judgment of where to land the ball. It could be on the front edge of the green or 50 yards short. If you can't land it short because there's a stream or bunker in front of the green, the best you can realistically expect is to go to the back of the green or over it. But that's not so bad. It's better than getting wet or chopping about in a pot bunker.

Walking back down a steep mountain can almost feel as tough as climbing up. Similarly, playing downwind can often be as tricky as hitting into it.

CROSSWINDS

There are two schools of thought for playing in a crosswind. The first is to counter a left-to-right wind by hitting a draw, and a right-to-left wind with a fade; meaning that the ball should fly fairly straight and stop quickly. The second is to play a normal shot, simply allowing the wind to push the ball in the direction it's moving.

I'd say the second option is probably the safer of the two for most amateurs, but bear in mind if you do go "with" the wind your ball will effectively be traveling downwind toward the end of its flight, so won't stop quickly.

PUTTING

In a strong wind, putting becomes extremely tricky as not only does the wind

---

Long Way Out, Easy Home

On a chilly November day a few years back, my mate Dave and I took on the Old Course at St Andrews in a howling gale. We considered spending the day in the local inn, but I'm very glad we didn't.

Those familiar with the 1st hole know it's not much more than a drive and pitching wedge in normal conditions, but on this day I hit a career drive followed by a career 4-iron and made it over the burn in front of the green with just about a foot to spare. To reach the par-5 5th, I needed a driver, two 3-woods, and a 6-iron while I went over the back of the 530-yard 14th with a driver and a 5-iron.

My score wasn't fit for this or any other publication, but I don't remember too many rounds as enjoyable as this one.

---

affect the ball it also makes it difficult to keep your body and head still. So first of all, for better balance just widen your stance slightly. Also, hover the putter just above the ground when you address the ball, because if you ground the club and the ball moves or oscillates in the wind you are deemed to have moved it and must add a penalty stroke.

With a wide base, the wind can't blow you over.

GETTING A GRIP

If the grip of a club is worn and shiny, you'll hold the club tighter to prevent it from slipping. A tight grip leads to tight forearms, tight forearms lead to a poor release of the clubhead, and a poor release usually ends up short and in the trees.

Some pros change their grips every week, which strikes me as a touch overzealous, but I suppose if my livelihood depended partly on my equipment I'd want to keep it in tip-top condition as well. Weekend golfers should re-grip their clubs at least once a year and wash them with warm, soapy water once a month. With a clean, tacky grip your hold on the club will soften automatically, and you'll release the clubhead powerfully once again.

Many take their clubs to the pro-store to be re-gripped. But it's not exactly rocket science, and you can find all the necessary bits and pieces online, so if you want to save some money, do it yourself. You'll need:

+ A utility knife. Use a hook blade on graphite shafts to avoid damage.
+ Grip solvent. White spirit works well, but odorless, non-toxic, non-flammable products are preferable.
+ Two-sided ¾-in-wide grip tape.
+ A vice and a rubber vice clamp.

PROCEDURE

First, choose the grip. Make sure the butt end is the correct diameter and that it's the right thickness for your hands — if you have large hands and/or consistently hook the ball, try a thicker grip. Slicers and those with small hands should try a thinner grip.

Place the club in the vice, using the rubber vice clamp. Starting at the thin end, cut along the length of the grip, peel it off, and scrape away the old tape.

Spiral wrap the tape around the shaft making sure not to go down further than the end of the new grip, and extending the tape about a half inch past the butt end. Peel the back off, and twist the end of the tape inserting it into the end of the shaft to prevent solvent getting in.

Cover the grip's vent hole with your finger (or plug it with a tee) and pour solvent into the grip. Then pour the solvent from the grip over the tape, and quickly slide the new grip on to the shaft.

Make sure the grip is aligned correctly. Give it a twist if necessary.

Finally, leave it to dry overnight.

TEXAS SCRAMBLE

There are more ways to score at golf than there are pages in this book, and I couldn't possibly tell you what they all were even if I had the space. However, the Texas scramble is a personal favorite, and you should give it a try.

Since I moved to America, my favorite format has been the extremely popular four-player scramble, ideally Texan, in which a certain number of drives from each member of the team must be used — a restriction that adds an element of strategy and means that nobody goes home feeling a complete loser because none of their drives were used.

Many readers will be familiar with the scramble, but for those who aren't I suggest you enter one as soon as possible, as this particular format involves just the right mix of feisty competition and team bonding. You and your teammates will celebrate your birdies and curse your missed putts in unison, and any time four men or women celebrate or commiserate together a real bond can be formed.

One of the many beauties of the scramble is that you can take four otherwise hopeless golfers and turn them into a 65-shooting dream team by combining their rare solid drive, occasional sound approach, and sporadic good putting with the huge dollop of luck needed for each of the players to stagger their flashes of good play effectively. Thus you get teams in which only one, maybe two, members are playing well and end up with 60 or, by failing to take advantage of good approach play, you can have teams with 15 birdie putts and three eagle putts, but who end up only four under par, which is what happened to a team I was part of last year. To say that was frustrating doesn't quite capture it.

Among my other favorite games are Stableford, Shamble, String, Skins, and Switch, which, you'll probably notice, all start with an "S." I don't think that's a prerequisite for a good game, but you never know.

The great thing about Texas scramble is that you stand or fall as a team. Mind you, if someone misses a six-footer to win, you can blame it all on them.

WHERE TO BUY YOUR EQUIPMENT

I've bought from on-course pro-stores, high-street golf superstores, online retailers, online auctions, and even a "for sale" ad in the local newspaper. Not surprisingly, I've had varied results.

The general rule is never to buy so much as a tee without trying it first. Well that's not quite true; feel free to buy a tee, just never ever buy clubs without hitting them first, ideally on a golf course where you can see the flight of the ball. A driving range is okay, but bear in mind you'll probably be hitting off mats that give a slightly unrealistic feel at impact. Nets are no good for testing as you have no idea where the ball might have ended up.

Like racquets, rods, and cues, every golf club is unique. Two may look exactly alike, have come out of the same factory, be the same length, loft, and lie, and have grips the same thickness, but somehow they just feel different. While one might not sit quite right with you, another might just have that "feel" about it. In short, you need to hit both to find the one you like.

If the pro lets you out on the course to test new equipment, offers helpful, friendly advice, and matches or is close to the price on the high street, I see no reason to go anywhere else.

IN THE PRO-STORE

In a perfect world I'd buy all my equipment from pro-stores. I could test everything on the adjoining course prior to making any decisions and honor the hard-working pro who's struggling to compete with the superstores. The prices on the high street or online are simply too good to ignore a lot of the time, but to combat this, many pros band together to form buying groups that can often meet the superstores' prices. Find one of these and your search may be over. The combination of low price, knowledgeable service, and being able to test is invaluable.

THE HIGH-STREET STORE

They offer a superb variety and invariably great prices, but often the only place a high-street store will let you test the club is in their nets. If budget is your only consideration and you don't mind the possibility of souring your relationship, you could ask your club pro if you can test a club at the course then go and buy it somewhere cheaper; but don't expect the same kind of friendly service next time you pop in.

ON THE WEB

Again, the Internet offers great prices and choice, but you can't test anything before you shell out what could be some serious cash. Most retailers offer a money-back guarantee, of course, but returning clubs can be tedious in the extreme.

ONLINE AUCTIONS

The price is usually right if you're familiar with online auction sites such as eBay. But what happens when the club arrives and the picture you saw on the Web site turns out to have been somewhat misleading? You may have a money-back guarantee, but you'll probably have seven days to notify the seller; while some don't specify a return policy at all. Although I had many reservations, I did buy a driver in an online auction once. Luckily, it fitted me well, but it took a lot of patience to find it, and a very late night to win it.

There are thousands of sites selling golf equipment on the Internet. If you know what you're looking for, are confident an online fitting is adequate (or have the specs from a more thorough fitting to hand), you can find what you need at a fantastic price. You just have to keep your fingers crossed that what arrives on your doorstep is what you think you ordered.

THE LOCAL PAPER

This is not the most sophisticated way to find clubs, but if it's a rusty set of second-hand clubs with the 5-iron missing that you're looking for then it can't hurt to have a look. Actually, I bought some clubs from a guy advertising in the paper once. They were horrible clubs in terrible condition, but I didn't know them from a set of brand-new Forged Callaway X-Tour Irons at the time. So what did I care?

GOLFING MATTERS

Walk if You Can

You have to take these stats with a very large pinch of salt because everybody's metabolism is different and every course is different, but even when riding a cart, the average golfer will burn an average of 300 calories an hour. Carry your clubs and walk and you'll burn up to twice that amount.

Golf gets a bad rap for its limited athletic demands, but apparently one hour of walking a golf course has the same effect as an hour of ballroom dancing. That seems incredible to me, but I've got the figures right here in front of me. My reliable source also informs me that I could use up exactly the same number of calories playing golf as I would scrubbing the kitchen floor on my hands and knees for an hour. I know which I'd rather do.

Whatever anyone says, carrying your bag and walking the length of a golf course with its numerous ups and downs is very good exercise. Sure, it's not running a four-and-a-half-minute mile, playing soccer, or cycling up a mountain. But it certainly beats sitting on your butt watching television.

⛵ THE WET STUFF

Whether it's a tempestuous ocean or tranquil mill pond, the sight of water can wreak havoc with a golfer's sensibilities. We see getting wet as so final, so absolute, so irrevocable. And Bobby Jones didn't help matters when he said the difference between finding a bunker and a water hazard was like the difference between a car crash and a plane crash.

Sure, you may think there's no way back from the watery depths; but this is dangerous territory. After all, if you find the water on a par 3, play another ball from the drop zone, then hole the putt you can walk off with a bogey four — the same as if you'd hit a nice shot to the green but three-putted. Likewise, on a par 4 you can find a stream short of the green, drop, pitch and putt for a five, or even on a par 5, you can walk off with a par if you pitch and putt after dropping.

Of course, I would never recommend finding the water, but doing so needn't carry with it such an air of finality. As we've seen above, the penalty for finding a lake, stream, pond, or sea can often be no worse than three-putting or chunking a chip. And you're actually better off than the poor chump who sailed over the water and the green and flew out of bounds. He doesn't have a drop zone up near the green to help him. He's got to go all the way back to where he played the original shot and face that daunting carry over the water again.

I think part of the reason we get so intimidated by water, besides the unhelpful notion that we will automatically lose the hole or make a double-bogey should we find it, is that the feeling of making it over to dry ground is so uplifting that should we fail it might ruin our day. Fine, I might be clutching at straws, but I know that's sometimes how I feel when I arrive on the 6th tee at my local course. I know that if I fly the water and land on the green my tea will taste that bit better, regardless of what I do the rest of the round. The solution, I suppose, is to somehow blot the water out.

Just imagine the pounding surf and crashing waves aren't there. It's merely another flat, dull par 3 — no big deal at all.

TAKE IT TO THE COURSE

No doubt you're familiar with the routine. As you hammer range balls far into the distance, you have total command of your swing. Every ball bows dutifully to your whim. The trick is to take that form onto the course.

A five-yard draw, you ask? No problem. A high, looping fade? Exactly how high and loopy would you like that? Between the legs, ricochet off your golf bag, five-yard draw, and a high looping fade before dropping like a stone next to the hole? Well, perhaps not, but nevertheless you still feel good on the range.

As you move to the 1st tee, however, the good feelings drain away and the silky, powerful move you had going ten minutes before has turned into a lurch. You slice your opening drive onto a parallel fairway and it continues like this for six holes at the end of which you're ready to rip up your scorecard. Of course, from the 7th to the 18th you play like a dream.

What happened to the on-demand fades and 300-yard drives? It's a mental thing, obviously. Not overly concerned with results on the range — you know that a bad shot won't affect your score — you grip the club lightly, ease the club away smoothly, and hit through the ball like Ernie Els. On the course, however, your thinking changes entirely. Apathy turns to anxiety because your shots have now become extremely important.

It does you no good to jump so quickly from calm indifference to acute nervous tension. You need to adopt similar habits

If the 1st tee shot looks anything like that at Machrihanish in Scotland, it will help if you know what to expect and have imagined the shot before you arrive. Otherwise you are going to get one heck of a shock.

on both the range and the course to make the move from one to the other less significant. The pre-shot routine is so important that you should use it for every shot that you hit, wherever you are. It may also help to mix up the shots that you hit on the range when you are warming up. Don't hit a lot in succession with the same club. Always aim at something. And try to picture what you'll be facing on the course, especially your 1st tee shot. Now, when you get to the 1st tee, it probably won't seem so scary and you will hopefully hit the ground running.

T-SQUARES AND WEIGHTED CLUBS

Sometimes pounding balls on the range just isn't enough. You have to introduce something different to stimulate your practice session. Drills are great and a training aid can help too. Just don't go spending all your money on useless gadgets and gizmos.

Time was when a white plastic ball with holes in it was all the practice aid one needed. You'd take it out to the back garden and swing away freely knowing you couldn't hit it hard enough to clear the back fence let alone smash any windows. They were safe, cheap, and who knows, might even have helped you with your golf.

The ludicrous number of training aids that are now available serves to illustrate just how bad at golf we all are. After all, if we were any good, we wouldn't be buying these things and encouraging more would-be inventors to introduce their latest, greatest contraptions to help us with a part of our game we didn't know needed help.

By purchasing dozens of training aids, you are, in a way, convincing yourself that you are rubbish. That may or may not be true, but I'm not convinced a closet full of swing vests, swing balls, swing setters, speed sticks, and hinged clubs is the answer to your problems. I'm not saying that buying a training aid isn't a good idea — far from it, there are many fine products out there. But overloading on the stuff just reminds you what a desperately difficult game it is we play, and remembering how difficult golf can be is not going to help you master it any quicker.

My suggestion is to limit yourself to one, maybe two, training aids, namely a weighted club and a T-square. (The "Crotch Hook" which attaches to your head and genitals and pulls sharply on the latter should you raise your head too early might also be an option for golfers who look up before impact.) The weighted club not only develops the muscles you

Danger: Golf

My dad used to own a training aid that clearly wasn't meant for a dumb kid like his own. It consisted of a golf ball attached to a length of elastic attached to a long spike that you stuck in the ground. When you hit the ball, it flew round in a circle and, the idea was, landed right back at your feet.

One day, I absent-mindedly pulled on the ball and the spike came flying out of the ground. Fortunately my face was concealed behind my arm, through which the spike traveled. It all happened so quickly that it was perhaps five or six seconds before I realized the spike had entered one side of my arm and come out the other. I ran into the kitchen and calmly asked my father if I was going to die. He said probably not, but that we should go to hospital just in case. I survived to tell the tale, but I hope the "Elasticized Golf Training Aid with Spike" didn't.

use to power your golf swing, it also helps you generate greater width and tempo; while the T-square ensures better alignment and ball position. Really, what more do you need?

Not only do you look a bit silly, you may not be helping your scores as much as you think.

The Irritating Golfer

Although I'd sooner be washed up on a desert island with a golfer than anyone else, there are factions of our subculture that do not toe the line, as it were — golfers who exhibit irksome, disrespectful, and just downright annoying habits.

I wouldn't say I'm overly picky or judgmental, in fact I hope I'm good company. But if you do any of the following, then I can see we're going to have a problem.

✦ Cheat.
✦ Repeatedly make or receive non-emergency calls on your phone.
✦ Step all over my putting line.
✦ Talk loudly.
✦ Keep giving yourself four-foot putts.
✦ Pace off the yardage to the hole and throw bits of grass in the air despite the fact you're 22 over par.
✦ Fail to replace your divots, rake the bunkers you play out of, or repair pitch marks.
✦ Give me a running commentary of your round.
✦ Tell me what I'm doing wrong and give me swing advice when I didn't ask for it.
✦ Curse strongly your bad luck and yourself for bad shots.
✦ Or in any other way be perceived as taking our little game way too seriously.

BOOKS

There are over 25,000 golf books in the USGA library alone. I hope you'll forgive me if I don't mention all of them here, but there is space to list a few that are definitely worth the read.

The Golf Library at home is coming on nicely.

The avid golf reader's library probably averages a dozen instruction books, far more than anyone needs or for that matter gets round to reading. Common to most collections are *Five Lessons: The Modern Fundamentals of Golf* by Ben Hogan, and Harvey Penick's *Little Red Golf Book*. I own both and have, at different stages of life, benefited greatly from both — *Five Lessons* when I was young and open to complex theory, *Little Red Golf Book* more recently when I needed small chunks of wisdom that didn't require me to sit down and think too hard.

Among other classic instruction books are Jack Nicklaus' *My Golden Lessons*, Ernest Jones's *Swing the Clubhead* (see pages 26–7), Percy Boomer's *On Learning Golf*, and Tommy Armour's *How to Play Your Best Golf All the Time*. For putting, you can't really beat Dave Pelz's *Putting Bible* unless, of course, you think a book this thick is slightly over the top for the art of hitting a ball into a hole with a stick.

Those golfers who are in need of help with the psychological side of the game should try reading Bob Rotella's *Golf Is Not a Game of Perfect*, or Gio Valiante's *Fearless Golf: Conquering the Mental Game*. I read Rotella's book recently and it certainly helped me to unclog a few synapses.

Every golfer's coffee table needs a huge, doorstop picture book weighing it down. Several worthy of the most discerning coffee tables have been published lately, the most notable being Jim Finegan's enormous *Where Golf is Great*. Another beauty is *Golf Courses: Fairways of the World*, which features photographer Dave Cannon's superb images.

MY ALL-TIMERS

My favorites among the hundreds of golf books in my house are neither instructional nor collections of great photographs, however. *The Greatest Game Ever Played*, *The Grand Slam*, and *The Match*, all by Mark Frost, are superbly researched and real page-turners. But my absolute number one is a collection of 31 silly short stories featuring characters such as Rollo Podmarsh, Cuthbert Banks, and the "Oldest Member." First published in 1973 and subsequently reprinted 19 times, P. G. Wodehouse's *The Golf Omnibus* is as enjoyable now as it was the day I bought it 18 years ago. I've only read it once this year though, so I might just dust it off this evening.

 *ON TEES*

Before William Bloxsom and Arthur Douglas patented the first ever portable teeing device in 1889, golfers had to shape a small mound of sand in order to raise their ball off the ground. Bloxsom and Douglas's tee was a fairly crude design, but it set the world of tees in motion.

Today there is a vast range of lengths and shapes to choose from: 2⅛ in, 2⅜ in, 2¾ in, and 3¼ in standard shape, 7mm, 12mm, 19mm, 25mm, 32mm, 40mm, and 50mm Castle tees, thin shank/small head tees, Brush Tees, Rip Tips, Eco tees, Velocitees, KORECTEES, Ti-Tees, PerfectTees, E-Tees featuring an internal spring, A-Balance Tees, Stinger Tees, CertainTees, Bazooka Hybrid Tees, and so on. There's even a tool called the T-Rite that uses the "latest breakthrough in consistent tee height setting technology" to ensure you tee your ball at the correct height every time (one imagines a mob of mad scientists working furiously in a secret laboratory in the Nevada desert to take tee-height setting technology to the next level).

The tee pocket in my bag is full of white, wooden, 3¼ in jumbo tees. You need these extra-long ones in order to tee the ball high enough for your mega-headed titanium driver. Some players, most notably Sergio Garcia, tee the ball very low — the top of the driver is higher than the top of the ball. The shape and speed of his swing is very different from most amateurs', however, so do yourself a favor and perch your ball up nice and high.

There are, of course, shorter tees available that are designed for use with an iron, say on a par 3, but you know what I do? I just push my 3¼ in jumbo tee further into the ground.

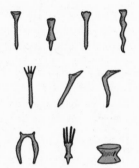

One wonders about a world with quite so many different types of tee to choose from.

DIFFERENT HEIGHTS FOR DIFFERENT SHOTS

For all the complexities of the golf swing and the various parts that can go wrong, the accuracy of your shots could well be affected by nothing more complex than the height at which you tee the ball.

If you hook the ball with your driver, try teeing it a little lower. This encourages a slightly steeper attack from outside the target line which results in a high slice. If you slice — and who doesn't? — try teeing it higher. This promotes a shallower path from inside the target line and consequently a sweet little draw.

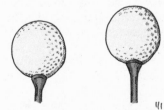

To encourage a fade, tee it low; for a draw, tee it high.

There are loads of devices, both electronic and mechanical, available to help you practice at home. Most of them are expensive and probably unnecessary. Cheapskate that I am, I prefer to use stuff I already have, like mirrors, walls, and chairs.

You may not actually hit any balls, but there's a lot you can do in the comfort of your own home, with the television on in the corner and a pot of coffee brewing, to improve your golf.

MIRRORS
Facing a mirror, you can check:

+ Your grip.
+ Ball position.
+ The length of your backswing.
+ Extent of your hip and shoulder turn.
+ How your head moves.

Then side-on you can make sure:

+ That your shoulders, knees, and feet all line up.
+ Your posture is sound.
+ You don't bring the club back too far on the inside (a common problem with slicers).
+ Your swingplane is good (the angle of the shaft halfway back is the same as the shaft angle at address).
+ Your hands are nice and high at the top of your backswing.
+ The clubface is square (45° to the ground) or close to square at the top of the backswing.
+ Your right knee remains flexed as you take the club up.

If you're going to separate your swing into sections, the place to do it is in front of a mirror. Make sure you're getting the club into the desired positions and swing the club in slow motion to reinforce the feeling you want to replicate on the course.

Don't just style your hair in the mirror. Put it to better use by checking your grip and posture.

WALLS
A wall (I'm assuming you have these in your house) is excellent for helping you with swingpath. Stand facing a wall a few feet away and take your club to the top. Come down slowly making sure the clubhead gets no closer to the wall than it was at address. Do that slowly a hundred times and the over-the-top move that produces pull-slices will slowly disappear. Another way to establish a downswing that attacks the ball from the inside is to address a ball (an imaginary one is just fine) with your back to the wall. Take your club slowly to the top until the clubhead rests against it. Pull

the club down slowly until your hands are about hip-high with the clubhead still touching the wall. By now, slicers will have thrown the clubhead out in front of them, but you're approaching the ball from the inside and in good position to hit a gentle draw.

CHIPPING
Chipping balls into an easy chair, an upturned umbrella, sand box, under or over a swing, or lobbing them over the fence (which only works if your next-door neighbor is understanding) is a great way to improve your feel for shots around the green.

PUTTING
Putting into a glass or your kids' plastic golf holes always works, unless your carpets have some heavy decorative weave that throws your ball off line. There are even ingenious devices such as the "Puttacup" that allow you to putt into an actual hole.

Get a feel for the speed of Augusta National's greens by putting on hardwood floors.

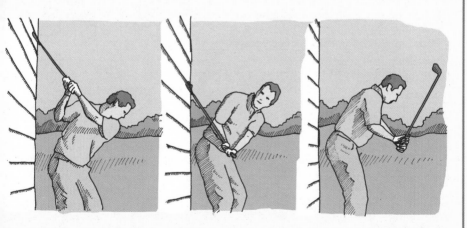

By repeating this drill over and over you will learn what the correct downswing path feels like and eliminate the over-the-top swingpath (on the right).

THE UNHELPFUL LESSON

I'm sure we're all inherently good people, so when we see a friend hacking their way to another triple bogey we instinctively feel a desire to offer some assistance. The trouble is we often don't wait to be asked.

But here's the problem, or rather problems. Years spent playing golf badly doesn't really qualify amateurs to teach the game, and the "lesson" they have to offer is probably based on some swing analysis they saw on the television or read in a magazine, meaning it's factually correct but perhaps not relevant to the person they're teaching. They also tend to forget their "pupil" is not a professional athlete, doesn't practice every day, and doesn't own custom-built clubs; rather they are a stiff, slightly overweight, once-a-weeker who hasn't had a lesson in years and with a collection of clubs based on low price rather than high performance.

BACKWARD IN COMING FORWARD
I'd suggest biting your tongue unless your buddy asks for help. Most problems are best addressed on the range after the round, not while it is still in progress.

Out on the course just concentrate on getting your stricken partner back to the clubhouse without him or her

"No mate, you're doing it all wrong. You've got to do it more like me."

upending his or her bag of clubs into the lake (which is in any case where most of his or her balls now reside). However, if there is a useful piece of advice then try to choose an appropriate time to remind your playing partner of the importance of tempo. It's most likely that as your partner's grip has tightened his or her rhythm has all but disappeared and all-round game has disintegrated.

Keeping your head down is common sense, right? Actually, making a conscious effort to do so might be bad for both your back and your shot.

COMMON SWING MYTHS
Of all the tips ever offered between well-meaning but misinformed friends, "keep your head down" and "keep your left arm straight" are unquestionably the most common. These old chestnuts have been doing the rounds for decades and while both sound perfectly reasonable they can be extremely toxic.

GOING OFF TRAIL

I've done some dumb things in my time, but none dumber than this. I was in the eastern Washington town of Spokane for a short break with my wife when I turned on the radio and listened to a guy talk about a tournament taking place on a ski hill just to the north. It all went wrong from there.

The man on the radio said that if listeners could get there within a couple of hours they could still enter. It sounded promising and we had nothing planned, so I turned the car around.

Arriving at the 49 Degrees North Ski Resort, I learned that rather than playing a legitimate course over flattish junior slopes at the base of the 5,774 ft mountain, we would in fact be taking a lift to the very top and playing up and down black runs with names like Last Chance, Tombstone, and Crusher.

After an hour-long ride I jumped off, looked around for a golf hole and began wondering what in God's name I had gotten involved in. The 1st measured well over 1,000 yards and dropped almost 1,000 feet.

I watched as a school teacher in the group ahead of mine hit a tee shot with a 3-wood that hung in the air for 25 seconds or more, before eventually landing just a few yards to the right of the target — a white painted circle some 20 ft. in diameter. A golfer for only a short time, he was pleased to learn his 1,000-yard 3-wood was roughly three or four times longer than any 3-wood Tiger Woods had ever hit.

In stark contrast, my opening tee shot sliced way right into a dark and eerie forest in which I took numerous hacks only to emerge cut to ribbons by brambles and pointy branches. The rules did account for such misfortune, allowing players to place their ball within a club's

Ski hills were meant for one thing... and it wasn't golf. Sadly, the UX Open was last played in 2004. I say "sadly," but somehow I don't miss it that much.

length of where they had found it. But a single club was never enough to find a half decent lie amongst the weeds, thistle, and assorted shrubbery growing on the "fairways."

The 5th was without doubt the hardest "golf hole" I've ever played — about 800 yards long up a near 45° incline with about 25 yards of space between the pines. It took me 45 minutes to make a 12.

Almost hyper-ventilating, I finished the ten holes in 68, 29 over par and in third-to-last place. My wife asked if it had been fun. "No," I said.

THE GOLF TRIP

In 1963, Eddie Pola and George Wyle composed "It's the Most Wonderful Time of the Year," a jolly jingle about Christmas. I suspect Messrs. Pola and Wyle weren't golfers. Sure, Christmas is great, but nothing beats the golf trip with your mates.

I think a good golf trip should be taken once a year and become a tradition, something you get excited about months before you leave. And it should be recorded electronically or in a scrapbook; anywhere but your failing memory. That way you'll never forget Bob's hole-in-one at La Manga six years ago, or the time Bill fell flat on his face on the 1st tee at Ballybunion following a particularly heavy evening at McMunn's on Main Street.

WHO'S GOING?

For it to become something really special, the same people should be involved each year, though you should expect some change in personnel as diminishing finances, failing health, and growing family ties will all inevitably take their toll as the years go by.

The ideal number for a trip is four, or multiples of four, so you can play together every day. If there are five, seven, or nine, you'll have to split up, which makes scoring and bonding that bit more difficult. You know who the ideal four are, and it doesn't bode well if you have a hard time deciding who should go.

WHERE TO GO?

The world is your oyster nowadays, but it obviously depends where you are starting from and how far your budget will stretch. The UK and Ireland always have plenty to offer. In Europe, Spain and Portugal are old favorites, but Turkey is coming on strong, while France, Italy, or the Czech Republic offer something a bit different.

Dubai is also seriously gearing up for golf tourists, South Africa is definitely worth the flight, especially if you like wine, and playing in Australia is a must at least once in your life. New Zealand possesses some of the world's most beautiful courses and is worthy of a trip

For a few days every year, you're as free as a bird — just you and your buddies playing golf. Good times.

in its own right, but can also be combined with a trip Down Under.

Thailand, Malaysia, Vietnam, and China are probably best for the party that has played everywhere else, although the region's swelling number of golf resorts is making this once improbable trip ever more enticing.

Then there's America. Home to roughly two-thirds of the world's courses, the US is relatively inexpensive, has a superb infrastructure, and a wealth of accommodation options. The courses are invariably well maintained and, as long as you go to Arizona, South Carolina, Florida, or California, the weather is good year round.

If you're going by plane, you need to decide if you're taking your clubs with you, sending them to your destination with a luggage-handling company, or hiring clubs when you arrive. Personally, I think the trip is expensive enough without shipping or hiring clubs, so I take mine with me in a heavy-duty golf club travel bag.

If you can only spare a weekend there are plenty of Web sites offering packages. Just try to make it at least a two-night stay so you can really get out of your everyday routine.

ITINERARY

On a five-day trip, I'd say you should be playing golf on at least three of them, if not four. You can play 36 holes all five days, of course, just don't include me. After three or four straight days of golf I prefer to do something different

and come back to the course on day five raring to go again. Alternatively, plan 18 holes for early mornings and have "free time" in the afternoons. As for eating, it makes for a more memorable trip if you can all eat together in the evenings, provided you're all still getting on with each other.

PACKAGE OR INDEPENDENT?

It makes sense to have all your tee-times and accommodation pre-booked and, if you can afford it, a vehicle and driver to ferry you about. If you're driving yourself, hire as big a car as you can afford (big enough for four players, four golf bags, and four sets of luggage) and take it in turns to drive.

I have been on a trip where the only thing that was pre-booked was the flight (we didn't even know which courses we were going to play) and while it was great fun, I wouldn't choose that approach again. It's far less hassle to book and pay for everything (apart from drinks, tips, new golf balls, and gifts for the family) in advance.

FORMAT

You really should have a tournament in which individuals accumulate points as the trip progresses. Vary the format each day — Stableford, foursome, better-ball, individual gross, two-man shambles, and so on — and add in all sorts of side shows like birdies, fairways hit, greens in regulation, and number of putts. Have fun creating your own scoring system and award prizes at the end of the trip.

HANDICAPS

It is perfectly possible to enjoy a lifetime's golf without ever owning an official handicap. However, although that is certainly true, it doesn't quite paint the whole picture, as it isn't possible to experience everything the game has to offer without one.

I'll be perfectly honest and say that, currently, I do not own a handicap. Why? Several reasons really, most of them centering around a woeful lack of time for "hobbies" and a lack of ready cash. These days, you actually don't need piles of money to get a handicap as you don't necessarily have to join a private golf club. You can just sign up with any of the commercial entities that offer a handicapping service (more of that later). But though I'll forever love the game and play whenever gaps in between work and family commitments allow it, I must admit I do not place as much importance on acquiring, keeping, and improving a handicap as I used to. I know it's merely one of life's many phases, however, and that when the kids have flown the nest, I'll be back on the course every day sweating over every 0.1 of a stroke.

REASONS TO GET A HANDICAP
With a handicap you can:
+ Play at most courses around the world. Anyone can play at municipal and pay-and-play courses, but if you want to tee it up at a private club you'll invariably need some proof of your ability, and that means a handicap certificate.
+ To measure your performance more consistently over time.
+ Accurate, official handicaps help prevent you coming up against bandits — golfers who say they're off 18 when, in actual fact, they're nearer a 10.

HOW TO GET A HANDICAP
Join a private club that is affiliated with a handicapping body (such as CONGU in the UK). It's unlikely any private club is going to have you, however, unless you already have a handicap.

Handicap Bandits

A bandit (sandbagger in the US) is the untrustworthy bounder who intentionally doctors or lies about his true handicap in an effort to win valuable prizes and bets. When the stakes are low he will purposefully play badly, or he will not enter his better rounds into handicap maintenance software and thus artificially inflate his handicap. When the big money game or tournament with the big first prize rolls around he now has a few "extra" strokes to play with. At worst, the bandit is a cad, a cheat, and a two-bit hustler; at best... a cad, a cheat, and a two-bit hustler.

There's a difference, of course, between someone who has an unexpected good day and beats their handicap handily and a committed, calculating bandit. Members of the first group are to be congratulated. Members of the second must be identified and run out of town.

This used to create a bit of a chicken or egg-type conundrum — you couldn't get a handicap unless you were a member of a golf club, but you couldn't join a golf club unless you had a handicap. Now, however, beginners and transient golfers can pay annual dues to one of several handicap certificate suppliers.

You'll need one of these to prove to the club that although you're only passing through, you're no hacker. It's a good idea to contact the club in advance though to make sure your handicap certificate will be accepted.

MAINTAINING A HANDICAP

If you think I'm going to waste valuable space by explaining how your handicap is set and can then increase or decrease under the system, then I'm afraid you are very much mistaken. I couldn't possibly summarize it in a few short lines, so just let me point you in the direction of www.congu.com and www.handicapmaster.org, which will tell you all you need to know.

THE ART OF GIVING

My drawers are full of golf gifts. I'm grateful for the thought, of course, but really my heart sinks as I unwrap yet another trinket.

I've seen golf-themed light switch plates, coasters, key racks, mugs, cufflinks, shower curtains, mailboxes, towels, dressing gowns, lamp stands, doormats, salt and pepper shakers, teapots, plant pots, flasks, picture frames, fireplace sets, cutlery, watches, soap dispensers, and house number plaques belonging to golfers who just don't have the heart to tell the giver that they really don't want this stuff and the money would actually be much better spent on a pair of socks.

If you can't summon up the courage to tell them yourselves, then just leave this book open on this page for them to find. Now, for all non-golfers reading this, do the golfer in your life a favor and get him or her a sleeve of balls instead. They're much easier to lose than some of the garbage you've given them over the years.

The motif gifts that actually do something like hold pens or mail are one thing. The furry frog with red and white cap and putter ornament is quite another, however, and should be outlawed.

CARRYING THE BAGS

Every now and again it's nice to have a caddie take you round. Besides performing the usual caddie duties, he or she could save you a few shots with some timely advice.

The last time I hired a caddie was at Pacific Dunes in Oregon two years ago. Rod was a strong young lad who not only carried my bag but also that of my partner.

At the 1st, 2nd, and 3rd he was encouraging despite a barrage of bogeys. When dense fog rolled in at the 4th, he steered us well to the left of a precipitous clifftop off which we could very easily have fallen had we been by ourselves. At the 6th, he understandingly looked the other way when I found an impossibly deep bunker and failed to get out not once, not twice, but three times.

Somewhere on the back nine he told us the story of a gentleman he had caddied for who shot 188. "At least, that's what he said it was," said Rod. "I reckon it was nearer 250." Then he told us about carrying for PGA Tour player Kirk Triplett, who had visited the course a few weeks previously. In terrible weather, Triplett shot 88 the first day, but improved to 64 the next.

I could go on but you get the picture. Rod was friendly, supportive, consoling, a well of information, full of good stories, and ever optimistic that my game might pick up at any moment. By the end of the round, we'd had such a good time, my mate and I had no problem bumping his fee up a little by way of thanks.

Having a caddie makes you feel like a professional — until you top your drive into a ditch that is.

NOT ALL CADDIES ARE CREATED EQUAL

On another occasion, having somehow gained permission for a round at an extremely exclusive private club (its amazing what a well-worded letter can do), I ended up with an old geezer who arrived a few minutes late absolutely reeking of drink and who wasn't entirely sure where he had spent the night.

We didn't see eye to eye. I played poorly and he let me know it. He didn't actually tut or throw his hands in the air in disgust, but I could tell that he wanted to. A relic and an anachronism, he was a blast from the distant past, a far cry from today's usually polite and professional caddies.

Your Caddie Has Seen Worse

The first time you hire a caddie it's likely you'll spend the first few holes worrying about the state of your golf and whether or not they've ever witnessed anyone play quite as badly. You'll want to perform as much for your caddie as yourself, and probably won't settle down until you've hit a few good shots or your caddie has told you that yes, he's caddied for dozens of golfers worse even than you.

Caddying Yourself

If you're ever roped in to caddying for your dad, a friend, or maybe Tiger Woods, you need to know the caddie's three most basic instructions; show up, keep up, and shut up. Turn up well before the tee-time, don't lag behind and, as a general rule, don't speak unless spoken to. Of course, there are exceptions, and if it's your dad you are caddying for, feel free to tell him how ridiculous his no-pleat, drain-pipe trousers and fat white belt look on a man of his age.

GOLFING FOR COUPLES

Plenty of couples get along just fine on the course; however, unfortunately for my wife and I, we are not among their number.

About ten years ago my then fiancée, now wife, and I went for a quiet round, her first. Much to my pleasant surprise, by about the 3rd hole she was lofting the ball into the air as if she had been playing the game all her life. I began to envision the two of us forming a killer mixed foursome, hoisting all sorts of trophies and taking golf holidays together.

She seemed equally excited and, on the 5th, claimed golf was an easy game, and that if I were to give her lessons, well who knows...

It seemed like a reasonable idea at the time. I had been a teacher, after all, and it would be a wonderful opportunity to spend time together.

Our first lesson started smoothly enough, but after altering her posture she began shanking the ball. Quickly, things turned nasty. I became "a total idiot who can't teach" while she was the "nightmare pupil who thinks she knows it all but can't take instruction."

The lessons stopped and for nine years she never once mentioned the game. Recently, however, she has started watching it on TV with me. I'd love for her to play again, and I still haven't ruled out those golfing holidays. But if she ever talks about lessons, I think I'll tell her about a teaching professional I know.

IT'S ALL IN YOUR MIND

We've seen how good course management can benefit your score without you having to lift a finger, and here's something else that could improve your golf with very little physical enterprise on your part. This game gets easier by the page.

Until fairly recently few people knew much about sports psychology and most of us had no idea that thoughts moving in and out of our heads might help or hinder our performance. None of us knew, for instance, that repeatedly cursing our own luck could poison our minds and prevent us from playing to the best of our ability. None of us knew that telling ourselves we were brilliant and that the last shot we played was truly a work of genius might actually help.

Now, of course, psychologists are as much a fixture on the driving range at tour events as swing gurus. Getting a little down on yourself? Quick, bring the mental coach in to perk you up. Need some inspiring words or a good mental image? The good doctor will see you now.

Pros are using anything they can within the rules to optimize their games and players not seeking the services of a sports psychologist are becoming

A psychologist is very much part of a tour player's entourage nowadays.

increasingly uncommon. But you're just a regular weekend player, so what's this got to do with you? What on earth do you need with a sports psychologist?

Alright, so maybe your unique style of play doesn't quite warrant the expense of a fully fledged sports shrink; but that doesn't mean you can't pinch a few of their tricks. After all you work on the physical side of your game, so why neglect the mental challenges?

The "remain positive" mantra common to all sports psychologists' teachings will certainly help you. Okay, "remain positive" might be a little vague, and in need of fleshing out — but it's a start.

Calmly tell yourself you can hit this shot, that you've done it before and can do it again. As psychologist Joe Kolezynski says, if you desire to change a negative belief into an empowering belief, you must rewire the negative neural track that already exists in the brain into a positive one by using self-talk and affirmations. What does that actually mean? Simple, you need to stop the self-condemnation, identify parts of your game that need improvement and create affirmations that you can say over and over to yourself. Make them short and specific. "I am a putting machine and hole all 15-foot putts," is better than "Yeah, I do okay. I hole my share of medium-range putts, but I suppose I could be a lot better. I'm pretty good at reading greens and aiming correctly, and if I could just get the speed right..." Kolezynski suggests the following process:

"I am Tiger Woods. I am Tiger Woods."
Positive affirmations can certainly be good for your game, but make them realistic and wait until the house is empty before talking loudly to yourself. You could scare the kids.

+ Sit upright in a comfortable chair.
+ Close your eyes and take a couple of minutes to relax.
+ Release your body's tight, sharp focus on the physical world by taking yourself to an even deeper level of relaxation.
+ Speak your affirmation aloud five times.
+ Do all this as often as possible.

Be patient with this. Don't expect results overnight — but keep at it and they'll arrive soon enough. In his book *The Art and Zen of Golf Learning,* Michael Hebron takes it a step further, advising golfers to favor pictures and feelings over words of instruction. Picture how the club should move, he says, not the body.

RELAX, EASY, SMOOTH... OR NOT?

As well as telling them to keep their head down and their left arm straight, golfers are in the habit of urging their underperforming partners to relax, slow down, and swing easy.

A lot of the time that's wise counsel, for who doesn't occasionally lose their rhythm? Sometimes, however, the words "slow," "relax," and "easy" can be misinterpreted. Ernie Els might appear relaxed, even carefree, but rest assured, he is concentrating hard; and by the time most amateurs get their club to the top of the backswing, Els has already thundered through impact. He hits the ball incredibly hard, but his even tempo and supreme balance make his swing look easy.

Jack Nicklaus, among others, suggests that instead of swinging easy or relaxing, you should actually swing as hard as you can "while still swinging rhythmically enough to keep the clubhead under control."

There's a line between hard and reckless. When you catch the ball cleanly, pass the 280-yard mark, and are still in perfect balance you'll know you're on the right side of it.

Swing like this and not only will you miss the fairway you'll do yourself a serious injury too.

THE HOME OF GOLF

The Old Course has been mentioned often enough in this book, and there's a fair chance you know all about it already. So let's find somewhere else to play and then, when we're done, head off into town to see what we can find.

At the time of writing (early 2008) the St Andrews Links Trust operates six golf courses. By the time you read this, there will be seven as the highly anticipated Castle Course, sandwiched between the east end of town and the privately owned St Andrews Bay golf courses, will be open. I've only seen pictures so can't really say too much about it other than if it plays as good as it looks then it's likely to run the Old Course a very close second in terms of popularity. That means the New Course will be demoted to third.

If you can't get a tee-time on the Old, don't worry, the New is nearby. It costs half as much to play and is very nearly as good.

How a course as good as the New could possibly rank as low as third in a town of just 14,000 people is obviously a large part of what makes the place so special. The Jubilee is fantastic too, if a little difficult, and the charming Eden holds some very special memories as the first links course I ever played. The short Strathtyrum and par-3 Balgove courses

complete the Links Trust set, but the golf in the area certainly doesn't end there. Just east of town is Kingsbarns, another of the world's best links courses, while a bit further inland is the superb Dukes Course, and on Fife's south coast, just 20 minutes drive away, are Craighead, Balcomie, Elie, Leven, and Lundin.

After the game, it's worth stopping by the Jigger Inn at the side of the Old Course's 17th green to watch a few stragglers trying to extricate themselves from the depths of the Road Hole Bunker. As night falls why not head to the Dunvegan for a bite to eat and a look at the photographs of famous golfers who have called in down the years.

Then head back to your digs, ideally Rusacks on Pilmour Links overlooking the Old Course's 18th hole, or, if you're really in the money, the Old Course Hotel where, if it's July and you're in the Royal & Ancient Suite, you'd better have a very deep purse.

When you're done playing golf, check out the cathedral ruins and the grave of Young Tom Morris who won the Open four times between 1868 and 1872, but died at 24 on Christmas Day 1875, three months after the death of his wife and newborn baby.

CHANGES I'D LIKE TO SEE

It could be argued that golf is currently enjoying something of a golden age. The number one player in the world is the most recognizable figure in all of sport, while better equipment has made the game more fun for everyone. We shouldn't let it all go to our heads though.

In his absorbing book *The Future of Golf*, respected commentator Geoff Shackelford paints a bleak picture, saying the game is becoming too slow, too expensive, and too boring. Five-hour rounds and ever-increasing greens fees — inflated by "signature" designs carrying the name of big-name players — are discouraging people from trying golf and forcing many existing golfers away, he says. The USGA and PGA Tours' insatiable appetites for cashing in on Tiger Woods' prominence is also sucking the drama out of the sport, turning it into an insipid vehicle for blue-chip advertising. Modern equipment is condemned, meanwhile, for reducing the game to an unsophisticated slug-fest and thus all but eliminating the need for finesse. The USGA and R&A are criticized for letting that happen.

Shackelford, an American, is talking primarily about the state of the game in the US, but figures for the number of people taking up golf in the UK, and many other countries in the world, are similarly stagnant.

Of course, many of the problems are the inevitable result of capitalism, which, I'm guessing, most readers would like to keep. Greens fees are as high as they are because enough people are willing to pay them. The same goes for our drivers, technological masterpieces that are superseded just a few months after we buy them.

Barring big changes in demographics and golfers' growing inclination to spend more time with their families, that's unlikely to change. What we must put a stop to right now, however, are the overuse of water and chemicals — fast-running courses are more exciting than lush dart-board courses — four- or five-hour rounds, and tedious 7,000-plus yard layouts with no personality (we don't enjoy them, so please don't build them).

As for clipping equipment's wings, I understand why many people want that to happen. But I'm surely not alone in hoping it doesn't, not for amateurs anyway. Perhaps bifurcation: one ball for tournament pros, one for the rest of us, is now a very real possibility, perhaps it is even a necessity?

No matter how good equipment gets though, most of the world's golfers will forever struggle. But in spite of that, or perhaps because of it, we'll always find a way to enjoy ourselves.

Oh well. Maybe some other round, another day.

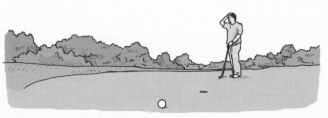

INDEX

To Sam — Looking forward to our first proper game together.

A big thank you to Jeff Shelley and Dave Castleberry for their suggestions and encouragement.

THE WAY OF
THE BULL

OTHER BOOKS BY LEO BUSCAGLIA

THE WAY OF
THE BULL

by Leo Buscaglia

Published by Charles B. Slack, Inc.

Distributed by Holt, Rinehart and Winston

This book is dedicated to…

Those with no concern for the Way;
Those temporarily lost on the Way;
Those diligently seeking the Way;
Those who know, but are unable to
    follow the Way;
Those who simply live the Way;
For all of us are one.

TABLE OF CONTENTS

INTRODUCTION

T he title, THE WAY OF THE BULL, was suggested by
a Zen book, *10 Bulls*, written in the 12th century by
the Chinese Zen master, Kakuan. In his story the
bull represented life energy, truth and action. The way
concerned the steps which man might take in the
process of seeking insight, finding himself, discovering
his true nature.

During the years of my life I have been schooled by
our society in many things. Mostly, I learned and never
questioned. Surely my teachers, who purported to love
me, would not lead me down false paths into dead
ends, away from myself into loneliness and despair.

A few years ago, I became suspicious. I began to
believe in my own senses, to trust my own mind. It
soon became painfully obvious that much of what I

had been taught had served as the greatest deterrent to joy and finding myself and had led me rather into my greatest fears, disappointments, confusions and pain.

For example, my society had taught me that man's worth was to be measured by the things he possessed. If he owned a "big" car, a "lavish" home and an "impressive" bank balance, he must be an important and worthy man, and was to be emulated. I was never told that man "possesses" nothing, only himself. I began to wonder: If man is his "things," what happens to him when he loses them or they are taken away from him?

I was also taught that life had no meaning unless it was goal-oriented and that my life, to be meaningful, had to be spent in creating goals, making decisions about those goals and charging toward them, through mud and muck if necessary, to achieve them.

Time and experience revealed to me that life was a trip, not a goal. That often one became so fixed on the end that he totally missed life along the way, and found, only too late, that when he had scaled the mountain there was only another mountain, and another, and another. What a pity that he had never stopped long enough to breathe the new, clean, fresh air and admire the spectacular view. I had to question: If life is a continual trip, does it matter if one ever "gets" anywhere?

Society also created confusing dichotomies for me: good and bad, mature and immature, reality and fantasy. I was then forced to select, supposedly for my own well-being, one over the other. I was told that society's morality was always superior to my own, though my true nature was compelled to question this. I asked, for example: Does it make sense that wars are fought to preserve peace?

The idea that maturity came with age, that experience meant wisdom, that youth could never be wiser than their elders, conflicted with my experience, which saw no real correlation. Had the wise elders really made our world a better place for us to live in?

The constant advice that I "get out of my fantasy world" into "reality," that I "face reality" often proved frustrating, since society's reality constantly seemed more unreal than my fantasy. I pondered: Wasn't reality nothing more than the freezing, the firming up, of illusion?

But so successfully had I learned these lessons, heard and responded to these teachings that it was only a little more than ten years ago that I decided to listen to myself, follow my own voices, and go the WAY that seemed to be most congruent with me and my true nature. In other words, I decided to take THE WAY OF THE BULL.

This WAY has not always been easy, though it has been wondrous, full of excitement and discovery, even though I now know that one need never "go" anywhere to find himself, for he is already "there."

Along my WAY I have read many books, experienced a million amazing things and met wondrous people in strange lands. Each has served to open my mind and head and heart. From each I have learned much. I know, now, for instance, that my existence is to be found nowhere but in myself for my existence *is* me. I know that I need not hold onto experience to make it mine, the experience is enough.

I have learned, most importantly, that a WAY will only have reality as it relates to living in the now for, as stated above, life isn't the goal, it's the voyage, and the only reality seems to lie in change. But if all things that are, are already ours, then even change is an illusion, and the WAY becomes simply an unfolding, like the opening of a flower for all things necessary are already a part of us and to discover it we need but nurture the flower, be patient and continue to grow.

THE WAY OF
THE BULL

Chapter 1

JAPAN

The new and the old have value to man only as they relate to the present. Yesterday made him what he is today, tomorrow is his dream. To live for either is to lose his only reality, the moment.

*T*here are several Buddhist monasteries in Kamakura, the city of the Giant Daibatsu. Here among the giant bamboo and tall pine, students of Buddhism wander, ponder and perform the many functions which aid in the complex process of "seeing into the self." In this city there are numerous fantastic temples with carved ceilings, straight, clean architecture and clear-lacquered woods in beautiful natural settings.

3

The sea rumbles just a few steps from the city's center, and the wind rustles the trees pushing them into odd, distorted patterns like oversized bonsai. From time to time the train from Tokyo passes noisily on its way to Yokohama — whistling through the city, breaking the silence only long enough to drop off passengers and the continual hordes of sightseers who come and go; but most of the time the city sleeps naturally and peacefully in the lap of nature, very much at home in the small rolling hills that surround it.

I was the guest of Mr. and Mrs. Hito, a middle-aged and charming couple, who clung to the old and the quaint of Japan as naturally as the flowers that graced the garden in which their home was located.

The house was a rather large wooden structure, surrounded by a neat, trim, dwarf garden that rolled in green mossy splendor between tiny stone paths, among large rocks, around little bridges, and finally down over the banks of a miniature stream. A large fish pond was active with bright, fat, golden and silver fish. The fence which enclosed the garden was of bamboo, old and brown with the color of time but still sturdy and well kept.

There were three large bedrooms, a room for cooking, with a huge hibachi that also served to heat the house, and a bathroom with a deep sunken tub of natural stone. Every wall was so made as to fold quickly to one side and at once make each room a part of the garden.

I had met Mr. Hito when I was guest lecturer at the English Speaking Society of a major university in Tokyo. In addition to serving as faculty advisor for the Society, he was a lecturer in comparative literature. He had studied in America, where he and his wife spent many happy and interesting hours learning what they called, "The Way of the Westerner."

After my lecture, Mr. Hito approached me, "In the

4

real sense, are not all schools of psychology simply a search for the self? They seem to claim that man is incapable of pursuing the 'self' alone, that he needs the aid and guidance of another."

"My interest stems from the fact that I am at present paralleling the teachings of psychology with our Zen Buddhism," he continued. "Do you know Zen?"

Our first discussion led to several meetings at tea rooms and beer halls all around Tokyo, and the final inquiry, "Would you like to visit a Zen monastery? I can arrange it, you know. Near my home in Kamakura is one of the very finest Zen schools in the country. Onomito is one of the great teachers and he speaks English. I think it may prove very interesting to you. I believe it has something to offer your Western mind."

I told him I would be excited to have such an opportunity and within a few days all was arranged. I would live for a period with the monks in the monastery spending the remaining time in Mr. Hito's home which would be more comfortable while I continued my study.

Onomito, my teacher, was a short, quite powerful man with a shaved, well-shaped head and keen eyes. His hands were strong and his fingers smooth, long and thin. His kimono was wrapped about him with determination, his back was straight and — though it seldom happened — his lips always seemed on the verge of parting into a warm smile. His command of English was good though the pronunciation was difficult for him. He spoke slowly, choosing his words carefully.

"Since you are here so brief a time, you can only look," Onomito said. "Without help you will see only the things you are ready to see. I will try to help you perceive things as they are, but when days must be counted, perception is shadowed by time. If you came here as a novice, you would wait for several days be-

5

fore admission to Brotherhood would be granted. You would be asked to wait for a week or ten days outside the gate. We would discourage you from waiting. Our meditation hall is always full. Our modern youth, like yours in America, find it difficult to wait. Zen has not and has never had a popular appeal in Japan for it is difficult for most men to wait. Zen calls for discipline and requires that one have great courage and perseverance; that one be able to postpone the sought after goal for an indefinite period of time without the security of knowing that he will ever attain it. There are no diplomas for the enlightenment achieved, no graduation exercise for those who have successfully pursued and found the self, and there is no monetary recognition. For this reason, it does not appeal to everyone. Hours, even lifetimes, are spent in meditation. The most important task in a monastery is learning the skill of zazen, meditation. This, with the proper teacher, can help the novice gain personal insight; it is only for this reason that such a monastery as this has any reason for existing."

We went through the monastery. Meditation halls, like large unfurnished classrooms, made up the greatest number of the cluster of buildings. There were simple rooms for lodging, a large bath, and a small kitchen. Comforts, or any signs of luxury, were conspicuously absent.

I was given a kesa (robe) and taken to the guest room. This room, like all the others, was but four walls and a series of tatami mats. Traveling monks were always allowed to stay here at least one night while en route. They were allowed the same privileges as the host monks, but stayed in the guest room.

The routine of the monastic life was given me. Basically, it was a life of prayer and meditation. Three meals, small and simple, were taken during the day. "The mind does not work well when the stomach is overfull. A full stomach is conducive only to sleep."

There are definite hours for meditation. The monks are required to sit in the proper formal posture, right foot over the left thigh, left foot over the right thigh. The hands, too, have a definite place, right hand on the left leg with palm up and on this the left hand is placed, with the thumbs pressed together over the palm. With head up and back erect but not rigid, eyes slightly open and tongue on the roof of the mouth with lips closed, one relaxes and breathes regularly.

Relaxation in this position sounded impossible to me and — for my tall, stiff body — was just that. Everyone else seemed to feel the prescribed position was surprisingly comfortable and extremely conducive to contemplation, for with each part of the body being strictly disciplined in its proper place, there was no need for fidgeting or readjusting. In position, I felt like a badly tied Christmas package about ready to come undone. It was necessary for me to concentrate so completely on staying in position that contemplation on anything else was obviously impossible. Least of all did I seem or feel peaceful and at ease, which, after all, was the objective. I was allowed, after a few tragically comic attempts, to assume the half-crossed leg position: left leg on the right thigh. This was less difficult. "The position is, in reality, only a tool and not a necessity," I was told.

Work is also a regular part of the daily routine. Each monk has his task. Tools are simple and no mechanization is allowed. Simple physical labor is the goal. Each monk, too, must go out for takuhatsu (alms). This serves a two-fold function. Since the use of money is not allowed in a monastery, the food obtained through begging is the sole source of subsistence. Even more importantly, begging teaches that one is dependent upon the good will of others and teaches humility.

There is silent prayer and there are periods of communal prayer. All prayer concerns a plea for "Right Knowledge" and for the ability to hold firmly to a desire for truth.

The meals were simple — gruel, pickles, rice — but eaten in quiet decorum with the greatest reverence.

While in the monastery, I was allowed no more freedom or special privilege than any other monk. From the moment Mr. Hito left me on the first day, I was assured I had no more significance than the grains of sand which surrounded the large pine trees that shaded the monastery. There was a Westerner on the grounds, that was known as I was introduced to the entire assemblage, but it was also indicated that this was nothing special.

I saw Onomito, my sensei, only on a pre-arranged interview schedule. The rest of the time I was alone. I was to spend my first days trying to "feel" what was about me in the darkness of my room. This was to be accomplished through quiet — indifference to my own presence, strict silence and the inner and outer peace which these things would create. I was to rid myself of mind and achieve a state of no-mind. At first, the result was totally adverse. The feeling of being alone and unguided was completely devastating. I felt lost, confused and frightened. I longed for direction — a book to read, a person with whom to converse. I had no idea what to do with my new found stillness. I had no idea how to begin the process, if indeed it was, of ridding myself of my mind. I wished for a book of directions to read, a how-to for no-mind. But faced with nothing but myself and the most simple routine, I began to settle down. Although I had nothing to "do" and was not to "think" (the only ready tools I had ever used to accomplish any task), I found that there *was* another way to learn to "see."

My first trip from my room was beautiful. All at once, everything seemed to become alive, as if I were seeing it all for the first time. The tall pines took on subtle details. Rays of sunlight through their branches became spotlights for dancing dust. Bits of green moss took on delicate designs beneath small round dots of dew. Insects spread their tiny legs to the warmth of the sun. Puddles of water became bottomless seas with sunlight swimming in them. Shadows on smooth wood accentuated the wood grain until it seemed to hold great canyons of light and shadow. The curve of the bamboo leaf and the cascade of the motionless branch seemed to give sound in silence. Nothing was insignificant. It was necessary at times to close my eyes to keep from going sight-mad but there was no turning it off. It was all still there. I welcomed it. Why would I wish to turn it off?

I had my first interview with Onomito on the third day. He was pleasant, formal, much like the first time I had seen him. We talked of many things; my panic in silence, my difficulty in letting my mind go, and the deep awareness which had suddenly become mine.

"Yes, it is such a great waste. This ability to 'see' belongs to everyone," he said quietly; "it is always there but cannot come through the great haze of confusion until we do something to clear the haze."

Onomito explained the importance Zen places on the moment. "It is difficult for the Western mind to understand Zen primarily because of the difference in emphasis on the value of the moment. For Zen, nothing is of greater value than the moment. Life is now. Yesterday is past and gone and therefore unreal, only real in its effect on the moment. The future is not real, and possibly it will never be more than simply a dream. This leaves simply the now, the moment, as reality. "Yet," he said, "so many people live only under the shadow of the successes or mistakes of the past or the possibilities and hopes of the future. They do not seem to realize that when they deal with these worlds of the

9

unreal, they are missing the 'moments,' the accumulation of which make a life. Life, then, becomes a series of moments, either lived or lost. Since moments pass, as time, there is soon nothing left and life is over, leaving some poor, unfortunate souls having never lived at all."

He then gave me a koan to ponder. These are spiritual lessons not to be answered by analytical means or scientific method or with knowledge, but by simply allowing the mind to arrive at truth intuitively and spiritually. For me, there was nothing simple about this process.

The first koan went something like this:

> There was a Buddhist monk who one day found himself running from a hungry bear. The bear chased him to a cliff. There was nothing for him to do, if he did not desire to be food for the bear's hungry stomach, but jump. He did so and was able to catch hold, as he fell, of a branch of wood growing from the cliff's side. As he hung there, looking up at the hungry bear above, he heard the roar of a famished lion far below who was already waiting for him to tire, lose his grip and fall to its hungry jaws.
>
> As the monk hung suspended, hungry bear above and starving lion below, he noticed the heads of two gophers appear from the cliff's side. At once they began gnawing on the small stump of wood to which he clung so desperately.
>
> All at once the monk saw that just a stretch away was a small clump of wild strawberries. He calmly reached out, plucked the largest, reddest, and ripest of the berries, and put it into his mouth.

"How delicious!," he said.

I had lost all awareness of time when I was told that it was time for my final interview with Onomito. Had I been there a week? A month? A year? He was more talkative than he had been during our earlier interviews. He said many things.

- I believe it is quite impossible to practice Zen, in the real sense, in your country, but there is much good in the knowledge of it.

- It will take you some time to integrate what you have learned here with your life. Your cup is full to the brim with Western ideas. Perhaps you are now more ready and less frightened to pour out a bit and make a place for new ways.

- Pattern your life after the giant bamboo. The exterior, though smooth and lovely to the touch, is tough and resistant to the sword. Within, it is soft, pliable, with much empty space for continued growth. It grows neatly and ordered, never cluttered. Alone, it rises tall and straight, always upward to the sky. There, it spreads its beauty to the sun. It leans on nothing. It makes its own way, perhaps near others, a part of others, but very much dependent upon its own strength and force. So pattern your life.

At the appointed time, Mr. Hito came for me. It was dusk. I had put on my Western clothes; they felt tight and uncomfortable.

We left the quiet monastery without farewells. Mr. Hito walked silently by my side along the small sand path which led up the hill to his home. The late afternoon was windy but the darkening sky was clear.

The sea was in the air. The twisted trees waved their branches in a noisy, modern, rhythmical dance to which the shadows responded silently. We exchanged not a word.

Mrs. Hito prepared a fine dinner for me that evening. She knew what I had been eating and felt it was time for a good, substantial meal with salad, sushi, shrimp tempura, string beans and squash flower.

After dinner I felt that I should discuss my feelings with Mr. Hito but found it impossible to do so. Mr. Hito only smiled, expecting nothing. I remembered Onimoto's statement, "You don't talk Zen, you live it."

"I have questions only, no answers," I said.

"There are no answers, only questions." Mr. Hito smiled. "Words are created," he continued, "to stand for reality. Often, after enough use, they become real for the individual, the true reality. But they are only words, so man is trapped."

My next few days were spent watching the living Zen. The Hitos' entire life was a constant illustration of it: the beautiful amalgamation of the old and the new, the joy in the trip to Tokyo and the peace of afternoon walks through fields of bamboo near the sea, the calm of the tea ceremony along with quiet hours of meditation, the joy in the company of others, the peace of the garden and the single flower.

When the time came for my return to Tokyo, Mr. Hito took me to the Kamakura train station.

Somehow farewells in Japan were never the same as those in any other place in Asia. There was always, of course, the nostalgia of parting with a friend; however beyond that there was a feeling that the person was not holding onto you, that he had enjoyed you, learned from you, perhaps shared some ideas with you, and that now he was quite ready, if it was to be, to let you go on to others.

When I mentioned this to Mr. Hito, he commented

that Buddha had spoken of this in his Parable of the Rhinoceros in the Khaggavisha Sutta. He quoted from memory: "Let therefore one who dislikes separation, which must happen sooner or later from those beloved, walk alone like a rhinoceros."

What Mr. Hito did not quote from this parable was the sole section in the long sutta in which Buddha does *not* conclude that man should "walk alone like a rhinoceros":

> If a wise man secures a wise friend who will act in concert with him, being firmly established in good principles, he will live happily with him, overcoming all afflictions.

Chapter 11

JAPAN

The only thing that is certain for man is change. To battle change is to waste one's time; the battle can never be won. To become the willing ally of change is to assure oneself of life.

When I entered the modern office the group was already waiting in the conference room to greet me. There were two girls and six men, all quite young or seemingly so. It was impossible for me to guess the age of any of the Japanese. They rose and bowed as I entered. The sensei, or teacher, was a most wonderful looking man. He had a broad smile which revealed all of his treasured gold front teeth. The deep wrinkles at the edge of his eyes made him appear somewhat puckish. He asked if I would do them the honor of sitting among them and simply conversing in English so they might see how much they could participate.

I seated myself among them. "Good evening," I said to one of the boys, following my instructions. "What is your name?"

"Good evening," he answered in measured, practiced cadence after a moment's hesitation, his head down, eyes on the floor, "My name is Senure Abe."

Abe was a short, dark-haired, muscular individual. His well-shaped head and powerful shoulders were erectly supported by a strong back and chest; his cheekbones were high, his eyes thin concave slits of light, and his rather thick lips curved gracefully and serenely into a relaxed smile.

"Where do you live, Abe-san?" I asked.

"I live in Yokohama."

"Where do you work?"

"I work here in the import-export business," he answered.

"What do you do for fun?"

"For fun?" He looked at me with surprise. "For fun, I practice Judo. I go to Judo school." He smiled broadly as I passed on to the next person in line. A triumph! Not one serious mistake. He glanced toward his sensei for approval.

I moved on from one person to another. One was an artist, another a master of the tea ceremony. One said that he was courting a girl who was very difficult and he had no fun at all. Another claimed that he drank beer for fun. They responded freely, quickly catching the spirit of the conversation. There was much laughter.

The lesson was a great success. At seven o'clock, the hour for dismissal, they wanted to remain and, in turn, find out about me. The sensei suggested that we move on to a beer hall, which seemed a most proper thing to do, and that we continue our class there.

Chattering together, we walked out into the Tokyo night and headed toward the Ginza area, only a few streets away. There we entered the lobby of a large building and took an elevator to the beer hall on the roof. It was very crowded. Colored lanterns blew in the breeze amid the flash of neon. Chairs were collected from here and there and a table appeared from nowhere, carried overhead, singlehanded, with little effort by Abe-san. We arranged ourselves about it. The sensei sat directly across the table from me, obviously very proud that his students had been so successful in their test of fire. He explained, "The students wish to have you come back to us again while you are in Tokyo. We shall be happy if you can spare the time to so honor us."

I assured them that I would be happy to continue the lessons provided that occasionally I could use our sessions as a source for the information I would need to see Tokyo and the rest of Japan properly.

Abe-san immediately offered to take me to the Judo school if I were interested. One of the young girls invited me to a tea ceremony. Another said she would be happy to escort me to a section of the city near the University, where I could find old books and prints. Others wanted me to taste the best sushi in all of Japan or to show me a lovely private garden. They were all interested in helping to satisfy my desire to see more of Japanese theater and made plans to take me to Kabuki and the Noh play.

Hours later, when we returned to the street, now more crowded than ever, everyone bowed to everyone else and went his way — except Abe-san. "Have you hunger?" he said.

"Yes," I answered, "I always have hunger."

"I know a restaurant where good noodles are made."

We started down the street together, with Abe-san pointing out the sights as we went along.

The noodles were excellent. We each had two large bowls which I learned to eat with chopsticks, to the delight of the restaurant staff who stood around and observed my every awkward movement. After we had eaten, we sat and talked. I was surprised to learn that Abe-san commuted from Yokohama daily. I had thought Yokohama was a great distance from Tokyo, but he assured me that there were express trains every few minutes from the Ginza Station which could get him home within an hour.

I expressed my amazement at Tokyo. "The city has come as rather a shock to me," I said. "I expected something different."

Abe-san laughed, "Temples? Kimonos? Tranquil tea gardens?"

"I knew Tokyo was one of the largest cities in the world, but I had hoped that some of the Japan of the Westerner's dream remained."

"Oh," he said, "there is still much to see of the Old Japan."

Abe was a university student in law and was typical of modern Japan in a state of change. He was most adamant that Japan must regain its status as a great international power, and he understood that this would mean complete industrialization. At the same time he wanted Japan to remain Asian in philosophy and way of life.

He loved the little things, the simple beauty, the peace of the inner life; he yearned for the kimono, though he saw the impracticability of this in a modern office. He loved the acres of gardens, but saw the need to use every available inch of land to improve living conditions and for the construction of giant buildings to deal with the ever-increasing population problem and the demands of the world market. He worshiped the ancient arts of archery, Judo, flower arrangement, classical dance and the tea ceremony, but he also felt the need to bounce with rock and roll. He was a mass of contradictions and he knew it. He was amazed and delighted with my knowledge of the ancient arts and culture of his country and appalled by my ignorance of modern industrial Japan.

"Imagine quiet gardens in the Ginza!"

Before we parted, we made arrangements to meet again the following day. He planned to take me to visit the Judo Institute.

Tokyo's Judo Institute is a mammoth structure, a mass of training rooms, stairs, hallways with glass-like polished floors leading to observation galleries, lockers and showers. Men and boys of all ages move lightly through the building, each identifiable in terms of skill by his belt. They ranged from beginner to champion with all the gradations between.

When Abe-san appeared, his small waist was encircled with the belt of a champion.

There were no pre-arranged bouts; one looked about for an equal and, with only a nod, challenged him. Abe went about the large room, watching, challenging, matching his skills with others. His ability was obvious. He was fast, alert, lithe, sensitive to each move, and powerful. Every encounter was performed with great ceremony, characteristic of the practiced art which Judo is. At the end of each bout, Abe-san would turn to me, with a wide smile, before returning to the task at hand which took his complete concentration.

As we walked to the shower rooms Abe said, "You must learn Judo. It makes one feel one's self."

The language classes continued to be an adventure. The students were more relaxed at each meeting. I planned the sessions with particular goals in mind: conversations about the home, the business, the garden, the visitor, the school, the city, directions and so on. For half of the period we would discuss the pronunciation of words and the correction of defective consonant sounds which the Japanese find so difficult: "th," "r," "l." For the remainder of the session, the students were free to bring in their own questions. I fully expected simple questions of grammar and word order. The questions were always well prepared, memorized with great care and quite impossible for me to answer.

"Doctor, please be so kind as to tell us. Why is it that it is not all right for Russia to have missile bases in Cuba, because it is too close to the United States; but on the other hand it is all right for the United States to have missile bases in Japan, which is not too much further from Russia?"

"Doctor, do you believe it ethically right for a country to maintain its position through power; for example, money and bombs of great destructive potential?"

"Doctor, do you think that communism can be kept out of Asia? I speak of Chinese communism as contrasted to Russian communism."

These questions were asked with a sincere desire to know and without malice. Each was sufficient to bring about enough conversation for the remainder of the time allotted, as well as our usual several hour adjournment over cold beer.

One Sunday, Abe-san suggested that I meet him in Yokohama for a visit to the famous Susenski garden. He was waiting for me when I arrived at the station. He had removed his Western garb and looked superb in a long beige kimono and getas. We took a tram and descended on a narrow paved road through the outskirts of the city. The road was lined with tiny wooden homes, simple and beautiful in design, which were typical of those one sees everywhere in Japan.

The garden was enchanting with its tea houses, wooden bridges, twisted bonsai and blooming azaleas. In the rear of the garden was an authentic sixteenth century farm house, complete with open fireplace, tatami, movable panel walls, finely constructed stairways. It was late afternoon and most of the visitors were gone. We removed our shoes and entered. We sat in an open section which looked out over the green at bamboo patches, tiny lakes, and waterfalls.

"This is the Japan I love," Abe said softly. "It worries me that we are now in a position where to survive and compete with the rest of the world, we must become like it, which means that we must be willing to give up all of this and the wonders of our past. It is a difficult decision to make. This is a problem that we are not yet ready to solve. My parents see what is happening, but know that they can do nothing about it, so they retreat into the past which is familiar and, in small ways, fight the future. I see the advantages of the future, but I resist parting with the past."

He looked for a long time at the garden. "If this is all gone, we shall be like everyone else. Then where shall we go for quiet?"

Abe-san had made arrangements to take me to his home. The house was hidden behind the usual high wooden fence, on a quiet dirt road. A small gate led us into the garden. Moss covered the ground. There were small bonsai and a rather large fish pond where several golden and orange fish swam noiselessly. The only sound was the quiet splash of a small waterfall which ran over a few well-placed stones into a pond. I stood for a moment and watched.

Abe-san's mother and father (both in kimonos) walked out onto the open goza-covered porch from which the screens had been pushed back and bowed to us. We bowed back and were welcomed into the house. We entered a twelve mat room (Sizes of rooms in Japan are determined by the number of tatami mats they contain.) There were three solid walls and one sliding wall by the garden which served as the entrance. The ceiling was low and there was little furniture — a few lacquered tables and a small Takonoma. The walls were bare except for a large scroll of calligraphy which hung above a beautiful classic flower arrangement of three simple flowers in the leafy branch of a maple tree.

I was given a pillow from a pile in one corner and knelt down with my hosts. Abe's mother and father spoke no English. His mother busied herself with a large hibachi and some water in a heavy brass pot.

"My mother is going to do a tea ceremony. She is very good with tea, a master," Abe told me.

We settled ourselves, after a short while, in a straight line, each on his own pillow. Abe's mother, looking very serene and beautiful, placed each coal in its proper position with long-pointed sticks. This done, she took the huge pot of water and set it on the coals. We waited for some time, listening to the sound of water beginning to boil and to the sounds of nature outside. The noise of a flapping fish tail in the pond seemed magnified ten-fold in the silence.

The tea implements were set before us, each of exquisite beauty and each in its proper place. With practiced strokes Abe's mother went through the ceremony: the measuring of the green tea, the pouring of the water, the quiet mixing, the wiping of the implements. All seemed to put us into a trance. At last she offered the first cup of tea to her husband who had quickly moved to her side. He passed it to me, and showed me how to take the cup, how to move it to the correct position so that I could see its design at best advantage, and how to drink the tea. He gave me a very sweet cookie which Abe explained was necessary to neutralize the tea's rather bitter taste.

During the ceremony a young girl — Abe's sister — entered and quietly seated herself next to him. She wore a brightly-colored kimono with a golden sash; her hair was cut in the usual school girl fashion, with long bangs over her forehead. She was offered tea, after Abe had finished his; then the parents drank theirs and the ceremony was over. It seemed that it had been a matter of a few minutes and I was amazed to find that it had taken over an hour. Abe explained that the length of the tea ceremony is dictated by the mood. Some are brief, as nature and feelings do not commune, while others may last for hours when all is in tune.

I rose from my pillow with much effort. My cramped legs occasioned much laughter and comment.

The rest of the afternoon was spent in pleasant conversation, with Abe translating for his parents and sister. His sister was learning flower arranging and had done the arrangement now in the room.

Dusk in the garden was exquisite and I well understood Abe-san's reluctance to part with such beauty.

During my remaining weeks in Tokyo, I visited many families and found that most maintained the old traditions in their homes. There was great respect for the family. Each house, no matter how poor or how rich, had a unique beauty, always simple, plain and amazingly in tune with its natural setting.

The people were wondrous. There was Mrs. Hito who taught classic dance, who herself always seemed to be in a graceful dance position. There was Mrs. Ono who practiced the ancient art of weaving silk materials of great beauty. And Tomoyo whose job it was to take care of me at my inn. She was always waiting up no matter how late I returned and saw to it that my bath was never too hot, serving me at the moment of my request with great ease and beauty. She taught me patiently, and with constant ripples of laughter, how to eat, how to bathe. Then there was Fumio, educated in the United States, who had returned to Japan more determined than ever never to lose its spirit. These and many others just as wonderful made up the world of Japan in which I was still such a child.

With the aid of my friends, I made out a complete list

of cities, towns and villages to be experienced and was ready to leave Tokyo.

The class gave me a farewell party at a most elegant Japanese-style restaurant, and escorted me, en masse, to the train.

As I left the station I thought I was beginning to see a possible answer. Tradition, the ingrained teachings of centuries, is not an easy thing to eradicate. Perhaps a compromise would be reached. The necessity of growth and the obvious advantages of improvements and modernization were weighed on one hand against the traditions of beauty, quiet, peace and individuality on the other. Could they be amalgamated?

Japan would find an answer in its own wise way. Abe had stated the problem: "If this is all gone, we shall be like everyone else. Then where shall we go for quiet?"

Chapter III

HONG KONG

As long as man has hope, he has direction, the energy to move, and the map to move by. He has a hundred alternatives, a thousand paths and an infinity of dreams. Hope-ful, he is half-way to where he wants to go; hope-less, he is lost forever.

WONG

A few hours after arriving in Hong Kong, I met a spindly, pale, soft spoken Chinese boy. His name was Wong; he was nineteen years old. I had come to see the sunset over the bay and found him seated beside a railing overlooking the harbor. He sat quietly, apparently oblivious of the noisy crowds that hurried to and from the Star Ferry, ready to cross from Hong Kong to its sister city, Kowloon.

Wong worked in a small toy shop twelve hours each day, starting at dawn and finishing just before sundown. Even so, he was able to wander each afternoon to the Kowloon ferry landing in time to watch the sunset.

I noticed that he fondled a small, well-worn Chinese-English dictionary.

"Do you speak English?"

"A little," he replied shyly. "Now, I teach myself. Soon maybe study in school. I have no chance for practice. To learn language one must practice." After some conversation and with much effort he added, "You teacher. You teach English me, I teach Hong Kong."

Thus our friendship started. Through Wong a terrible world opened up before me with Hong Kong as the backdrop before which a battle for the maintenance of man's dignity was enacted each second by unsuspecting amateurs before a hard and indifferent audience.

With Wong as my guide, the several cities of Hong Kong, laid out amid ocean, rugged hills and lush New Territories began to unfold. The first city was that of fantastic shops, opulent hotels, gourmet restaurants, rich mansions, colorful tree-lined avenues and handsome people.

Another city was that of the business world, of money-hungry, desperate executives who measured wealth by the dividend and success by the profit, of the white collar worker who in the most modern office buildings worked in air-conditioned panic on the world market, with all the anxieties of a New York commuter.

There was the city of the middle-class merchant who depended upon the throngs of tourists for his livelihood; who ran a small novelty shop, restaurant, a well-kept hotel or spotless tearoom.

Abhorred by the wealthy, ignored by the middle class, hidden from the casual observer, and inconceivable to the simple tourist was the city of the refugee. This was Wong's city. A place of pride and poverty hidden behind the papier-mâché and glitter of Hong Kong glamour. Introducing me to the many-faceted city was Wong's part of the bargain.

My part of the agreement, to teach Wong English, began with evening walks of incredible variety. I taught him language of the street by way of the waterfront world of Suzy Wong, with its blaring night bars, and narrow alleys lined with street stalls and prostitutes; the language of the beautiful by gazing into windows alive with jewels from Europe, diamonds from Africa, trinkets from India, rugs from Persia, silks from Thailand; the language of money by way of the money changer — the French franc, the English pound, the American dollar, the Indian rupee, the Chinese yen. "Buy money with money." "Sell money with money." It was all handled in one simple transaction, with the speed and efficiency of an expert cook though with far less measured concern. Five dollars, four hundred, two thousand, forty thousand! We learned the vocabulary of travel by walking past miles of airline offices, steamship lines, tourist agencies, consulates, studios for passport pictures, offices of American Express and Diner's Club.

During our walks I learned more about Wong. There were ten other children in his family, all younger than he. They had been raised in Peking where their father was a well-to-do merchant until, to escape Communism, the family had left for Hong Kong and the home of a friend. When they arrived, the friend was compelled to turn them away; he had already used all of his resources to help the many others who had arrived before them. It was necessary, with their by then limited funds, to live in a small hotel until a permanent room could be found; but it was not long before they realized that finding a room was impossible in Hong Kong and were forced to take to the street or wherever they could find a plot of ground or temporary shelter. Money ran out and jobs were impossible to find; several members of the family became ill; a smaller brother died. Each move was to a place more desolate than the last until finally they were compelled to enter the dreaded refugee camp.

Each night after our wanderings, Wong accompanied me to my hotel. He seemed afraid to allow me to return alone. One night, as we approached Nathan Street through a small alleyway full of carts, bicycles, rickshaws and a million bodies in constant motion like jittery flies, he turned suddenly and asked, "Would you like to meet family of Wong?"

"Yes. Yes, I would."

"Sunday, at tea," he said, and after a quick, shy goodnight, he turned and walked briskly in the direction of his home.

On Sunday, we met at a small tea house near the port on the Kowloon side. Only Wong's mother, father and four older brothers came. We bowed to each other and sat down to tea. Wong acted as interpreter. Our conversation was simple and rather hesitant; we discussed the fact that I had never been to China, that I liked Hong Kong, that I was amazed at the number of people who lived in such a small area, and that I planned to remain for only a few more weeks. The brothers ate their food quietly with occasional shy glances in my direction. Wong's father had brought a gift for my mother, a small mandarin-style cotton house coat, obviously sewn by hand. There was embroidery on the collar and on the long, loose sleeves.

Wong's father told me how grateful he was for all that I was doing for his son. He felt it was important that all his family learn the language of their new home. Soon he would be making more coats like the one which he had given me for my mother and which was an original design. With the help of the entire family, he could supply the coats to a local merchant who was selling to tourists and English was imperative. Wong's father considered the present moment in Hong Kong a new world, a time to create anew, in whatever manner possible. It was no time for pride, self-pity or fear.

Much too quickly our tea was finished and, with bows, the family left.

Several days later Wong and I were wandering through the old section of Kowloon near the new multi-million dollar airport. The area was one of ragged beggars with frightened, fantastic faces. Its sky was composed of the converging tops of high crumbling tenements and clothes lines where wash, strung like hanged phantoms, dangled and flapped in the breeze. As we neared the end of one street, Wong commented, "This is one of refugee places. It not seem part of Hong Kong." I looked at the area to which he was referring. It was a walled section — the wall, a patchwork of bits and pieces of cartons, tin, cardboard, piled stone and cement hunks, was shadowed by the surrounding ruined tenements. There were occasional small openings in the wall, just large enough for a human form to enter into what resembled a maze or labyrinth constructed of the same patchwork. It was a cubist's nightmare sketched in dull browns, hard grays and deep blacks.

"No law here. No police. Much bad and crime," Wong said, adding, "Will you see inside?"

We entered between crates, piled high. Wong knew his way and I followed. Only a discerning and practiced eye could have identified the proper directions. As we walked through the cardboard-box, tin-roof, broken-board community, slanted eyes sunken into drawn faces peered quietly at us. Here there was an almost ghostly stillness. Everyone seemed huddled together in frightened groups as if there were no place to hide. Spindly children with bloated bellies ran naked over piles of garbage. Sad-looking women sat on dirt floors and looked through us with dead expressions. A mass of tiny girls approached, screaming as much to Wong as to me. They were child prostitutes, some of them not even nine years old. Their little fingers were covered with dirt; their overly-long dresses were torn, soiled and ragged; their little feet were black with soil, scabby and infested with sores; their voices were shrill and desperate — and they grabbed at our bodies with eager, knowing hands.

The dirt paths were endless, branching crookedly in all directions like long arthritic fingers. They were covered with puddles of strong-smelling urine, piles of feces — the delight of swarming flies — bits of dried vegetable rind, cobs and discarded open tins. The odors were so strong that they pierced the senses into a painful numbness. Everything appeared devastated, dead, senseless — void of color or life. Adult prostitutes with still youthful bodies compressed within tightfitting, sweat-stained mandarin dresses stood against paper walls without smiles and solicited sexlessly. Once beautiful faces were now masks, expressionless, blanched, untinged. The strong sweet smell of opium, mixed with the fumes of fires, dung, spoiled food and garbage, clouded the air.

Sometime later settled safely in a tearoom, I turned to Wong. I was stunned, speechless.

"There is no place else," Wong said simply.

"Who are those people?"

His answer was a whisper, "That is where I live."

Wong stayed with me that long night. We sat quietly in the dark of my noisy hotel room. I remember that during the evening he said, "Do not be sad. We work to find good life again. We work to make beautiful."

I wondered what there was about life so precious that a living horror was valued more highly than the peace of death. Perhaps what Wong said was true. Perhaps each man had his unconscious dream of beauty to which he strived and he will endure hunger, pain and untold suffering and degradation for its realization. Perhaps this dream was Wong's only reality. Perhaps only through his dream could he continue to feel and to believe in something. From dreams, changes can be made.

Wong told me that the government was building apartments but the waiting lists were long and the houses were filled beyond capacity before they were even completed. Greedy landlords were charging high prices for hovels, which could only be afforded if several families moved in together, making the situation little better.

My last few days in Hong Kong were spent enrolling Wong in a good night school for English lessons and supplying him with books on English grammar and conversation.

It was not an easy thing to leave Wong. He was so much more than nineteen years old: proud, independent, gentle, affectionate, kind and responsive. The day I left he met me at the airport. He had taken the day off from work and was waiting for me. I went through all the necessary formalities without looking at him until we retired with a cup of tea to a corner of the luxurious coffee shop. The atmosphere was unreal as if we suddenly had become strangers, as if we had revealed ourselves too completely and now were ashamed. It was as if we somehow had to recover ourselves, to replace the facades which protected us against nakedness and guilt. At last Wong spoke.

"Will some day you come back to Hong Kong?"

"I hope so. I don't know."

"I not write English too well. I study much. Someday I repay you for nice things you do for me and family. You will see."

The plane was called. We embraced.

"I bring you present," Wong said, and handed me a tiny package. "It is a little package, but a big gift. You open on airplane, please. Do you know where I go tonight?" he asked as I started to the gate. "I go to Star Ferry where I meet you. I watch sunset."

I boarded the plane, and with superjet efficiency was off and overlooking the faint outline of Hong Kong on the sea. I took out Wong's gift and opened it. It was a small Buddha. The Buddha was fat and smiling.

I leaned back in my seat and thought of Wong. I could clearly see his thin body seated quietly on a bench amid the frantic pre-dinner rush at the Star Ferry, his drawn, sad, rather pale face and his shining eyes, orange in the sunset. I put the Buddha in my jacket pocket.

Strange, but I felt good.

Chapter IV

THAILAND

To deny ourselves the knowledge even of a single man is to lose the central piece of the jigsaw puzzle.

KANOKE

*T*hailand is virtually unique among the countries of Asia. Its people have never known colonization, mass hunger or oppression. They are prosperous, relaxed and happy.

Bangkok, the capital of Thailand, stands like an Oriental Disneyland. Its hundreds of temples are exotic, each one unique. Their grand, colorful silhouettes can be seen for miles spreading across the horizon.

The Chao Phraya River runs through the city like a

jade snake pin. From it, canals jet out like the sticks of a fan forming colorful islands. These islands keep the city alive with activity and form the famous floating markets.

The entire city is surrounded with marshy rice fields, added security against poverty.

With the temples, the islands, the more than four hundred exotic monasteries, the towering Royal Palace with its vast chambers in silk and velvet, Bangkok turns the ancient tales of the gold-laden Orient into reality.

This is the land of the Reclining Buddha, the shaved-headed, saffron-robed Buddhist, and the powerful cemented Roc.

There are fairs, carnivals and religious holidays aplenty to keep the fun-loving people happy as well as a spring-like atmosphere between festivals to keep them active. The Thai have the reputation of being the friendliest and most hospitable people in Asia, and they have created an ideal setting in which to enjoy these gifts.

For the tourist, the city is a heaven. Transportation is cheap and efficient. Hotels are ultra-modern and offer every convenience. Restaurants serve Oriental and Western foods with equal ease, cooked to vie with the best anywhere in the world. There are bars with blaring juke boxes where one can sit in air-conditioned comfort and sip dry martinis prepared to taste. Coffee houses prepare Maxwell House in electric percolators or expresso in giant machines. One can shop in opulent surroundings, buy silks of any length, style or color desired. If what you seek is not displayed, it can be made to order and delivered to your hotel within hours.

Bangkok offers pleasures of a different, more modest nature for those who cannot afford first class, pools and air-conditioned comfort. There are hotels, shops, and restaurants to suit any budget. These can be found down most side streets or alleyways.

A lean budget and sparse accommodations compelled me to share the luxuries of such a hotel with another gentleman, an American salesman. The hotel was a small wooden structure in what seemed to be a patio behind a series of business establishments which lined a main street. Our tiny, neat room was equipped with two wrought iron beds, each with a sagging, lumpy innerspring mattress, one window, and a sink marked with hot and cold spigots from which you could always be assured of a full supply of cold water, whichever spigot you tried. In addition, and at no extra charge, the guests were treated to several varieties of bugs, a small temperamental fan which usually did not work and, on the hotel grounds, a noisy bar with several available prostitutes.

The management was always ready to smile, to listen, to nod about such complaints as "There's some sort of animal on the ceiling," "The door doesn't close," "Could you please ask the fat prostitute to stop coming into my room." But nothing was ever done.

Mack, my roommate, was in his late forties. He did not seem to be bothered by any of these small inconveniences. "Hell," he would say, "this ain't the Waldorf Astoria. Anyway, I save money this way. I like it here. I can't stand those damn tourist hotels full of virgin school teachers and their damn guidebooks."

Mack was tall, husky, fair-skinned, and blond, the physical type best loved and immediately recognized by the Asian as American. He had been in Bangkok several times on business trips for his U.S.-based pharmaceutical firm.

"This is quite a place, Bangkok. That Buddha and the Palace are real nice but the best things are the dames. I know plenty of 'em, kid. Sexy, cheap and clean. Say the word and I can fix you up."

41

"What the hell ya wanna travel here for, anyway, kid? Me? I take care of my business, play around a little after hours and get the hell out."

On the first evening I spent with Mack, he took me to a Western-style restaurant. "Damn good American food," he assured me. "You've got to stay away from that Thai crap unless you want to get the creeping 'dingle dangle.' "

After dinner he took me to a bar near the river. "I get a real kick outta this place," he chuckled. His entrance caused quite a stir.

"Mack, my honey!" the women swarmed to him. "Mack, my stud! My bull!"

He received them with obscene gestures, slapped them on their fat bottoms and exclaimed, "Now, ain't she something? And a tiger in bed!"

He pulled a rather fleshy woman in our direction and pushed her at me. "Feel," he smiled, "Smell. Doesn't she have it all over them Indian whores?"

The woman reeked of a rather cheap flower perfume. She did not move but struck what she imagined as a provocative pose right out of a Harlow movie which I found wonderfully amusing though I hesitated to smile for fear it be misinterpreted.

"Really something," Mack said and slapped her backside. "Plenty for your money, too. Want it?"

It was apparent that our taste in both women and travel was quite different. Many evenings Mack didn't return and I was often gone before he showed up in the morning. I could tell when he had been there, as the room was always strewn with the clothes he left about in his rush to get to work.

When he departed after a week, the hotel manager approached me meekly to ask if I would mind sharing my room with a Thai gentleman.

"He's a clean, young businessman," the manager assured me. "One of our steady customers."

I told him I wouldn't mind.

In this way Pricha and I were introduced. He was a small man in his late twenties, dark, thin and pleasant looking. His clothing was neat and conservative; his manner was straightforward and formal. "My name is Pricha," he introduced himself. "I am Thai."

It soon became a habit for us to have dinner together. We went often to a small Thai restaurant on Chak Ching Road, where he was known and ate fantastically exotic and delicious foods. Since Pricha was aware of everything about him and seemed to be able to literally "smell out" the excitement in the city, there was never a problem as to where we would spend the evening, be it a Chinese opera, a carnival or a new street magician.

After dinner one evening, Pricha suggested that we take a boat trip on the river. He explained that the real beauty of the great river and the floating market section was to be seen at night. We went to a small dock off a side street where several sampans about the size of Venetian gondolas were tossing about in the river. Pricha requested a boat and we were at once deluged with offers of various prices. He finally selected a sampan owned by a rather young boy, more pleasant and less aggressive than the other boatmen. Then Pricha walked to a food stand to purchase several items while the boy lit a small lantern and waited, smiling at me warmly. We pushed off into the river and almost at once the boat was caught by the current and pulled quietly downstream.

The city's thousands of colored lights were reflected at our feet in a shimmering watery blur. The large temples bordering the river now resembled giant black monsters hovering over us, ready to strike and devour. All the gaudiness and color of the daytime Bangkok was now but an Oriental shadow play, dark and graceful.

The night was warm and the lamb and chicken

which Pricha had bought tasted good even on a full stomach. He had purchased several bottles of beer which we shared with our boatman. The only sound was that of the oars gliding through the water. The lantern flickered continuously.

The beer was potent and soon the silence was broken by the boatman's lusty singing. His repertoire, made up mostly of Western songs which he sang in a relaxed pidgin English, was delightful and pleasant. "Don' ya' nose..." We could not help but laugh.

As we passed through narrow canals cutting through the lush, nearly deserted market district, we could see the many occupants of the floating town going about the business of living, laughing gaily. Small groups of people stood chatting, arguing or listening intently.

At one point, Pricha asked the boatman to stop.

"Since you are interested in people, shall we rest here awhile?" He was referring to what looked like a small inn floating on a marshy island. Inside, the room was filled with men, smoke and the smell of beer.

"So the workman spends his nights like workmen all over the world I suppose, with friends, a cigarette and a bottle of beer," I thought.

The group greeted Pricha with a friendly welcome, though they obviously did not know him. They surveyed me oddly but immediately included me in the circle on the floor.

After so many days, Pricha and I had become fast friends. He told me of his family and friends, of his dreams for the future and his fears. His dreams were simple like those of any man, anywhere; his fears were rather unique but none the less real, understandable and human.

After a week, Pricha made plans to visit some of his relatives, farmers who lived a very different kind of life from that which I had seen so far in Bangkok. He asked if I cared to go with him.

"They are not poor people," he said proudly. "They have fields of rice, only their lives are more simple than ours."

We took a crowded, noisy streetcar from our hotel and then a bus to the end of the line. We were more than an hour's drive from the center of Bangkok, which had faded to a dim glow on the horizon. At the end of the bus line were several small cars, old retired taxis, repaired to run an additional million miles, again serving their original function outside the city from which they had been outlawed. For some time Pricha talked with several drivers, obviously concerned about the price and our destination. When everything was finally arranged, we climbed into one of the ancient cars and started off in a rumble down a dirt road.

Abruptly, the road came to an end in the midst of moonlit rice paddies. The tall rice plants hid the muddy water below which slushed mysteriously, unseen in the dark.

"From here we must walk," Pricha informed me. "The taxi will wait for us. I think it would be wise for you to remove your shoes, socks and trousers. We shall have to walk on wet, slippery boards in the dark. You are likely to step into the mud now and then and it will be better if you don't get your clothes ruined." I did as he suggested and we started off down the planks which — edged occasionally by a single, weakly constructed handrail — seemed to lead nowhere. There was neither light nor house in sight.

It was much like walking a blind maze. Pricha led and I followed close behind, one hand on the rail and the other on his shoulder as he had instructed.

The planks were jagged and veered first to one side, then the other. I could feel the mud push its slimy way between my toes and the tops of the rice plants brush against my ankles. We attracted thousands of insects. I neither dared nor cared to stop for even a moment. I was afraid to let go of Pricha or the rail to swat them. Rather than let go, I allowed them to bite and suck away.

Several times we came upon a fork with planks going in two directions, but Pricha always knew without hesitation which branch to follow.

The walk was much farther than I had imagined. At last, seemingly growing out of a rice swamp and completely surrounded by it, there emerged a cluster of small wooden shacks, scattered about on what appeared to be a tiny island.

Pricha called out, "Kanoke!"

In a moment, a young man draped only with a white cloth about his slim waist emerged from one of the shacks and stood momentarily silhouetted in the dimly lit doorway.

"Kanoke! It's me, Pricha," he seemed to be saying.

The young man, obviously delighted, approached with open arms to plant a kiss on Pricha's mouth. Pricha introduced us. He could not speak English, but I was surely welcome for he kissed me firmly on the mouth just as he had his relative.

He led us into the shack, lit with a single oil lamp. The room was empty except for some farming tools and a few open bed rolls. There were two windows which were closed to the night and a mat in the center of the floor on which we sat, almost in darkness.

The two men spoke quickly and at once. There was great warmth and animation in their conversation. At last it occurred to Kanoke that I was being excluded. He reached out and took my hand warmly in his. His hand felt rough and strong.

"He regrets that he cannot speak to you," Pricha translated. "He wants to awaken his family to have you meet them, but I will not allow it. They work very hard all day and would be very tired."

Kanoke rose and started for the door. He took the

lamp in his hand and motioned for us to follow him. "He insists that you at least see them," Pricha said. "He's very proud of his family."

We walked out into the night which now seemed a bit lighter. The fields of rice which surrounded us were vast and silent and only the glow in the sky from the distant city reminded me that we were still part of this century.

Kanoke walked directly to a small shack and opened the door. With the candle, he lit up the faces and relaxed, sleeping bodies of several children. None of them stirred. Their expressions were soft, peaceful. In another room, a short distance away were two older boys in their early teens. Their bare shoulders and chests were exposed, strong, dark and firm. One of the boys sat up slightly and spoke, but with the assurance of his father's response, lay back and seemed to fall asleep again instantaneously.

Kanoke looked proudly at me and smiled.

At last we met his wife. She looked like one of the children, youthful and shy. She wore a loose-flowing petticoat; her feet and ankles were bare.

She busied herself at once, fixing tea with quick, sure movements.

For a long while we sat outside in the now friendly darkness, drank the hot tea and ate small rice cakes. Pricha and Kanoke spoke in soft tones.

When the time came to leave, Kanoke insisted upon walking back with us over the long-planked path to the road. Pricha guided me from the front and Kanoke supported me from the rear. I was, indeed, well guarded from everything except the insects that feasted themselves greedily on my still unhardened skin.

When we arrived at the road, Kanoke led us to a trough where we could wash the mud from our feet and legs. The taxi driver, who had fallen asleep at the wheel, seemed a bit disappointed and annoyed that we had returned so soon.

Kanoke kissed us both with great tenderness. He looked at me deeply, smiled nodding his head from side to side approvingly, and then impulsively kissed me again.

We left Kanoke in the soft darkness of his strange world and started back to town.

"He is a fine man. He liked you very much," Pricha said. "He felt that you were comfortable in his home. You are the first Westerner he has ever known. You have given him great honor."

All at once I thought of Mack, loud, insensitive, rough. How sad that he would never know Kanoke's kiss.

Chapter V

CAMBODIA

Man will find the greatest riches where he finds the joy in living; since we serve God and ourselves best in joy, it seems to be the only sensible goal in life.

Hôtel de la Paix

Phnom-Penh is the Asian city of the Emerald Buddha, with a dash of France, her colonizer.

Large, graceful temples lining the horizon; spicy-smelling marketplaces selling everything from cheap images of the Buddha to Chanel No. 5 and Gillette Blue Blades; dark-skinned natives cycling quickly through congested, dirty streets; and nearby the great river rushing through the city, teeming with activity; all this Phnom-Penh.

It is a full day's bus trip from Phnom-Penh to Siem Reap. The native bus is open to the elements, has wooden seats, stops any time for everyone and everything and is, in spite of this, quite reliable.

We left Phnom-Penh at dawn when it was still cool. I had packed a small lunch of French bread, cheese and fresh fruit as I had learned that there were no such things as lunch shops and no schedules to advise the traveler when the trip would end. When I inquired about time schedules, my questions were met only with queer looks, grunts, groans and "me no know what is schedules!"

At dawn, as we left, the streets were just beginning to take on life. Bicycles were standing idle; sweepers who tried continuously to keep the roads clean pushed their brooms along in tired, steady rhythms, as if they knew it was in vain; shopkeepers sleepily opened their shutters.

The bus passed through these morning rituals with quick indifference and left the city. Almost at once we were plunged into jungle which was to surround us throughout the trip, broken only momentarily by a small village, a stream, or a river.

The seats on the bus were all reserved, but this did not include those passengers who were standing or hanging on outside. The luggage was tied high on the roof, like a pyramid of multi-colored, odd shapes. I was seated next to the only other person on the bus who was not a native. She was a short, severely dressed, neatly groomed woman. Her face was small with delicate features, except for her lips which were full and well shaped. She wore a skirt and blouse, both gray, well pressed and clean. Obviously, she was not a fellow tourist, usually recognizable by the wash-and-wear quality of the press in his clothes and the tense, almost pathetically lost quality of his expression.

I introduced myself, "Would you rather sit by the window?" I asked.

She thanked me, "No. I have been on this road many

times. It is a lovely drive, but I am sure that you will enjoy the window more than I. I am Madame Clote. I live in Siem Reap."

I explained, during the drive, that I understood there were two luxury hotels in Siem Reap, both very good, but very expensive and far beyond my means. I had heard also of a third hotel which was much cheaper but quite nice.

She knew the hotel about which I spoke, "The Hôtel de la Paix." Yes, it was located in the city itself, quite some way from the ruins of Angkor which she assumed I had come to see. "Why else would someone go to Siem Reap?" She smiled. "I am surprised that you spent time in Phnom-Penh. To the Western world, except for a few of us who have lived here for many years and love it, Cambodia is just a vast jungle of uncivilized people with nothing to recommend it but the massive ruins of ancient Angkor."

We talked for some time. I was embarassed to learn that she and her husband were the proprietors of the city's most expensive and most coveted hotel. She did not seem at all disturbed but rather amused by my discussion of expensive hotels, commenting, "One pays for quality — even in the jungle."

She, too, had brought food and combining our lunches we had quite a feast. She supplied a bottle of wine, a real necessity as the heat of the day increased. The wine, the food, the heat and the swaying of the bus lulled us into afternoon naps. When we awoke we were entering Siem Reap. It seemed more colorful, less congested, and less dusty than Phnom-Penh.

Madame directed me to the hotel which was just a few hundred feet from the bus station, and I saw her step into a large, chauffer-driven car which drove off in a spray of dust.

Alone, I was immediately pounced upon by several

bicycle drivers, all wearing variations of a small pair of shorts, usually too large to be held up by their flat bellies and narrow hips, always ready to fall about them on the ground.

"I take you to ruins," they all shouted in perfect English.

"You come with me."

"I take you cheap."

"I be your guide."

"I'm going to the Hôtel de la Paix," I said.

They seemed confused. Obviously, this was not a part of their practiced dialogue. They looked from one to the other, then followed in silence.

The Hôtel de la Paix was a rather small, box-like, two-story stucco structure. The lower level was partially devoted to a large restaurant and, outside, there was a four-table sidewalk cafe. The sign on the wall was broken and read, "Hôt de..."

"Oui," said the proprietor, who spoke only French, "Nous avons une chambre."

He took me up the flight of stairs into a narrow hall. My room was at the far end, with windows on two sides. One, facing the rear of the hotel, overlooked the yard of a very large, very noisy native family and their menagerie of chickens, cows, pigs, motor scooters and children. The other window looked across a mucky field to the dense jungle which vied successfully with the yard for animal noises.

There were a small, single bed with a torn mosquito net hanging loosely over it, a dresser and a table. The toilet had a basin, shower and commode, all crowded together in a space so cramped that one could perform all functions with hardly a move of the body.

"Tres jolie, n'est pas?" the proprietor beamed.

I took the room, together with two meals, for a dollar and a half a day. A good price, indeed, I thought.

After my first night I was not so certain. The native

family seemed to be having a perpetual orgy with a record player screaming out into the night, obviously not only amusing the many guests but also delighting the animals that answered in their own spirited tones. Women laughed, children cried, men argued. Each spoke as if everyone else were deaf.

It was no better inside the hotel. The hallway was like the Rue de la Paix for which the hotel was named. Doors opened with creaking sounds and slammed shut. Men whispered loudly, women giggled and screeched with joy. Feet pattered, objects fell and windows crashed.

At one point, there was a loud knock at my door. "Who is it?" I asked angrily.

The knock was repeated. I rose, put a shirt over my sweaty nakedness and answered the door. A very young girl, not over fifteen, pushed her way into the room. Her garbled French was incomprehensible, but her purpose was obvious.

After much discussion, none of which she understood, I had to remove her bodily from the room, cursing myself for having fallen into this age-old trap, so common among Asian prostitutes.

When I finally fell asleep it was almost morning.

The sun was already unbearably hot when I awoke and light was pouring through the shadeless windows. I struggled through my morning ritual, the cold water actually feeling good over my tired, insect-drained flesh. Finally, I got myself downstairs for breakfast.

The proprietor was busily packing things in an old fashioned ice box.

"Bonjour," he said. "Et alors?"

I mentioned that there certainly had been a great deal of noise during the night.

"Oui," he smiled, "c'est merveilleux!"

The manager directed me to the ruins. He advised me about bargaining with the cyclists and motorbike drivers and felt that for no more than two dollars I should be able to hire one for the day. They could take me on a pre-planned tour which included La Grande Cercle, Angkor Wat and some of the major sights and La Petite Cercle, some of the more remote ruins. This, he felt, I could see in two days; if I wanted to really see and feel it, it would take five; while if I wanted to see, feel and perceive, it might take a lifetime.

He went out and hired a motorbike. The driver was a spindly boy whose half-naked body appeared dried by the sun. His head seemed too large for his thin frame, but he had a pleasant face, soft and peaceful. I liked him. He spoke only a few words of English and a few more of French, but I felt sure that we would be able to communicate adequately for the relationship we would be having in Angkor. His name sounded like Noke.

After breakfast of good hot café au lait and fresh French bread, I piled into the buggy. The motorbike sputtered and spat as we left in a cloud of dust, with Noke smiling broadly in front of me.

It was a wonderful morning. The sky was clear and a deep blue. The jungle looked rich and dense, like a fantasy land.

Noke pointed out one of the modern hotels. It was white, tall, well-kept. The gardens were beautiful and full of colorful tropical flowers. Well-dressed, camera-carrying tourists sat about the veranda reading, talking or simply staring at the large open space around the hotel.

"Much francs," Noke said as we sputtered by. Cars were waiting in front of the hotel to take the guests to the ruins in cool comfort. "Why you no stay there?"

"No francs," I answered. He laughed, "Moi aussi."

We traveled dustily down the narrow main road, completely lined with giant trees and shrubs, alive with the high-pitched screech of insects. At the end of the road, bathed in the hot mid-morning sun, stood the great side gate of Angkor Wat. A large staircase poured down into a vast, moss-flower, insect-infested moat. The walls extended almost endlessly on either side. Towers, stairways and paths made interesting patterns against the skyline and gave steady support to hungry vines and bushes.

The main entrance was tremendous and led to the vast central sanctuary through several walls, magnificant gates and courts within courts. All along the stone walkway were exquisitely carved sacred naga serpents, menacingly guarding the sanctuary — a central group of rooms and towers of beautiful symmetry and giant size.

In the afternoon sun, Angkor Wat turns orange and seems like a jewel set carefully in a wild jungle setting. Undisturbed, one can sit for hours on one of the central towers, high above the complex of buildings and view a city which, though built in the 12th century, was being eaten by the jungle, slowly and hungrily, until only a century ago. Here, the Khmer Empire blossomed for some 600 years, rich and exciting, creating artistic and architectural masterpieces with hordes of slaves. Vast irrigation systems were set up, great cities of incomparable beauty flourished in the shadow of overpoweringly lovely temples protected by the seven-headed naga. Then suddenly, inexplicably, all was seized by the jungle's hungry fingers; it was all hidden, vanished.

Angkor Wat is only one of hundreds of monuments and temples covering an area of six hundred square kilometers. Awesome, magnificent, defying time and jungle, they remain almost intact and allow modern man a chance to glimpse a vanished civilization and bask in its mystery.

The hordes of tourists were disconcerting: grumbling about the heat, the endless steps and the vastness of the city; dashing through the fantastic setting, hurrying to make it fit within a one- or two-day itinerary.

However, time did not permit them to remain too long in any one place, and no sooner had their rumble and dash disturbed the peace than it moved on and out of earshot, leaving one to continue his journey in silence.

Saffron-robed priests from nearby Buddhist temples wandered quietly alone or in small groups through the temples and gazed at the fantasy of their past culture before returning to the simplicity of their tiny wooden temples, dwarfed and insignificant in comparison with these ancient buildings.

Madame's hotel was directly across the road from Angkor Wat. I walked in, looking for her, and was told that she was in the kitchen supervising the preparation of lunch. When she saw me she greeted me as an old friend. "How do you like your hotel?" she asked.

"Well," I answered, "there is very little 'Paix,' but I think it will be fine."

She laughed. "You are brave."

We talked for a few minutes, experiencing several interruptions. Her staff spoke both the native tongue and French.

"Madame, Mrs. Charles in Room 18 says her air-conditioning makes too much noise."

"Mr. and Mrs. Smith want to know if you have arranged for the station wagon so that they can go to Bantai Serei tomorrow."

"There is not enough coffee for lunch and dinner. We need more."

"Should I take the elephant out this afternoon? The children of the couple in Room 16 want to ride him and take pictures."

"Miss Barsi says the crickets are too loud."

"I must go," Madame said finally. "Come to dinner here tonight. I would like you to meet my husband and a few friends. Nine o'clock? Oh, yes, and you must visit Bantei Serei. I have a station wagon which takes my guests. It is too far for a motorbike. If there is an empty seat, I shall save it for you."

I waited that day to watch the temple turn a bright yellow-orange-red in the light of the setting sun. I wandered through its deep, heavy, ancient halls and then out onto a small path which led to the simple Buddhist monastery adjacent to the ruins. I thought I heard the sound of voices and laughter and, although the ruins seemed deserted, followed it up a large stone staircase to the top of a wall along the side of the moat which separated the ruins from the surrounding roads and jungle. The laughter and voices grew louder. Twenty or thirty young monks, heads shaved, naked bodies the color of the ancient walls, skin glistening in the orange light, were lying in the tall grass, splashing in the muddy water of the moat, running up and down the stairs with happy, boyish laughter, and using tall stones, crumpled with age, as impromptu diving boards.

Unseen, I watched them for some time. I did not want to inhibit their spontaneity or dampen their joy. I could still hear their laughter as I re-entered the temple and started back to the motorbike which Noke had parked under a tree.

Returning to my hotel, I changed for dinner. When I explained to the manager that I would be eating at the Hôtel du Temple, he seemed rather disappointed. "We have much better food here than they do at the du Temple," he said. "There they wash out all the goodness and cook everything to death for the tourists who will not eat anything unless it's mush. You will see." He seemed sincerely hurt.

"I'll certainly eat here tomorrow," I assured him.

"I will have something special for you," he said.

Dinner at Madame's was excellent. I had been eating bread and cheese for so long that to have salad with oil and vinegar, fresh-made soup, chicken with potatoes and fresh vegetables, and real ice cream was a joy. The conversation was most exciting. I had revealed my intense desire to know the Cambodian people. My companions at dinner agreed that the Cambodians were certainly worth knowing, that they were warm people with a simple yet profound way of life.

One of the gentlemen present asked if I cared to meet a friend of his who lived on the lake. "Lake people have the true essence of the real Cambodian, untouched by either colonizer or tourist." I was delighted. Arrangements were made for me to bicycle to the lake and I was given a letter to the friend who spoke French fluently.

The next few days I spent with Noke puttering from one great wonder to another. The enchanting Ta Prohm, the mystery of Bayon, the glory of the Terraces of the Leper King and the Elephants — with its immense terraces and galleries topped with the two hundred colossal stone faces of the gods, serene, smiling and at peace whether in a thriving civilization, overrun by the jungle, or the object of the tourist gaze.

I took the long trip to Bantei Serei, the pink temple lost until 1914 from the gaze of man, and to the temples of Beng Mealea, Pheah Kahn and Koh Ker.

Each trip was full of wonder. Noke seemed proud, as if each temple belonged to him personally. He was free to show, reveal, defame or slander if he chose. With a true flare for the dramatic, he took the most glorious approaches through wild dense jungle, stopping here and there to reveal an area which as yet had not been excavated and which, he felt sure, was full of wonders even more fantastic than those we had been viewing.

After a week I set off on a borrowed motorbike along the river from Siem Reap to the lake. The Tonle Sap is a gigantic body of water covering about one-third of the territory of Cambodia. The river was one of the main tributaries. Life along the river was wonderful to watch. Small, well-built shacks with their water wheels, women washing, men and children bathing, vendors — all the things which made up the slow-paced life of the people who knew pretty generally what tomorrow would bring and were not too concerned about it.

I followed the river, as instructed, never leaving the main road. Soon I left the city behind and cycled for what seemed like hours through level brush-swamp country. Finally, in the distance I could see a tiny city of shacks on the shore of the lake. It was late afternoon. The fishing boats had returned and some of the men were working on them, while others were mending nets, large sacks or boxes. Several children came to greet me shouting with joy and puzzlement. The men continued to work, but obviously were aware of my presence. "Monsieur Gilwee?" I asked.

"Làbas," one of the men answered, and the others laughed at his use of French.

By this time a rather short, husky, middle-aged man with a thick crop of black hair hanging over his weathered face was walking toward me.

He spoke in flawless French: "My name is Gilwee."

I told him who had sent me and why and asked if this was a good time for a visit or if I had come in a very busy, inconvenient season.

"Now is always a good time. There is no bad time to welcome friends," he answered.

We moved down a dirt road which followed the shore of the lake. It was lined with small wooden shacks on tall posts that kept them standing high above the water. They all seemed to have only one room with open windows and to contain little furniture.

"Our life here is very simple. We fish, we plant small gardens, and we reap what we sow. When our catch is good we sell to the merchants who come from Siem Reap, but mostly they cheat us and it is not worth the trouble to sell the fish. The fish feed the people here and we must make sure that we do not allow the lake to become barren."

Gilwee's shack was like the others, small and empty, with one large window giving an unobstructed view of the giant lake and the tall masses of pussy willow lining the shore.

"It is truly beautiful, is it not?" It was a statement, not a question. "I hope you can stay for some time. You are very welcome here."

He took me out onto the lake in his small motor-propelled fishing boat. En route, we saw boats at anchor, and endless living. There were women squatted on buoys to wash the children in their arms. They smiled as we passed. Young boys paddled about in the muddy lake like pollywogs. The entire scene was movement.

When we had lost sight of the shore, Gilwee stopped the motor and let the boat float soundlessly in its own ripples. "This is our lake," he said simply. The sun was setting and the colors danced on the calm water. There was no sound except the occasional slap of a wave against the boat's side.

"In such calm it is hard to imagine that this lake becomes a demon during the monsoon. The waves are too high and dangerous for these tiny boats. Sometimes our houses are washed away and we must live together, depending on each other for our very lives. Each year's monsoon seems worse than the year before, but we know it is only our memory which forgets the unpleasant, remembering only moments like this." I sat back in the boat and listened to the silence.

The next few days were mostly spent in watching. I found it amazingly simple to be assimilated by the community. The children followed me everywhere, the men fought to have me in their boats or to invite me to join them at their work. Love and security were as apparent and refreshing as the cool breezes that blew off the lake and the fresh smell of the fish which were unloaded on the dirt road from the tiny boats.

Gilwee explained, "We seem to have nothing, but we have no use for anything more. Nature, when you live so close to her, tells you that there is no reason for things. Things are destroyed in storms and taken away from you. Feelings and knowledge and closeness with God are what we seek, for these are the only things which remain with us even in famine and flood or when all seems lost. We are Buddhists. These are the things we believe."

After a few days, I left. I had become attached to them, and they had enjoyed me. But there was no pain in leaving because somehow these people had been trained to hold on to nothing, for all things eventually must go.

When I returned to Siem Reap, I was already an old friend at the Hôtel de la Paix. The noise had long since ceased to bother me and busy days lulled me to sleep with their rich, vital experiences. The prostitute and her friends were constant dinner companions.

The meals at the La Paix were grand. Each day the manager posted a long list of what was to be served. He always went through the act of asking, "And what would you have today?" At first, I would examine the list carefully and he would announce, "The tripe is excellent today."

"I think I'll have the rabbit."

"I'm sorry but the rabbit is all gone."

"Then I'll have the coq au vin."

"It is gone, too."

"Well, then what do you suggest?"

He would brighten up, "The tripe is excellent."

"Then it will be the tripe."

Soon I understood that the list was a dream, that there was always one dish which one must allow him to suggest and then follow his suggestion. This presented no problem as the food was uniformly delicious.

On my last day, I said goodbye to all of my new friends at the Hôtel de la Paix. We exchanged addresses, then I climbed into the seat behind Noke who looked very sad. I had loved the hotel and felt a deep sense of losing something very real. In spite of the bites which covered my body, the strange nonexistent menu, and the not too efficient clean-up crew, the hotel had real charm, truly French Cambodian: not actually French, yet not Cambodian. It was something like the country, not poor and not rich, but proud, full of life and the love of life.

The little one-shack airport was bustling with tourists. The two or three Cambodian officials checked us through slowly with little concern about complaints and accusations of inefficiency. They were proud and polite, but left no doubt that Angkor was theirs. They could not be shouted at, bought or attacked. This, after all, was their country.

Chapter VI

SAIGON

Man must learn to let go as easily as he grasps or he will find his hands full and his mind empty. Though every hello is the beginning of a goodbye, do not lose heart; for every goodbye may also be the beginning of another hello.

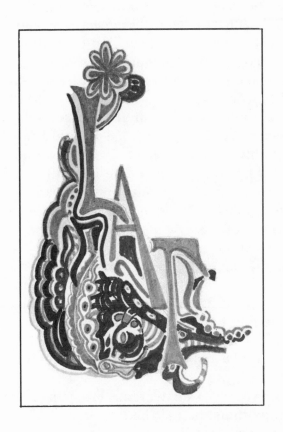

*T*he most fantastic thing about Saigon is its women. Neither Asian nor European, they have the best qualities of both cultures. They are small, well built, slim, graceful, feminine, literate and a joy to be with. Their dress is the most gracious in the world. They wear the ao dai, a tight sheath dress which flows to the ground, usually of a single color, pale blue, pink, green or yellow. A slit from the floor to above the hips allows the front and back panels to fall loosely and **gracefully** about them. Under the dress there is a pair of dark, loose-fitting, pajama-type silk trousers. On their feet they wear high heels. No sight is more lovely than watching one of these small, beautiful women riding on the back of a motor scooter, holding on to her boyfriend with her head tossed back, a smile on her face, hair tied neatly in place, and the tail of her dress flapping loosely behind her in the wind.

Lat was such a girl. I first saw her from a distance as she led four tourists through Saigon's giant zoo, pointing gracefully to this animal and that with the gestures of a dancer. As she approached I could hear the singsong quality of her voice which sounded most pleasant. She was not over five feet tall and weighed no more than ninety pounds. Her hair and eyes were dark; her skin, a golden tan. She seemed to be constantly smiling.

"These are but a few of the Manu birds we have in Vietnam," I heard her say. "The colors are amazing, too, no?" She paused, giving the tourists an opportunity to inspect the birds, then added, "Now we will go to the snake section, perhaps the most interesting collection in Asia." To my surprise, she turned to me. "Have you seen the snake collection? It's just over there," she pointed.

"No, I haven't," I answered. "I'm going there next."

"Come with us, then," she said matter-of-factly. The group moved after her and I followed.

"Are you a tourist?" she asked.

"Yes."

"Alone?" She looked at me with large, almond-shaped eyes. "No tour?"

"No," I answered, "no tour, and, yes, alone."

She led us to the snake section and again began her melodious explanation. When she had finished, she backed away, allowing her group to take a closer look.

"They are beautiful, I think. Most people believe there is nothing so terrible as a reptile, but we grow up with them in Southeast Asia," she said. "Have you ever seen any so large or so colorful?"

"You are not a soldier?" she asked after a moment.

"No," I answered.

"I didn't think you were American at first. Americans seldom travel alone. I thought you must be French or even Italian. Americans here are either soldiers or very old or school teachers. Which are you?"

She did not wait for an answer but turned to her group. "There is a refreshment stand over there and some benches by a lovely lake. Perhaps you would like to rest a few minutes before we go to the temple in the city."

The group seemed eager to comply with her suggestion and sauntered off with familiar dialogue...

"I'm tired!"

"I don't know why I came on this tour, anyway. An animal is an animal."

"She's cute, but it's too damn hot."

"Did you ever see so many god-awful snakes? I hate snakes!"

They vanished in the direction of the refreshment stand.

She turned to me. "My name is Lat. What's yours?"

I told her my name which she had great difficulty pronouncing. When she finally succeeded, she laughed at it. I have never since heard my name spoken so beautifully.

"Will you be long in Vietnam?" she asked.

"I don't think so," I answered. "With the curfew and the travel restrictions there isn't much to keep me here. I'd like to get out into the countryside; I'd like to meet the people, but there is no chance for that now."

"Yes, that is true. There are many restrictions. Some even we do not understand, but some are necessary. There is a war. But there are many things one can do in Saigon, even now."

She asked me many questions, as a child would,

without regard for their personal nature. "What do you do in the United States? Why are you making this trip? Where did you get all the money necessary to travel so much? Are you very rich?"

I explained to her about my profession, told her of my limited bank account and my reason for making the trip. She listened attentively, as if she would later be asked to repeat all she had heard. She accepted everything except the part about my limited resources.

"Americans are all very rich, I know. Sometimes they give me more in tips than my wages for the week. And you must have a great deal of money just to come so far. America is a very long distance from here. With the money for your passage, many Vietnamese could live very happily for a long time."

There was a moment of awkward silence. "I must go now," she said. "I have many things to show my group."

I wanted to see her again, but felt reticent, since I was unfamiliar with Vietnamese protocol. "Can you recommend a good restaurant for French food?" I asked clumsily.

"Yes, many."

"Would it be proper to ask you to dinner?"

"Do you want to ask me?"

"Yes."

"Then it is proper."

"Will you have dinner with me tonight?"

"Yes," she said simply. "Where is your hotel?"

"I'd be happy to pick you up," I said.

"I don't think so," she answered, matter-of-factly. "I'll meet you at your hotel."

I told her the name of the hotel and we agreed to meet at 8:30. "Au revoir," she said, and walked toward her group. I watched as, with great ease, she reassembled them, took the arm of a complaining woman, and started off toward the gate.

I was ready by seven. As it was much too hot to wait in my room, I wandered down onto the hotel veranda. It was crowded with people, mostly military, having their aperitif. They were noisy and seemed carefree. On a raised platform at the foot of the garden, a small orchestra played French songs badly. I ordered a cold drink and sat at the only empty table. It was one of the first times I had worn a tie and coat for quite some time, and I felt hot, uncomfortable and conspicuous.

I was there only a few moments before an American couple approached me. "There doesn't seem to be any room, fella," the man drawled, "can me and the little lady join you for a drink?"

"Sure," I said, and stood up to introduce myself. They were Mr. and Mrs. Condon from Texas. They both ordered Scotch and soda, a most expensive drink in Asia. He drew out a large number of bills. "These piasters sure are a joke!" he said. "We just get used to one kind of money and it's time to start using another. The wife here is the bookkeeper."

"It's nothin'," she said, "you just divide by..." and she continued with a long explanation of how money was converted in each of the countries they had visited. They were on a six week tour which had somehow qualified them as experts on Asia.

"Why most of the places are filthy holes, dirty as hell!" Mr. Condon said. "The people are all crooks and after only one thing — the American dollar. I hate the goddamn place, can't wait to get home. And that damn Calcutta. Did you ever see such a hole? Why the wife and I arrived and left the same day. Didn't even unpack our bags. Just got the hell out!"

"All those poor starving children," Mrs. Condon added sadly. "Why don't they do something? It's terrible! And the beggars! They're so dirty! Thank God for Western hotels! At least there you can have a shower and meet some civilized people."

"There wasn't one nice hotel in Calcutta," Mr. Condon said.

"Yes there was, dear," his wife corrected him with finality, "our agent just couldn't book us there."

The conversation continued in this vein for some time.

Mrs. Condon: "The Taj Mahal was nice but they should spend their money on feeding some of those skinny children."

Mr. Condon: "What they need in these countries is some American know-how and get-up-and-go. I think the whole damn bunch are lazy, and it gripes my behind that they wait for us to give them handouts."

Mrs. Condon: "What's there to buy in Vietnam? I need a million souvenirs to take home. We have to get something for the kids, you know. We have six grandchildren. Show him the pictures, dear."

Mr. Condon: "And everything's so damned expensive here. You can't turn around without having one of those smelly Chinks with his hand out. Terrible!"

Mrs. Condon: "I think the people are awful. There are a few nice ones, I guess, but there isn't one of them who wouldn't profit from a good bath, a bottle of deodorant and a dentist's office."

I was relieved to see Lat walking up the stairs. I stood as she approached. She walked directly to the table. She was wearing the native dress, this time in deep blue. Her hair was loose and down over her back.

"This is Lat," I said, as I did not know her full name. "Mr. and Mrs. Condon." They greeted her pleasantly.

Mr. Condon offered her a drink which she accepted, seating herself at his side.

"You are from Texas," she laughed.

"That's right. How did you know?"

"Oh, I can always tell a man from Texas, he's so big and strong and talks so slow and nice."

I thought I saw Mrs. Condon squirm slightly in her seat.

"Are you from these parts?" she asked Lat.

"Yes, I am Vietnamese. I was born in Saigon." After a moment of silence, Lat spoke again. "Oh, Mrs. Condon, what a beautiful pin. Where did you get it?"

Mrs. Condon beamed, a bit more at ease, "Just a little something I picked up in Bangkok."

"It's lovely."

The conversation became more animated. Lat's presence made even the Condons more palatable. She laughed and listened attentively, from time to time glancing toward me as if she could sense my uneasiness.

"It's so nice to meet the people of the country," Mrs. Condon said. "We haven't had much of a chance. We've got six weeks, and though that's a lot of time, Asia's pretty big."

"Six weeks for all of Asia?" Lat asked. "On a tour?"

"No sirree," Mr. Condon answered, looking proudly at his wife. "We're on our own. No tour for us. All ya do is get herded around like cattle. No, the Mrs. and I decided we'd do it alone. Our travel agent arranges everything for us, of course, hotels, local tours, plane reservations, the works, but we're on our own. They meet us at the airport in each country, of course. We've never seen so damn many markets and temples and historic places in our lives."

"Shall we go, Lat?" I said.

"Oh, won't you have another drink," the Condons pleaded, as though dreading the thought of being faced with another evening alone together.

"We really haven't the time," I said.

"Well, it's sure been nice," Mr. Condon said.

"Yes," Mrs. Condon echoed. "See you again."

We left the veranda in silence. When we reached the street Lat turned to me. "I feel very sorry for them," she said. "Would you like to ask them to join us?"

"I think not," I said, a bit thankful to be away.

"Americans are like children," she said. "I like them very much. They make me feel like a very large mother, and I want to take care of them. The French are very independent. The Germans are forceful and know their own minds. The Italians are very relaxed and enthusiastic and don't much care. But the Americans always need someone!"

The restaurant of Lat's choice was comparable to most on the Champs Elysées in Paris. The decor was French, with the large menu in French and Vietnamese. All the waiters spoke English as well as French and Vietnamese.

The dinner was cooked to perfection and the wine tasted especially fine after so many months. When we were presented with the bill, Lat commented, "You see, you are a wealthy man!" I didn't explain that I could easily live for a week on the cost of this single meal but after several weeks of rice, dahl, chapate, gruel and sushi, it was well worth the expense.

"You would like our Vietnamese food," she said. "It's really very fine."

The night was beginning to cool and we walked down one of the main boulevards, brightly lit and busy with people taking their evening promenades. It was hardly imaginable that somewhere, not far off, a war was raging. Saigon was still "The Paris of the Orient." It was well planned and lovely with long, broad tree-lined streets, busy sidewalks swept clean and well-lit, superbly arranged shop windows. The traffic and crowds were as noisy as those of Paris and almost as plentiful.

"No one even seems aware there is fighting going on," I commented.

"Oh," Lat said, "we are aware. But what would you have us do? I am nineteen years old and I have never known anything but war. It has been going on in one form or another for over twenty-five years. One simply lives. In Saigon, except for the soldiers on leave, occasional bombs or fires and some grumbling, it's the same as ever."

She was silent for a long while. "It is very difficult under our present regime. It is very much disliked, especially by the Buddhists. I am a Catholic, a Christian, so it is easier for me, but for the Buddhists life is unbearable." She looked very seriously at me and continued. "I do not understand politics, but I wonder why your country continues to remain here. Have you seen the bombed palace? My people are trying to say how unhappy they are, but. . . ." her voice trailed off into silence.

"I guess our government thinks you'd prefer this to the Communists," I said.

She looked at me, incredulously. "Communism?" she asked, "for Buddhists and Christians? I think that all we really want is freedom, to eat, some peace. We are all tired of war. We are happy people. I want to dance again before I forget how. I will be an old lady before I can go to another party!" she laughed. "But we are being so serious. I'll take you to something very interesting, a Vietnamese opera."

The opera had already begun. The theater was packed and extremely noisy. The production, half-spoken, half-sung, was more like an operetta. The story was easy to follow, a variation on the usual horse opera in an exotic, royal setting. It had the inevitable villain dressed in black, the very pure heroine and hero in white, the confused parents and abused citizenry, and the corrupt go-between. Action was the most important element. The hero gouged out his eyes within full view of the audience. Blood and cries of anguish were the delights of the evening. Stabbing, torture and brutal murders were all performed with carefully contrived special effects; the more real, gory and gruesome the action, the more delighted and noisy grew the audience, as if they were experiencing some special emotional release. They cheered the hero, hissed the villain, and had a great time.

It was very late when the opera ended. Much to my surprise, Lat asked to be put into a taxi and would not allow me to see her home. She thanked me, promised to call the next day, and sped off into the crowded streets.

The next day I waited for Lat's call, never wandering far from the hotel. I found excuses to wash the clothes which had been accumulating in a plastic bag in my suitcase, to write letters to people who surely must have given me up for dead, and to lie about on my bed and watch the palms on the veranda stand stately still in the heat of the day.

There was no call that day.

That evening I again met the Condons. We had a drink together at their invitation. They had been most intrigued by Lat.

"I only wish I were young and fancy free again," Mr. Condon said.

Mrs. Condon giggled.

"We're going to see Saigon at night tonight. The tour is picking us up at 9:00. 'Course, I don't know what there is to see in Saigon that's worth twenty-five dollars, but at least it's better than sitting around this dump!" Mr. Condon rumbled. "Thank God we leave in the morning. We're off to Cambodia to see some damn place called Angkor Wat. Know the place? Our agent told us we had to see it. What is it, some damn temple?"

I tried my best to explain a bit about Angkor, never taking my eyes off the desk for a possible call.

The night was hot and sultry. When the Condons left, I took a short walk. The street noise seemed especially loud and irritating; the motor scooters, deafening. I was amazed that I had not really noticed them before. I was beginning to find Saigon oppressive.

I returned to the hotel to find a note from Lat. It read simply, "Work did not permit me any free time to see you again. Thank you for the nice evening. Continue to have a good trip. You are really very nice. Return to Saigon after the war. Lat."

A few days later, I left Vietnam.

Chapter VII

BALI

In the Inn of the world
there is room for everyone.
To turn your back on even
one person, for whatever
reason, is to run the risk of
losing the central piece of
your jigsaw puzzle.

I arrived in Bali on the day before Christmas. The bus driver, with a broad, betel nut stained smile, stopped at a fork in the road. He pointed down a narrow paved street. Like most roads in Bali, it cut straight into the dense jungle, only to vanish in heat mist. "Ubud," he said.

I thanked him, shook his hand, waved goodbye to my fellow passengers, and waited as he started the small rickety bus with a loud blast and disappeared down the main road.

The morning was still relatively cool. December was

a good month for Bali, with hot days, balmy nights and long afternoons ending in spectacular, multi-colored sunsets.

From what I had been told in Denpasar, the palace of the Agung was less than an hour's walk down the road. In Asia, distance is measured by time.

I took a firm grip on my suitcase and started out. Brown-skinned Balinese draped in gorgeous batik began to appear from nowhere, carrying bundles of fresh fruit, bottles of various colored liquids, animals in various stages of approaching death, and plump, smiling naked infants. The almond-eyed, bare-breasted young girls moved quickly like ballerinas, while handsome hard-bodied boys, whose skin glistened like deep waxed mahogany, ran and chattered together.

Occasional dirt paths cut their way into the jungle from the narrow road, suggesting the location of small settlements here and there in the brush. Small wooden shacks, partially hidden between bushes on the banks, towered precariously over the road. Crooked stone steps rose to doors which stood open, welcoming the cool early morning darkness.

Houses became more frequent, more people appeared, and soon I approached the center square of Ubud. There, towering over everything in pink beauty was the wall of the palace compound, facing what seemed to be a large open-air assembly area. On the opposite side of the road were several small shops selling wood carvings and the famous paintings of Bali.

The Agung had received a letter from one of his hundreds of relatives throughout the islands of Indonesia and was expecting me. He was a rather jolly, rotund man, dark-skinned, with a friendly smile whose favorite expression, learned while attending school in England, was rather shockingly, "Gee, goodness me!"

"Gee, goodness me," he greeted me, "I knew you

were coming, but I did not know exactly when. Welcome."

Two little boys ran out and attached themselves to his fat legs below the drape of his knee-length sarong. "These are my sons," he said proudly, "and those playing there are also my children. And, gee, goodness me, those women on the veranda are my wives. You will meet them tonight. Tonight we talk."

There was a moment of silence as he detached his children gently from his legs and lifted them affectionately in his arms. "Ratab," he called. "Ratab is my best servant." Ratab appeared dressed in Western-style clothes, all in white. His face was round, dark, alive with dancing eyes, a broad smile, and even, white teeth. Ratab stood staring at me while the Agung continued, "Will you stay here on the palace grounds or will you take one of the cottages on the hill near the river?" He did not wait for my answer but continued, "I have many interesting guests now, an American school teacher on vacation from Sumatra, an Irish painter who came for a week and has been here for seven years, and a very important person from the Consulate in Djakarta. There is still room in the palace. There is no one in the cottages."

"I think I'd like a cottage, if it means no additional trouble."

"Gee, goodness me, no. Ratab will be there with you, to take care of what you may need. It will be good for him, too. It will give him a chance to practice his English. We will send a servant ahead to get the place ready, and Ratab will show you how to get there. It is not too far."

As we started out of the court he called, "Gee, goodness me, come to dinner at seven."

We reached the road and started up the slow incline which led to the cottages. Ratab explained that he was seventeen years old, had a secondary school education and was now studying English in Denpasar. He was neither shy nor aggressive, but had a simple honest quality which was most charming. "You will like the cottages," he said. "I'm happy that you chose to stay there. There are many flowers and birds, and all is green. You get no dust from the road, and at night, when all is quiet, you can hear the song of the river. I stay there only when we have a guest. I am happy that you chose the cottage."

"It's beautiful here," I said. "It's a perfect place to spend Christmas."

"Christmas?" he asked. "What is Christmas?" This was unexpected. I had forgotten that there were many in the world who had never heard of Christianity.

"Christmas is the birthday of the Christian God, Jesus."

Ratab was perhaps the most curious individual I met in all of my travels. Not simply a child-like curiosity but a deep interest obsessed him which was not satisfied until he understood exactly, with no question, what was implied or stated. He would never allow a question in his mind to remain unanswered.

"Who is the Christian God, Jesus?" he asked.

"Like your God, Vishnu. Well, sort of."

So started a rather simple telling of the Christmas story. Until this time, as often as I had heard the story, I had never realized what an exciting, charming and delightfully mystical tale it was. As I spoke, we walked through a dense rain forest of lush ferns, tall tropical trees and shrubs which easily dwarfed us, and flowers which hung everywhere in splashes of orange, yellow, pink, red, all entwined in the deep green of the landscape.

"I hear the river!" I interrupted my tale.

"Yes," Ratab answered. "It flows beneath the rope bridge ahead. But why would not the people allow Mary and Joseph to share their bed?"

I explained that neither Mary nor Joseph knew anyone in Bethlehem. This did not seem to make any difference to Ratab who insisted that someone should have made room for them in their bed.

"But they did not know that Mary was to give birth to their God, Jesus."

"That is not important," Ratab insisted matter-of-factly. "If Mary was traveling, if she was going to have a child, what matter if it were God or not? They should have given her a place to rest." There was certainly no arguing with this statement and I realized that there were some things I would never be able to explain to Ratab. I changed the subject, telling him about the significance of the Christmas tree. He was delighted with the idea and the giving of gifts, and laughed at the thought of a "jolly old Santa Claus," though I was not quite able to explain the connection between Santa Claus and the God, Jesus, to his satisfaction. "Why does not Santa Claus dress as Jesus?" he asked.

In a few moments we had come to a steep gorge, green and rich with color. At the bottom rushed a clear river, purring its way over and around rocks of odd shapes and sizes.

"This is our river," Ratab said. "It is a most sacred river because all our ancestors are buried here and their remains flow in the stream. We bathe here each day. You must bathe with us."

We crossed over the shaky rope bridge. Below were groups of naked people, splashing happily in the river, washing their sarongs or drying their brown bodies in the warm sun.

"Tell me of the snow in Bethlehem," Ratab said suddenly. "Of what use is snow? And then you must explain why they would not let Mary and Joseph stay at the inn."

After crossing the bridge, we made a sharp turn to our right and down a steep stairway. There, in a natural garden of grass and flowers, stood four square, thatch-roofed cottages.

"You must take the top cottage," Ratab told me. "From it you can see the mountains, the river, the valley and the sky."

Each cottage had a large living area covered with palm branches and open to the jungle. The bedroom was half as large, with wall-length, pull-up shutters and a small Western-style bed. The bathroom had a cesspool and a stone sink into which fresh water was poured daily for washing. The water was carried up from the river. All about the rooms were small oil lamps made of clay. The hard dirt floor was swept clean.

It was now shortly after noon. The sun was hot, but pleasant. Ratab went off for awhile to send the house-boy for food. The Christmas story had made a great impression on him. He accepted it without question except for the fact that Mary had been denied lodging. "Certainly, two persons do not take very much space. It is very strange, indeed."

I looked out into the afternoon. The sun's rays pierced through leaves and flowers livening each one with design and color.

When Ratab returned he was followed by a tall, thin young man with shy and downcast eyes. His brown body of drawn muscle and bone was partially covered with a fading batik loin cloth. His long legs were straight and muscular. He carried a tray covered with small dishes of exotic foods, which he set before me. Then, he left without a word.

Ratab sat beside me and explained each dish as I ate the subtle tasting, savory mixtures. Now and again one could hear the sound of footsteps and laughter as the natives walked down the cliff on their way to the river. Some paused to look at us, seemingly delighted that one of the cottages was again occupied.

When I finished eating, Ratab said, "Now you must rest. Later, I will take you to bathe. If you want anything, call Adja. He will be here with you all the time, night and day." He had no sooner said this when Adja appeared to remove the tray he had brought. He did not raise his eyes as we were introduced.

I stripped and climbed into the bed. From a reclining position I could see the tops of the tall palms, some orange and purple bougainvillea, the fluffy edge of a very white cloud, and the blue sky. As the heat became more intense, the afternoon awakened all at once with the myriad sounds of life in Bali: the buzz of the insects, the murmur and splash of the river, soft footsteps, voices, and laughter. Adja entered silently and lowered the shutters. I fell asleep instantly.

It was late afternoon when Ratab awakened me. It was still hot and my sheets were wet with perspiration. "It is time to bathe," he said. He carried a patterned batik which he helped me tie around my body.

The path down along the cliff to the river was only wide enough for one person to move along, with caution. It was patted firm by the many hard-soled bare feet that mounted and descended each day. Ferns and flowers bordered it, hanging gently just out of reach.

What before had been the constant sibilant sound of the river became a roar as we descended into the gorge. From above, the river had seemed narrow and gracefully bouncy, but at close view it revealed its rushing strength. In some places the water was clear enough for us to discern the stone bottom; in others the river floor vanished in foam and deep color. Clever damming created the bathing areas. A group of men in various bathing postures, tanned and hardened by the sun and streaked with soap foam, greeted us as we reached the river. Ratab pointed to a clear spot on a large rock. "Here," he said. We stripped and under the curious eyes of the other bathers plunged into the cold water. The initial shock brought the usual reaction causing the others to laugh, relax, and resume what they were doing before our arrival.

When we had soaped and bathed and were lying in the sun to dry, the group assembled about Ratab with expressions that seemed to ask, "Well, who is this strange white man?" Ratab explained with understandable gestures that I was staying in the cottage on the hill as the guest of the Agung, and that I was from far-off America. One by one they glanced sideways at me, my smile meeting theirs in a language of its own.

Through Ratab we all learned a few simple facts about each other: I was a professor from America, one was a painter, another made wood carvings, others worked their fathers' rice fields, and so on. As our initial strangeness wore off, we each found our own language to tell our story.

"House." "Your." "There."

"Water." "Cold." "Nice."

"This rock better, smoother."

"Sun warmer here."

"Come, lie with us here."

Soon I was surrounded by naked, shining bodies, by lips murmuring in a strange wondrous language, and by smiles rivaling each other for warmth and beauty.

Calmly Ratab began to talk. He was obviously telling them something which meant a great deal to him. The group was intent on every word. I found myself listening along with the others. Every now and then I seemed to hear, "Jesus," "Mary," "Bethlehem," and it became clear that he was telling them the Christmas story. I lay back and closed my eyes, lulled by the sounds of the lilting language.

We all left the river together, walking up the path directly toward the setting sun. As it dropped into the trees, it seemed to cling to a group of drooping palm leaves, then reluctantly release them and dip out of sight behind the rain forest, leaving the sky a hundred colors. I said goodbye to the group at my cottage door and stood listening to their laughter and watching them as they scaled the last small incline and vanished into the sunset. Ratab said he would return in a few hours to escort me to the palace for dinner.

As I dressed that evening I seemed to hear a soft moan, or was it a strange weeping? I walked out into the dusk. The cry seemed to be coming from the dense rain forest across the river where there was certainly no human habitation. At first I felt sure that it must be the breeze which had suddenly come up, but then it sounded too human, too desperate. Night came suddenly with a deep purpleness which covered everything. I only then realized that the oil lamps in the cottage were lit. I had neither seen nor heard Adja though obviously he was very much present. Entering the bedroom I found him lighting another small lamp.

The weeping sound seemed even louder now. I took Adja by the arm and pointed toward the sound in the blackness. He did not immediately understand, but after a moment he nodded. Then, for the first time he spoke. His voice was at once excited and animated. Of course, I understood nothing. Upon finishing his complicated explanation, which he assumed I understood, he took me into the bathroom and showed me the clear water he had carried from the river for my shave.

Shortly Ratab arrived, dressed in a richly-colored sarong. His dark hair was partly hidden under a small two-cornered hat of red silk. His chest was bare, broad and smooth. He carried a small oil lamp to light our way to the palace. We crossed the footbridge in silence. The night noises were overpowering. The river's voice sounded clear and constant although the river could not be seen. I wondered about the moan which was no longer audible, but I did not want to disturb the night mood with my questions.

The Agung was silhouetted in the palace entrance when we arrived. He seemed younger.

"Gee, goodness me," he said. "You have come at last. It is the birthday of my youngest son. They are waiting for us." He took my arm and led me through the small, dimly lit square and into a cluster of trees and flowers.

"Ratab told me that you related the Christmas story to him. Yes, it will be Christmas. I have ordered a Christmas dinner for you. You seem to have won over the young men of the village. You will find them very sincere and very good. I am happy that you want to know them."

We entered another court, typical of the inner courtyards in Balinese homes, surrounded by tall walls and containing several small structures — huts, a place of worship, and studios. In the rear of the compound was a small elevated stage. Informally seated about it were all of the Agung's children, twenty or more, and several beautiful women. On the platform were an old priest, a woman and the birthday child.

The Agung mounted the platform, kissed the child, and sat on a large chair. He insisted that I follow him and sit next to him in a place of honor. The ceremony was short and consisted mostly of sharing an odd tasting drink and murmuring a short prayer. This was followed by much rejoicing on the part of the children and by the eating of wondrous sweets and savory fruits.

A large white sheet was then stretched across the platform and after everyone had gathered before it, a puppeteer worked behind it treating us to a fantastic shadow play. The story was simple and required only a word or two of explanation. The Agung was delighted that I was acquainted with the Ramayana, as it was an episode of this epic which was being produced. For about fifteen minutes Rama battled the forces of evil with those of good, and the children watched entranced as he succeeded. The puppeteer supplied all the voices and manipulated the various graceful, grotesque puppets with ease.

The Agung rose when the performance was over. "You must see the truly great stories done by the master." He smiled to the assembled group. A child ran to the Agung to be picked up and hugged to his bare shoulder. "Gee, goodness me," he said, handing the child to one of the women. "Let us go to dinner."

We walked back to the palace dining room which was lit with oil lamps of great beauty. There, on a large round table were more than twenty dishes with a large, crackly suckling pig in the center. The odors were fantastic. Seated on cushions around the table were the other guests. The American school teacher was about thirty years old and wore Balinese dress. He was obviously trying hard to appear Indonesian. The Irish painter had a long, straggly beard, spoke with a brogue and smiled deeply and calmly as if he had achieved some secret insight from his seven years in Bali. Only the Indonesian dignitary from the Consulate was in Western-style clothing and seemed strangely out of place in the group.

When the introductions were over I was seated on a pillow at the table and two graceful women silently began to serve us. The Agung cut the pig, taking great pains to see that each of us had his share of the crackling skin. Each dish was elegant: fish, vegetables, rice, fowl, fruit.

After the dinner, the group relaxed on their pillows and the conversation started. The Agung's participation revealed his facility with the English language, his keen wit, his clear mind and his exciting ideas about life.

"Here in Bali things have not changed as in other

parts of Indonesia. Somehow we continue to live as we please. It is true there is some hunger and poverty, but this is not a new condition among our people. We have learned to live with nature. We are a people who love happiness. We need little: we dance, we play our music, we work. Art comes easily in Bali, for all is art, and the search for beauty is not difficult. It is everywhere. Beauty is our way of life. If you say, 'growl not, stomach, there is nothing to put in thee,' long enough, the stomach learns and growls less. In Ubud we are better off than most, for we are a colony of artists. My people are painters and dancers and wood carvers. Tourists come to look. We show them our beauty. We have changed our painting in some cases to suit their taste. Therefore we have to some small extent compromised with the rest of the world. But compromise enables us to eat, sleep and live as we please. We are a superstitious people. We are affectionate without being passionate. We are strong without forgetting how to be dependent. We are proud without losing sight of the strength in being humble. I hope," he said to me, "that you will stay long enough to know us."

The evening passed too quickly. Ratab came out of the nowhere into which he had disappeared carrying another oil lamp.

"Ah, how quickly time passes. It is time for us to go already," the Agung said as he rose and rubbed his round belly. "Merry Christmas to you all, and to all a good night."

"Is that not Charles Dickens?" he laughed.

The night had become lighter. The sky was filled with stars. We returned to the cottage in silence. Ratab put his arm warmly about my shoulders and held the lamp before us. "It is a beautiful Christmas night," he said. When we reached the incline, Ratab preceded me down the side and helped me toward the cottage. In the doorway stood a banana tree which had been trimmed into the shape of a pine tree. On each branch were tied several flowers of assorted colors and scattered about the tree were small clay oil lamps like tiny stars. "Your Christmas tree," he said simply.

I stood in the darkness before the tree. The lamp lights flickered slightly in the warm breeze. My eyes welled with tears. Ratab watched me closely. Assuming this was the tradition he mustered tears and joined me in a good cry. After some time we entered the cottage. The room was crowded with some of the same boys I had bathed with and others I had not seen before. Each, Ratab indicated, had brought me a Christmas present, bananas, coconuts, papayas, pieces of batik, paintings and even oil lamps of various shapes and sizes.

I sat on the floor among them, and the conversation never stopped. They all wanted to hear the story of Christmas from me. With Ratab translating, no more flowery presentation was ever made. When the story was told, I passed the fruit and, while they were eating, went into the bedroom. What did I have to give them? I had so little with me. I took everything that I could give away from the suitcase, my T-shirts, briefs, shirts, socks, no matter what — it was the spirit. They were all delighted with their gifts and discarded their elaborate batiks to put on jockey shorts and T-shirts, all too large for their slim bodies. They began to dance and sing and were pleased when I joined them.

In the midst of all the laughter the sounds from across the river could again be heard. This time I felt sure the sound was a human weeping.

"What is that, Ratab?" I asked.

"Oh, it is the spirits," he said simply. "Bali has many spirits. The forest is full of them. They are everywhere. The spirit you hear is a very sad one. They say that he was Dutch and that he loved a girl from Ubud and was killed in the war. The girl leaped from this very cliff into the sacred river, so she too has never died. Do not have fear. Spirits who love, do no harm. Bali is a land of spirits."

The festivity continued for a while and then Ratab announced that I must be tired and that it was time for sleep. Then he explained that several of the guests had asked for the honor of staying overnight.

"When you have made a new friend," he explained, "it is bad manners to leave him." The bed was small but Ratab picked six of the guests to join me. They put me in the middle and arranged their bodies about me. Like joyfully exhausted children they fell asleep instantly: one holding my hand, another with his head on my shoulder, another with his leg over mine.

I stared up at the thatched roof and listened to the even breathing of my bed partners. The light of a single oil lamp danced about the room. Outside the Christmas tree glittered beneath the stars.

Ratab, who had taken the place of honor at my side, slid his arm under my head. "I still don't understand why they could not make room for Mary."

After a moment of silence he said, "Well, Merry Christmas," and fell asleep.

Chapter VIII

CEYLON

Happiness, for man, has its own measure, though beauty and riches can often tip the scale.

*T*he buses streamed in until the large square overlooking the lake in Kandy was completely
congested. Dark, dhoti-clad worshippers, some
with painted faces, walked toward the Temple of the
Tooth. Gaily colored elephants in festive regalia
swayed clumsily along the shore of the lake. Chants
were already arising from the large temple where
thousands of worshippers had come to prostrate
themselves before the Sacred Tooth of the Great
Buddha.

The large hall just outside the ornately decorated
sanctum sanctorum where the Tooth was housed was
completely filled with bare-chested, sweaty bodies:
kneeling, sitting, lying, standing in wait.

Flowers were everywhere and each worshipper carried at least a handful of brightly colored flower petals. Many had leis strung around their necks and wrists and blossoms between their toes.

The women in the group wore their best saris, often of brightly colored silk which glistened in the light with indefinable color, like a magician's handkerchief which changes to red, blue, green, before your eyes.

Noise and activity dominated the scene: the unintelligible instructions shouted over blaring microphones to the oblivious mass, the chants of the worshippers, the shouts of the members of the press, and the screams of young boys scrambling through the crowds or over the temple walls like small, agile lizards.

Saffron-robed priests, unmoved by the rising excitement, proceeded toward the temple gates at an even gait, each chanting and praying as if he were alone in the vast square.

The intoxicating odors of burning woods and incense together with their light smoke added a misty haze which gave the scene the aura of pre-dawn light.

The ceremony continued throughout the day. People pushed impatiently in every direction through the assembled worshippers, in long lines forming snake-like patterns of bodies in the crowd. Each person was finally admitted into the holy room in noisy procession. As each entered he threw his petals on the golden altar, hesitated a moment for prayer, and was impatiently pushed out by those behind him. There was time for a quick look at the Holy Relic on its tray of gold, then in an instant one was out of the temple, down the stairs, and back among the thousands still waiting in the square.

By dusk everyone had seen and prayed before the Sacred Tooth of Buddha, and all crowded back on their buses which moved slowly as they had come, back over the jungle road to Colombo or another village along the way.

By moonrise, the tiny city by the lake was again submerged in the stillness of the surrounding mountainous jungle, the moon shadows and the warm breeze.

That had been my first day in Kandy. I had arrived by train the day before expressly for the ceremony. I met Mano on the ramp in Colombo, perhaps the most handsome boy I had seen in Asia: features dark and perfect, a combination of well-shaped lips, heavy black brows and hair, and large, almond eyes set apart by a sensitive nose. His skin was a light, smooth chocolate brown with a dash of color over his cheeks. His body was slim, strong and agile. He spoke clearly and distinctly.

"How do you find my country?" he asked me in lieu of formal introduction.

"I really don't know yet," I answered. "I've been here only a few days and I understand one can't judge Ceylon by Colombo."

"Oh, I agree," he smiled. "Wait until you see Kandy, I am sure you will find it enchanting. I was born there. My name is Mano Sahayam. Are you going to the Ceremony of the Tooth?"

"Yes."

"I, too, am going. These are our holidays from school."

"Are you at the University?"

"Yes, in law. That is the field my parents have chosen for me. I have no interest in law."

The train pulled up to the platform.

"Do you have a third class ticket?" he asked.

"No, mine is for second."

"Well," he said, "they will allow you to sit in third class with a second class ticket. Come with me." He took my suitcase and we boarded a large car, clearly marked "Third Class." To my suprise, it was the newest and most well-equipped of the train's cars. The seats were soft and luxurious and situated so that one could get the maximum view through large, tinted windows.

"This is the most beautiful third-class car I have seen in my travels," I commented. "Are they all like this?"

He laughed. "Indeed, no. Look at first class over there. It is terrible — old, worn, and ready to crumble. This car is a gift from the People's Republic of China to the people of Ceylon. It is one of many given expressly for our workers who must otherwise ride in third-class filth." He waited for my expression and reaction.

"A very clever bit of propaganda, indeed," he said for me. "The Americans have given us a great deal more, but I don't think the people who ride these trains have ever seen a thing from you which they could really understand. American aid has become a joke in Ceylon. You built a gigantic dam which has been abandoned dry. I forget how many thousands of dollars it cost. You assume that our needs are like yours, a rather silly assumption."

"I hope," Mano added suddenly, "that I do not offend you, speaking this way. The Americans I have met always speak freely."

I smiled.

He was pleased and continued to talk.

"We have come a long way in Ceylon, but we must go our own way. I don't believe we are ready for democracy in the American sense, at least not as I understand it. The British governed us like infants and left us as children. We are now seeking to find who we are. We are not sure who we are or where we want to be. When we find out, then we can make a choice. My father is a conservative. I am, perhaps, more of a socialist."

Thanks to Mano, the train trip was informative and

delightful. As we neared Kandy he asked, "Where will you stay? You are a professor and can stay at the University. It is vacation time and there is much room. The food is terrible, but you can come to my home for meals."

There was a small university station before the train arrived in Kandy. We left the train there and walked a short distance to the campus. It was simple for Mano to arrange a room for me in one of the large dormitories, mostly vacant due to the recess.

Mano left me in the hands of several students who seemed more than eager to assume the responsibility and left for home on a borrowed scooter.

Life at the University was like that on any campus during a vacation period: quiet, deserted, with few students who appeared only for meals. Food was served family-style at communal tables — a few simple curry dishes accompanying mountains of steamed rice.

About sundown, Mano arrived with his usual smile. "I have my father's car. You are cordially invited to dinner."

It had rained that afternoon and everything shone, washed and fresh. The lake and the rain forest in the distance reflected the hues of the multi-colored sunset as we drove up the hill leading to Mano's home.

"The main part of the city is there," Mano pointed. "All roads lead to the temple. There, beyond the residential section, the jungle begins. There, you'll find the elephant baths. Have you been on an elephant yet?"

Mano's father was very sophisticated, handsome like his son, and spoke clipped British English. His mother and two sisters, all wearing saris, resembled each other with large eyes, deep olive skin and soft smiles.

"We are very happy to have you here," the father said, "my son told us about you. I, too, am an educator. I run a private school for several hundred children.

Our home is part of the school which extends back for several meters. It is a pity that school is not in session or you could visit. We are on the British system, of course, and..." he continued.

Dinner was served. The food was hotly seasoned, but varied and delicious. The conversation at dinner mostly concerned Mano, and the problems he posed for the family. The parents felt that it was time for him to marry and settle down to raise a family. They had already chosen the girl whom I was to meet later. She was from a good family, was highly educated, and had a fine dowry. Mano was objecting, they said, though all during dinner he said not a word.

When the meal was over we moved into the living room for coffee and shortly Mano's bride-to-be arrived with her parents. She was a very young girl, not over thirteen. Her body was small and shapeless within her neatly folded sari.

Mano did not say ten words the entire evening, nor did he once look at his chosen bride. Later, in the car, he said anxiously, "We are not living in the days when people could be bought and sold. I will not marry that tiny nothing!"

We drove in silence for some time. Finally he added, "I love someone else."

We stopped in front of a two-story white structure with a long stairway rising across the front to a second level.

"Come," he said.

We climbed the stairs to a large porch where Mano let himself into the house without even a knock. There were four attractive young people in the room, three girls and a boy, who all greeted Mano enthusiastically.

"We heard you were home."

"When did you return?"

"How long will you stay?"

Mano answered their questions briefly, then

introduced me to the group. They all spoke excellent English.

One of the girls, fairer and taller than the others, wore a bright, orange sari. Her hair fell in a long dark braid over her back. Her manner was carefree and her smile warm and pleasant. Her name was Silva. It was instantly apparent that she was Mano's girl.

Within minutes the young people were engaged in animated conversation which led to dancing to precious records by Elvis Presley. They were enraptured by his garbled speech which they asked me to translate.

Several hours later, Mano drove me back to the University. He spoke eagerly of Silva. "She's an Indian, not Ceylonese. She works as a receptionist at our best hotel in Kandy. Her family lives in Colombo."

"Indians," he continued, "are looked down upon in Ceylon as an inferior race, without education or sophistication. They are mostly servants. My family would not speak to anyone of Silva's class and would certainly never consent to our marriage." He fell silent like any hapless lover.

I saw Mano with Silva often. They were delightful together. Their relationship was never discussed. They were always relaxed and full of fun. Together we took trips to the lush highlands and tea plantations of Nuwara Eliya, to Pulanerua and to Anuradhapura, where we sat under the ancient banyan tree beneath which Buddha had contemplated.

During these trips I met some delightful people. One was a young waiter who took great pride in showing me his daily gift to the Great Buddha. Each day he offered a small glass of precious Coca Cola, placing it with great care before the special altar decorated with sacred pictures, tiny candles and flowers in the tiny closet-like room he called his own. Another was a baker who worked in primitive splendor before a giant fire-lit oven making bread fit for the best tables in Europe; yet another was an American Peace Corps volunteer with a severely infected leg he did not wish to report because it might take him away from his work in a tiny rural school.

Silva enchanted everyone she met. She was vivacious, charming, intelligent and helpful. She was, indeed, as precious as Mano considered her.

One afternoon, when we were alone, she confided, "Mano is a very unhappy boy — spoiled, too. Nice, of course, and pretty, but spoiled. He wants to marry against his parents' wishes, you know, but he fears being disinherited. His family sees me as unworthy. They are trying to preserve a custom which is fast vanishing from Ceylon. Mano knows this, but he is weak. He wants me, but not enough. He will marry the little one, you will see."

On the day before I was to leave Kandy, we went to the elephant bath. The road leading to the bath was partly paved, winding through the jungle for about three miles. Here, near a large muddy bank, stood several elephants. Some were stomach-high in the stream, others considering whether to brave the stream's rush, while others, prodded about by boys with huge sticks, moved slowly along the bank. Each, in his turn, was urged roughly into the stream until he had his fill.

We returned part way to Kandy by elephant. I wore only walking shorts affording no protection between my legs and the elephant except his coarse, hairy, moist, rough, hot skin. He slid about under me like a large mold of warm jello: a uniquely unpleasant experience.

Regretfully I left Mano, his family and Silva to their common dilemma and returning to Colombo moved into the Y.M.B.A. (Young Men's Buddhist Association) in the center of the city. From my window I could see the busy harbor. Several times each day the silence was broken by the sound of jets roaring into the airport several miles away. It was rather a jolt, for during my few weeks in Ceylon, I had viewed the most primitive and the most modern — from primitive medicine man to modern jet age technology — within a very small area.

Mano drove to Kandy for my departure. Before I left he said bravely, "I shall marry Silva and you will be our best man."

I was touched. I thought of the enormous changes taking place in his country, changes in attitudes, feelings, and visions of the future. Perhaps with time, I thought, even the fulfillment of Mano's wish was possible.

Chapter IX

SOUTHERN INDIA

Pride and impatience in
man may not be virtues,
but sometimes there is a
certain beauty in both.

KASHMIR

PROF GUPTA

MALABAR

CEYLON

*T*hose who have known only the India of the north have not known India. One must wander the streets of Tiruchirappalli, watch the sun rise and set over the sea at Cape Comorin, experience a Madras bazaar, talk with student groups in Trivandrum, stroll the beautiful esplanade of Ernakulum, paddle the canals of Cochin or spend some time in the giant temple of Madura. Then go north and you may get a feel for this great subcontinent." His eyes sparkled with pride. Although his words sounded like those of a travel folder, I could not help feeling his enthusiasm and deep concern for my well-being.

When my plane from Ceylon landed in Tiruchirappalli, I was the only tourist in the group. During the confusion of customs inspection, I was given some advice by a young man, Mr. Matriam, a Southern Indian. "There are many things about staying in India." he told me, "that you should be prepared for before you set out alone. In the first place, it is like no other country in the world. The way of life is different, the philosophy is unique, the food and clothing, even your accommodations will be a new experience. Prepare yourself."

"Station rest houses are comfortable and convenient," he continued. "They are very inexpensive, too. Trains are the best means of transportation, though buses are fine."

We went together by bus as far as the train station where he left me, explaining that he was continuing to Madras on a later train.

The station faced the square and was surrounded by shops and small offices. The building had two levels with the train platform, luggage and mail rooms below while several small guest rooms, a restaurant and the hostel office were located on the level above. The woman in charge of rooms seemed quite impatient and abrupt. I later learned that this was merely the voice quality and manner of the Indian. She briefly surveyed her reservation list and said, "I have a double room. You must be prepared to share it, if you plan to stay longer than two days."

The room was narrow and very long with windows at each end. The rear windows overlooked the train tracks and those at the front looked onto the square. It was a clean room. The beds had sheets and were covered by neatly patched mosquito netting. Not far from the room, on a small porch, were a toilet and shower. In all, it was as I had been told; not luxurious, very clean, pleasant and certainly not expensive.

The city, Tiruchirappalli, is referred to, even by

some Indians, as the "cesspool." It owes its infamy to over-population, dirty streets, lack of water, unbearable heat, poor sanitation and the prevalence of disease. I was prepared for the worst when I left my room and walked toward the central part of town.

By evening, I had strolled the length and breadth of the city. It was true that the roads were mostly unpaved and dusty, that the heat was intense, that people and animals defecated in the streets, that everything was dry, that odors were pungent and rank, and that insects were everywhere. But there was also a contagious excitement that permeated the atmosphere and tempted me to look beyond such depressing externals.

The center of the city, before the temple, was the focus of excitement. Here, one could find everything at any time of the day or night. The temple entrance was through a high red and white wall. Men were dressed in the Indian dhoti, a white cloth wrapped loosely around the body and tied at the waist. Feet and trunks were bare, bodies strong and black. The women wore saris of orange, red, green, purple, white, some of dull, faded cotton showing many washings in muddy river water. Others wore crisp silk that swished and crackled with each movement. Fingers, toes and arms were covered with rings, ringlets, bracelets, armlets, anklets; all jingled and jangled with every movement.

The children were mostly naked and ran freely through the crowds, joyful and unafraid. Animals were everywhere — sacred cows, decorated red, white, green; elephants with faces painted like happy clowns; goats; chickens; frisky, mischievous monkeys; and stately, disinterested bulls. As at a flower festival, men had leis about their necks and women wore them in their hair. Like animated centerpeices, vendors were seated in their stands surrounded by fresh fruit. They wore blossoms in their heavily greased dark hair and between each toe. Long garlands of blooms hung in batches like rainbows at the temple entrance.

The temple itself rose like a medieval fort, visible from every point within the city and from far off into the vast deserts which surrounded it. It was carved from and built into a massive rock, hollowed into levels joined by a single, steep stairway through the center. Each floor had its cool room of stone: one dominated by a huge carving of the dancing, multi-armed Krishna with a wise, smiling face; another by the God-elephant holding a nude female figure on his knee; a third by Krishna again, depicted this time as a voluptuous woman with firm breasts and shapely body. Above this level there was still another room crowded with noisy worshippers where a group of musicians sat cross-legged on a stone altar, playing beautiful but strangely dissonant music.

There were several smaller chambers, too, all filled with people reciting repetitive incantations or chanting prayers before a caged phallus or carved statue.

There was little inhibition, abstraction or refinement in the style of worship. It was personal and human, each man busily seeking salvation in his own way, through one of the innumerable sects, cults and philosophies which comprise modern Hinduism. They prayed or performed the necessary exercises loudly, with passion and a childlike trust in what they were doing. Their religious path, as their God, was comprehensible to them: full of human frailty, some humor, and inevitable pain and desire. After all, was not Vishnu often found as a man? And certainly Shiva, the God of demons, was never reluctant to enjoy human favors.

The activities of the temple seemed to me like India herself: individual, real, beautiful, sensual, colorful and mystical. The Indian learned early from his scriptures that life would pass and that life's only reality was the illusion that it existed. It was his role to accept life as illusion, to lose himself as simply a man among men. Everywhere there was evidence of the vitality of this belief.

My head was spinning with the color and confusion and wonder of Tiruchi. When I returned to the hostel that evening I found a note, very formally written, from a Professor Gupta who was interested in making my acquaintance.

After dinner, I followed his written directions, given so precisely, to a small college on the outskirts of the city. I asked for Professor Gupta. After some time an extremely overweight, very dark, middle-aged man appeared. He was dressed with a Western-style coat and tie even in the evening's oppressive heat. "I am Professor Gupta," he said, extending a pudgy hand. As I took it I felt rings on all but two fingers and a palm clammy and wet with perspiration. "I was told of your arrival by Mr. Matriam, the young gentleman you met at the airport." He spoke formally, in an American style of speech rather than the usual English of his countrymen with its British accent.

He ushered me into his small office, turned on the overhead fan, and motioned for me to be seated. Dropping his large frame into his desk chair with rather a thump he added, "I'm a professor here but my home is in Madras. I was educated in America, of course, as you can tell from my accent. I'm always interested in any Americans who come through Tiruchi. They are so very few." He spoke as if he were reciting a memorized speech.

He patted his forehead gently with a large white handkerchief, folded it neatly and replaced it in his pocket with much effort. "It's damn hot this evening! This place can be deadly. Only insects thrive on the conveniences of this city. A cesspool! Would you like a short walk?"

"Yes, very much." I was not sure I liked Mr. Gupta. He seemed distant, formal, cold. After all, he had requested the meeting; yet he seemed almost annoyed by having to entertain me, as if I were an added inconvenience. Each movement pained him in some way.

It was not much cooler outside than in his office. The streets of Tiruchi were now brightly lit, still crowded and noisier than ever. It was obviously time for food. For a few rupees one could buy rice and curry or some delectable candy made from coconut and honey and wrapped neatly in leaves, ground ices sweetened and made colorful with artificial flavors, freshly squeezed juice of sugar cane, or, of course, betel nuts.

Mr. Gupta saw all these things as additional personal annoyances: the cane squeezer crowded the sidewalk, the cooked coconut smelled rancid, the sight of the curry made him ill, and the ground ices were surely lethal.

"My major field is American literature. I am something of an expert on Whitman, Emerson, Melville and Thoreau. Of course, I know the minor authors such as Hemingway and Steinbeck, but I feel that modern American literature has not had a single important person since Twain, don't you agree?" He never afforded me an opportunity to answer. "Just people who satisfy themselves with badly written, best-selling trash about perverted sex," he grumbled as he plodded along the dusty road. "I suppose you find Tiruchi rather disgusting?" he added.

"Not at all," I assured him, "I find it exciting. Fascinating. I've never seen anything like it. A bit mystifying."

"Like a strange animal in a zoo?"

His remark caught me off guard. "I like it here," I said at last, not trying to hide my annoyance. "I came here because I wanted to experience India."

"Frankly, I can't understand anyone coming here of his own free will. I find this city depressing." He reached for his handkerchief but did not use it. Instead, he nervously replaced it in his pocket.

"I spent the day in the temple," I told him, changing the subject. "I don't know when I've seen such feeling for life. So much color and joy. I don't find the city depressing at all."

"The heat is depressing, the dirt is depressing, the people are depressing. I can't speak for the temple as I've never been in it myself." He said this so condescendingly that had he not been serious I would have thought that he was trying to be amusing, like a cynical character from an Oscar Wilde play.

"I could understand someone visiting Madras, Mysore, Bangalore, perhaps even Cochin if the weather were favorable, but what can one possibly find here? I can only suspect that you came to be amused by staring at the natives."

Suddenly he stopped, sighed deeply and said, "I'm parched; I must have a cup of tea. I know a place where we might risk a cup of tea. Tea is boiled, you know — clean. My dear Doctor, I fear you must learn to forgive these primitive conditions if you plan to spend any length of time in Southern India."

We entered the tea shop and sat at a small wooden table. The waiter, a thin, dark boy, came immediately.

"Cha," Mr. Gupta pronounced distinctly, adding several specific instructions which I was unable to understand. His tone was disdainful, firm. "You must instruct these people precisely. So stupid, you know."

He stared at his hands, fingering his rings with pudgy fingers as he spoke. "So, my dear Doctor, you are planning an extensive trip through mysterious India. Well, I hope you find what you are seeking. And I am still wondering what that might be."

"Well," I started, but he did not allow me to finish.

"The temple at Madura. That is really quite lovely, but now the fools are painting the damn thing like a Christmas tree. Finally it will look like nothing less than a giant pyramid of circus characters. Pearls to swine!" he said, "Pearls to swine! Madras is lovely, but the sea makes any place bearable, isn't that right?" The tea came. The waiter placed it before us cautiously and left.

"Well at least they make a decent cup of tea here," he sighed.

When I left Gupta that evening, I was angry and did not care ever to see him again, so I was surprised when he invited me to join him the next morning on a trip to visit the Temple of the Bull in Tanjore.

"I shall try to get a car," he said, "but we may be required to take the blasted bus." He did not wait for my reply, but forced a smile, extended his sweaty, fat hand and said in his best Western American manner, "So long! See you tomorrow," and, with great effort, plodded off down the dirt road toward the college, mopping his forehead continuously and grumbling.

I hoped he would not come in the morning. I tried to think of several excuses not to go but when he arrived, sweating and puffing, it was impossible to reject him. He was very apologetic for being unable to get a car. "We shall have to take that damn bus," he said.

Actually the bus was rather pleasant. It was overcrowded but we had seats and with the warm air blowing on our faces through open windows, it was not too uncomfortable. I was relieved to find Gupta not as talkative as he had been during our previous meeting, which afforded me the pleasure of watching rural Indian life without caustic comment.

We passed mile after mile of parched earth, where not even a weed seemed to grow. Animals whose skin sagged over sharp bones and whose frothy mouths attested to their need for food and water, stood like statues before dry water holes. Nearly naked farmers worked with crude implements on small patches of green. The sky was sparkling clear, cloudless. The sun beat down fiercely, as if magnified, determined to scorch man and his earth.

In contrast to this, even Tanjore's bareness seemed an oasis with its small cluster of brave structures washed white by the sun, standing as shady shelters against the heat.

The temple was closed. "What nonsense," Markham fussed, "we'll have it opened at once." He waddled over to the caretaker's house and, with much gesture and vocalization, obtained permission for us to enter. The caretaker made it clear, however, that we could not enter in Western clothes.

"Stupid, childish nonsense!" Gupta shouted, but on this point the man was adamant. Gupta led me to a small store where we could purchase dhotis, mumbling all the way. "Stupid! Stupid! Stupid! I have not worn one of these things in years. I feel damn ridiculous!" he complained, tying it around his fat hairy belly. "Stupid superstitions! When will we grow up?"

Within the temple on a high pedestal rested the giant bronze bull.

"You probably know that the bull was the animal chosen to carry the God Shiva to earth. So you will find him honored all over India. A sacred bull, indeed!"

Gupta conceded that the bronzed animal was impressive in its appearance of strength and expression of gentle, refined wisdom. "You wouldn't expect to find such subtlety of craftmanship on a bull, would you?" he said, studying it closely as if seeing it for the first time. "Yes, I thought you should see this. It is quite lovely."

Gupta continued to confuse me. His attitude toward his country and its people was less than tolerant, kind and accepting. His attacks were vicious, yet he seemed very concerned that I enjoy and see carefully the very things he attacked. Although he showed no pleasure in his self-appointed position as my personal guide, he continued to insist on showing me as much as possible. It was as if he were almost afraid to allow me to miss something or perceive without guidance.

He consented, after several invitations, to have dinner with me one evening. He arrived mopping his forehead as usual. Each time we met he seemed a bit more relaxed. Now, he even smiled occasionally.

"Good evening, my dear Doctor," he said. "I'm famished!"

As we dined in Tiruchi's best restaurant, Mr. Gupta proved that there was good reason for his rotund shape. He requested second helpings of almost everything. "The food here is quite good. Our college food is atrocious! But that's true in the States, too. Fit only for the empty-headed youths it sustains. I, for one, love to eat. I always think it is such a pity that those of us who do have a passion for food and no vanity about the results cannot live in a place like Italy or Paris where food is respected and cooking is an art. Give me a good stuffed goose, fresh trout almondine, vegetables with hollandaise and a fluffy soufflé."

"Actually, the life you see now in Southern India has greatly improved since my youth," he continued. "As a child I remember seeing people die in the streets of hunger and disease. My family was always well off and we were never worried about our next meal, but you can't live among the homeless and the starving without becoming involved. Especially when you know that it is all so unnecessary. Such a damn waste!" He was silent for a while and then took out his handkerchief and blotted his dark brow. "There is so much undeveloped potential in India; for instance, here in Southern India our mills have removed the danger of starvation. Almost any man who is willing to work can eat and afford a place to stay. More people send their children to school. This would be good if only we had a meaningful education to offer them. If only we could shake off our stupid superstitions and cultural lags! Stupid!"

I decided that I would take advantage of what seemed to be one of Gupta's more pleasant moods. "But what about the dominant philosophy here, the acceptance of life as it is?" I asked.

"That sounds like a paraphase of a freshman's analysis of Hinduism," he replied. "How ignorant you Westerners are of these beliefs. Of course one accepts — when one has no other choice. If a man can better himself, he does so. Only the holy man, who by some mystical means believes he knows the wish of God, would be willing to die of hunger without a battle. If you are really interested in the Indian, and for some strange reason I truly believe you are, observe him closely. Not with your Western eyes, but with empty, sensitive eyes. You'll find him like a child. Even the most humble and poor of them can find something to smile and laugh about. They seldom question. They are good workers. Perhaps, in a sense, they do accept, but only what is known and possible to them. I use 'them' because in a very real sense, I am not like them. I cannot be. I am not a Hindu. I have a Western education and my background is upper middle class."

We talked of many things that evening as another side of Gupta was revealed. He was interested, allowed me an opportunity to air my views and ask questions, and was much less abrupt than during our previous meetings.

"Let me help you to plan your trip through Southern India. First, I think you must see..." And so with Gupta's help, using Tiruchi as a base, I planned trips to the mill town of Ernakulum and the university town of Trivandrum.

In Trivandrum, I was asked to conduct a short seminar at one of the many universities for twelve graduate students in psychology, young men and women. Gupta had warned me, "Indian education is based upon the English system. That means that education is measured by the extent to which one is able to learn facts, not the meaning, just facts. Not the thinking processes, heaven forbid! It's a sad state of affairs. The student passes examinations, one after another, until he is finished with his formal education. Then he is educated, but for nothing useful. He is at a loss as to what to do with the isolated facts he has learned. Most go to work for a bank or Shell Oil of India. It's a stupid shame!"

His analysis became dramatically apparent in my seminar. The students were intelligent and alert, knew all the facts, the labels, the definitions. They knew a great deal about the causes and treatment of mental illness, but confessed that they had never seen a real mental patient. I suggested that we visit a local mental hospital. They were first shocked, then intrigued by this proposal.

It was not surprising to find the mental hospital in Trivandrum suffering from the problems of such institutions throughout the world: it was overcrowded and understaffed, lacking both funds and professional help. The visit impressed some of the students deeply. Several felt that they might volunteer their help. They admitted, quite frankly, that they had never guessed their knowledge of psychology would ever have any real or practical value. Most of the students were from upper-class families where education was simply for its own sake. Several planned to join the family business, whatever that might be, while most of the girls would marry, run households.

Each day students came to my hotel to talk about their feelings and about the excitement of their new found work at the institution. They generally agreed that Indian education, as it existed, had little, if any, effect whatsoever; that an educational revolution was the only hope for the country's future, but still was a long way off. They were eager for change, but had no idea from where it would come. I was relieved that it would not be my responsibility. We had problems enough in the United States with higher education. The job seemed so great that it became easier to understand why Gupta took refuge in feigned disinterest and grumpy impatience.

"I'm happy you saw what you did," he said, when I returned. "It's important that you know why we're moving so slowly. It's like the village women who are given lectures on birth control. They listen attentively, then go home and imagine that it did not pertain to them, that it concerned only their neighbor, and go right on having children. I gave up years ago! It's very difficult to fight the system. It's usually run by people who fear the new and hold to the security of the old. The college here is small but liberal. I try to use the American system, not the English. I will not compromise my ideas. I make my students think. I don't give one damn if they don't know the location of Walden Pond as long as they know how Thoreau's philosophy applies to them. Damn heat!" he added, reaching for his handkerchief.

I rested for a week in Cochin, a delightful city on the Bay of Bengal. Like a tropical island, it was covered with palm trees, flowers, and waterways of great beauty, fringed by small, sparsely inhabited islands. One of the oldest cities of India, it was an important port for centuries. The influence of the amalgamation of the cultures of many peoples was still apparent: the Jews, the Christians, the Moslems, the Hindus. Architecturally, it was a hodge-podge of Victorian buildings, 1950 modern, and grass huts. Little boats went from one wondrous island to another; vanishing into jungle beauty, playing near clear deserted beaches, or past parties of naked natives busily damming, cutting, or fishing through tiny canals amid dense, wild patches of vegetation like abandoned gardens.

I went by waterway to the city of Ernakulum, and from there took a bus to Cape Comorin, where I sat among hundreds of awed observers on the vast sandy beach as the sun rose and set in the same rough, blue sea. Here, too, the mystical Temple of the Diamond Devi stood and defied the giant waves, its diamond headdress glittering magical rays out to sea and guiding the sailor safely home.

"I'm glad you think my country beautiful. But the finest of all the wonders of Southern India, as I told you, is the Temple of Madura," Gupta said, "that is, if you can ignore that damn paint job!" He gave me a letter to a professor at a medical school in Madura. "Samutri is an old friend. He will take good care of you."

I arrived by train in Madura, right at the scheduled time, as always. It was late afternoon, steamy and humid. Haze danced over the hot streets and even the flies had lost their vitality, resting quietly in the shadows, on huge dung heaps. The towers of the temple, visible from the train depot, were sun-yellow and deep purple in the distance. It was a simple process to find one's way in well-planned Madura. The temple was at the center of the city from which the roads paralleled, street by street, to the city limits.

At close range the temple was overpowering. Its four giant towers, each intricately carved with tiny figures of humans at work and play, rose like beacons over the city. The red and white painted outer wall contained several tall gates which gave access to the main inner chambers. Each chamber was vast and housed enormous statues of Gods. In the center court was a delicate reflecting pool, the largest in India. Inside, the worshippers moved in flowered splendor, traversing long hallways to enormous chambers, to intimate altars. Here and there sat gurus, surrounded by avid pupils. Their lips moved slowly, softly, proudly and devotedly, articulating the ancient wisdom of the Gita or the code of the Mahabarata, part of a religious heritage established hundreds of years before the Christian era.

Stately priests with wise, dancing eyes, blessed the eager pilgrims gathered about them and performed their religious rites with practiced agility.

Wedding parties accompanied by noisy bands and dancing transvestites moved through the crowds on their way to all-night festivities.

Beggars sat in the coolness of the temple among animals which yawned or defecated before giant altars as if the temple had been built solely for their pleasure and use.

Odors of sandalwood, dung, incense, sweet-smelling perfumes, and human perspiration permeated the air.

Outside, the stairs led to the center court and the delicate reflecting pool. It was crowded with half-naked throngs busily preparing themselves for religious rituals, primping, washing their clothes, simply basking in the sun, chatting, or cooling themselves half-submerged in the dirty, greenish water.

Dr. Samutri's house was in what might be called the suburbs since the more modern, larger homes were on the outskirts of the town. He was expecting me.

"Oh, yes, you found us. Good. Come in. Gupta told us you would be coming. Come in! Come in!" He was a large muscular man in his forties, graying prematurely, with large eyes, warm and vibrant. "This is my wife, Gretchen," introducing his blond, blue-eyed wife whom he had met while studying in Vienna, "and our daughter, Lisa." Lisa was perhaps the most beautiful child I had seen in my travels, with the best features of both handsome parents.

When I was seated they gathered eagerly about me. "We are dying of curiosity. How on earth did you ever meet Gupta? He's such a loner. I never thought he ever spoke to anyone, least of all a stranger. He seems to have such a keen interest in you. His letter was glowing. What is it?"

I described our meeting. "I really don't know why he has been so kind. He's been great."

Samutri laughed. "Gupta has become a romanticist in his old age. An Indian at last. He really is a good chap, you know. It is just that he is rather a snob. People fear him a bit and don't relish having him around. Happily for him, he enjoys being alone. One must know him before his real charm and sense of humor can be appreciated."

"We love him," Gretchen laughed. "We find him so refreshing. He hates everything so. Actually, he is the warmest person we know. I call him the Indian Robert Morley. He looks like him, don't you think? All those chins, the sour expression covering the puckish look, the way he swaggers when he walks."

"He claims he hates India," Samutri cut in. "He calls the Indians by his favorite expression, 'stupid.' Actually, he loves his country. It is just that he feels frustrated. Like so many of us who have seen the world, Gupta and I would like to shove our people out of their dormant state. But we find that to wake someone who has been asleep in the cool shadows for so long is not easy. We have to be patient. We must be willing to offer him time. Gupta has no patience, so it drives him mad! You know, he could get a position almost anywhere in India if he were willing to put up with the system, but he chooses to make less money and live amid the discomforts of Tiruchi for the freedom of living and teaching what and how he pleases. There are many like him in India. Abhorred by the sophisticated Indian because he makes him look at himself, feared by the poor Indian because he will not be pushed. So Gupta exists in a world apart. But what about you?"

That evening we had Wiener schnitzel for dinner, then went to the roof of the house where we sat on a swing and listened to Beethoven's Ninth Symphony while watching the mystical Madura Temple change colors with the approaching night.

My final stops were in Madras, Bangalore and Mysore. As Gupta had said, they were the three most physically beautiful cities in the South of India. All offered the old and the new in pleasant, flowered surroundings: ancient weed-vine covered temples and shrines, together with patterned, pampered gardens. Simple shacks crumbled in the shadows of maharajas' vast marbled palaces. Vendors with dime store trinkets sat on boxes in front of luxurious shops selling jewelry of solid gold and precious stones, available on credit.

On my return to Tiruchi, I informed Gupta that it would be necessary for me to move on. He seemed strangely different to me now and it had become easier to ignore his peculiar mannerisms, his odd outbursts and his wicked lashing tongue.

"So," he said, "how did you find Southern India? Did you discover the mystery and glamour you came to find or was it just a dirty, overcrowded bore?"

I am sure I sensed true pride in his expression as I spoke of my strong attraction to his country, its art, its culture, but especially its people.

"Yes, India is beautiful but it's changing," he said. "From the untouchable who still wanders the streets in his nakedness, sore-infested and sick, to the rich mill owner who sits on his fan-cooled veranda and complains about taxation, we are all changing. From the maharaja, looking back to the time when his dilapidated marble palace was stacked with chests of precious jewels and crowded with elegant maharanies, to the field worker and the rising white collar worker, we all are having to face this change, each in his own way. No one can escape it. But it's so damn *slow,* this process." He mopped his brow. "The hell with it!" he said. "Anyway, I'm happy you came to the south and we have become friends." He mumbled this in a rather embarrassed manner, staring at his rings.

The last time I saw Gupta, he was mopping his brow furiously and cursing the station porter for handling my luggage so carelessly. "Stupid man!" he said in English. "When will these people wake up?"

Chapter X

CALCUTTA

Don't spend your precious time asking "Why isn't the world a better place?" It will only be time wasted. The question to ask is "How can I make it better?" To that question, there is an answer.

CASE FAMILY

*O*n first impression, Calcutta seems to be the most crowded, dirtiest, ugliest, and most depressing city in India. It has neither monument, nor fresh sea, nor beautiful garden, nor fantastic temple, nor obvious rich culture to recommend it. It is large, sprawled out, a colorless industrial city where the air is heavy with dust, smoke, and stench. Sacred cow and naked child defecate in the main street; crowds move indifferently, through throngs of starving, maimed, crippled beggars. Autos, buses and taxis speed through garbage-infested streets with equal indifference toward stray child, lame old man or dog. The sun beats down unmercifully most of the year, drying the land so that even the open spaces seem like vast deserts; the river flows through the city black with oil and smelly debris. The lawns of the parks are dirt-dust brown and the trees cry for attention, punishing those who ignore their need with little shade.

It is a city of great wealth and desperate poverty, of great concern and callous indifference, of great promise and lack of all hope, of over-fed and starving, of silk saris and shriveled peasant nakedness. It is a city where, daily, endless streams of hopeless humanity wind their way, fighting for a section of sidewalk or deserted road on which to settle their tired bodies.

Calcutta is India in transition, the India of the intellectual, the new thinker, the West; like the Chicago of the twenties, Paris of the eighteen hundreds, Naples of the forties. Whatever else it is, Calcutta is not basking in the decaying ruins, or the fly-infested dung heaps. It is moving.

The day I arrived in Calcutta was a scorching, hazy, dusty one, when all activity seems forced and frantic, when people, hot and sticky, feel maximum indifference.

Although I had written to the YMCA well in advance, I was informed that they had no reservation for me and had no time to answer requests for rooms. It was suggested that I go down the road to a church hostel. Perhaps they would have something, if I were not too particular.

Back on the street, I was immediately surrounded by a mass of beggars, by those who wanted to direct me, to carry my luggage, to introduce me to a house of prostitution. Twisted figures, faceless, voiceless, squirmed about me like hungry sidewalk reptiles.

"Baksheesh! (Money!)" they moaned.

The walk to the hostel became a nightmare. I

gathered beggars like a pied piper and found myself becoming vicious and cursing at them to leave me alone, which they refused to do. Even my light suitcase weighed upon me and prevented my pushing my way past the group.

The flight of steps leading to the hostel seemed to act as an artificial barrier, causing the beggars to scatter and vanish as mysteriously as they had appeared.

In a small room at the top of the stairs, at an old Victorian desk, sat a very young, very dark Indian boy.

"Do you have a room?" I asked.

"I call Miss Case, Sahib," he said, and vanished through a strangely decorated dining room. It was a large room, dark and cluttered with assorted odd pieces of furniture. The room opened onto a balcony which overlooked the narrow street below. It seemed cooler here.

After a few minutes the boy reappeared.

"Miss Case come soon, Sahib. You wait, please."

He stared at me innocently. To break what seemed to me an awkward silence, I smiled at him and asked, "Have you lived in Calcutta long?"

He smiled a large white-toothed smile, "All the life."

At that moment Mrs. Case appeared. She was over-powering, at least as tall as I and twice as heavy, a solid, firm heaviness. Her light hair was cut in a mannish bob, short and combed straight back over her head, accentuating a long, rather sensitive face and deep blue eyes. Her voice was low-pitched and her inflection was almost unfriendly.

"I'd like a room," I said. "The YMCA suggested that I come here in the hope that you might have a place for me to stay."

"I have a room," she said, matter-of-factly, with an American accent. "How long will you be?"

"I don't know; I have no particular schedule."

"It doesn't matter."

She handed me a large book and asked me to register. "Remember, this is not a luxury hotel. You will have to 'do' for yourself except for meals. The food is Indian and you may have to share your room."

"This is a non-profit hostel," she continued, "as it is, we just manage to keep open from day to day. We're here primarily as a mission."

In fluent Bengali she instructed the boy where to take me.

We crossed the dining room into a hall and ascended a very narrow wooden staircase. The boy opened the door, which had no lock, and led me into the room. It had two beds and a small dresser. The walls were of stucco, clean and plain. On the dresser was a Bible, the only item other than the basic furniture. There was one small window which looked directly into an apartment house just a few yards away, where smoke rose seemingly from nowhere, as if the rooms were on fire.

Then I was guided up another long flight of stairs to a bathroom. Again, no frills: sink, a clean but broken mirror which distorted everything, a shower head reaching out like a thin, wrecked arm from one wall, and a Western-style toilet bowl with no seat.

I expressed my mixed pleasure to the boy with a "Namaste" and a broad smile and returned to my room.

"Dinner start at seven, Sahib," he informed me, closing the door behind him.

It quickly became apparent that my first impression of the room's coolness was only due to the contrast with the intense heat outside; I could feel beads of perspiration forming over my back and running slowly down my body in trickling streams. I removed my clothes and dried myself with a towel, to no avail; in a few moments I was again dripping wet.

It was now late afternoon and I prepared to go out into the city. Certainly Calcutta had more to offer than the horror I had seen in the few streets I had walked.

I started out through the dining room. Two boys were busily setting tables for dinner. One I recognized as the boy who had greeted me upon my arrival. He brightened up. "Doctor," he shouted, "you doctor? You write doctor on book."

"Yes," I said, "I'm a doctor."

"You help me please," he said and led me into the adjoining kitchen. As he began to undo his trousers it occurred to me that he thought I was a physician.

"No," I said, "not that kind of a doctor. I am a doctor of philosophy."

It was no use. His trousers were down around his ankles exposing his extremely thin trunk, sunken stomach and long, dark, spindly legs. He ran his fingers through his pubic hair and pointed out tiny red bites, indicating his discomfort by going through the motions of scratching, then looked at me questioning. It was easy for even a layman to diagnose crabs, and anyone who had traveled through the Orient, staying in small local hotels and hostels, was normally well equipped to handle them. I smiled. "I cannot show Mama Case," he said simply. "You have medicine?"

I indicated that he should pull up his trousers and come with me. We returned to my room where I gave him the necessary instructions and the bottle of liquid which I carried.

"Namaste, doctor," he said.

I walked out into the blinding afternoon. The sun was hotter than ever. Crowds of unwashed and dirty people moved slowly through the streets, seemingly without direction.

Most of the streets were narrow, dusty and littered with the accumulated trash of weeks.

I moved amid stalls and past walls lined with vendors. Children were engaged in the game of begging. They followed for blocks whining "baksheesh" with dirty palms extended, and seemed to revel in the irritation they produced, growing ever more aggressive and pleased with themselves. Suddenly I was confronted with a tall, rather impressive building, the Calcutta Opera House. It faced a large covered market offering everything from the finest silks to the most base, twisted sweet potatoes. With everyone engaged in bargaining, searching, and shouting, it was very much like other Asian markets, only perhaps more congested, unkempt, filthy and smelly.

Strangely patterned streets took me past long queues waiting before hundreds of movie houses blaring dissonant music and covered by advertising placards showing richly-garbed, heavily-jeweled and painted maharanies with their handsome maharajas. I finally emerged into a large open space which I recognized as Victoria Square. The streets around the square were lined by shops, restaurants, and the more expensive, air-conditioned movie houses with shorter queues.

The park only suggested what it was intended to be. Its grass had given way to dirt from misuse and lack of water. Sacred cows moved slowly across the dry field, searching dumbly for something, seemingly not certain what. Groups of people huddled around, on the dirt, talking, selling, buying.

At one end of the square was a row of buildings, black with soot and dust and the terminal for noisy streetcars. At the opposite end was the Victoria Government House, before which passed busy streets and tram tracks, leading to the river and beyond.

I started back to the hostel slowly; both because of the intense heat which precluded speed and the deep depression the city had imposed upon me.

When I arrived, dinner was already being served. I sat at one of the unoccupied tables, but was shortly asked to join the group at a table near the balcony.

"It's cooler here," a fair man with a British accent told me.

He introduced me to the others, all of whom were staying as guests of the hostel. Two were missionaries visiting Calcutta for just a few days from an area near Hyderabad in central India. There was an English family, husband, wife and two teen-aged boys, who had once lived in India and were now visiting with friends and feeling rather nostalgic about the "old" way. The other member of the group was a rather plain young girl from an American university, who was touring India to research the dissertation she was writing on comparative religions.

"How long have you been in India?"

"Several months."

"How long will you stay?"

The routine questioning.

"I don't know."

"Do you like it?"

"I loved the south and central parts," I said, "I could have stayed in Cochin, Ernakulum, Trivandrum, Cape Comorin, or even Madura, forever. I like the central part, too, but I'm not sure, if Calcutta is typical, that I shall love the North."

"Give it a chance," said the plain girl. "It's glorious! So fantastically alive and earthy."

"Rather too alive and earthy for my taste," the Englishman with the family commented dryly. "It's changed since the war. Funny, but it's rather the way a house changes when the builders move."

"The builders!" the young minister exclaimed. "Do you mean we British? You know, though it's apparently still not understood by some of our countrymen, the Indians were here even before the British."

The American student laughed gaily. None of the others joined her and she became quiet.

The conversation safely returned to me as we ate.

"Are you going to the service?"

"I wasn't planning to," I answered.

"You should go at least once," the American girl said. "You must see Mrs. Case work. It's a real experience."

After dinner, I joined the English family and we descended the stairs to the street level. We walked up a dirt drive to a large hall where the service was to be held.

In a room completely devoid of furniture or ornament, at least fifty Indians, perhaps more, were seated cross-legged, hungrily eating rice and curds with their fingers off sections of banana leaves. Two Indian boys scurried among them with pots of food and with agile movements poured second helpings of food onto the small shiny leaves.

As those present finished their meal, the boys gathered the leaves, depositing them in a large cardboard box which they dragged from the room. Everyone then settled themselves, facing now in one direction, and waited. After a moment, Mrs. Case appeared. She wore a white robe and, over it, a heavy cape of black.

The room was hot and smelled of sweating, unwashed bodies and food. Mrs. Case's forehead was covered with dots of perspiration but she appeared cool and comfortable. In one hand she carried a Bible which she did not open. She stood before them and began to speak with smooth, caressing ease, in what I surmised was the Bengali dialect.

They sat before her in silence and deep respect. It was not clear from their expressionless faces whether they understood her or not. The English family seemed to understand what she was saying and responded every now and then with a murmured "Amen, sister," but no one else seemed particularly to hear.

After ten minutes, Mrs. Case smiled, folded her hands in a "Namaste" sign over the Bible and walked into the group. The listeners rose, adjusting their clothes which were stuck to their skin by sweat. When the last of them had gone, Mrs. Case walked over to us, greeted the English family, and smiled at me. She seemed softer, kinder, than she had that afternoon.

"I'm glad you came," she said. "I understand you are a physician."

"No, I'm a Ph.D."

"Oh, I'm sorry," she said, "I thought I could put you to work if you were a real doctor. There's not much use for another Ph.D. here. There's enough philosophy already in India. Too much, in fact!"

She wiped her brow. "It's not much cooler outside," she said, "but if you have no other plans, would you like to join me for a stroll?"

The English family excused themselves and we walked together into the humid night. The sun was gone but its heat remained.

"It's been a hot day," she said, fanning herself with her handkerchief. We walked for some distance in silence.

"Vishnu said you gave him some medicine," she said.

"Not medicine, really," I answered. "He has crabs. I gave him something that will take care of them. I told him I'm not a medical doctor, but he doesn't seem to accept the fact."

She laughed, a deep-throated laughter. "How could you ever expect someone like Vishnu to understand? He saw your signature in the book, and it said 'Doctor.' As far as he is concerned, there is only one kind of doctor."

As we continued our walk, she asked me none of the usual questions: Why was I traveling? Did I like India? How long would I be there?

When we arrived at the river, she led me to a small boat landing. The street lights were on, with neon signs on the buildings advertising Coca Cola, shoes, silks. The air was no cooler but seemed fresher. Night color swept Calcutta clean, and the young people walking along the bank and in the surrounding shadows might have been lovers in any of the world's large cities. Cars and motorcycle cabs putted by, while the inevitable pimps and prostitutes sauntered alone, conspicuously, slowly.

"This is the only time this poor city is beautiful, when it takes on the color of the night," she sighed. She was very relaxed, woman-like.

We talked for a long time.

"My husband and I came here more than twenty years ago from Iowa. He was newly ordained. We were in the south of India near Poona," she told me. "It was beautiful there. Actually, we didn't do much converting, but when people are sick and hungry there isn't much time for preaching. I hated India at first, but there is something very special about it. From the way you spoke a little while ago, I think you know what I mean. It creates an excitement, a passion, that makes one more aware of life." She looked into the swiftly moving black river.

"My husband died in Poona. Some strange disease. Actually, I think it was more like a depression. He was a big man, even bigger than I. Football player and all that, but underneath he was too soft. I think he found the task too great and his contribution too small. I think he just gave up one day and died. At first, I thought I'd go home, to the States, but then I heard about this mission in Calcutta. The people who had been running it just quit. They couldn't seem to understand the Indians. They kept feeling they should want to help themselves! People assured me it would be better for me to be in a city like Calcutta, but I think India is fine almost anywhere for a woman alone. Here it's not the rapists and thieves who keep you off the streets, but

138

the beggars. Anyway, I find that after a while the beggars get to know you and leave you alone. They are a pretty smart lot, especially the children and the cripples. Some say that they are the only ones, except the rich, who eat regularly in Calcutta."

We wandered back to the hostel. At times it was necessary for us to walk in the street for the sidewalks had become the hotels of the poor, and for blocks in all directions they were lying along the road, grouped together like rows of corpses.

"How can the officials keep Calcutta clean, or any other city in India for that matter? When almost one-third of a city's population uses the sidewalks for their home, when the streets become their kitchens, their garbage cans, their toilets?" As she spoke, we turned into the hostel drive. Vishnu and three other boys were seated on the steps.

"Namaste, Doctor," Vishnu said. Mrs. Case and I laughed.

Early the next morning Vishnu knocked on my door. "Sahib," he said, "I bring two friends to see you." He entered with two Indian boys in their early twenties. "They need doctor. You look see." He spoke to the boys. One lifted the shirt which hung over his dhoti and exposed huge sores, pus-filled and inflamed. The other losened his dhoti to display a large, chancrous penis.

"Much hurt," said Vishnu, the self-appointed Florence Nightingale.

I knew there was no use in trying to explain that I was not a physician so I asked them to return in a few hours. I showered. I ate my breakfast. Vishnu served me with great pleasure. Obviously he considered me a godsend, and it became apparent that I was given more of everything being served. He loved the title, "Doctor," using it at every opportunity.

After breakfast, I gathered up Vishnu's two friends

and set out to find a physician. I found one on the main square, an English-speaking Indian with accent and bedside manner imported directly from London's West End. After I explained the situation to him, his initial response was to direct me to the nearest dispensary. The two boys, not understanding a word, stood by nervously. At last he agreed to look at them. He did not speak to either, but conducted both examinations roughly, forgetting his smooth manner. Finally, he wrote prescriptions for both and told them what they had to do. He also instructed them to go to the dispensary in the future.

Later that afternoon Vishnu came to see me. "Why not you take care of friends?"

I felt that I should stop this at once, before I found myself "doctor" to all the infirm of Calcutta, a tall order for even a massive team of physicians. Through gestures and simple words I told him that I could not treat anyone, that all my tools and medicines were back in the United States and that he should tell his friends they need not fear the dispensary, that care there was good — and free. He listened to my explanation with only a degree of acceptance.

Each day Calcutta grew more hot and seemingly more crowded. Thousands of immigrants arrived daily and there seemed no way to stop the flow. Small tents of rags were set up in almost every open space; after nine in the evening, the sidewalks were almost impassable. The city stifled me. I longed for an open space, a single moment of silence and peace, a tree, or something that was clean and dust-free or beautiful.

One afternoon I met a wealthy Indian in a theater where I had gone to escape the terrible heat. He was a very kind man and was most interested in my reactions to India. We spent several evenings in his garden-surrounded, fan-cooled home, talking about birth control, relief for the needy, medical care for the sick; but the magnitude of these problems was so great that every attempt toward their solution was very much like killing a single flea on the tail of a giant elephant. Our talks, though interesting, always left me somewhat ill at ease, confused and frustrated.

But Mrs. Case obviously felt that something could be done. Her days were full. In the early morning she set out on her daily trek to solicit help from the more fortunate. "Indians who have money never refuse a Westerner who is begging," she told me. "They give almost freely as if by giving they are passing some of the responsibility on to someone else and alleviating their own frustrations and guilt." With this money in her hand, and accompanied by her four adopted sons, headed by Vishnu, she would shout her way to bargains in the marketplace. Here she was known as "Miss Case of the loud voice and the strong arms," but she was obviously well loved.

Upon arriving home, she fed her hostel guests, helped to keep the place in order, supervised the work and the daily menu, and finally set to the task of cooking for the fifty or sixty hungry street dwellers she would gather up for the evening meal.

The fact that she was feeding the poor was well known throughout Calcutta, and some of the hungry were always assembled at the dinner hour, waiting for what would be their only meal of the day.

"First you feed their empty bellies, then you preach to their minds. I'm sure half of them don't understand my Iowa Bengali. But they sit quietly and they are fed and that's really all that matters, isn't it?"

As the days passed my feelings about Calcutta changed. I no longer felt horror at the sights I saw, merely defeat. The beggars no longer bothered me, I simply ignored their terrible whines and pleading cries. Even the heat felt almost pleasant when one stopped trying to fight it.

Finally, I told Mrs. Case I was leaving. She seemed unhappy. "I'm sorry to see you go. I thought you might end up being another of our crazy crusaders, but I guess you see the joke of it all," she said. "I know I'm not *really* doing anything important, but I feel that just to keep forty or fifty people alive for one more day is something. Who knows the answer?"

She looked at me apologetically, almost ashamed.

When I left, Mrs. Case and her family lined up to say goodbye. Vishnu did not understand why I was leaving after so few days.

"I'm a coward," I said. He looked puzzled.

I avoided looking at Mrs. Case when I shook her hand; I picked up my suitcase and left quickly.

Chapter XI

KASHMIR

To see a man as he really is you must love him unconditionally. Unless you do so, he may not reveal himself to you and you will miss him forever.

KATIE

We were told that due to the severity of the weather no flights had been able to complete the trip from Delhi to Srinigar during recent weeks. Srinigar, situated as it is, surrounded by gigantic mountains, had been snowed in and was inaccessible. However, most of the well-dressed passengers had come at least half-way around the world to know, firsthand, the mystery of the Valley of Kashmir, and the flight was full.

One passenger stood out among the rest. She was in her middle twenties, wearing a black angora turtleneck sweater, far too large for her and too warm for the climate. It hung loosely over her thin body and clung to her wide hips and thighs. Tight-fitting ski pants covered her plump legs. On her large unkempt and unwashed feet were loose Indian sandals that slapped the floor when she walked. Her hair, predominantly blond, hung in multi-colored tangles as if it hadn't been brushed in days. Her nose was too long and too pointed, her lips too thin; her face plain, pale and showing no sign of care or makeup. She was obviously alone, oblivious and unconcerned.

When our flight was announced, most of the passengers, in pairs or groups, rushed to be first on board. After the scramble was over, I boarded and found myself sitting next to Katie.

She was an English sociologist, she told me, on a tour of India, studying the effects of English colonization on the Indian. After this short, polite identification, she seemed to have nothing else to say and no desire to continue the conversation. The trip was made in silence. She all but buried herself in her book.

By the time the plane was approaching the mountains, the weather had become impossibly rough forcing us to land at a small airport at the base of the mountains. The passengers were incensed upon hearing the announcement that we could either re-board the plane for a return flight to Delhi, stay there at the airline's expense on the chance that the weather would clear the following day, or take the local bus on to Srinigar. The storms in the mountains were reported to be so violent that there was some question whether even the bus would be able to make the trip.

"You must take us there! We came all the way from Ohio."

"This is unforgivable, it's the height of inefficiency. I'll speak to the French Consul about this. This is no way to treat a French tourist."

"This would never have happened if the incompetent Indians were still under us British, I tell you."

"But I'm on a tight schedule, I can't wait."

Having thus expressed their indignation, the passengers all decided to return to Delhi and still grumbling, filed back to the plane. I was determined to try the next day; if this were impossible, I had decided to trust the bus.

The airplane motors sputtered insecurely and the plane took off and vanished into the gathering black clouds.

I turned back toward the building. There, squatted against the wall like a thin black spider, was the only other remaining passenger, Katie, still calmly reading her book.

"You decided to stay, too?" I asked rather stupidly.

She looked up from her book, squinted and smiled. "I decided that back in England."

The airline agent, a dark, stout Indian with a clipped British accent, drove us to the hotel over a roughly paved road.

"This is not Delhi," he explained superfluously, obviously annoyed at the inconvenience which our remaining there would cause him.

The one main road of the city was lined with the usual open-front shops, made beautiful with multi-colored materials hanging in broad drapes from the ceilings, and piles of hand-crafted materials in shining brass, copper and stone. Small roads with residences of stone, wood or stucco, led in straight lines off the main street and up the hills which framed the village. Above the town stood a massive mosque, like a huge copper monster, with thin armlike minarets raised to heaven asking protection for the infant city curled in the lap of the mountain. We were now in Moslem country.

The desk clerk assured us that although the hotel was not like those in Delhi, rooms would be readied for us. The rooms were enormous: each with a sink, a private toilet and windows which overlooked the residential area of the city. The beds were Western-style with mattresses caved in at the middle and brown with use.

"Well," said the agent, "I told you it wasn't Delhi. You must take your meals at the restaurant across the road."

Sparsely-clad servants moved leisurely about: Katie lay quietly on her unmade bed, watching them intently with her small, bright eyes. "Aren't they wonderful people?" she commented when I looked in on her. "Even the poorest and the most uneducated Indian seems to have his own private world which he shares with no one. A hundred million mysteries." She watched them for a few moments in silence.

"Look at the way they clean the dresser. I'm sure they think it's an ornament, never used inside. I noticed a maggoty bowl of rice in the drawer. I'll bet they don't even think of opening a drawer." We watched until the servants left. The room was quite clean, the maggots undisturbed. "Ha! Just as I told you. Isn't that wonderful?" she laughed gaily and bounced on the bed. It was a fine laugh, unaffected, intelligent, warm.

The rest of the afternoon we walked through the narrow back streets of the city. Most of the time we were silent. Katie, in her spider-like garb, drew more than casual attention from the Indians, who, with child-like curiosity, stared as we passed. Naked children followed us up the streets, laughing and chattering among themselves until they lost interest, then disappeared down another noisy road to find their way home.

We stayed up late, watching the color of the city fade into cold night and talked.

Katie questioned everything but wanted answers to nothing. She wondered if there were any answers at all. She struggled with the need to free herself from her own culture in order to truly see, feel and understand India.

"I feel as if I have lived here before. Perhaps in another life," she mused.

"In spite of poverty, illness, wars, political and religious differences, the Indian has somehow managed to hold onto what life is all about," she continued softly. "There is such a **reverence** for life, as if each day one walked the path from birth, at dawn, to death, at night, only to be reborn the following day."

"They have a very different concept of love and beauty, you know. Heavens! They see beauty even in me. I always thought I was one of the few girls who could travel all over the world and be as safe as I am in England. Even Italians don't pinch me. But, God, I found I was wrong about that in India. They think I'm great. For an Indian, love and sex are very different things. Very uncomplicated," she snapped her fingers simply. "I have been in India a year and I have been proposed to by hotel clerks and bus drivers, propositioned by businessmen and policemen, and seduced by a man who claimed that he was the Maharaja of Jaipur. I knew differently, of course, but it was a great seduction. And such romantics! They weep with passion and joy. They love to give flowery speeches. Really, quite grand."

It was a strange, wonderful night. We found that we were communicating, enjoying that rare experience of finding another human being who hears you. I soon realized that Katie was much like the India she loved — poor, unkempt, ragged, but unconcerned, and full of the beauty and vitality of life.

In the morning the hotel manager awakened me to report that the plane was not even going to leave Delhi, the flight had been permanently cancelled, and that if we hurried we would still have time to catch the bus.

Katie was already up and sitting outside in the cold morning air, absorbed in her book. She looked less tired than the previous day, but just as unkempt.

"Have you heard?" she asked. "I think the bus will be a lot more fun anyway, don't you?"

News travels fast in small Indian villages and before we could leave for the bus station, a new Mercedes drove up and a fat, rather pleasant looking Indian stepped out. He bowed, "Allow me to introduce myself. I am Mr. Atal," he said. "I am on my way to Srinigar by car. I have business there. Business, you can be sure, is not ruled by weather," he continued in a clipped British accent. "I must be in Srinigar by this evening. I heard that you were looking for a ride. May I have the honor of offering you the comforts of my car? It will be company for me and for you it will be superior to the bus which is dirty and very cold."

An almost disappointed Katie, after looking at me in desperation and finding no escape, nodded her consent and we took our places in the luxurious car. Mr. Atal seated himself between Katie and me, with his daughter who was accompanying him, on his lap. He held her small body close like a lover; she folded herself, like a limp doll, to the contours of his pudgy body and remained awake but silent, only moving to occasionally readjust her long, neatly-tied braids.

The road was in terrible condition, the weather vile, and the trip took almost fourteen hours. We seemed to wind endlessly through one mountain range after another. Mr. Atal talked continuously of everything from his love of mother England, to literature and religion, emphasizing that he was a Christian.

A few times we stopped for tea in very small villages. Mr. Atal had obviously passed this way often and was well known. His manner was always curt and his tone one of impatience. "These biscuits are stale! Take them away! Can't you serve the tea hot? Do you not know how to make tea yet?" He would turn to us: "You must forgive these people, they are truly uncivilized. True civilization left India with the British. Now we are left with pseudo-sophisticated bores and dull-witted peasants!"

Except for a few pleasantries, Katie said not a word during the entire trip.

The roads through the mountains became more icy. Icicles hung from roofs and electric wires, and snow covered the mountains and fields in all directions. The lakes were mostly frozen and showed gray beneath the crisp, now moonlit, sky as we arrived in Srinigar.

"Where will you stay?" Mr. Atal asked.

"On a houseboat," Katie and I answered, almost together.

"A houseboat? That is no place to stay in mid-winter. You will freeze to death; besides, they are all closed."

Eventually he realized that we would neither accept his invitation to stay in his twelve-room house, which he generously offered, nor move into the city's one open Western-style hotel. He shrugged indifference and ordered his driver to pull over beside the low stone wall which edged the lake. He wrapped a heavy blanket around him and stepped out into the night. "Houseboat!" he called impatiently into the darkness.

At once the night became alive with lights, lanterns and small boats. These soon formed at the foot of a series of steps. Mr. Atal stood above the assembly like a general addressing his troops. After a few moments, he returned climbing back into the car and slamming the door loudly against the cold.

"Habib is a good houseboat manager, he will let you have his best boat for a bit more than two dollars American or," to Katie, "one pound English, a day for the two of you. That, of course, includes all meals, a houseboy, and a cook, and Habib himself will be your guide as part of the price."

We removed our suitcases from the trunk, and after offering our thanks and a brief goodbye, we stumbled down the steep steps to be greeted by Habib, holding a lantern.

He was of medium height, dark, mustashed, rather plump. He had a happy smile that showed his pride at having been chosen from all the other houseboat owners, who stood about in frustrated defeat, to house such illustrious guests at such an out-of-season time.

He rowed us to his boat, "This is My Sunshine, my finest houseboat," he said. "My brother and me own four boats, but this is the best of all. It will not take too long to get it ready. I will get the cook to make you some tea while you wait. You will be pleased with my boat."

The houseboy met us at the cabin door. He was barefoot. The upper part of his body was covered with an old green pullover under a loose, white jacket, and a white dhoti hung below his thin waist. He took our bags into the living room, where he started a fire in a large pot-bellied stove. Habib had vanished, and Katie and I were alone.

"A houseboat in Kashmir," she exulted. "Old Katie has made it at last! I couldn't care less if we froze to death here. Isn't it grand? God! The thought of staying with Mr. Industrialist, saved Christian, expert in philosophy, culture and the living arts, made me cringe."

But Mr. Atal had been right. It was freezing cold, but at the moment that seemed unimportant, for the boat was a true beauty. We examined every inch. The living room was large and Victorian in decoration. The furniture was heavy and formal but comfortable. In the center of the room was the large wood stove, now rumbling with fire-life. Lace curtains hung from the windows and drooped to touch spectacular, soft Kashmir rugs, of intricate pattern and rich color.

All along the port side of the boat ran a narrow passage, which gave access to the many rooms, including a dining room, furnished with heavy, carved table and chairs of oak. Separated from the dining room by an ornate door was the kitchen where we could hear Habib talking softly with the houseboy or cook. Adjacent to the dining room were two large bedrooms, each with double beds and separate bathrooms containing huge sinks and baths. It was true luxury.

The houseboy served us English tea, strong, hot and welcome. Habib, who had returned, sat cross-legged on the living room rug in his loose flowing trousers and tent-like wool coat, beneath which he held his individual fire pot, providing him with his own built-in heating system.

"You both must have such coats. Then I'll give you fire pots like mine and you will always be warm."

Tired, but too excited for sleep, we sat by the stove and talked late into the night. Habib, like all the Kashmiri, was Moslem. Although India was his country, the mountains and the religion made Kashmir a separate world. He was completely different from the Hindus I had known.

"I shall take you everywhere," he promised. "I am free. I have much time. In the summer and spring, life is very busy. Wealthy people from Delhi come to Kashmir, but they are very difficult to please. I prefer to have foreigners on my boats. They are more easy to make happy. Tomorrow we shall see many things. First, we shall make you coats so that you will be warm. It will be cold for many months yet. Why did you not come in the summer? It is most beautiful in the summer, when all is garden. But you will find it nice now, too. This is the time when the city again belongs to its people. We shall have many good times," he said. "How long will you stay?"

"We don't know yet," I answered. "We shall see. Is that all right?"

"All is all right," he replied. Thus assured, we slept well that night.

The following days were clouded over by a dream-like, gray-white haze that settled over the lake and sliced the surrounding mountains in two. Occasionally, patches of blue sky became suddenly visible; then, from between mountain peaks, black clouds would move silently into the valley and drop their pale gray-white moisture over the city.

I had a coat made, as Habib suggested. It had a small collar which buttoned tightly at the neck then fell like a large tent, to below the knees. Katie insisted that she did not need one but was finally persuaded to drape a long wool blanket over her turtleneck sweater, changing her spider-like garb to that of a brown-winged lady bug. We were supplied with fire pots which we were instructed to carry under our coats above stomach level which made us both look nine months pregnant. But, as everyone in Srinigar carried fire pots, we were no more conspicuous than the others.

We spent our days eating wonderfully exotic foods, huddled around the wood stove in our living room; sailing with Habib over the rippleless, icy, gray lake and narrow canals; strolling through the maze of wooden structures, stores, stalls, temples and mosques which made up the city; walking under trees whose giant branches hung nakedly above the muddy streets and through large gardens which revealed only a skeletal suggestion of the multi-colored lushness of the summer and spring to come.

The streets were always marvels of activity. In spite of the cold and the constantly falling mist or snow, they were crowded and alive with ghost-like white-garbed women and drably-dressed men, bulging with fire pots. The children seemed like children the world over, oblivous to the weather as they ran, dashed and screamed between the crowds through the crowded narrow streets. All this was the Kashmir we had become so much a part of.

Spice stalls full of bags, bottles, and shiny tins containing powders, seeds and acrid spices offered a spectrum of colors and odors which Katie pecked at like a little bird. Though it was impossible to question or discuss sensation with the vendors, our expressions and gestures provided the necessary communication. "You must taste this," gestured the storekeeper. "It's very bitter," answered Katie's expression.

Families of rug makers were huddled together behind paper thin walls, their agile fingers flying over intricate patterns which would soon become expensive Kashmiri rugs. We listened in icy silence as the leader chanted the colors to be added in a dull sing-song voice and the half-frozen group responded in conditioned, unquestioning silence to his commands, still in ignorance of what the final results would be.

Katie was a worshipper of the senses. Things were not real, did not exist, until she had smelled, felt and tasted them. At times she seemed almost mesmerized, entranced, by the feel of a deep wool rug or the odors drifting from earthen pots of hot food steaming over crackling fires along the road.

"The city seemed, at first, washed water gray," she commented one day, "as if its colors were all resting for the winter on the clouds of the mountains, but now it shimmers red and orange everywhere."

At night Habib would join us in the living room. Katie would curl up, cat-like, on the heavy couch or sit on the floor and pull her large legs up under her chin. With the wind tossing the rain softly against the window, we would talk about many things.

"But we were promised," Habib would say. "They

said that after the emergency we could decide either to remain as part of India or go with Pakistan. There is no doubt that the decision was made a long time ago. We are Moslems, we are not Hindus. It is only that we live in India, but we are not truly Indians. Yet we must be silent and not talk about it."

It was during this conversation that we learned of Habib's brother, Alam. Alam was a radical, a deeply religious man who was determined that Kashmir, which seemed more their homeland than did India, must become a part of Pakistan. He was an expert on the Koran and believed this change was preordained. He was deeply respected in the valley.

In her quiet way, Katie revealed a deep knowledge and understanding of the politics and religions of India. Habib and Alam were constantly caught off guard by her ability to quote directly from the Koran and her keen interpretation of the words she quoted as by her general knowledge of their country and its social and political history.

Alam joined us in our evening talks. He was very thin, pale-faced, with sunken deep-black eyes, a mass of even deeper black hair and a several days growth of beard. His lips were heavy and moved slowly around the English words which he pronounced with great care. Some evenings he would read to us softly, in Arabic, the holy words of the Koran. As he read, the language sounded like a soothing morning raga.

Though he had a great disdain for women generally, Alam's respect for Katie grew. After several evening discussions, he began to look upon her as almost his equal and used her to supply the knowledge which he so eagerly wanted in the areas of psychology, philosophy and the social systems of the world.

"Are people truly free?"

"How can it be that all men are equal?"

"Is it true that you believe in one God, and that you

believe He is the *only* God for all men on earth?"

He listened closely to Katie's intelligent, simple answers. His black eyes became even darker and deeper with each word and lit up when a thought was finished and he had been able to bring it within the scope of his understanding.

For almost two months Srinigar seemed like an island, separated from the rest of the world by an icy sea. Days passed and even the buses failed to arrive. The mountains became whiter and their reflection on the frozen, glass-like lake challenged the observer to determine which was reality. All Srinigar seemed topsy-turvy, at the mercy of winter.

Then, for several days the sun shone and the activity of the thaw took over the city. The ice cracked and melted into watery pools, the brown frame houses took on a golden look, the gray of the city became touched with orange and blue, and the people began to move a bit more quickly, toward the new work to be done. Little boats loaded with vegetables appeared from nowhere as if by magic. Houseboats were cleaned, scraped and readied for the spring and summer visitors.

Katie took part in the new activity, visiting schools, institutions and homes. She talked with public officials and businessmen, politicians and religious leaders. Her enthusiasm each evening was contagious and, no matter how seemingly mundane, each experience held some new wonder for her.

These were also days for hikes into the mosque-topped hills surrounding the valley. The mosques were always cold, and vacant, with large carpeted rooms, fantastically carved walls of stone, and hardly a window through which the now warm sun could shine. There were more boat trips on the lakes and canals and walks through the bazaars.

One evening Habib informed us that the plane from

Delhi would probably be able to come in the next day. I had already stayed in Srinigar much longer than planned and, since the possibility of another freeze was imminent and a ticket could be arranged, I made plans to leave at once.

That night we had an unusually elaborate feast and invited several of the friends we had made, during our weeks in the valley, to be our guests. It was a clear and beautiful night. The moon was white, lighting Srinigar with a soft white-black winter glow.

The party was a noisy, happy one. Mr. Atal and several of the other guests made advances to Katie which she smoothly rebuffed, smiling at me with bright eyes and a wink. Left to themselves the men embraced happily, danced together and kissed each other joyfully. It was late when the festivities ended. Goodbyes were flowery and affectionate, with embraces, kisses and speeches about love, fellowship among nations, and the inevitability of future meetings.

Later, when we were alone, Katie told me, "I'm leaving the boat, too. The price is going up and Habib needs it for some of the passengers from the plane. It's better that way. What would I do on this Queen Mary alone? I'm going to that little hostel near the museum. Do you remember it? It has a great view of the canal. There are still so many things I want to do and understand here, but it will be strange without you."

The following morning Katie walked with me to the airline bus station. The cold room was full of people, anxious to be on the first plane leaving for Delhi in several weeks. Habib, always the businessman, was planning his strategy to capture some of the incoming tourists for his boats.

When the airline bus was announced, Katie hastily left me with a promise, "I'll write on your birthday."

As the bus pulled out onto the slushy road, I looked back. Katie was walking toward the hills, away from the lake. She had left her blanket on the boat that morning and was dressed as I had seen her the first day in her baggy, black angora sweater, too tight ski pants and Indian sandals, splashing in the slush as she walked.

We left Srinigar on schedule, rising slowly above the valley with the plane's two motors straining for height and speed. Below, the streets seemed empty; the boats along the river, scattered among the lake islands looked like colored squares on a black-brown rug.

When we passed the hill of the mosque, it seemed to me I could see a black-clothed figure of a girl seated on the steps. Her arms were encircling her legs which were pulled up under her chin. Her head was raised, face upward. For an instant we seemed to feel each other's vibrations. She remained motionless as the plane turned to bank between two towering mountains and veer off into the clouds.

Chapter XII

NEPAL

Man need not climb the mountain to see into the valley. All things to be seen can be found in a simple shared bowl of rice.

What I really came here for was to hear a crystal-clear temple bell ring across the Himalayas in the early dawn," I told him jokingly. Mohan looked very serious. "Why should you not hear such a bell?" he asked.

I had been in Katmandu for only a week and had met Mohan at the small hotel annex where I was staying. He was hotel manager, tour leader, kitchen boss, host and the general do-all. He was twenty years old, a very handsome, extremely dark-skinned Indian who had become weary of his country and emigrated to Nepal. His family lived in Delhi, and he had been living alone for several years in this new country which he loved.

The annex he managed was a part of a more expensive, more centrally located hotel. It had only four rooms, to accommodate any overflow from the main hotel, one bath and a small dining room. There were only two others staying at the annex, a rather jolly, retired German gentleman and his wife, both very young looking, brimming with energy, activity and life. After a few hours we had all become fast friends and formed a close-knit family with a home of our own.

On the afternoon I expressed a desire to hear the temple bell, we were resting in the hotel garden which faced the giant Himalayas. The sun was warm. It was the month of March, spring.

"I have a good friend who was born in this valley. He would know where we could go to hear your bell," Mohan told me. "Shall we visit him tonight? He is a student and it is now vacation time so it is well to go at once."

"Ja! You must go at once!" the German woman echoed in a throaty tone. "We are not young enough to go along, but you must experience dawn in the Himalayas. We already know the valley floor. There is not a street we have not walked through in Patan or within twenty miles. So why not go?"

That evening we visited Tara in his rooms off the main street in the center of Katmandu. He was a small boy, not over sixteen years of age, with a rather round, almond-eyed face which made him look even younger. He had a winning smile and fine even teeth. As he was studying English in school, he was pleased to have someone with whom he could practice. He was delighted by our visit.

"Yes, I can go at once," he said. "When shall we start?"

It was as simple as that. We made our plans for the end of the week, just a few days off.

"I know many beautiful villages," Tara told us. "We shall follow the river through the great valley, then go up into the mountains to the tiny village of the bells."

Our German friends hired a jeep, and on the morning of our departure, drove us to the end of the road. Here a narrow, well-worn path began which led up a slight incline before abruptly plunging down into the spectacular valley of Nepal.

It was dawn and in the distance, washed orange and blue, stood Annapurna, Everest and others of the world's most lofty and beautiful mountains.

Tara had instructed us to bring only a wool blanket, and the clothes we had on and Mohan had packed a lunch to tide us over until we reached the first village late that afternoon.

We said goodbye to our friends and started our descent into the valley. In the distance we could see a silver snake of river winding along and finally vanishing into the mountains.

"We follow that river," Tara said.

For the next several miles we chatted gaily, sang in English and Nepalese, and spoke of our dreams.

Mohan was content to stay in Nepal forever. He had met a girl, eleven, who was now going to school but would soon be ready to marry. The hotel would be their home. They would always have food and warmth. They could have many children.

Tara, on the other hand, wanted to see the world. He was eager to see great India. The United States was far too remote for his young dreams, but of course he would some day like to go there. He would never marry.

At mid-day we stopped and had our lunch of Indian chapate and curried vegetables with cold rice, and drank from the icy mountain streams which seemed to follow the path into the valley. The sun was warm and the valley below appeared totally uninhabited.

When we reached the river it was late afternoon. The sun still was hot, our bodies were warm and the single wool blanket we each carried had taken on gigantic proportions. We were delighted to stop at the river's edge, drop our blankets, strip and bathe in the icy stream. Mohan produced a bar of soap and we all scrubbed ourselves free of dust and dirt. Tara washed his clothes, too, then we all lay naked in the sun. The only sounds were those of a small waterfall that dropped its meager burden into the river's flow, and of the river itself which rushed through the valley at great speed, as if it had some place to go, some rendezvous to keep.

Tara asked me to sing a song he loved, one I had sung casually for him a few days earlier, and often since, at his request.

"Summertime, when the living is easy..."

He listened intently and finally said, "I must learn that song. I like it much."

We reached the first village at nightfall. It was a simple cluster of wooden structures, each two stories high with narrow ladders leading up to large communal rooms. The lower stories were divided, with one open room and the other closed for eating and sleeping.

Our arrival caused a crowd to gather, which looked like the entire village population. Very animatedly, Tara talked with them. It soon became clear that Tara was explaining our presence, telling them who I was and that I came from a far-off land, the United States. He also explained, he told me later, about the crystal-clear bell. No one questioned this motivation, rather they offered suggestions as to where the best bell could be found. They smiled warmly, welcoming us.

A place for us to sleep was arranged on the upper

level of one of the houses. One side of the room was open to the night. A candle was brought and then food was carried to us on a large wooden tray. It was rice and dahl, a mixture I was to eat frequently during my stay in the valley. The dahl, though it varied in appearance and consistency, most often seemed like glue and tasted like chives and exotic spices. I was shown how to mix the rice and dahl with my fingers and feed myself by the finger load. It was warm, rather good and always filling.

Tara chattered freely with the group which gathered to watch us eat. He asked them to sing. Their songs sounded tunefully romantic, without the dissonance of Indian music — romantic yet not Western. They sounded rather sad. It did not surprise me then that they were delighted with "Summertime" which they insisted I sing for several encores.

As soon as the sun was out of sight, the night turned icy cold. We finished our dinner in the candlelight, washed it down with hot tea and then Tara announced it was time for us to sleep. He explained that we had a long, difficult journey the next day. The group dispersed. Mohan spread one of the blankets over some straw, placed me in the center with Tara and himself at either side, then pulled the remaining two blankets over us. We were happy, excited, exhausted, and sleep came easily.

There was much activity outside when we awoke the following morning. Small fires were burning with streaks of smoke rising to the cold, gray, still sunless sky. Everyone seemed to be busily moving about but I was uncertain as to why or to where.

We rose and Tara led us directly to the river for the ritual of the daily toilet; washing our hands, face, chest and brushing our teeth in the icy water.

When we returned to the house, chapates were waiting for us, filled with a tasty, firm cream, and followed by very hot tea. There was also a strong goat cheese.

By the time we finished our breakfast, it seemed as though the entire village population had disappeared. The huts and shacks were empty except for a few very old men and women who sat huddled about the fires and several small children whose flat, slanty-eyed faces seemed to be forever enlivened by smiles. I cannot remember ever hearing one of them cry.

We gathered the blankets and resumed our trip across the valley floor. We stopped only for lunch which we had purchased in the morning and for a short swim and rest in the afternoon. Tara seemed pulled in an unknown direction, seemingly into nowhere, but there was never any doubt that he knew exactly where he was going. Our goal that evening was to reach the end of the valley and start the ascent of the tall mountain which already blotted out most of the sky before us.

The paths were deserted, except for occasional groups of Nepalese, with giant loads on their backs, going or coming, from nowhere, it seemed, to nowhere. We also passed several Tibetans, colorfully garbed, with masses of jewelry and tattooed faces.

At dusk, we reached our destination, simply a dozen stone houses. Somehow, villages seemed to appear from nowhere just when we felt we were too tired to go on.

As before, people came out to meet us and ask the usual questions. Fires, to which we were welcomed, were soon lit and the smell of food filled the night air. Lodging was never any problem. Everyone seemed pleased to share what he had, though it was clear that there was neither much spare room nor any excess of food.

Our host that evening was a small man and, like most of the Nepalese I had seen, it was impossible to guess his age. His frame was solid and his muscles strong. His eyes were narrow and bright, his face round, and his head was topped by a pointed hat which made him look like a bright pixie. His name was Lato.

As we walked toward his house he questioned Tara about me, stealing quick glances in my direction, smiling, and shaking his head in what appeared to be a gesture of approval, which he repeated many times.

The house was simple, again with two levels. We were taken upstairs where there were two sleeping rooms, both quite small and windowless. There was no furniture in the house. A hole for a fire and some large iron utensils were the only frills.

We laid our blankets on the straw at one end of the room and prepared for darkness when, from necessity, much activity must stop.

Lato was married and had two small children. His wife was not over sixteen years old, thin, and extremely shy, with a pretty young face. She moved about the house quickly, with few lost motions and the agility of a small squirrel. Lato told us that she would fix chicken and we would have a real feast; she would also fix fresh chapate, dahl and get milk from the cow.

In less than an hour everything was ready, and she shyly placed the food before us. Lato had seated himself next to me and continued cementing our friendship with glances of warmth and gentle smiles. He praised his wife and pointed out the high quality of her cooking. From time to time he questioned Tara.

"How far was this United States, in days, from Katmandu; on foot, of course?"

"What was life like there?"

"Did they eat such good dahl?"

Lato was a person for whom words were superfluous. His every look communicated far beyond the limit of spoken language.

"Take more food, please. I am concerned that you have not eaten enough," Tara translated unnecessarily. "I am so pleased that you have chosen my house to honor with your presence. You are welcome to stay forever."

Lato served the dinner, first to me, then to the others and finally to himself, taking what was left. I was becoming very fond of Lato and wanted to know more about him. When he left us for a few minutes, I asked Tara to tell us what he knew about our host.

Like all the others in the valley, Lato was a farmer. He was wealthier than the others and had several animals, among them a cow, two pigs and several chickens. His house was in a most advantageous position, quite near the water pump. He had been born in the valley and had traveled as far as Katmandu only once in his life. Neither his wife nor his children had ever been so far. All of his children attended school for a portion of the day, the rest of the time he taught them the skills necessary to maintain his position as one of the valley's best farmers. He was highly respected in the village, not only for his skill as a farmer and his strong back, but also for his keen mind. So much was this true, that a retired teacher from Katmandu, who had come to live in peace in the valley, had chosen Lato as his best friend and intellectual companion.

When Lato returned, the village was already in total darkness. The moon was almost full and cast a soft white over the dirt streets. The houses, having assumed the night glow, seemed less harsh and ragged.

Lato had brought us two prizes: the teacher who, to my delight, spoke good English, and several bottles of the celebrated Nepalese rum.

In what seemed no time at all, we were feeling the effects of the warm conversation and the potent drink. The teacher was never at a loss for words. He was a

Hindu and as the magic of both communication and rum took effect, he shouted freely from Hindu scriptures, addressing no one in particular.

Lato listened intently as if there were an opportunity at this moment to gain some new insight, to learn about some new mystery.

"A man should not hate any living creature. Let him be friendly and compassionate to all. He must free himself from the delusions of 'I' and 'Mine,'" the teacher shouted.

He poured himself more rum, then continued. "Wisdom is the secret of secrets. Knowledge is the holy of holies, the god of gods, and commands the respect of crowned heads; shorn of knowledge, man is but an animal."

The philosopher kissed me squarely on the mouth, "Oh, who has created the two letters mitram (friend), which are more precious than a mine of gems?" He was very drunk by this time.

During this period our host had, in the manner of the Nepalese, cuddled close to me, and with his hand in mine, rested his head on the stone wall behind us. He seemed to breathe in the joy of the scene like a lover.

As more liquor flowed, the group rose and danced. How strange it seemed that, high in Nepal, at the very base of the Himalayas, a group of people, hardly able to communicate, who just yesterday had not even known each other, were now singing and dancing in the night like brothers.

In the midst of the gaiety a voice called from the street below. Tara explained that it was Lato's young wife calling him to come to bed. Lato told her that I was a very special guest, that there would be no sleep that night, that she should go to bed and stop her absurd sniveling. She became silent at once, but from time to time she could be seen below, her tiny figure silhouetted by the bright moonlight, waiting.

One by one, we fell in exhaustion onto our blankets and, huddled in each others' arms, fell asleep. The teacher muttered drunkenly in my ear, "Remember, one should not see the sun at the time of rising...so say the Purnas and so does the Lord require." Having said this, he pulled a corner of the blanket over his head and instantly emitted a large snore.

We awakened late the following morning. Our host was outside waiting for us to rise. At his signal his wife shyly brought breakfast and set it beside us. Except for the teacher, none of us felt much like eating but, not wanting to insult our hostess, we forced the food into our mouths and swallowed it as best we could. I tried to tell her how grateful I was for everything that she had done for us. She seemed to understand and smiled delightfully.

Tara insisted that it would be bad taste to try to pay for their hospitality and taught me to say "thank you" instead. When I accomplished this, Lato's face broke into a broad smile. He embraced me tightly, almost crushing the wind from my body, and kissed me. There were tears in his eyes.

All the village came out to watch our morning toilet. They gazed at me in wonder as the teacher told them about the stranger. Lato supplied us with some hard-boiled eggs, freshly cooked chapate and crisp apples and we were ready to continue our voyage.

"Will you not stay, just for a few days?" Tara translated, but we assured Lato that we were in a great hurry. When we embraced for the last time, it hurt me deeply that I would never see this man again — he, to whom I had been so close, who had shared with us his home, his food, his love, with no hesitation or thought of gain, simply for the pleasure of knowing another human being. This time, we both cried.

The climb to the next village was not an easy one. Indeed, there were moments when I began to wonder if this had not been a rather insane idea. The ascent, like most of those in Nepal, traced the shortest distance between two points, regardless of the steepness of the path or the dangers involved. This time, as we climbed, we could not even find the energy to sing.

From time to time we came upon other travelers, always friendly and willing to stop for a short chat with Tara. If there was a girl in the party, Tara and Mohan would make teasing remarks, to which everyone would respond with childlike glee. Except for a short stop for lunch, we continued climbing for the entire day.

Occasionally Tara would ask, "What comes after 'fish are jumping and the cotton is high'?"

Mohan would answer, "Your daddy's rich and your mother's good looking."

"Oh."

Then we would proceed in silence.

By late afternoon we had reached the mountain peak. It was flat, as if nature had leveled it off for the city to be built with a view which could not be surpassed by any other. The main road wound past several impressive buildings, a three-storied palace, a building which Tara referred to as the city hall, and a beautiful, rambling temple at the far side of the city.

Tara had hoped we could stay at the palace, but upon inquiry, found that this was not allowed. Instead, we were directed to a large rest house along the main street. It looked out, without obstruction, over the valley several thousands of feet below, and the mountains which surrounded it.

The proprietor was delighted with his guests and gave us an attic room with no furniture. It had two large windows with heavy shutters which looked out over the cliff edge. A small stairway led down to the remainder of the house. The room was cold and a fire was started at once.

Though it was still early afternoon, it already was so cold that we were compelled to wrap ourselves in our blankets in order to walk through the village.

We went directly to the temple. It sat precariously at the very edge of a cliff which fell, without obstruction, to the valley floor. The walls were of thick stone. Stairs led us upward to a large, vacant worshipping room with several small adjoining chambers. The usual statues of Shiva, the bull, the dancer, the eunuch, and the inevitable lingam, were all there. The wooden ceiling was intricately carved with naked men and women in complicated positions of sexual intercourse. Tara laughed at these and explained that they were done hundreds of years ago to shock away the sensitive, virginal goddess of lightning.

In an anteroom of the temple, in an open space in the wall, hung two very large bells.

"Here is where you will hear your temple bells," Tara said. "These are very fine bells and can be heard almost to Katmandu."

We descended a stairway to the temple basement, now serving as a schoolroom and crowded with children from seven to seventeen. The teacher himself was very young, not over seventeen years old. Each child held a different lesson, a book, a scrap of news-paper, or a bit of written script. Each read his own material aloud with all the others. Some seemed to know their material from memory and seldom looked at the papers they held, but rather watched us with curious eyes. The room echoed with the loud sing-song chant. The teacher wandered back and forth, seriously, before the group, waving a large stick as if he were conducting a choir.

When we left the schoolroom, the sound of the youthful voices followed us through the village streets, echoing from the small huts which lined the road, down to the water fountain on the hillside.

The water fountain seemed to be the center of activity. Here, half-naked villagers washed their yellow-brown bodies, and women chatted as they filled their water pitchers; several women were laundering clothes, while others just stood about, watching and chatting. Tara and Mohan entered easily into the spirit of things and were soon taking part in the general activity.

"I have asked a few of the villagers to come to our room this evening," Tara told me later. "They are interested in talking with you. They would like to hear about your country and your people."

After our usual rice and dahl dinner, the guests began to arrive. I was introduced to the Mayor's son, the school teacher, the inn keeper and his two sons, and several others whom I had seen at the fountain. They all sat cross-legged before me in silence, waiting for me to speak. It was very difficult to know where to begin or what to say. In trying to find something we seemed to have in common, I decided to start with the family and the home. The group listened carefully to every word, as if they actually understood me, and responded to Tara's translations with audible wonder and gestures which seemed to say "Did you hear that?"

Their questions were simple but revealed that there had been communication. It was apparent that a bridge between our cultures was a difficult one to grasp, so differently did we live, feel, perceive.

Tara had ordered rum which was passed around. The bottles made several journeys through the group and soon we all became a bit noisier, more responsive and affectionate. We began to sing. Instruments were produced and the room became filled with the plaintive music. By the time the dancing began, we had a great deal in common: we were a group of happy human beings.

Morning came much too quickly. An orange sun

streaked into our dark room to announce the dawn. At once, loudly, beautifully, a crystal-clear temple bell rang out through the cold morning air. I jumped to my feet, shouting to Tara and Mohan, then rushed down to the street to follow the sound of the bell. The temple was bright orange, as was the whole village. Shadows of pale purple and faint colors of blue and red made accents of shadow spots.

The bell rang with a measured clearness. It seemed quickly to reach the distant peaks of Annapurna and Everest in the distance and awakened the dawn to fill the valley with morning light.

Tara and Mohan watched the scene with sleepy eyes. We felt great empathy. People are easily united in beauty. No one spoke. We were at one with everything and words were not needed. The bell continued to ring for some time into the unknown and seemingly beyond.

We walked back to the rest house in silence. I had heard my temple bell ringing across the Himalayas in the early dawn.

All at once I was very tired, drained, exhausted. I blamed it on the altitude, the excitement, the rum. I thought of Lato, somewhere in the valley. Did he, too, hear the bell? Was he still wondering about me and my world as I was about him? Could either of us ever truly explain to anyone else what we had experienced that evening together?

I suddenly longed to lie between Tara and Mohan, under our wool blankets, close my eyes and sleep.

EPILOGUE

Traveling THE WAY OF THE BULL leads nowhere. If one needs to attach a meaning, it lies merely in traveling the WAY creatively — in wonder, in joy, in peace, and in love.

This book described a short part of my voyage, some of the teachers I met along the WAY and what they taught me. It is neither a guide nor a map and if you follow my WAY you will surely get lost. It is merely a sharing. For my WAY can only be mine, as, some day, if I stay with it, it will lead me back to myself. Your WAY can be equally exciting, as it will lead you back to you, the only place where you can ever *become*.

Travel joyously.

Leo Buscaglia